Michael Hanisch

On German Foreign and Security Policy –
Determinants of German Military Engagement in Africa Since 2011

Michael Hanisch

On German Foreign and Security Policy – Determinants of German Military Engagement in Africa Since 2011

2015
Carola Hartmann Miles-Verlag Berlin

Bibliografische Information der Deutschen Nationalbibliothek
Die Deutsche Nationalbibliothek verzeichnet diese Publikation in der Deutschen Nationalbibliografie; detaillierte bibliografische Daten sind im Internet über www.dnb.de abrufbar.

© 2015 Carola Hartmann Miles-Verlag
www.miles-verlag.jimdo.com
email: miles-verlag@t-online.de

Titelbild: Hanisch

Herstellung: Books on Demand, Norderstedt

Alle Rechte, insbesondere das Recht der Vervielfältigung und Verbreitung sowie der Übersetzung, vorbehalten. Kein Teil des Werkes darf in irgendeiner Form (durch Fotokopie, Mikrofilm oder ein anderes Verfahren) ohne schriftliche Genehmigung des Verlages reproduziert oder unter Verwendung elektronischer Systeme gespeichert, verarbeitet, vervielfältigt oder verbreitet werden.

Printed in Germany

ISBN 978-3-945861-20-2

Table of Contents

I.	**Introduction**	**15**
	A. Major Research Questions	19
	B. Importance	20
	C. Literature Review	25
	1. Continuing the "Culture of Restraint" or Becoming a "Normal Ally"?	27
	2. Reflexive Multilateralism or Domestic Politics?	33
	3. National Interests—Which, Where, and How?	37
	4. Policy- and Decision-Makers—Movers and Shakers?	40
	D. Problems and Hypotheses	41
	E. Methods and Sources	43
	F. Study Overview	44
II.	**German Foreign and Security Policy Decisions for International Military Engagements—An Explanatory Approach**	**47**
	A. Integrative Three-level Model: Influences on Foreign and Security Policy Decisions for International Military Engagements	48
	B. Determinants on the External Level	51
	1. International Power and Security Environment	52
	2. National Interests and Strategies	58
	3. Multilateral Integration	63
	4. Evolution and Status of Military Engagement	70
	5. Mission Framework	76
	C. Determinants on the Internal Level	81
	1. Strategic Culture and Conception of National Role	82
	2. Parliament and Political Contestation	91
	3. Public Opinion	96
	D. Determinants on the Actor Level	103

III. Libya—A "Normal" Special Case: Ambivalent Premises of German Foreign and Security Policy   109
   A. Context and Framework of the Decision-Making-Process   114
   B. Evolution of the International Environment and Germany's Decision-Making-Process   119
      1. Acceleration, Germany's Skepticism, and France's Turnaround   119
      2. European Division and Germany's Growing Military Reluctance   121
      3. U.S. Switch and the Shift toward "All Necessary Means"   124
      4. Germany's Misinformed Political Debate and Public Refusal   125
      5. UN Negotiations and Merkel's Determination against German Participation   128
      6. From Nonparticipation to Abstention   130
   C. Analysis of the Relevance and Interplay of Determinants for the German Decision for Nonparticipation   133
      1. Determinants on the External Level   134
         a. Power and Security Environment   *134*
         b. National Interests and Strategies   *138*
         c. Multilateral Integration   *140*
         d. Evolution of Military Engagement   *144*
         e. Mission Framework   *146*
      2. Determinants on the Internal Level   149
         a. Strategic Culture and Conception of National Role   *150*
         b. Parliament and Political Contestation   *152*
         c. Public Opinion   *156*
      3. Determinants on the Actor Level   158
   D. Conclusion—Libya: The Ambivalence in a German *Sonderfall*   162

IV. Mali—A Standard Case: Germany's Return to Consistent Patterns of Decisions for Military Engagement — 167
  A. Context and Framework of the Decision-Making-Process — 173
  B. Evolution of the International Environment and Germany's Decision-Making-Process — 180
    1. Coup d'état, Deteriorating Security Situation, and Slowly Evolving International Response — 181
    2. France's Push, the International Struggle toward a Military Engagement, and Germany's Quest for Participation — 184
    3. Operation Serval and Germany's Ambivalent Position to Support — 191
    4. From Indirect Support to Decisions on Contribution to EUTM Mali and AFISMA — 195
  C. Analysis of Relevance and Interplay of Determinants for the German Decisions for Participation in and Contributions to the Military Missions in Mali — 199
    1. Determinants on the External Level — 199
      a. Power and Security Environment — *200*
      b. National Interests and Strategies — *203*
      c. Multilateral Integration — *206*
      d. Evolution of Military Engagement — *210*
      e. Mission Framework — *213*
    2. Determinants on the Internal Level — 216
      a. Strategic Culture and Conception of National Role — *217*
      b. Parliament and Political Contestation — *223*
      c. Public Opinion — *226*
    3. Determinants on the Actor Level — 227
  D. Conclusion: Mali—A German "Standard" Case — 235

V. Germany: A Responsible and Restrained "Shaping Power"	241
A. Germany's International Role in Action	245
B. Responsiveness and Responsibility	249
C. Germain Restraint	254
D. Reflections	256

Appendix   **259**
List of References   **264**

List of Figures

Figure 1. Integrative 3-Level Model of Determinants for Decisions on German Military Engagement (model drawn by the author)   51

List of Acronyms and Abbreviations

AFISMA	African-led International Support Mission to Mali
AWACS	Airborne Warning and Control System
AU	African Union
CAR	Central African Republic
CDU	Christian Democratic Union
CFSP	Common Foreign and Security Policy (EU)
CMC	Crisis Management Concept (EU)
CSDP	Common Security and Defense Policy (EU)
CSU	Christian Social Union
ECOWAS	Economic Community of West African States
EFSF	European Financial Stability Facility
EFSM	European Financial Stabilization Mechanism
EU	European Union
EUBG	European Union Battle Group
EUCAP Nestor	European Union Regional Maritime Capacity Building Mission in the Horn of Africa and the Western Indian Ocean
EUFOR Althea	European Union Force Althea
EUFOR DR Congo	European Union Force Democratic Republic of Congo
EUFOR RCA	European Union Force République Centrafricaine

EU HR	European Union High Representative of the Union for Foreign Affairs and Security Policy
EUSEC RD Congo	European Union Security Sector Reform Assistance Mission République Démocratique du Congo
EUTM Mali	European Union Training Mission Mali
FAC	Foreign Affairs Council (EU)
FDP	Free Democratic Party
FHQ	Force Headquarters
FRG	Federal Republic of Germany
ICC	International Criminal Court
IFOR	Implementation Force (NATO)
ISAF	International Security Assistance Force (NATO)
KFOR	Kosovo Force (NATO)
MINUSMA	United Nations Multidimensional Integrated Stabilization Mission in Mali
NAC	North Atlantic Council
NATO	North Atlantic Treaty Organization
NRF	NATO Response Force
NSC	National Security Council
OAE	Operation Active Endeavour (NATO)
OEF	Operation Enduring Freedom (NATO)
OHQ	Operational Headquarters
SFOR	Stabilization Force (NATO)
SPD	Social Democratic Party of Germany

UN	United Nations
UNAMID	United Nations and African Union Mission in Darfur
UNIFIL II	United Nations Interim Force in Lebanon II
UNMIS	United Nations Mission in Sudan
UNMISS	United Nations Mission in the Republic of South Sudan
UNOSOM II	United Nations Operation in Somalia II
UNSC	United Nations Security Council
UNTAC	United Nations Transitional Authority in Cambodia

Acknowledgements

This book comments on controversial points that have been of discussion among politicians, scholars, historians, journalists, and others interested in the foundation and making of German foreign and security policy. It also presents a novel explanatory model that aims to address the complexity of German decision-making for the use of military force. While the author cannot hope that all readers will agree with his interpretations, deductions, and conclusions, he notes that this work is thoroughly based on years of engagement with the topic as a long-serving member of the German armed forces, as a student at two different universities on two different continents, and as an interested German citizen.

I owe a particular debt to Professor Donald Abenheim and Professor Carolyn Halladay from the Naval Postgraduate School in Monterey, California, who with patience, knowledge, and experience, gave me invaluable support and continued guidance, based on their expertise of the material from years of studies of the political, social, and historical sciences. Their challenges and comments on my drafts were essential for the academic depth and richness of this work. Outstanding academics like them make the Naval Postgraduate School an exceptional and unique place to guarantee excellence through knowledge. It is also their merit that international students as myself are integrated into the academic community at NPS.

I especially owe a debt of gratitude to my beloved wife, Annett Hanisch, who accompanied me to the United States and suppor-ted me with patience and understanding that were paramount preconditions for the success of my entire academic year in Monterey.

In the end, my family, my friends in Monterey, and the thoughtful cooperation I shared with professors and students made this work possible.

I. Introduction

At the 50th Munich Security Conference in 2014, high-level politicians spoke publicly and plainly about a more "responsible" and a "more active" German foreign policy.[1] While asking whether Germany does enough to stabilize its "neighborhood," both in Europe's East and in Africa, Federal President Joachim Gauck argued that Germany "should make a more substantial contribution, and it should make it earlier and more decisively if it is to be a good partner," to

---

[1] Niels Annen, "Eine Militarisierung unserer Außenpolitik findet nicht statt, *Internationale Politik und Gesellschaft*, September 14, 2014, http://www.ipg-journal.de/schwerpunkt-des-monats/interventionen/artikel/detail/eine-militarisierung-unserer-aussenpolitik-findet-nicht-statt-587/; Arvid Bell et al., "Früher, entschiedener und substanzieller?: Engagiertes außenpolitisches Handeln und militärische Zurückhaltung sind kein Widerspruch," *HSFK Standpunkte* 1 (Frankfurt am Main: Hessische Stiftung Friedens- und Konfliktforschung, 2014); Josef Joffe, "Friedensarbeit 2.0: Gauck rüttelt an deutschen Selbstgewissheiten – und niemand tobt," *Die Zeit*, February 6, 2014, http://pdf.zeit.de/2014/07/gauck-rede-aussenpolitik.pdf; Hanns W. Maull, "Intervenieren?," *Internationale Politik und Gesellschaft*, September 1, 2014, http://www.ipg-journal.de/schwerpunkt-des-monats/interventionen/artikel/detail/intervenieren-557/; Rolf Mützenich, "Gemeinsame Erklärungen reichen nicht aus!: Weshalb wir in der Außenpolitik statt einer deutschen Kultur der Zurückhaltung eine europäische Kultur der Verantwortung brauchen," *Internationale Politik und Gesellschaft*, February 10, 2014, http://www.ipg-journal.de/kolumne/artikel/gemeinsame-erklaerungen-reichen-nicht-aus-255/; Günther Nonnenmacher, "Deutschland und die Militäreinsätze: Gaucks Leitfaden," *Frankfurter Allgemeine Zeitung*, February 1, 2014, http://www.faz.net/aktuell/politik/deutschland-und-die-militaereinsaetze-gaucks-leitfaden-12778867.html; Christian Nünlist, "Mehr Verantwortung?: Deutsche Außenpolitik 2014," *CSS Analysen zur Sicherheitspolitik* 149 (Zürich: Center for Security Studies, 2014).

maintain an "open world order" and to make it fit for the future.[2] His thoughts were echoed by Minister of Defense Ursula von der Leyen, who claimed that not "indifference" or "to sit tight," but "commitment and … responsibility" are the options for Germany in times of crisis and conflicts. She also advocated for a stronger military engagement in Africa—if indicated and necessary.[3]

While Minister of Foreign Affairs Frank Walter Steinmeier explicitly emphasized a necessary reticence as far as the use of military means is concerned (as part of a strategic culture that is skeptical about the efficacy of military force and the ends of war in the international system), he also underlined that a "culture of reticence for Germany [must] not [become] a culture of 'refrain from anything'"

---

[2] Joachim Gauck, *Germany's Role in the World: Reflections on Responsibility, Norms, and Alliances*, speech by Federal President Joachim Gauck at the opening of the Munich Security Conference, January 31, 2014, 4, accessed November 6, 2014, http://www.bundespraesident.de/SharedDocs/Downloads/DE/Reden/2014/01/140131-Muenchner-Sicherheitskonferenz-Englisch.pdf?blob=publicationFile.

[3] Ursula von der Leyen, *Rede der Bundesministerin der Verteidigung anlässlich der 50. Münchner Sicherheitskonferenz, 31. Januar, 2014*, 5, accessed November 6, 2014, http://www.nato.diplo.de/contentblob/4123416/Daten/3885836/redevdleyensiko2014.pdf; see also Julia Leininger, "Mehr Einsatz in Afrika," *Die Aktuelle Kolumne* (Bonn: German Development Institute, February 11, 2014); Johannes Leithäuser, "Mehr Verantwortung für Afrika," *Frankfurter Allgemeine Zeitung*, January 26, 2014, http://www.faz.net/aktuell/politik/von-der-leyen-plaene-mehr-verantwortung-fuer-afrika-12770671.html; "Reformulation of Germany's Foreign Policy towards Active Military Engagements Is Likely over the Next Three Years," *IHS Jane's Intelligence Weekly*, March 20, 2014, http://www.janes.com/article/35743/reformulation-of-germany-s-foreign-policy-towards-active-military-engagements-is-likely-over-the-next-three-years; Ulrike Scheffer and Albrecht Meier, "Verteidigungsministerin setzt auf mehr Auslandseinsätze," *Tagesspiegel*, January 27, 2014, http://www.tagesspiegel.de/politik/bundeswehr-verteidigungsministerin-setzt-auf-mehr-auslandseinsaetze/9386838.html.

because "Germany is too big simply to commentate on international politics from the sidelines."[4]

The words, if not the deeds, have some recent history in Germany. In January 2011, as Germany began its fifth term as a nonpermanent member of the UN Security Council, then-Minister of Foreign Affairs Guido Westerwelle reassured the international community that his country would be a "reliable, responsible, and committed partner."[5] However, less than three months later, when it came to prove its stance in response to the worsening civil war in Libya, Germany opted not to join its NATO allies in voting for the United Nations (UN) Security Council Resolution 1973 on March 17, 2011, which approved establishment and enforcement of a no-fly zone over the country. Instead, it joined India, Brazil, China, and Russia in abstaining. This unprecedented event was one of the most controversial German foreign policy decisions since 1989 and provoked vigorous domestic criticism and international concerns about Germany's po-

---

[4] Frank Walter Steinmeier, *Rede des Außenministers anlässlich der 50. Münchner Sicherheitskonferenz, 01. Februar 2014,* accessed November 6, 2014, http://www.riga.diplo.de/contentblob/4118688/Daten/3880778/Download2014RedeBMSteinmeier.pdf.

[5] Permanent Mission of Germany to the United Nations, "Responsibility, Reliability and Commitment: Germany in the UN Security Council," *Auswaertiges Amt*, updated January 3, 2011,
http://www.auswaertiges-amt.de/EN/Infoservice/Presse/Meldungen/2011/110102_DEU_Sitz_VN_Sicherheitsrat.html.

tential shift toward becoming an unpredictable and nonreliable partner or a return to bad habits of the diplomacy prior to 1945.[6]

Since then, however, Germany has changed course again. It was not only eager to reemphasize its obligation to assume international responsibility,[7] but also became engaged in more military missions well beyond its borders—especially in Africa—than ever before. To the present, German military personnel were active in up to nine such African missions as the European Union (EU) training missions in Mali and Somalia, the EU Operation Atalanta for protection of humanitarian aid and antipiracy operations at the Horn of Africa, and the UN peace support missions in Sudan and South Sudan. Six of

---

[6] Sarah Brockmeier, "Germany and the Intervention in Libya," *Survival: Global Politics and Strategy* 55, no. 6 (2013): 63–90; Joschka Fischer, "Deutsche Außenpolitik: Eine Farce," *Süddeutsche Zeitung*, March 24, 2011, http://www.sueddeutsche.de/politik/2.220/streitfall-libyen-einsatz-deutsche-aussenpolitik-eine-farce-1.1075362; "German Foreign Policy: The Unadventurous Eagle," *Economist*, May 12, 2011, http://www.economist.com/node/18683155; Helmut Kohl, "'Wir müssen wieder Zuversicht geben:' Helmut Kohl über eine Außenpolitik, der es an Verlässlichkeit mangelt," *Internationale Politik* 5 (September/October 2011): 10–17; Hanns W. Maull, "Deutsche Außenpolitik: Orientierungslos," *Zeitschrift für Politikwissenschaft* 21, no. 1 (2011): 95–119; Alister Miskimmon, "German Foreign Policy and the Libya Crisis," *German Politics* 21, no. 4 (December 2012): 392–410; Constanze Stelzenmüller, "Germany's Unhappy Abstention from Leadership," *Financial Times*, March 28, 2011, http://www.ft.com/intl/cms/s/0/2490ab8c-5982-11e0-baa8-00144feab49a.html#axzz3F6o3ea00.

[7] See Angela Merkel, *Deutschland weiß um seine Verantwortung in der Welt: Rede der Bundeskanzlerin anlässlich der Festveranstaltung zu '50 Jahre Bergedorfer Gesprächskreis' der Körber-Stiftung in Berlin am 9. September 2011*, accessed March 12, 2015, http://www.bundeskanzlerin.de/ContentArchiv/DE/Archiv17/Reden/2011/09/2011-09-09-rede-merkel-au%C3%9Fen-u-sicherheitspolitik.html; Angela Merkel, *Rede von Bundeskanzlerin Angela Merkel anlässlich der Tagung des zivilen und militärischen Spitzenpersonals der Bundeswehr in der Akademie der Bundeswehr für Information und Kommunikation, am 22. Oktober 2012, in Straussberg*, accessed November 7, 2014, http://www.bundesregierung.de/ContentArchiv/DE/Archiv17/Reden/2012/10/2012-10-22rede-merkel-bundeswehr.html.

these nine engagements were first approved in 2011 or later, that is, after Berlin refocused on Africa.[8]

A. Major Research Questions

The mixed and ambivalent policy outcomes since 2011 raise the urgent question about contemporary German military engagement in general, and particularly, in Africa: what are the main determining factors that explain *whether* and *how* Germany has engaged militarily in certain missions in Africa, yet not in other cases of crisis and conflict since 2011? In doing so, this study analyzes the character of German foreign and security policy on the continent of Africa with a particular focus on the decision for participation in military interventions in a collection of case studies that have received little scholarly attention.

On the macro level, this study also examines the following question: how does German military engagement in Africa after Libya

---

[8] "Einsatzzahlen: Die Stärke der deutschen Einsatzkontingente," *Bundeswehr*, updated May 18, 2015, http://www.bundeswehr.de/portal/a/bwde/!ut/p/c4/04_SB8K8xLLM9MSSzPy8xBz9CP3I5EyrpHK9pPKUVL3UzLzixNSSKiirpKoqMSMnNU-_INtREQD2RLYK/. The German participation to the EU civil-military advisory and support mission EUSEC RD Congo ended after nine years on September 30, 2014. The mission EUFOR RCA ended after 11 months on March 23, 2015.the military contribution to the maritime capacity building mission EUCAP NESTOR ended on April 2015. See "Closing Ceremony of EUFOR RCA," *European Union External Action Service*, updated March 23, 2015, http://www.eeas.europa.eu/csdp/missions-and-operations/eufor-rca/news/archives/20150323_en.htm; "Demokratische Republik Kongo—EUSEC RD Congo," *BMVg*, updated September 30, 2014, http://www.einsatz.bundeswehr.de/portal/a/einsatzbw/!ut/p/c4/LclBDoMwDAXRs3CBeN9dbwHdWE7yFaJQG8UpSJy-VKpm9TT0ojuVoxYZ1VQ2mmlJ9RHPEM8MRlWXcd2UWOBp3cwd-h8YF0LG21rnjp2babGAjyNxz5x-pL09py-aZ9F0/; "Die EU-geführte zivile Mission am Horn von Afrika—EUCAP Nestor," *BMVg*, updated April 1, 2015, http://www.einsatz.bundeswehr.de/portal/a/einsatzbw/!ut/p/c4/04_SB8K8xLLM9MSSzPy8xBz9CP3I5EyrpHK9pPKU1PjUzLzixJIqIDcxKT21ODkjJ7-4ODUPKpFaUpWql1qanFiQl1pckl-kX5DtqAgA8A74Ag!!/.

(and particularly since beginning of 2014) correspond with—and must be understood in relation to—Berlin's stance for a (more) responsible foreign and security policy? Thus, the present project provides explanatory approaches for guiding principles that shape Germany's position and behavior in matters of foreign and security affairs—in Africa and elsewhere as well as regarding the use of military force and other policies.

B. Importance

The evolution of German foreign and security policy after the Cold War can be seen best in the "political and geographical dissolution of boundaries" of military engagement amid a changed domestic political environment as well as an international system in which war has reasserted its place.[9]

Framed by a controversial political, scholarly, and public discussion about role and mission of German armed forces after the end of the Cold War, the Bundeswehr has gradually transformed from the bulwark of continental forward defense in the Cold War mode into

---

[9] Sven Bernhard Gareis, "Militärische Beiträge zur Sicherheit," in *Deutsche Sicherheitspolitik: Herausforderungen, Akteure und Prozesse*, 2nd ed., ed. Stephan Böckenförde and Sven Bernhard Gareis (Opladen, Germany: Verlag Barbara Buderich, 2014), 116; Johannes Varwick, "Bundeswehr," in *Handbuch zur deutschen Außenpolitik*, ed. Siegmar Schmidt, Gunther Hellmann, and Reinhard Wolf (Wiesbaden: Verlag für Sozialwissenschaften, 2007), 246.

an instrument to guarantee Germany's "capability for action in the field of foreign policy."[10]

Germany's multilateral out-of-area engagements began in a policy of small steps and ranged from humanitarian aid and peacekeeping support in Cambodia and Somalia in the early 1990s, through the breakthrough peace-enforcing operations in the Balkans in the mid to later 1990s, protection of maritime routes against piracy at the Horn of Africa, to the participation in the Afghan war—with or without a clear UN mandate.[11]

This change of policy broke with the NATO centric focus of the Bundeswehr from 1955 until 1990 that resisted any attempt by, say, the French, the Dutch, the British, or the Americans to be drawn into postcolonial wars, or "out of area" operations (i.e., Korea, Vietnam, the 1970s Middle East, and so on) that would diminish the defenses of Central Europe. Throughout its increasingly self-confident evolution, however, Germany also decided not to deploy troops to several UN-led missions, particularly in Africa, as well as to some NATO, EU, or coalition-led missions, such as in Iraq in 2003, in Chad and the Central African Republic (CAR) in 2007-2008, and most recently

---

[10] Federal Ministry of Defense, *The White Paper 2006: On German Security Policy and the Future of the Bundeswehr* (Berlin: Federal Ministry of Defense, 2006), 53; Sven Bernhard Gareis, "Militärische Auslandseinsätze und die Transformation der Bundeswehr," in *Deutsche Außenpolitik: Sicherheit, Wohlfahrt, Institutionen und Normen*, 2nd ed., ed. Thomas Jäger, Alexander Höse, and Kai Oppermann (Wiesbaden: Springer Fachmedien, 2011), 148–70; Hans J. Gießmann and Armin Wagner, ed., *Armee im Einsatz: Grundlagen, Strategien und Ergebnisse einer Beteiligung der Bundeswehr* (Baden-Baden: Nomos, 2009); Ulf von Krause, *Die Bundeswehr als Instrument deutscher Außenpolitik* (Wiesbaden: Springer, 2013), 167–363.

[11] Bernhard Chiari and Magnus Pahl, *Auslandseinsätze der Bundeswehr: Wegweiser zur Geschichte* (Paderborn, Germany: Schöningh, 2010); Gießmann and Wagner, ed., *Armee im Einsatz*; Stefan Mair, ed., *Auslandseinsätze der Bundeswehr: Leitfragen, Entscheidungsspielräumen und Lehren* (Berlin: German Institute for International and Security Affairs, 2009); Germany participated with war planes in the NATO Operation Allied Force in former Yugoslavia from March 1999 until June 1999 without a UN mandate. See Gareis, "Militärische Beiträge zur Sicherheit," 156–58.

in Libya in 2011. This had happened regardless of whether a UN mandate existed or whether Germany had agreed before to establish those military missions.[12]

Diplomats, policy planners, decision-makers, and scholars alike are consternated when a state does not behave according to their expectations of it, in part determined or at least inflected by its own commitments.[13] Predictability and coherence become even more critical in international relations when the engagement of military forces is concerned. Still having one of the largest armed forces in Europe, Germany continuously faces demands by allies and partners for more substantial contributions to military operations, as well as criticism for insufficient spending on its military capabilities.

The majority of the few analyses that aimed to explain German decisions on military intervention, however, often remained generic or stressed single factors rather than the complexity of, and the linkage between, many determinants that are especially germane and useful to the German case at hand. Because public, political, and scholarly debate alike have been concentrated on German engagement in

---

[12] Even if it had not prevented missions of UN, NATO, and EU, between 1990 and 2011, Germany agreed in 17 cases to establish a military mission, but decide afterwards not to contribute to them. The majority of the cases (13) relate to relatively small UN missions, mainly in Africa. For more details see Klaus Brummer, *Die Innenpolitik der Außenpolitik: Die Große Koalition, 'Governmental Politics' und Auslandseinsätze der Bundeswehr* (Wiesbaden: Springer VS, 2013), 21; Deutscher Bundestag, *Schriftliche Fragen: mit den in der Woche vom 4. April 2011 eingegangenen Antworten der Bundesregierung*, Drs. 17/5422 (Berlin: Bundesanzeiger Verlagsgesellschaft, August 26, 2011), 5–9, http://dipbt.bundestag.de/dip21/btd/17/054/1705422.pdf; Von Krause, *Die Bundeswehr als Instrument deutscher Außenpolitik*, 357; Regarding the European Union Force (EUFOR) Chad/CAR, it should be noted that Germany, like the United Kingdom, despite an UNSC resolution and the implementation of the Joint Action by the Council of the European Union, decided not deploy any troops into the theater and instead only contributed with four soldiers at the operational headquarters in France.

[13] Oliver Schmitt, "Strategic Users of Culture: German Decisions for Military Actions," *Contemporary Security Policy* 32, no. 1 (2012): 59.

the Afghan war, analyses for other regions and missions, such as in Africa, also are lacking. This study fills these gaps by presenting a synthetic explanatory model of the determining factors that shape and influence German policy decisions on participation or nonparticipation in military interventions in Africa, and elsewhere.

Focusing on the two recent Africa-related cases, the present work analyzes whether the decisions chiefly resulted from the specifics of the case, reflecting Germany's search for its own security policy identity hinging on national interests, or whether the decisions were based on patterns that reflect continuing paradigms, evolving qualities, and inherent contradictions of contemporary German foreign and security policy.[14] Consequently, this project broadens the view of determinants that shape German policy decisions, promotes a better understanding of the significance of military inventions as an instrument of German foreign and security policy, and serves to classify future governmental decision more accurately.

The analysis of the current relationship between Africa and Germany is particularly important for several reasons. First, a clear majority of all ongoing EU-led Common and Security Defense Policy (CSDP) and UN missions are conducted on the African continent.[15] Committing itself to pursue security objectives and interests only in multilateral cooperation, German military participation reflects this

---

[14] For the argument that Germany is still searching for its security policy ("sicherheitspolitischer Suchprozess") see Klaus Naumann, *Einsatz ohne Ziel?: Die Politikbedürftigkeit des Militärischen* (Bonn: Hamburger Edition, 2010), 27.

[15] "CDSP Map: Mission Chart," ISIS Europe, updated October 2014, http://www.csdpmap.eu/mission-chart; "CSDP Note: Overview Ongoing CSDP Missions," International Security Information Service Europe, updated October 2004, http://isis-europe.eu/wp-content/uploads/2014/06/CSDP-Overview-October-2014.pdf; "Peace Operations 2013/2014," zif-berlin, accessed October 17, 2014, http://www.zif-berlin.org/fileadmin/uploads/analyse/dokumente/veroeffentlichungen/ZIF_World_Map_Peace_Operations_2013.pdf.

intensified international engagement.¹⁶ The present work reveals whether and to which extent decisions on military engagement or nonengagement were mainly driven by external, internal, or actor-related factors.

Second, a comprehensive strategic German understanding of its interests in, and relations with, Africa is relatively new. Although broadly active in Africa in the deeds of Lettow Vorbeck or Rommel, Germany has no coherent or unitary Africa strategy before 2011; in contrast, the inaugural 2011 strategy has already been updated—in mid-2014.¹⁷ Thus, the examination of German military engagement since 2011 provides a deeper understanding of how these policies have been implemented in reality in terms of security politics as well as whether and how they have affected the decisions in reality.

Moreover, amid the proclaimed change of the African continent's nature from "hopeless" to "rising,"¹⁸ discussions about Germany's

---

16 Federal Ministry of Defense, *Defense Policy Guidelines: Safeguarding National Interests—Assuming International Responsibility—Shaping Security Together* (Berlin: Federal Ministry of Defense, 2011), 5, 11.

17 Bundesregierung, *Deutschland und Afrika: Konzept der Bundesregierung* (Berlin: Ministry of Foreign Affairs, June 2011), accessed August 7, 2014, http://www.auswaertiges-amt.de/cae/servlet/contentblob/581096/publication File/155321/110615-Afrika-Konzept-download.pdf; Bundesregierung, *Afrikapolitische Leitlinien der Bundesregierung* (Berlin: Bundesregierung, 2014), accessed August 7, 2014,http://www.monrovia.diplo.de/contentblob/4246600/Daten/4317323/Afrika_Leitlinien_Engl.pdf.

18 "Africa Rising: A Hopeful Continent," *Economist*, March 2, 2013, http://www.economist.com/news/special-report/21572377-african-lives-have-already-greatly-improved-over-past-decade-says-oliver-august; "Hopeless Africa," *Economist*, May 11, 2000, http://www.economist.com/node/333429.

international role either as a "Europe's central power,"[19] as a "shaping power,"[20] or as a "geo-economic power,"[21] were accompanied by some scholarly claims that Germany may better fit to assume a more active role in Africa than other European powers because of its marginal colonial history.[22] Thus, the present work provides insights into whether Germany's engagements in Africa since 2011 adequately reflect Germany's role, its increased international weight, and its aspirations to shoulder more responsibility in global security.

C. Literature Review

Questions of "why states intervene, when, where, and how lie at heart of international relations," but also significantly drive the social and historical sciences.[23] However, influenced by the continuing wide-

---

[19] Rainer Baumann, "Deutschland als Zentralmacht," in *Handbuch zur deutschen Außenpolitik*, ed. Sigmar Schmidt, Gunther Hellmann, and Reinhard Wolf (Wiesbaden: Verlag für Sozialwissenschaften, 2007), 62–72; German Institute for International and Security Affairs, and German Marshall Fund of the United States, *Neue Macht—Neue Verantwortung: Elemente einer deutschen Außen- und Sicherheitspolitik für eine Welt im Umbruch* (Berlin: German Institute for International and Security Affairs, 2013), 9.

[20] Bundesregierung, *Globalisierung gestalten—Partnerschaften ausbauen—Verantwortung teilen* (Berlin: Auswärtiges Amt, 2012), accessed January 15, 2015, https://www.auswaertiges-amt.de/cae/servlet/contentblob/608384/publicationFile/169965/Gestaltungsmaechtekonzept.pdf.

[21] Hans Kundnani, "Germany as a Geo-Economic Power," *Washington Quarterly* 34, no. 3 (Summer 2011): 31–45.

[22] Stefan Mair and Denis M. Tull, *Deutsche Afrikapolitik: Eckpunkte einer Strategischen Neuausrichtung* (Berlin: German Institute for International and Security Affairs, 2009), 38.

[23] Wilhelm Mirow, Strategic Culture Matters: A Comparison of German and British Military Interventions since 1990, Forschungsberichte International Politik 38 (Berlin: LIT Verlag, 2009), 1.

spread "societal indifference"[24] concerning the armed forces and the tendentious lack of a strategic debate about foreign, security, and defense policy in Germany,[25] the scholarly work on German military engagements with particular focus on regions and missions does not belong to the mainstream of contemporary security studies. Hence, the factors that determine Germany's participation or nonparticipation in military interventions, and particularly in Africa, must be analyzed within the framework of general principles and sources of contemporary German foreign and security policy and their alleged continuation, modification, or alteration. Several factors, which include considerations of the role and relevance of the Bundeswehr in international affairs, dominate the scholarly debate. They include the strategic culture and the conception of national role, competing international and domestic imperatives and constraints, national interests, and national decision-makers.

---

[24] On occasion of the commanders' convention of the Bundeswehr in October 2005, then–Federal President of Germany, Horst Köhler, spoke about a "friendly indifference" of German society towards its own armed forces and called for broad societal debate not over the Bundeswehr, but over German foreign, security, and defense policy. Horst Köhler, *Einsatz für Freiheit und Sicherheit: Rede von Bundespräsident Horst Köhler bei der Kommandeurtagung der Bundeswehr am 10. Oktober 2005 in Bonn*, 6–7, accessed October 3, 2014, http://www.bundespraesident.de/SharedDocs/Reden/DE/Horst-Koehler/Reden/2005/10/20051010_Rede_Anlage.pdf;jsessionid=A4F37B017%205C96252B7B4FBBAA1872E91.2_cid388?__blob=publicationFile&v=2.

[25] Christopher Daase and Julian Junk, "Strategische Kultur und Sicherheitsstrategien in Deutschland," *Sicherheit und Frieden* 30, no. 3 (2012): 153; Gareis, "Militärische Beiträge zur Sicherheit," 143; Hans J. Gießmann and Armin Wagner, "Auslandseinsätze der Bundeswehr," *Aus Politik und Zeitgeschichte* 48 (November 2009): 7; Michael Rühle, "In was für einer Welt leben wir?: Sicherheitspolitische Folgerungen aus einer globalisierten Welt," in *Bewährungsproben einer Nation: Die Entsendung der Bundeswehr ins Ausland,* ed. Christoph Schwegmann (Berlin: Duncker & Humblot, 2011), 22–24; Varwick, "Bundeswehr," 247; Von Krause, *Die Bundeswehr als Instrument deutscher Außenpolitik*, 337–39.

1. Continuing the "Culture of Restraint" or Becoming a "Normal Ally"?

Whether the literature refers to "political culture" or "political-military culture," all concepts of strategic culture focus on a body of norms, ideas, attitudes, and practices, shared by both elites and society, that shapes, under domestic and external influences, a persistent set of preferences and "internal predispositions" for achieving security and defense objectives.[26] These strategically prioritized options include orientations for role, relevance, and efficacy of the use of force in international affairs.[27]

---

[26] John S. Duffield framed the term "political culture," whereupon Thomas U. Berger introduced his analytical concept of a "political-military culture." The study will make use of the more common term of "strategic culture" as introduced by Kerry Longhurst and others. See John S. Duffield, "Why Germany Confounds Neorealism," *International Organizations* 53, no. 4 (Autumn 1999): 765–803; Thomas U. Berger, *Cultures of Antimilitarism: National Security in Germany and Japan* (Baltimore: John Hopkins University Press, 1998), 15–19; Kerry Longhurst, *Germany and the Use of Force: The Evolution of German Security Policy, 1990–2003* (New York: Manchester University Press, 2004), 17. See also John Glenn, "Realism versus Strategic Culture: Competition and Collaboration?," *International Studies Review* 11 (2009): 530; Christoph O. Meyer, *The Quest of a European Strategic Culture: Changing Norms on Security and Defense in the European Union* (New York: Palgrave Macmillan, 2006), 20. Moreover, this study does not intend to participate within the ongoing scholarly controversy about definitions and the effects of strategic culture as an independent variable on a state's behavior. For an overview of the discussion, see Tobias M. Wilke, *German Strategic Culture Revisited: Link the Past to Contemporary German Strategic Choices*, Forschungsberichte International Politik 36 (Berlin: LIT Verlag, 2007), 17–24. For the "internal predispositions" of a country and the linkage with conditions of the external environment, see Wolfram Hanrieder, "Compatibility and Consensus: A Proposal for the Conceptual Linkage of External and Internal Dimensions of Foreign Policy," *American Political Science Review* 61, no. 4 (December 1967): 971.

[27] Alastair Lain Johnston, "Thinking about Strategic Culture," *International Security* 19, no. 4 (Spring 1995): 46; Longhurst, *Germany and the Use of Force*, 17; Mirow, *Strategic Culture Matters*, 6–7.

Proponents of this "continuation" school of thought argue that Germany's strategic "culture of reticence,"[28] the symptoms and causes of which include an aversion to unilateralism and a deep skepticism on the use of armed forces, influenced and persistently affects decision-making and opinions while addressing international crises and conflicts, all of which is a legacy of the epoch 1945–1989 in the development of the Federal Republic of Germany in this period.[29] They claim that the persistent cultural-normative dictates are most visible in Germany's reluctant and only slowly evolving participation in multilateral, out-of-area missions since unification.[30] Although gradually expanding the nature, scope, and geography of military engagements as the result of the imperative to slowly change what had been until 1990 a central tenet of political life and the international order, Germany's decision-makers and public alike maintained their

---

[28] Duffield, "Why Germany Confounds Neorealism," 788. Sometimes also named "Culture of Restraint." See Rainer Baumann and Gunther Hellmann, "Germany and the Use of Force: 'Total War,' the 'Culture of Restraint,' and the Quest for Normality," *German Politics* 10, no. 1 (April 2001): 61–82.

[29] For an overview of detailed features of Germany's strategic culture, see Longhurst, *Germany and the Use of Force*, 17, 47; Schmitt, "Strategic Users of Culture," 65; Björn Conrad and Mario Stumm, *German Strategic Culture and Institutional Choice: Transatlanticism and/or Europeanism?*, Trierer Arbeitspapiere zur Internationalen Politik (Trier, Germany: Lehrstuhl für Außenpolitik und Internationale Beziehungen, 2004), 32–33.

[30] Study examples on impacts of strategic culture on decisions for German participation or nonparticipation in military interventions can be found in Wilke, *German Strategic Culture Revisited* and Baumann and Hellmann, "Germany and the Use of Force." For specific case studies for German military engagement in Africa, see Schmitt, "Strategic Users of Culture"; Mirow, *Strategic Culture Matters*; Sandra Pillath, *Motive und Rollenkonzepte deutscher Außenpolitik: Die Auslandseinsätze der Bundeswehr im Kongo und Libanon*, Studien zur Internationalen Politik, ed. August Pradetto, Anette Jünemann, and Michael Staack (Hamburg: Institut für Internationale Politik an der Helmut-Schmidt-Universität, 2008), 39–60.

preference for political and more or less nonviolent resolutions of conflict and for military means only as a last resort.[31]

In contrast to this careful adaptation of German strategic culture to increased external commitments under continued domestic antimilitary sentiments, proponents of "change" school of thought see significant and structural adaptations.[32] Germany's participation in the NATO air campaign in the former Yugoslavia without a UN mandate in 1999, the unilateral abstention from several international military operations since 2003, and especially the commitment in the Afghan war after 2001, marked turning points and contributed to unprecedented shifts in the general outlines of German foreign pol-

---

[31] Schmitt, "Strategic Users of Culture"; Longhurst, *Germany and the Use of Force*; Mirow, *Strategic Culture Matters*; Kai Oppermann, "National Role Conceptions, Domestic Constraints and the New 'Normalcy' in German Foreign Policy: The Eurozone Crisis, Libya and Beyond," *German Politics* 21, no. 4 (December 2012): 509; Robert von Rimscha, "Ein Land tut sich schwer: Bundeswehr-Einsätze seit 1991," in *Bewährungsproben einer Nation: Die Entsendung der Bundeswehr ins Ausland*, ed. Christoph Schwegman (Berlin: Duncker & Humblot, 2011), 73.

[32] Longhurst argues that Germany's strategic culture has not changed, but successfully adapted after the end of the Cold War. Overhaus, Harnisch, and Katsioulis argue that the "culture of restraint" continued even after the increase of participation in military interventions, but the ties between Germany and its allies have loosened. Baumann and Hellmann, however, argue that specifically the increased participation of Germany in multilateral mission illustrates not a mere adaptation to an evolving international environment, but a significant or even structural change. Roos, and Guérot and Leonard have recently supported this analysis. Longhurst, *Germany and the Use of Force*, 147; Marco Overhaus, Sebastian Harnisch and Christos Katsioulis, "Schlussbetrachtung: Gelockerte Bindungen und eigene Wege der deutschen Sicherheitspolitik?," in *Deutsche Sicherheitspolitik: Eine Bilanz der Regierung Schröder*, ed. Sebastian Harnisch, Christos Katsioulis, and Marco Overhaus (Baden-Baden: Nomos, 2004), 253; Baumann and Hellmann, "Germany and the Use of Force," 20; Ulrich Roos, "Deutsche Außenpolitik nach der Vereinigung: Zwischen ernüchterndem Idealismus und realpolitischem Weltordnungsstreben," *Zeitschrift für Internationale Beziehungen* 19, no. 2 (2012): 33; Ulrike Guérot and Mark Leonard, "The New German Question: How Europe Can Get the Germany It Needs," *ECFR Policy Brief* (London: European Council on Foreign Relations, 2011), 6.

icy. As a result, Germany's policies toward military engagements became not only more self-confident, but also more ambiguous.[33]

Originally related to, and still mainly focused on, foreign policy decision-makers,[34] conceptions of national role encompass societal shared "beliefs or images about the identity of the state."[35] These images include definitions of "appropriate orientations or functions of … [a] state toward, or in, the external environment."[36] Emerging throughout the postwar period, the "civilian power" theorem still dominates the scholarly discussion and the public understanding of Germany's foreign policy identity.[37] Framed by the key mottos of "never again," "never alone," and "politics before force," it promotes

---

[33] Duffield, "Why Germany Confounds Neorealism," 787–89; Conrad and Stumm, *German Strategic Culture and Institutional Choice*, 63; Von Krause, *Die Bundeswehr als Instrument deutscher Außenpolitik*, 352; Wolfgang Ischinger, "Germany after Libya: Still a Responsible Power?," in *All Alone? What U.S. Entrenchment Means for Europe and NATO*, ed. Tomas Valasek (London: Center for European Reform, 2012), 47–51. Germany's participation within the NATO Operation Allied Forces, in Serb 1999 and the abstention from participation in the Iraq War, 2003, are often raised as diametric examples."

[34] K.J. Holsti, "National Role Conceptions in the Study of Foreign Policy," *International Studies Quarterly* 14, no. 3 (September 1970): 233–309.

[35] Cameron G. Thies, *Role Theory and Foreign Policy* (Iowa City: University of Iowa, Department of Political Science, 2009), 1, 14–15. It should be noted, however, that national role conceptions can be contested both among foreign policy decision-makers and between the political elites and the general public. See Cristian Cantir and Juliet Kaarbo, "Contested Roles and Domestic Politics: Reflection on Role Theory in Foreign Policy Analysis and IR Theory," *Foreign Policy Analysis* 8 (2012): 5–24.

[36] Holsti, "National Role Conceptions," 246.

[37] It should be noted, however, that the concept itself was first framed after the Cold War. Hanns W. Maull, "Germany and Japan: The New Civilian Powers," *Foreign Affairs* 69, no. 5 (1990): 91–106. Including Japan as civilian power, the concept parallels the cultural approach of "antimilitarism." See Berger, *Cultures of Antimilitarism*.

multilateralism, integration, political solutions, and constrained use of force as guiding preferences in international affairs.[38]

Proponents of the concept argue that increased participation in military interventions outside the traditional NATO context of collective defense, as established in Articles V and VI did not reflect a fundamental departure from Germany's foreign and security policy identity as "civilian power." Instead, Germany was able to reconcile increased external demands and requirements of a changed security environment with its own core values. The continuity of essential paradigms, they claim, would even explain unilateral decisions against a participation in Iraq in 2003, Chad/CAR in 2007/2008, or Libya in 2011.[39]

Yet, another scholarly stream contests the applicability of "civilian power" as a guideline for contemporary and future German foreign and security policy.[40] In this view, Germany, beginning with red-green coalition under Federal Chancellor Gerhard Schröder from 1998 until 2005, underwent a progressive but dramatic change of its

---

[38] Hanns W. Maull, "Germany and the Use of Force: Still a Civilian Power?," *Trierer Arbeitspapiere zur Internationalen Politik* 2 (Trier: Lehrstuhl für Außenpolitik und Internationale Beziehungen, 1999), 4–9.

[39] Hanns W. Maull, "Außenpolitische Entscheidungsprozesse in Krisenzeiten," *Aus Politik und Zeitgeschichte* 62, no. 10 (March 2012): 36; Hanns W. Maull, "Deutschland als Zivilmacht," in *Handbuch zur deutschen Außenpolitik*, ed. Siegmar Schmidt, Gunther Hellmann, and Reinhard Wolf (Wiesbaden: Verlag für Sozialwissenschaften, 2007), 82; Hanns W. Maull, "'Normalisierung' oder Auszehrung?: Deutsche Außenpolitik im Wandel," *Aus Politik und Zeitgeschichte* B11 (2004): 19–23; Mirow, *Strategic Culture Matters,* 75; Thomas Risse-Kappen, "Kontinuität durch Wandel: Eine 'neue' deutsche Außenpolitik?," *Aus Politik und Zeitgeschichte* B11 (2004): 31. Proponents of the civilian power theorem argue that these unilateral deviations from the concepts could be explained as unique, contextual-based exemptions, but do not question the validity of the entire concept as such.

[40] Dieter Dettke, "Deutschland als europäische Macht und Bündnispartner," *Aus Politik und Zeitgeschichte* 15-16 (April 2009): 45; Werner Link, "Vom Elend des 'offensiven Idealismus:' Eine Antwort auf Hellmanns 'Traditionslinie' und 'Sozialisationsperspektive,'" *WeltTrends* 12, no. 3 (2004): 49.

foreign policy identity toward becoming a "normal ally."[41] This normalization manifests itself in increased aspirations to shoulder more responsibility, including participation in military interventions, but also in a much more emancipated, self-confident weighing between national interests and external expectations.[42] As a normal country, Germany considers contributions to military interventions as a basic requirement for its security policy, but is also able to oppose them.[43]

---

[41] Oppermann, "National Role Conceptions."

[42] Gunther Hellmann, Reinhard Wolf, and Siegmar Schmidt, "Deutsche Außenpolitik in historischer und systematischer Perspektive," in *Handbuch zur deutschen Außenpolitik*, ed. Sigmar Schmidt, Gunther Hellmann, and Reinhard Wolf (Wiesbaden: Verlag für Sozialwissenschaften, 2007), 36–37; Gunther Hellmann, "Das neue Selbstbewusstsein deutscher Außenpolitik und die veränderten Standards der Angemessenheit," in *Deutsche Außenpolitik*, 2nd ed., ed. Thomas Jäger, Alexander Höse, and Kai Oppermann (Wiesbaden: VS Verlag für Sozialwissenschaft 2011), 735–58; Roos, "Deutsche Außenpolitik nach der Vereinigung, 33–34; Oppermann, " National Role Conceptions," 506–507, 514; Wilke, *German Strategic Culture Revisited*, 12–13; Martin Wagner, *Auf dem Weg zu einer 'normalen' Macht?: Die Entsendung deutscher Streitkräfte in der Ära Schröder*, Trierer Arbeitspapiere zur Internationalen Politik 8 (Trier: Lehrstuhl für Außenpolitik und Internationale Beziehungen, 2004), 2. It should be noted, however, that some scholars refuse the concept of normalization. Their critique focuses on the question concerning appropriate parameters to compare the nature and the evolution of German foreign and security policy and demand a more nuanced perspective. See Sebastian Harnisch and Kerry Longhurst, "Understanding Germany: The Limits of 'Normalization' and the Prevalence of Strategic Culture," in *German Culture, Politics, and Literature into the Twenty-First Century: Beyond Normalization*, ed. Stuart Taberner and Paul Cooke (Rochester, NY: Camden House, 2006), 50; Stefan Fröhlich, "Herausforderungen der deutschen Außen- und Sicherheitspolitik bis 2030: Grundlegende Problemstellungen," *Zeitschrift für Außen- und Sicherheitspolitik* 5, no. 3 (2012): 404–405. For a critique to apply the term concerning military engagements see Von Krause, *Die Bundeswehr als Instrument deutscher Außenpolitik*, 245–46.

[43] Roos, "Deutsche Außenpolitik nach der Vereinigung," 27; Varwick, "Neue deutsche Außenpolitik," 15. One also notes that from 1950 onward, the young Federal Republic of Germany decided to arm itself in the Western alliance and bore an extraordinary burden of potential armed force not only of itself, but of its NATO allies and the enduring possibility of destruction in nuclear war.

2. Reflexive Multilateralism or Domestic Politics?

These thoughts echo in the literature of Germany's foreign and security policy the refrain of "two-level logic,"[44] arguing that paradigms and decisions alike, including those for the deployment of military forces, are shaped, incentivized, and constrained by both international and domestic imperatives and conditions. Depending on the context, however, international and domestic conditions may not only contradict themselves, but also their impact on policy choices may vary,[45] which causes inconsistent behavior.

Some scholars of the question contend that international demands and responsibilities still decisively influence, or even dominate, German foreign and security policy, including Berlin's decisions on participation in military interventions.[46] Chief among the external expectations of Germany's allies and partners since unification in 1990 have been the promotion of a European integration; burden-sharing within the transatlantic and European cooperation; and the translation of

---

[44] Robert D. Putnam, "Diplomacy and Domestic Politics: The Logic of Two-Level Games," *International Organizations* 42, no. 3 (Summer 1988): 427–60. See also Kai Oppermann and Alexander Höse, "Die innenpolitischen Restriktionen deutscher Außenpolitik," in *Deutsche Außenpolitik: Sicherheit, Wohlfahrt, Institutionen und Normen*, 2nd ed., ed. Thomas Jäger, Alexander Höse, and Kai Oppermann (Wiesbaden: Springer Fachmedien, 2011), 44; Von Krause, *Die Bundeswehr als Instrument deutscher Außenpolitik*, 16.

[45] Oppermann and Höse, "Die innenpolitischen Restriktionen deutscher Außenpolitik," 44–45.

[46] Markus Kaim, "Deutsches Interesse versus Bündnisverpflichtung: Zur Frage nationaler Handlungsspielräume bei Auslandseinsätzen der Bundeswehr," in *Armee im Einsatz: Grundlagen, Strategien und Ergebnisse einer Beteiligung der Bundeswehr*, ed. Hans J. Gießmann and Armin Wagner (Baden-Baden: Nomos: 2009), 177–83; Alice Pannier and Oliver Schmitt, "Institutionalized Cooperation and Policy Convergence in European Defense: Lessons from the Relations between France, Germany, and the UK," *European Security* 23, no. 3 (2014): 3-4; Bernhard Rinke, "Die Auslandseinsätze der Bundeswehr im Parteienstreit," in *Armee im Einsatz: Grundlagen, Strategien und Ergebnisse einer Beteiligung der Bundeswehr*, ed. Hans J. Gießmann und Armin Wagner (Baden-Baden: Nomos: 2009), 172–75; Longhurst, *Germany and the Use of Force*, 148.

Germany's economic-political heft into more global responsibility, including commitments in military missions, so as to end the Federal Republic's "check-book diplomacy"[47] (noticeable in the 1990–1991 Gulf War) as well as its much storied security free-riding—an old saw going back to the early days of the Cold War.[48] These expectations were reflected in Germany's normative and practical imperative to organize and implement foreign and security policy exclusively within multilateral frameworks, as all relevant strategic documents and government declarations repeatedly emphasize.[49]

This strong emphasis on the principle of collective action, Markus Kaim argues however, narrows Germany's room for manoeuver in international affairs, creating a "multilateralism trap."[50] Accordingly, after a collective decision for participation in NATO or the EU, Germany could not refuse to contribute substantially, even if the domestic context may prefer such nonparticipation.[51] Thus, as a kind of

---

[47] Longhurst, *Germany and the Use of Force*, 148–49.

[48] Helga Haftendorn, *Deutsche Außenpolitik zwischen Selbstbeschränkung und Selbstbehauptung, 1945—2000* (München: Deutsche Verlags-Anstalt, 2001), 386–431. For a recent claim see Jackson Janes, "Merkel 3.0: German Foreign and Security Policy in the Aftermath of the 2013 Bundestag Election," *German Politics and Society* 112, no. 3 (Autumn 2014): 88–91; Hans-Ulrich Klose and Ruprecht Polenz, "Wahre Werte, falsche Freunde: Deutschlands Partner sitzen im Westen—eine Erinnerung aus gegebenem Anlass," *Internationale Politik* 5 (September/October 2011): 18.

[49] Federal Ministry of Defense, *White Paper 2006*, 5–8; Federal Ministry of Defense, *Defense Policy Guidelines*, 5–8; *Deutschlands Zukunft gestalten: Koalitionsvertrag zwischen CDU, CSU und SPD, 18. Legislaturperiode*, Berlin: 2013, 168–71, accessed August 10, 2014, http://www.bundesregierung.de/Content/DE/ Anlagen/2013/2013-12-17-koalitionsvertrag.pdf? blob=publicationFile.

[50] Markus Kaim, "Deutsche Auslandseinsätze in der Multilateralismusfalle?," in *Auslandseinsätze der Bundeswehr: Leitfragen, Entscheidungsspielräumen und Lehren*, ed. Stefan Mair (Berlin: German Institute for International and Security Affairs, 2009), 43-44. See also Von Krause, *Die Bundeswehr als Instrument deutscher Außenpolitik*, 356; Gießmann and Wagner, "Auslandseinsätze der Bundeswehr," 7.

[51] Kaim, "Deutsches Interesse versus Bündnisverpflichtung," 177.

"reflexive multilateralism,"[52] Germany participates, and continues to be engaged, in missions that may not be justified by national interests or for which a broad political and public consensus may not exist. Political debates and public opinion surveys concerning military interventions in the Balkans, Africa, and Afghanistan from the late 1990s until 2010 seem to support these claims.[53]

Although Germany has maintained its preference for multilateral cooperation, other scholars argue that the nature of its multilateralism has changed. Embedded in gradual shifts of Germany's foreign and security policy self-conception, including a heightened sense of self-confidence and responsibility,[54] German multilateralism, they postulate, has become more pragmatic, selective, and instrumental.[55] The reticence to participate in missions in Iraq in 2003 and in Libya in 2011 may reflect a certain resistance to external expectations of unquestioning multilateralism.

---

[52] Roos, "Deutsche Außenpolitik nach der Vereinigung," 33.

[53] For role and relevance of external demands and internal alliance solidarity in contrast to the political debate and public opinion in the framework of Germany's participation in several military interventions since 1990, see Wilke, *German Strategic Culture Revisited*, 70–110; Mirow, *Strategic Culture Matters*, 31–75; Kaim, "Deutsche Auslandseinsätze in der Multilateralismusfalle?," 46.

[54] A vocabulary analysis that reconstructs the development of the German foreign policy practice between 1986 and 2002 on the basis of the foreign policy elite's discourse can be found in Gunther Hellmann et al., "'Selbstbewusst' und 'stolz': Das außenpolitische Vokabular der Berliner Republik als Fährte einer Neuorientierung," *Politische Vierteljahresschrift* 48, no. 4 (2007): 650–79.

[55] Rainer Baumann, "Multilateralismus: Die Wandelung eines vermeintlichen Kontinuitätselements der deutschen Außenpolitik," in *Deutsche Außenpolitik: Sicherheit, Wohlfahrt, Institutionen und Normen*, 2nd ed., ed. Thomas Jäger, Alexander Höse, and Kai Oppermann (Wiesbaden: Springer Fachmedien, 2011), 468–87; Rainer Baumann, "The Transformation of German Multilateralism: Changes in the Foreign-Policy Discourse since Unification," *German Politics and Society* 20, no. 4 (Winter 2002): 1–26; Oppermann, "National Role Conceptions," 507; Roos, "Deutsche Außenpolitik nach der Vereinigung," 33–34.

In contrast to the international dimension of Germany's two-level logic, another scholarly group sees a "domestic politicization"[56] of German foreign policy because electoral considerations, party and coalition politics, and public opinion increasingly influence and contest foreign policy choices.[57] Because the preservation of office concerns these leaders most fundamentally, decision-makers attentively and continually monitor the preferences of the German public and the mainstream media for direction in military solutions, aligning their behavior with the popular mood to avoid any harmful repercussions to their electoral prospects.[58] The general skepticism of the German public toward international deployments of the Bundeswehr—particularly if they involve high-intensity combat missions, as in Afghanistan[59]—appeals to decision-makers and parliamentarians alike, framing, constraining, and mediating their attitudes toward, and decisions about, the use of military means as an instrument in political affairs. Hence, public opinion facilitates, if not encourages, ambiguity in the face of critical decisions for military interventions.

---

[56] Oppermann, "National Role Conceptions," 509.

[57] Oppermann, "National Role Conceptions," 504–505 and 508–510; Oppermann and Höse, "Die innenpolitischen Restriktionen deutscher Außenpolitik," 48–72; Maull, "'Normalisierung' oder Auszehrung?," 21; Katy A. Crossley-Frolick, "Domestic Constraints, German Foreign Policy and Post-Conflict Peacebuilding," *German Politics and Society* 31, no. 3 (Autumn 2013): 43–75; Sabine Collmer, "'All Politics Is Local': Deutsche Sicherheits- und Verteididungspolitik im Spiegel der Öffentlichen Meinung," in *Deutsche Sicherheitspolitik: Eine Bilanz der Regierung Schröder*, ed. Sebastian Harnisch, Christos Katsioulis, and Marco Overhaus (Baden-Baden: Nomos, 2004), 201–225; Christos Katsioulis, "Deutsche Sicherheitspolitik im Parteiendiskurs: Alter Wein in neuen Schläuchen," in *Deutsche Sicherheitspolitik: Eine Bilanz der Regierung Schröder*, ed. Sebastian Harnisch, Christos Katsioulis, and Marco Overhaus (Baden-Baden: Nomos, 2004), 227-252.

[58] Oppermann, "National Role Conceptions," 504; For a recent survey see Körber-Stiftung, ed., *Einmischen oder zurückhalten?: Die Sicht der Deutschen auf die Außenpolitik* (Hamburg: Körber-Stiftung, 2014).

[59] Markus Kaim, *Deutschlands Einsatz in Afghanistan: Die sicherheitspolitische Dimension*, Note du Cerfa 76 (Paris: Institut Français du Relations International, 2012), 9–11.

Additionally, some scholars argue that Germany's foreign and security policy has become more volatile through the dynamics of party and coalition politics in the recent past versus the old order that was obtained in the pre-unified Federal Republic of Germany (FRG).[60] Since unification in 1990, Germany's executive and legislative branches both represent a more heterogeneous spectrum of foreign policy orientations. Whereas a Cold War consensus about security policy operated in the FRG from about the middle of the 1950s until 1989, post-unification coalition politics increased the pressure for consensus building, resulting in varying or even inconsistent foreign and security policy preferences toward military interventions after a governmental change, which influences decision-making processes. Furthermore, party politics may restrain Germany's international affairs as they reflect and intensify public debates for appropriate foreign policy reactions as well as imposing pressure on key actors within the decision-making process.[61]

3. National Interests—Which, Where, and How?

In his speech for the introduction of the new *White Paper 2006*, then-Minister of Defense Franz Josef Jung underlined that German out-of-area missions must correspond to the values of the Basic Law—as the Federal Republic's constitution is called; the objectives and responsibilities of international commitments; and national interests.[62] The orientation toward values and interests as guiding principles for Ger-

---

[60] Rinke, "Die Auslandseinsätze der Bundeswehr im Parteienstreit," 165–175; Torsten Oppelland, "Parteien," in *Handbuch zur deutschen Außenpolitik*, ed. Siegmar Schmidt, Gunther Hellmann, and Reinhard Wolf (Wiesbaden: Verlag für Sozialwissenschaften, 2007) 269–70; Crossley-Frolick, "Domestic Constraints," 58–61; Oppermann, "National Role Conceptions," 508.

[61] Oppermann and Höse, "Die innenpolitischen Restriktionen deutscher Außenpolitik Domestic political constraints of German foreign policy]," 68.

[62] Deutscher Bundestag, *Stenografischer Bericht: Plenarprotokoll 16/60* (Berlin: Deutscher Bundestag, October 26, 2006), 5784, accessed September 20, 2014, http://dipbt.bundestag.de/dip21/btp/ 16/16060.pdf.

man foreign and security policy in general, and in particular for decisions on military engagement, has been repeatedly emphasized in all official strategic papers as well as by politicians and scholars alike from the birth of such white papers in 1969 until the present.[63] However, international relations theory scholarly work rejects an overly generic definition of interests in the current policy documents, which fail to distinguish clearly between national and multilateral objectives, let alone elucidating when, where, and how Germany is willing to pursue them.

Most importantly, these critics charge that both strategic documents and political debates proceed without any coherent or consistent articulation of priorities among these interests for support of military engagements in certain preferred mission frameworks.[64] As a consequence, some argue, Germany's decisions to participate in the ISAF, KFOR, or EUFOR Congo missions were not derived from

---

[63] Federal Ministry of Defense, *White Paper 2006*, 21–22; Federal Ministry of Defense, *Defense Policy Guidelines*, 3–6; *Deutschlands Zukunft gestalten*, 168; German Institute for International and Security Affairs and German Marshall Fund of the United States, *Neue Macht—Neue Verantwortung*, 5–6; Michael Staack, "Normative Grundlagen, Werte und Interessen deutscher Sicherheitspolitik," in *Deutsche Sicherheitspolitik: Herausforderungen, Akteure und Prozesse*, 2nd ed., ed. Stephan Böckenförde and Sven Bernhard Gareis (Opladen, Germany: Verlag Barbara Buderich, 2014), 60–63; Rolf Clement, "Die neue Bundeswehr als Instrument deutscher Außenpolitik," *Aus Politik und Zeitgeschichte* B11 (2004): 42; Franz Josef Jung, *Deutsche Sicherheitsinteressen und die Rolle der Bundeswehr. Punktation des Bundesministers der Verteidigung bei der Konrad Adenauer Stiftung* (Berlin: Bundesministerium der Verteidigung, June 18, 2007), 9, accessed September 20, 2014, http://www.kas.de/upload/dokumente/2007/070618_jung.pdf.

[64] Bertelsmann Stiftung, ed., *Gut, aber nicht gut genug: Das neue sicherheitspolitische Weißbuch der Bundesrepublik Deutschland* (Gütersloh, Germany: Bertelsmann Stiftung, 2006), 9–10, accessed September 21, 2014, http://www.fundacionbertelsmann.org/cps/rde/xbcr/SID-1503D609-1DA671C6/bst/Analyse_Weissbuch.pdf; Gareis, "Militärische Beiträge zur Sicherheit," 164–65. A more positive analysis of pursued national interests in German foreign and security affairs is provided by August Pradetto, "Ganz und gar nicht ohne Interessen: Deutschland formuliert nicht nur Ziele—Es setzt sie auch durch," *Internationale Politik* 1 (January 2006): 114–21.

German national interests, as officially claimed; rather, these interests were "discovered" immediately before the start of the missions to legitimate domestically the deployment of Bundeswehr soldiers.[65]

The uncertainty about how to use military force within foreign affairs to pursue German national interests in the shadow of the NATO mission in Afghanistan culminated in media uproar and intense debate in May 2010, when then-Federal President Horst Köhler declared that Germany, as a foreign-trade–dependent country, must protect its interests, such as free trade routes, with means up to and including, in extreme cases, the military.[66] Although clearly referring to interests as stated in the White Paper 2006, a document that hardly any citizen of the FRG had ever read, Köhler's remarks were almost completely understood by his outspoken and populist critics as to call to return to German saber-rattling. Köhler ultimately resigned amid the continuing public furor, which characterized him as illegitimately promoting military interventions to enforce Germany's economic interests and to militarize German foreign policy.[67] Köhler had broken taboos about security policy and armed forces, and, at least in the eyes of his critics, had exceeded his role as federal president versus the chancellor and, in this case, her cabinet.

---

[65] Kaim,"Deutsches Interesse versus Bündnisverpflichtung," 179; Hanns W. Maull, "Nationale Interessen! Aber was sind sie?: Auf der Suche nach Orientierungsgrundlagen für die deutsche Außenpolitik," *Internationale Politik* (October 2006): 63.

[66] Hörst Köhler, interview by Christopher Ricke, *Deutschlandradio*, May 22, 2010, accessed October 31, 2014, http://www.deutschlandradio.de/sie-leisten-wirklich-grossartiges-unter-schwierigsten.331.de.html?dram:article_id=203276.

[67] Sebastian Fischer and Veit Medick, "Bundeswehr in Afghanistan: Köhler entfacht neue Kriegsdebatte," *Spiegel Online*, May 27, 2010, http://www.spiegel.de/politik/deutschland/bundeswehr-in-afghanistan-koehler-entfacht-neue-kriegsdebatte-a-696982.html; Reuters, "Militäreinsatz für deutsche Wirtschaftsinteressen?," *Zeit Online*, May 27, 2010, http://pdf.zeit.de/politik/deutschland/2010-05/koehler-bundeswehr-wirtschaft-2.pdf.

4. Policy- and Decision-Makers—Movers and Shakers?

Although the literature is divided about the extent to which leaders' dispositions, attitudes, and beliefs rather than situational factors determine their actions, it supports the significance of key stakeholders in shaping and changing general foreign policy guidelines, as well as their relevance within event-driven decision-making processes.[68] Scholarly work on Germany's participation or nonparticipation in multilateral military operations until 2011—from Yugoslavia in 1999, through Iraq in 2003, to Libya in 2011—shows that the triad composed of the federal chancellor, minister of foreign affairs, and minister of defense significantly influenced the political debate and the decision-making. Federal Chancellor Schröder's emphasis on more self-confidence and Foreign Minister Westerwelle's reluctance to depart from a "culture of restraint" may reflect two poles of German strategic thinking, which affected decision-making for military engagements.

D. Problems and Hypotheses

The majority of the literature focuses on the discussion of whether and to what extent continuity or change in the axioms of foreign policy explains contemporary German foreign and security behavior. The attempts to design approaches for the foundation, function, and scope of German foreign policy predominate. As the introduction to the literature review highlighted, however, scholarly work that conceptualizes the evolving role and relevance of armed forces and their engagement in military interventions as an instrument for German foreign policy is underrepresented. Moreover, many analyses remained generic or stressed single factors rather than the complexity of and the linkage between external and internal determinants within

---

[68] Robert Jervis, "Do Leaders Matter and How Would We Know?," *Security Studies* 22, no. 2 (2013): 153–79, http://dx.doi.org/10.1080/09636412.2013.786909; Putnam, "Diplomacy and Domestic Politics," 456–60.

the explanation for a specific policy decision. Among other things, the mission framework itself, the influence of current military interventions, and domestic conditions are undersold.

Decisions on participation in military interventions may be single-case political answers[69] to a set of interacting factors and/or they may reflect deeply ingrained tenets. Instead of isolating a predominant single cause, this study argues that within a complex and unique context for a decision-making process for German military engagements, factors on the external, internal, and actor level as well as the interplay between these factors determined, to a varying degree, the outcome. By doing so, the present work explains persistent and changing paradigms of German foreign policy behavior, but also the specifics of the particular case of German policy in Africa.

Anchored in the case studies of Libya and Mali, this study finally argues that within a complex interplay of determinants on three interrelated levels, six factors—strategic approaches (if applicable), multilateral imperatives, the mission framework, cultural and conceptual axioms, domestic politics, and policy-makers—chiefly inform Germany's decision-making-process on *whether* and *how* German soldiers should be deployed in a certain mission.

Magnified by an uncertain and shifting security environment, by the salient Afghanistan war experience, and by indecisive notions of interests, the question of *how*—under *what conditions*, in *which scenarios*, and for *what tasks*—German soldiers are expected to act plays a dominant role in the decision-making by makers of policy as to *whether* Germany should embark on military engagements—in Africa and elsewhere. Apart from collective defense efforts, modestly shaped and clearly delineated military contributions to such noncombat mis-

---

[69] Thomas de Maizière, "Regierungserklärung des Bundesministers der Verteidigung zur Neuausrichtung der Bundeswehr," in *Plenarprotokoll* 17/112 (May 27, 2011): 12816, accessed October 10, 2014, http://dipbt.bundestag.de/dip21/btp/17/17112.pdf.

sions as humanitarian aid, training support, or peacekeeping/peace-enforcing operations, will most likely constitute Germany's foreign and security policy touchstone on the use of military force between what is (mainly) externally required versus what is politically desired and indispensable, militarily affordable and feasible, and domestically justifiable. German participation in wars or in war-like operations as in the case of Afghanistan remains and increasingly becomes an exception.

Finally, this project concludes that the active but modest instances of Germany's military engagement in Africa after Libya, and particularly after the beginning of 2014, correspond with Berlin's stance for a more active and responsible foreign and security policy in a changed world. Such a policy plays out among three interrelated premises of contemporary German foreign and security policy in Africa: "empower others," "being responsible," and "being restrained."

The duality of the latter two tenets characterizes contemporary German foreign and security policy—particularly concerning the use of military force. At the same time, the tension between responsibility and restraint challenges state actors to find a balance.

E. Methods and Sources

To identify reasons and causes of a state's decision to participate or not to participate in an international military intervention requires investigation of the foreign policy decision-making process of the respective state. This project combines a historical-descriptive approach, trying to portray the overall picture of a state's foreign policy over or within certain phases, with an explanatory analysis of foreign and security policy by seeking to identify and validate factors that affect national foreign policy and determine the political decisions.

The decision-making process itself and the influencing factors serve as an explanation for foreign and security policy actions.[70]

To provide substance to the analysis, the present work follows the methodology of process tracing. Process tracing is a tool of qualitative analysis that seeks to identify and draw a causal sequences between one or more independent variable to one dependent variable based on qualitative data.[71] The core of the study is the extraction of facts through text analysis. Governmental sources, such as strategic policies, governmental declarations, protocols of parliamentary debates and decisions, and official statements of politicians, such as interviews and speeches, will not only serve as primary sources but also provide evidence for conditions and changes of governmental as well as individual perspectives on military interventions as an instrument in international affairs. Secondary sources, such as surveys of public opinion, media releases, and scholarly work, extent and deepen the insights.

The scope of the study encompasses three dimensions.[72] Based on text analyses, the descriptive dimension provides the narrative of context and sequence of events within the decision-making process. The analytical part of each case, the analytical-connecting dimension, explains the degree to which each factor influenced the decision and how the linkage between them affected the outcome. The final analysis, the comparative-generalizing dimension, summarizes, compares,

---

[70] Dirk Peters, "Ansätze und Methoden der Außenpolitikanalyse," in *Handbuch zur deutschen Außenpolitik*, ed. Sigmar Schmidt, Gunther Hellmann, and Reinhard Wolf (Wiesbaden: Verlag für Sozialwissenschaften, 2007), 815; Nik Milosevic, *Deutsche Kriegsbeteiligung und—verweigerung: Analyse der Einflussfaktoren im politischen Entscheidungsprozess der Fälle Kosovo, Afghanistan, Irak, und Libyen* (Hamburg, Diplomica Verlag, 2012), 7.

[71] David Collier, "Understanding Process Tracing," *Political Science and Politics* 44, no. 4 (2011): 823.

[72] Helga Haftendorn, "Zur Theorie außenpolitischer Entscheidungsprozesse," in *Theorien der internationalen Beziehungen: Bestandsaufnahme und Forschungsprozesse*, ed. Volker Ritterberger (Opladen, Germany: Westdeutscher Verlag, 1990), 402.

and assesses the results of the studies within the general context of paradigms for and evolutions in Germany's decisions on participations in military interventions.

The book encompasses two case studies of contemporary German decisions on military engagement in Africa since 2011: Libya and Mali, after having analyzed the chief developments in paradigms of German foreign and security policy until 2011. The cases, timeframe, and regional selections are based on two relevant aspects. First, the book seeks to explore the complexity of relevant factors for the decisions on military engagements as a potential answer to a new crisis and not to ongoing crisis management. Extension of existing mandates for participation in international military missions, even if intensively domestically debated, do not completely explain the interactions between external and internal factors. Moreover, not one single extension has been refused by the German parliament until today. Second, the scholarly work on developments of Germany's international military engagements lacks the analyses of contemporary cases, especially in Africa. Starting with the examination in 2011 will also allow for analysis of the impact and relevance of the two strategic concepts of the German government for Africa.

F.   Study Overview

The study consists of five chapters. After this introduction, chapter II introduces and elucidates the explanatory model for Germany's decisions on participation in international military interventions, as drawn by the author.

After a description of the context and an illustration of the sequence of events leading to the decisions on participation or nonparticipation, the explanatory model serves in chapters III and IV as roster to analyze the influence and significance of each determinant, the potential interdependences between them, and the linkages between the levels on the respective decision of the German government. Chapter III presents and analyzes context and decision-making process under the influence of factors in the external, internal, and actor level for the (official) nonparticipation in the NATO Operation Unified Protector in Libya in 2011. Chapter IV repeats the process for the German participation within the European Union Training Mission (EUTM) and the International Support Mission under African lead (AFISMA) in Mali. Briefly looking at the evolution of German military engagement in Africa up to 2015, the conclusion addresses the role of Africa in German strategic thinking and looks forward to the future nature of German foreign and security policy under Germany's aspiration for more international responsibility and under a shifting perception concerning the role and relevance of the use of military force within it.

II. German Foreign and Security Policy Decisions for International Military Engagements—An Explanatory Approach

For decades political scientists, foreign and security policy experts, and even historians have debated which set of factors most determines and influences the foreign policy decisions of nation states. Several competing theoretical paradigms stress either the importance of structural or material (power) conditions, institutional frameworks, domestic political constraints, political-strategic cultures and norms, or personality aspects. Whereas the neorealist school of thought still dominates the scholarly discussion, there exists today a widely accepted consensus that single-factor approaches lack the capacity for explaining political reality comprehensively. Instead, a complex and simultaneous interplay of several interlinked—supporting or competing—factors is more likely to illuminate the scope, direction, and timing of policy decisions. Such a generalization applies especially to German security and defense policies for the reasons examined below.

The controversy about continuity and/or change in Germany's foreign and security policy after 1990 reflects this international scholarly debate.. Explanatory models ranged between the poles of a power-political resocialization of Germany, emphasizing the maturation and normalization of a rational-calculated and national-interest orientated German foreign and security policy after 1990, and the theories of strategic culture and national role, stressing the continuing predominance of a civil power–related and military force–averse disposition of Germany's key stakeholders and general public derived from the experience of the age of total war.[73] This debate has been particularly nourished through controversial decisions about Germany's participation or nonparticipation in such international military missions as Iraq in 1990 and 2003, Chad/CAR in 2007/2008, or recently Libya in 2011. Accordingly, scholarly work has provided a variety of often single-level or single-factor explanations for these decisions, focusing on either structural, institutional, cultural, or actor-related determinants.[74]

Instead of isolating a predominant single cause, this study examines various approaches to German foreign and security policy decisions and introduces a synthetic explanatory model to capture the range of determinants that shape policy decisions—on German participation in military intervention in Africa, as well as others. In particular, the present chapter demonstrates the interdependencies between the three levels and the complex linkages between the determinants.

---

[73] For a controversial discussion of power-political resocialization of Germany's foreign and security policy, see Gunther Hellmann, "Wider die machtpolitische Resozialisierung der deutschen Außenpolitik: Ein Plädoyer für offensiven Idealismus," *WeltTrends* 12, no. 42 (2004): 79–88; Roos, "Deutsche Außenpolitik nach der Vereinigung," 10, 26.

[74] For a general overview of different approaches explaining decisions on missions of the Bundeswehr see Brummer, *Die Innenpolitik der Außenpolitik*, 20–24. For study examples on impacts of role concepts and strategic culture on decisions for German participation or nonparticipation in military interventions, see Wilke, *German Strategic Culture Revisited*; Baumann and Hellmann, "Germany and the Use of Force." For specific case studies for German military engagement in Africa, see Schmitt, "Strategic Users of Culture"; Mirow, *Strategic Culture Matters*; Pillath, *Motive und Rollenkonzepte deutscher Außenpolitik*, 39–60.

A. Integrative Three-level Model: Influences on Foreign and Security Policy Decisions for International Military Engagements

The political analysis of foreign (and security) policy lacks a unifying and universally valid theory. During the last five decades, several school of thoughts emerged that studied foreign policy, the action of states within the international system, from various perspectives and basically established three distinct levels of influence on a state's foreign policy: the international level, the domestic level, and the individual level of policy-makers.[75] The complexity of different paradigms for the analysis of foreign and security policy has brought up integrative and multilayer approaches, trying to systematically portray the effects of factors on different levels on foreign policies and decisions states.[76]

Starting out from Robert Putnam's metaphor of a "two-level game," German foreign (and security) policy is *formulated* and implemented between the poles of the international and domestic level, both simultaneously incentivizing and constraining the state's foreign and security policy actors in an interdependent relationship.[77] On the international level, German foreign and security policy actors basically attempt to achieve national interests and to influence the interaction of international political events with the governments of other states. The power and interests of their governmental partner will primarily restrict their opportunities to act. Simultaneously, governmental rep-

---

[75] For the levels of analysis of the foreign policy process see also Haftendorn, "Zur Theorie außenpolitischer Entscheidungsprozesse," 405.

[76] For example see Richard C. Snyder, H.W. Bruck, and Burton Sapin, *Foreign Policy Decision Making: An Approach to the Study of International Politics* (New York: Free Press of Glencoe, 1962); James N. Rosenau, "Pre-Theories and Theories of Foreign Policy," in *Approaches to Comparative and International Politics*, ed. R. Barry Farrell (Evanston, Ill.: Northwestern University Press, 1966); see also Andreas Wilhelm, *Außenpolitik: Grundlagen, Strukturen und Prozesse* (München: Oldenbourg, 2006), 21–24.

[77] Putnam, "Diplomacy and Domestic Politics," 427–60.

resentatives are urged to mobilize enough political support for their foreign and security policy actions on the domestic level, within the executive itself, the parliament, and the general public. These requirements limit the opportunities to act for the key state stakeholders on the international level as they need to implement a foreign and security policy measure within the state-internal process. The primary strategy of German foreign and security policy decision-makers thus is to conciliate the imperatives of the two levels so that they do not contradict openly.[78]

Although an integral part of the domestic level, state actors, in particular executive representatives, are key for foreign and security policy, including decisions for the deployment of military forces. Functioning as gatekeepers and binding elements between the two levels, political state actors finally make collectively binding decisions within international relations.[79] This project therefore extends the two-systems approach—external and internal—with a study of the actor level.

This study furthermore argues that the three levels, even if distinct definable, are not only interdependent, but also internally linked and mutually interpenetrated.[80] Following this approach, this book particularly addresses criticisms on two-level-logic analyses, which may lack to identify and to stress to relations between distinct determinants within the systems and the potential effects of the interrelations—reinforcing or contradicting—on the outcomes.[81]

---

[78] Oppermann and Höse, "Die innenpolitischen Restriktionen deutscher Außenpolitik," 44–45; Oppermann, "National Role Conceptions," 504.

[79] Gunter Hellmann, Wolfgang Wagner, and Rainer Baumann, *Deutsche Außenpolitik: Eine Einführung*, 2nd ed. (Wiesbaden: VS Springer Fachmedien, 2014), 43-44.

[80] For comparable approaches, see Hanrieder, "Compatibility and Consensus," 974; Jeffrey S. Lantis, *Strategic Dilemmas and the Evolution of German Foreign Policy since Unification* (Westport, CT: Praeger Publishers, 2002), 19. See also Putnam, "Diplomacy and Domestic Politics," 430–31.

[81] For a description of relevant issues, see Peters, "Ansätze und Methoden," 831.

Thus, first, across several issue areas of politics, including economy, finances, and security, the external and internal system have extended into the other domain and fused, thereby diminishing the clear distinction between international affairs and domestic politics substantially.[82] Second, determinants are mutually dependent, and hence, often need to be framed in relation to other factors. The constellation of national interests, for example, requires considering the status of the state within the international system, but also the key stakeholder's perception of the state's role in international affairs. A nation state's strategic culture will not only reflect domestically embedded norms and values, but also evolutions and foreign and security experiences in the external system. Likewise, the amount of domestic political consensus on the ends and means of foreign policy impinges upon which policy concerns receive primary attention, how policy goals are formulated, and which options are pursued.[83] As a consequence, foreign and security policy decisions are a response by political state actors to overlapping impulses or contradictions between external and internal referents rather than to single factors.[84]

In summary, German decisions on participation in certain military missions can fruitfully be analyzed through the lens of an extended, integrative three-level model, which incorporates determinants on the external, internal, and actor level (see Figure 1). The model presented here likely is applicable to all states. In the German case, however, the model well reveals the permanent interplay and the inherent tensions between imperatives and determinants of the external and internal level as well as the impact of state actors. This complex back-and-forth characterizes German foreign and security policy and its evolution, determines decisions on military engagements, and results in the

---

[82] Hanrieder, "Compatibility and Consensus," 979–80; Rosenau, "Pre-Theories and Theories of Foreign Policy," 53.
[83] Hanrieder, "Compatibility and Consensus," 977.
[84] Hanrieder, "Compatibility and Consensus," 980.

divergent, if not contradictory, policy outcomes at issue in this study.[85]

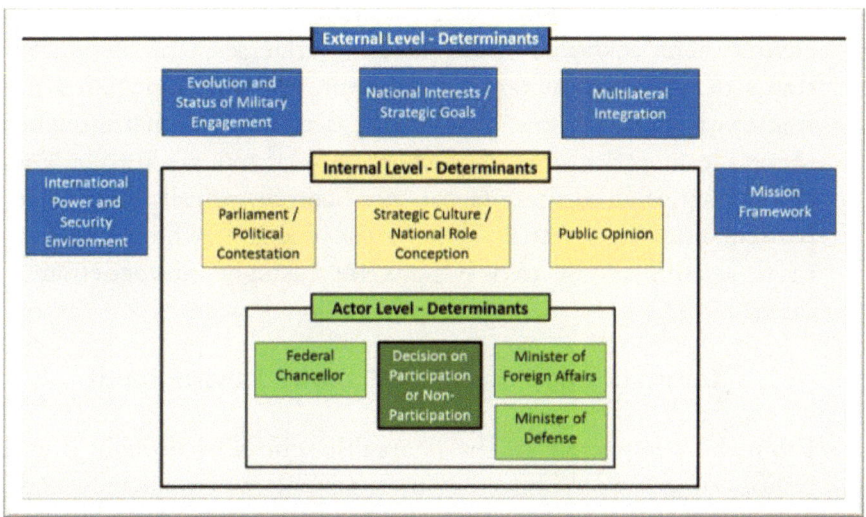

Integrative 3-Level Model of Determinants for Decisions on German Military Engagement (model drawn by the author)

B. Determinants on the External Level

Political science of the early twentieth century gave prominent weight to external influences on the foreign policy of states. According this

---

[85] Sven Bernhard Gareis, "Die Organisation deutscher Sicherheitspolitik: Akteure, Kompetenzen, Verfahren und Perspektiven," in *Deutsche Sicherheitspolitik: Herausforderungen, Akteure und Prozesse*, 2nd ed., ed. Stephan Böckenförde and Sven Bernhard Gareis (Opladen, Germany: Verlag Barbara Buderich, 2014), 106; Oppermann and Höse, "Die innenpolitischen Restriktionen deutscher Außenpolitik," 44–45; Von Krause, *Die Bundeswehr als Instrument deutscher Außenpolitik*, 352; Gießmann and Wagner, "Auslandseinsätze der Bundeswehr," 6–8.

perspective, a state's foreign policy behavior primarily depends on position it occupies amid the international system. The role of political and economic power distribution within the international system and the role of international institutions received paramount importance to explain a state's external actions.[86] Moreover, the security environment, national interests and strategies, the evolution and status of a state's military engagement, and the anticipated mission framework itself are key (and related) determinants that influence and shape German decisions for deployment of military forces. The relative impact of all of these factors has been historically interlinked with particularities in Germany's domestic domain, which became even more salient, as the two systems increasingly interpenetrated each other.

1. International Power and Security Environment

From the perspective of the neorealist school of thought, the distribution of power within the international system shapes and constrains a state's opportunity to act and the implementation of its foreign policy. In the absence of an overruling central power, the uncertain conditions of an anarchic system structure force states to act as egoistic units in a self-help system. Consequently, all states follow system-immanent incentives to accumulate those resources that secure their survival: power, security, and autonomy to act.[87]

The FRG's power position and security orientation after the World War II was determined by its status as a divided frontier-state within the East-West conflict, political standards and expectations of

---

[86] Peters, "Ansätze und Methoden," 817.

[87] Kenneth Waltz, *Theory of International Politics* (New York: McGraw Hill, 1979), 73–102; Robert Jervis, "Cooperation under the Security Dilemma," *World Politics* 30, no. 2 (January 1978): 167–214; Stephen M. Walt, "Alliance Formation and the Balance of World Power," *International Security* (Spring 1985): 3–43; Stephen M. Walt, International Relations: One World, Many Theories," *Foreign Policy*, no. 110 (Spring 1998): 29–46; see also Wilhelm, *Außenpolitik*, 95–104.

the Western allies, and its own efforts to break with its National Socialist past. International priority of all West, East, and later unified German governments since World War II has been to regain national sovereignty as well as to strongly integrate into multilateral Western institutions, hereby, projecting Germany's strong commitment as a reliable, respected, and benign partner and ally. Rooted in the raison d'état of the Federal Republic, post–World War II West Germany arose as a state that—politically and societally—deliberately renounced strong power politics[88] on the "classical" model, for example, the ambition for territorial expansion or for Great Power status. Instead West Germany committed itself to formulate and exercise foreign and security policy exclusively in political and economic cooperation with other states, based on the principle of the rule of law and the welfare of humanity, and with strong prioritization of peaceful against violent means in conflict resolution.[89] The new armed forces, created out of the rigors of the Cold War, were integrated in Euro-Atlantic defense in the 1950s. These core paradigms of (West) Germany's external actions gave rise to the societally internalized and politically implemented strategic "culture of reticence" which after 1990 became coalesced in the ideal of a "civil power," both reflecting the domestic-ideological dimension of Germany's self-restrained foreign and security policy.

With the end of the Cold War and the acquisition of its full sovereignty, Germany's position in the international, but especially the European, system changed dramatically in a manner that was not immediately apparent in the 1990s. The collapse of the Soviet Union and the gradual expansion of NATO and EU toward the East, shifted the reunified Germany back toward the center of an increasingly integrated Europe, strengthening its political potential as Europe's central

---

[88] Gareis, "Militärische Beiträge zur Sicherheit," 117.

[89] Helga Haftendorn, *Coming of Age: German Foreign Policy since 1945* (Lanham, NY: Rowman & Littlefield, 2006), 353.

power.[90] Simultaneously, with the impact of globalization and a focus on the Asia-Pacific realm to the detriment of Europe's former leading role, Germany gradually evolved to a strong "commercially realist"[91] or geo-economic power by defining national interest increasingly in economic terms, promoting the European political-economic integration, and partaking of an intensifying globalization of economic relationships. Economic strength—export-orientated commerce and trade in high quality manufactures—consolidated as a key source of Germany's international power; it played a dominant role in shaping Germany's foreign and security policy amid the reform of the German social market economy in the 1990s in the face of national unity, a single European market, and globalization. Consequently, as post–Cold War Germany has always used economic rather than military means to achieve its foreign policy goals, it became increasingly dependent on an unhampered international trade and global economic stability.[92]

The interdependency between a changing external power structure, intensified through the rise of such new powers as China, India, Brazil, and Russia at the close of the 1990s, and the increasing German power-potential in international affairs, led allies and partners to

---

[90] Baumann, "Deutschland als Zentralmacht," 62–72; Hans-Peter Schwarz, *Die Zentralmacht Europas: Die Rückkehr Deutschlands auf der Weltbühne* (Berlin: Siedler Verlag, 1994), 10–12.

[91] Stephen F. Szabo, "Germany's Commercial Realism and the Russia Problem," *Survival: Global Politics and Strategy* 56, no. 5 (2014): 119.

[92] Michael Staack, "Deutschland als Wirtschaftsmacht," in *Handbuch zur deutschen Außenpolitik*, ed. Sigmar Schmidt, Gunther Hellmann, and Reinhard Wolf (Wiesbaden: Verlag für Sozialwissenschaften, 2007), 85–87; Andreas Busch and Roman Goldbach, "Die Stellung Deutschlands in der Weltwirtschaft," in *Deutsche Außenpolitik: Sicherheit, Wohlfahrt, Institutionen und Normen*, 2nd ed., ed. Thomas Jäger, Alexander Höse, and Kai Oppermann (Wiesbaden: Springer Fachmedien, 2011), 278; Robert Kappel, "Global Power Shifts and Germany's New Foreign Policy Agenda," *Strategic Analysis* 38, no. 3 (2014): 345, doi: 10.1080/09700161.2014.8952; Kundnani, "Germany as a Geo-Economic Power," 30–45; Szabo, "Germany's Commercial Realism," 119–20.

demand that Germany transform its political heft into more global responsibility, including commitments in military interventions. This external influence remains strong until today.[93] To mitigate initial concerns of neighbors and allies about an overall powerful, ambitious, and possibly unpredictable Germany (German *Sonderweg of Schaukelpolitik*—swinging between East and West), on the other hand, German governments continually emphasized political continuity and that a united and stronger Germany remains a trustful and reliable partner who fulfils its obligations of solidarity and burden-sharing within the transatlantic alliance and the European cooperation.[94] The gradual extension in the 1990s of German participation in multilateral military out-of-area mission under the umbrella of the UN, NATO, and EU reflected these self-commitments. At the same, however, German foreign and security policy became increasingly ambiguous. Despite the self-imposed limitations of autonomous external actions based on the imperative of multilateral cooperation, Germany's foreign and security policies and decisions showed a "re-socialization to power-politics" (*machtpolitische Resozialisierung*),[95] a cautious and still restrained, but deliberate efficiency enhancement of national power in relation to other states. In a process often described as "normalization" or "maturing," Germany's foreign and security policy gradually evolved into a posture—a shifting national self-image in international affairs—that reflected a heightened sense of responsibility, self-confidence, national interests, and aspiration to shape, including a more rational view on the use of military force in international affairs.[96]

Besides the distribution of power in the international system, evolutions in the security environment influence the decisions on Ger-

---

[93] Janes, "Merkel 3.0," 88–91.
[94] Haftendorn, *Coming of Age*," 352–53.
[95] Hellmann, "Wider die machtpolitische Resozialisierung," 80–82.
[96] Roos, "Deutsche Außenpolitik nach der Vereinigung," 27–28; Haftendorn, *Coming of Age*," 353.

man military engagements. Regional or international crises have as "strategic dilemmas" the potential to challenge an existing status quo, such as international law and regional or global order, and hence, demand a response from the great powers and/or systems of collective security, which may involve the use of military force.[97] These challenges are strategic as they directly affect foreign and security orientations of states and organizations alike. They also are dilemmas as they demand attention, but allow a variety of means for a proper response, including those that confront national or domestic sentiments. In the case of Germany, these sentiments include constitutional challenges or the tensions among the strategic culture of (military) reticence, aspirations of more responsibility, national interests, and multilateral expectations.

Four dimensions of shifts in the security environment through strategic dilemmas are of particular importance for Germany's decision on military engagement. First, dramatic international events that have a great visibility, such as the 1990 Kuwait invasion, the Yugoslav war of 1991, the genocide in Rwanda in 1994, or the terrorist attacks in the United States in 2001, can pose "external shocks" that trigger major policy changes.[98] Affecting governmental actors, parliamentarians, and the general public alike, these events may constitute a catalyst for policy restructuring, resulting not only in debates, but also in changed perceptions of and guidelines for the use of military force. Some scholars argue that the crisis in the former Yugoslavia between 1991 and 1999 presented Germany with the most serious strategic dilemma of the post–Cold War era. Wars of independence in Croatia,

---

[97] This study applies and extends the concept of Jeffrey S. Lantis who analyzed the role of strategic dilemmas as catalyst for foreign and security policy change. Although policy restructuring is closely connected to decisions and variations of decisions on military engagements, it lacks the emphasis on the direct influence of strategic dilemmas on these decisions and the inter-linkage with other factors in the external and internal domain. See Lantis, *Strategic Dilemmas*, 19–20.

[98] Charles F. Hermann, "Changing Course: When Governments Choose to Redirect Foreign Policy," *International Studies Quarterly* 34, no. 1 (March 1990): 12.

Bosnia-Herzegovina, and finally Kosovo, caused fierce domestic debates about proper foreign policy responses.

Accompanied by the ruling of the Federal Constitutional Court, which allowed the deployment of German military forces within systems of mutual collective security, the German governments first decided to support NATO air strikes against the Serb artillery in 1995, to send Bundeswehr ground forces into peace enforcement operations in 1996, and finally to allow pilots to conduct air strikes within the NATO campaign against the Federal Republic of Yugoslavia in 1999.[99] With the first combat operation since the end of World War II, the latter decision marked a decisive shift in German foreign and security policy, intensifying the public debate about Germany's role in the world, its strategic culture, and appropriate political means.

Second, consequently, strategic dilemmas affect the public opinion and the political debate on adequate foreign and security policy reactions as they gain salience in the general public, which influences governmental actors and parliamentarians in their individual considerations in decisions about the use of military force.

Third, in a complex and interconnected security environment, international crises, such as regional conflicts, disintegration of states, or humanitarian crises, have an impact on the security of the international community as a whole.[100] The UN, NATO, and EU, as primary responder to international crises, can additionally cause and intensify pressure on Germany to act within their multilateral frameworks, including the participation in military operations on all levels.

Finally, strategic dilemmas particularly press and incentivize key stakeholders in the German government, especially the chancellor, minister of foreign affairs, and minister of defense, to mitigate between the two poles of external and internal demands and to develop,

---

[99] See Lantis, *Strategic Dilemmas*, 18–19.
[100] Federal Ministry of Defense, *White Paper 2006*, 14–15.

in coordination with international and domestic actors, policies which "do not openly contradict either of them."[101] As highlighted above, depending on the relations between all factors of the external and internal system within a strategic dilemma, the policy choices—the decisions on whether and how to participate in military operations—can be expected to vary.

2. National Interests and Strategies

Political and economic power gives a state the opportunity to implement its national interests. National interests are understood as the sum of demands and expectations that a state formulates toward the international system to safeguard and, if possible, improve its security and welfare.[102] Since they function as general guidelines for a state's external actions and orientation for decisions of governments, national interests should help to define short- and medium-term priorities of foreign and security policy, hence, the choice of appropriate instruments and means to achieve them, including the role and relevance of military force. National interests, however, are not fixed and sacrosanct, but underlie influences of changes in the international system and the domestic contestation.[103]

The significance of Germany's interests in foreign affairs as inherent and adequate reasoning for an international engagement of the Bundeswehr has been the subject of endless domestic debate for de-

---

[101] Oppermann, "National Role Conceptions," 504; Lantis, *Strategic Dilemmas*, 20; Putnam, "Diplomacy and Domestic Politics," 460.

[102] Sven Bernhard Gareis, *Deutschlands Außen- und Sicherheitspolitik*, 2nd ed. (Opladen, Germany: Verlag Barabara Budrich, 2006), 38.

[103] Staack, "Normative Grundlagen," 59–60.

cades on end.¹⁰⁴ This debate began promptly in May 1949 and has never stopped; it is marked by intense positions and a struggle for consensus amid much dissent. Two dominant aspects frame the ambivalent influence of this debate on the decision-making process. First, given the conditions of persistent and changing determinants of Germany's role in a changing security environment, all official strategic papers since the mid-1990s refer to values and interests as an orientation for German foreign and security policy in general, and in particular as a criteria for the decisions on military engagements, as it has been repeatedly claimed by the scholarly and strategic community.¹⁰⁵ According to the German Ministry of Defense *White Paper 2006*, interests of German security policy range between "preserving justice and freedom, democracy, security and prosperity for ... [German] citizens"; "preventing regional crises and conflicts that may affect Germany's security, wherever possible"; "help uphold human

---

¹⁰⁴ Staack, "Normative Grundlagen," 60–63. A detailed analysis of role and relevance of values and interests in German foreign policy can be found in David Bosold and Christian Achrainer, "Die normativen Grundlagen deutscher Außenpolitik," in *Deutsche Außenpolitik: Sicherheit, Wohlfahrt, Institutionen und Normen*, 2nd ed., ed. Thomas Jäger, Alexander Höse, and Kai Oppermann (Wiesbaden: Springer Fachmedien, 2011), 444–67. Maull, however, indicates that debates over "national interests" are implicit part of the political struggle for influence and interpretational sovereignty rather than an effort to gain more clarity of foreign affairs action. See Maull, "Nationale Interessen!," 64, 76.

¹⁰⁵ Stefan Mair, "Kriterien für die Beteiligung an Militäreinsätzen," in *Auslandeinsätze der Bundeswehr: Leitfragen, Entscheidungsspielräumen und Lehren*, ed. Stefan Mair (Berlin: German Institute for International and Security Affairs, September 2007), 16–17; Thomas Silberhorn, *Deutschlands Interessen und Deutschlands Verantwortung in der Welt: Leitlinien für Auslandseinsätze der Bundeswehr*, (Berlin: CSU-Landesgruppe im Deutschen Bundestag, January 10, 2007), 2, accessed December 10, 2014, http://www.thomas-silberhorn.de/fileadmin/pdf/positionspapiere/ 070201_Auslandseinsaetze_Bundes-wehr.pdf; Volker Perthes, "Wie? Wann? Wo? Wie oft?: Vier zentrale Fragen müssen vor Auslandseinsätzen beantwortet werden," *Internationale Politik* (May 2007): 20.

rights";[106] and "promoting free and unhindered world trade as a basis for ... prosperity." The *White Paper* also acknowledges that in an age of globalization German foreign and security policy interests "are not static, but contingent on international constellations and developments,"[107] and cannot be defined solely in terms of geography.

Although clearly connecting interests with goals of German security policy, including multilateral implementation, consolidation of the transatlantic alliance, and promotion of the European integration, German strategic documents, however, continually struggle to clearly operationalize when, where, and how Germany is willing to pursue or even defend them, as well as which interests and goals have priority.[108] The vague nature of German national interests in strategic documents and debates gives German key stakeholders the opportunity to interpret them differently, depending on their perceived need to mitigate between external and internal drivers. It further contributes to the fact that Germany may participate in military missions rather based on externally dominated factors instead of its own reasonable operationalized national interests. It also lends strong support to the claim that Germany's decisions to participate in the KFOR ISAF, or EUFOR Congo missions were not derived from German national interests, as officially argued; rather, these interests were

---

[106] Federal Ministry of Defense, *White Paper 2006,* 21–22; see also Federal Ministry of Defense, *Defense Policy Guidelines,* 3–6; *Deutschlands Zukunft gestalten,* 168.

[107] Federal Ministry of Defense, *White Paper 2006,* 21.

[108] Julian Junk and Christopher Daase, "Germany," in *Strategic Cultures in Europe: Security and Defense Policies Across the Continent,* ed. Heiko Biehl, Bastian Giegerich, and Alexandra Jonas (Wiesbaden: Springer VS, 2013), 147; Bertelsmann Stiftung, ed., *Gut, aber nicht gut genug,"* 9–10; Berthold Meyer, "Von der Entgrenzung nationaler deutscher Interessen: Die politische Legitimation weltweiter Militäreinsätze," *HSFK-Report 10* (Frankfurt am Main: Hessische Stiftung Friedens- und Konfliktforschung, 2007), 23, 32–33.

"discovered" immediately before the start of the missions to legitimate domestically the deployment of Bundeswehr soldiers.[109]

Conversely, the official and public reference to national interests as rationale for German foreign and security policy actions has significantly increased since reunification, giving them potentially a stronger influence on decisions for participation in military inventions. Beginning the end of the Helmut Kohl era, particularly intensifying during the term of office of Federal Chancellor Gerhard Schröder, and continuing today with Federal Chancellor Angela Merkel, the term *national interest* became an increasingly important reference to legitimize German foreign and security policy.[110] Although vaguely formulated and differently interpretable, stronger emphasized national interests may both be partly explained by and contribute to the evolved but simultaneously ambiguous notion of a more self-confident, power-oriented, and normalized German behavior in international affairs as well as a more pragmatic and instrumental understanding of multilateralism. The decisions on participation or nonparticipation in the multilateral military interventions in Kosovo, Iraq, and Chad/CAR reflect this change from 1998 until the present.

Despite the surfeit of single strategic concepts and its rather ad hoc, cabinet-oriented coordination of foreign and security policy,[111] over the last two decades, a united Germany has developed a strategic understanding of its policy implementation, aiming at interlinking and coherently coordinating all policy instruments within a comprehensive approach and within networked security structures—on both a national and a global scale—to an overall concept that is tailored to

---

[109] Kaim,"Deutsches Interesse versus Bündnisverpflichtung," 179; Maull, "Nationale Interessen!," 63.

[110] Baumann, "Multilateralismus," 477–79.

[111] Claudia Major and Elisabeth Schöndorf, "Umfassende Ansätze, vernetzte Sicherheit," *SWP-Aktuell* 22 (Berlin: German Institute for International and Security Affairs, April 2011), 3.

the problem.[112] Milestone documents that have introduced and manifested Germany's idea of "networked security," "comprehensive approach," and "whole of government approach,"[113] include the federal government's overall concept for "Civilian Crisis Prevention, Conflict Resolution, and Post-Conflict Peacebuilding"[114] (2000); the "Action Plan for Civil Crisis Prevention"[115] (2004); the "Over Sectoral Concept for Crisis Prevention"[116] (2005); the *White Paper*[117] (2006); and *Defense Policy Guidelines*"[118] (2011). Still, Germany continually faces challenges to implement its approach already on a national level, as institutional structures (diversity of governmental bodies related to foreign and security policy issues as exist in the Berlin Republic fed-

---

[112] See Federal Ministry of Defense, *White Paper 2006*, 6–7; Bundesregierung, "Gesamtkonzept der Bundesregierung: 'Zivile Krisenprävention, Konfliktlösung und Friedenskonsolidierung,'" in *Aktionsplan 'Zivile Krisenprävention, Konfliktlösung und Friedenskonsolidierung'* (Berlin: Bundesregierung, May 12, 2004), XVI–XVII, accessed October 11, 2014, http://www.auswaertiges-amt.de/cae/servlet/contentblob/ 384230/publicationFile/4345/Aktionsplan-De.pdf.

[113] Bundesregierung, *Krisenprävention als gemeinsame Aufgabe: 2. Bericht der Bundesregierung über die Umsetzung des Aktionsplans "Zivile Krisenprävention, Konfliktlösung und Friedenskonsolidierung," Berichtszeitraum Mai 2006 bis April 2008* (Berlin: Bundesregierung, July 16, 2008), 80, accessed October 11, 2014, http://www.auswaertiges-amt.de/cae/servlet/contentblob/384192/publicationFile/4340/Aktionsplan-Bericht2-de.pdf.

[114] Bundesregierung, "Gesamtkonzept der Bundesregierung."

[115] Bundesregierung, *Aktionsplan "Zivile Krisenprävention, Konfliktlösung und Friedenskonsolidierung*" (Berlin: Bundesregierung, May 12, 2004), accessed October 11, 2014, http://www.auswaertiges-amt.de/cae/servlet/contentblob/384230/publication File/4345/Aktionsplan-De.pdf.

[116] Bundesministerium für wirtschaftliche Zusammenarbeit und Entwicklung (BMZ), *Übersektorales Konzept zur Krisenprävention, Konfliktbearbeitung und Friedensförderung in der deutschen Entwicklungszusammenarbeit: Eine Strategie zur Friedensentwicklung* (Berlin: BMZ, June 2005), accessed October 11, 2014, http://www.bmz.de/de/zentrales_downloadarchiv/themen_und_schwerpunkte/fr ieden/krisenpraevention.pdf.

[117] Federal Ministry of Defense, *White Paper 2006*.

[118] Federal Ministry of Defense, *Defense Policy Guidelines*.

eral structure), constitutional regulations (for example, the ministerial principle, that is, the primacy of the Finance Ministry for the budget; the primacy of the Foreign Ministry for external affairs, and so on), and particular interests, can hamper an efficient and coherent horizontal and vertical coordination[119] as well as influence the intergovernmental decision-making process when compared to other leading powers.

Finally, Germany's struggle to define—and implement—an overarching national strategy[120] also influences German decisions on military engagements, as it complicates the formulation of a consistent national position on security issues as well as increasing the dependency on situational-contextual factors.

3. Multilateral Integration

Germany's normative imperative to organize, legitimize, and implement foreign and security policy exclusively within multilateral frameworks, based on international agreements, is an important but evolving factor for decisions on military engagements.

Based on the experiences of the world wars and the disaster of National Socialism, Germany's raison d'état during the Cold War was rooted in the conviction, championed by Konrad Adenauer and later by the SPD, that it could regain and maintain its capacity and sovereignty to act in international affairs only by embedding its foreign and security policy in Western-oriented international and supranational

---

[119] Major and Schöndorf, "Umfassende Ansätze," 6–7; Naumann, "Wie strategiefähig ist Deutschland?," *Aus Politik und Zeitgeschichte* 48 (November 2009): 13–14.

[120] For an overview concerning the strategy discussion in Germany, see Klaus Naumann, "Wie strategiefähig ist Deutschland?," 10–17; Malte Bruns et al., "Die strategische Kultur der deutschen Sicherheitspolitik: Brauchen wir eine nationale Sicherheitsstrategie?," *Policy Brief—Globale Fragen* (Berlin: Stiftung Neue Verantwortung, August 2009). In relation to the discussion about military engagements see also Naumann, *Einsatz ohne Ziel?*

institutions, hence, by refusing any unilateral power and interests politics or the swinging between East and West that had been the norm of German geography and power for centuries before.[121] Framed by the key mottos of "never again" and "never alone,"[122] it formed a multilateral-oriented political understanding that became one of the two most characterizing paradigms of German foreign and security policy.[123] Germany's strict orientation toward peaceful conflict resolution, strongly linked with the reluctance of using military force, is the topic of following sections.

Repeatedly emphasized in official papers and by politicians alike after reunification, the principle of multilateralism is thus often considered as one indicator of continuity of German foreign and security policy.[124] Consequently, Germany has continuously committed itself to pursue its foreign policies and security interests in coordination and cooperation with partners and allies, based on its integration into the UN, NATO, and EU, and to organize its participation in out-of-area missions exclusively within the multilateral context of these mutual collective security systems.[125].

As the sole universal international organization, the UN plays an outstanding role in guiding Germany's foreign and security policy and decisions on military engagements. Its charter not only provides the fundamental international law framework for international relations,

---

[121] Haftendorn, *Coming of Age*, 16–17, 40–41; Hellmann, Wolf, and Schmidt, "Deutsche Außenpolitik in historischer und systemischer Perspektive," 30–32; Gareis, "Militärische Beiträge zur Sicherheit," 117.

[122] Maull, "Germany and Japan," 91–106.

[123] Gareis, "Militärische Beiträge zur Sicherheit," 117.

[124] Baumann, "Multilateralismus," 468.

[125] See Federal Ministry of Defense, *White Paper 2006*, 6–11, 24; Federal Ministry of Defense, *Defense Policy Guidelines*, 8–10, 23; Kaim, "Deutsches Interesse versus Bündnisverpflichtung," 176; Sven Bernhard Gareis, "The Making of Germany's Security and Defense Policy: Actors, Responsivities, Procedures, and Requirements," in *German Defense Politics*, ed. Ina Wiesner (Baden-Baden: Nomos, 2013), 66.

but also defines the objectives, such as the safeguarding of world peace and international security, that generally legitimize the use of German military forces outside its own territory, through a mandate of the UNSC.[126] As its biggest financial contributor and based on its enhanced power position since reunification, Germany justifies its claim for a permanent seat in the council, without having yet achieved the goal. Germany's aspiration to shoulder more responsibility and to design UN policy more actively, however, still does not reflect the level of its actual participation in UN missions. Germany has indeed mostly participated in UN-mandated missions, but to a significantly lower degree in UN-led missions, most notably in actual participation or the level of capacities, particularly in Africa.[127]

NATO is the "anchor of the West" and the "cornerstone of German security and defense policy"; it formalizes the transatlantic partnership between Europe and North America and binds 28 of the most powerful states in the world along the principles of collective defense, mutual solidarity, political consultation, burden-sharing, and military integration.[128] Despite the buildup of European capabilities under the umbrella of the EU, NATO still constitutes the most important key framework for political consultation in the West and military alliance for Germany, resulting in the biggest contributions to

---

[126] Federal Ministry of Defense, *White Paper 2006*, 43–44; Federal Ministry of Defense, *Defense Policy Guidelines*, 5–6.

[127] Milosevic, "Deutsche Kriegsbeteiligung und—verweigerung," 16–17; Manfred Knapp, "Vereinte Nationen," in *Handbuch zur deutschen Außenpolitik*, ed. Sigmar Schmidt, Gunther Hellmann, and Reinhard Wolf (Wiesbaden: Verlag für Sozialwissenschaften, 2007), 734–40. For a overview of UN peacekeeping missions and the level of German participation as of 2012, see Johannes Varwick, "Deutsche Sicherheitspolitik im Rahmen der Vereinten Nationen," in *Deutsche Sicherheitspolitik: Herausforderungen, Akteure und Prozesse*, 2nd ed., ed. Stephan Böckenförde and Sven Bernhard Gareis (Opladen, Germany: Verlag Barbara Buderich, 2014), 375–77.

[128] Federal Ministry of Defense, *White Paper 2006*, 24–25; Federal Ministry of Defense, *Defense Policy Guidelines*, 6–7; Claudia Major and Christian Mölling, *German Defense Policy in 2014 and Beyond: Options for Change*, Note du Cerfa 113 (Paris: Institut Français du Relations International, 2014), 12.

military interventions since reunification, such as in the Balkans or in Afghanistan.[129] The solidarity and cohesion within the alliance remain the "backbone" of Germany's well-being, as it defines the ensured security of each single member as shared interests of all.

For Europe, and Germany within it, the EU represents a successful European political and security order, which is capable of assuring its members of stability, security, and prosperity. Intending to further strengthen the EU as "the core of the European area of stability," Germany has been a key proponent since 1992 of an intensified European integration through the Common Foreign and Security Policy (CFSP) as well as the Common Security and Defense Policy (CSDP), which seeks to develop and provide a broad spectrum of combined civilian and military instruments for international security-building missions, in parallel with and complementary to, but without redundancies toward NATO.[130] Multinational cooperation and incorporation under the umbrella of NATO and the EU has gradually extended Germany`s commitments toward reliable contributions to military capabilities within a combined headquarters, multinational command and control facilities, and standing crisis-response capabilities, such as the NATO Response Force (NRF) or the EU Battle Group (EUBG).[131] The duality of implementing German interests

---

[129] Johannes Varwick, "Nordatlantische Allianz," in *Handbuch zur deutschen Außenpolitik*, ed. Sigmar Schmidt, Gunther Hellmann, and Reinhard Wolf (Wiesbaden: Verlag für Sozialwissenschaften, 2007), 768–74; Olaf Theiler, "Deutschland und die NATO," in *Deutsche Sicherheitspolitik: Herausforderungen, Akteure und Prozesse*, 2nd ed., ed. Stephan Böckenförde and Sven Bernhard Gareis (Opladen, Germany: Verlag Barbara Buderich, 2014), 348–57.

[130] Donald Abenheim and Carolyn Halladay, "Stability in Flux: Policy, Strategy, and Institutions in Germany," in *The Routledge Handbook of Civil-Military Relations*, ed. Thomas C. Bruneau and Florina Cristiana Matei (New York: Routledge, 2013), 307; Federal Ministry of Defense, *White Paper 2006*, 33; Federal Ministry of Defense, *Defense Policy Guidelines*, 7–8.

[131] Federal Ministry of Defense, *Defense Policy Guidelines*, 11; Gareis, "Die Organisation deutscher Sicherheitspolitik," 107.

through European integration and transatlantic anchorage simultaneously often resulted in a "both-and-policy" (*Sowohl-als-auch-Politik*), which drew Germany repeatedly in a mediating role between NATO-maximalists and minimalists,[132] but also increased the external demands to put its weight into international military interventions.

Since the end of the Cold War, the general parameters of Germany's foreign and security policy have changed decisively with the disorder in the world, which framed, incentivized, and constrained its decisions to send the Bundeswehr beyond Central Europe, its Cold War strategic focus. Shifts of global power relations, the emergence of new security concerns, as well as the complex and continuously changing security environment, have led to dramatic extension and enlargement of such multilateral institutions as NATO and the EU, broadening their responsibilities and extending their scope for security and defense concerns. Policy and organizational changes of these institutions, which form the foundation of Germany's own foreign and security policy, have not only caused institutional and constitutional adjustments in Germany,[133] but also intensified the external expectations on Germany's self-imposed multilateral cooperation and integration, pulling its military capacities into new missions.[134]

With the theory of a "multilateralism trap" in mind, the expectations of security policy institutions substantially determine decisions on German participation in military missions, however, without causing automatic (and/or unilateral) German actions. Accordingly, collective consensus decisions for establishing a mission under the um-

---

[132] Theiler, "Deutschland und die NATO," 349–50.

[133] Abenheim and Halladay, "Stability in Flux," 305–308.

[134] Olaf Theiler, "Bundeswehr und NATO: Multilateralismus und Integration als Grundlagen deutscher Sicherheitspolitik," in *Armee im Einsatz: Grundlagen, Strategien und Ergebnisse einer Beteiligung der Bundeswehr*, ed. Hans J. Gießmann and Armin Wagner (Baden-Baden: Nomos: 2009), 186–87; Abenheim and Halladay, "Stability in Flux," 307; Gareis, "Making of Germany's Security and Defense Policy," 70; Kundnani, "Germany as a Geo-Economic Power," 34.

brella of NATO or the EU, pose high political costs for a refusal to contribute to it, even if the domestic context may prefer nonparticipation.[135] Consequently, decisions against a German participation within multilateral military engagements, especially against those based on the consensus principle, were and remain an exception.[136]

Germany lacks the willingness and the material capacities to sustain a decisive shift toward a unilateral approach for its foreign and security policy. Even a case-by-case abstention from multilaterally agreed military missions would reduce its credibility within NATO or the EU and might even lead, in the long-term, to political isolation. Simultaneously, Germany would lose influence on the institutional decision-making, partners and allies, as well as resources.[137]

Showing the linkage between external and internal systems, multilateral integration weighs particularly heavy in German political calculations because of its salience in Germany's strategic culture and officially formulated national interests, but also for reasons of political exertion of influence and responsibility, which gives a self-imposed push toward credible commitments in international affairs.

Germany deliberately seeks to increase and maintain transparency of, and trust for, its political actions through solidarity and burden-

---

[135] Kaim, "Deutsches Interesse versus Bündnisverpflichtung," 177.

[136] Until 2011, there were only four cases of German abstention from a mission under the NATO or EU umbrella: NATO Training Mission in Iraq in 2004; the EU-led EUFOR Chad/CAR 2007/2008; NATO Operation Ocean Shield in 2009, a maritime operation against piracy in the Gulf of Aden; and most recently Operation Unified Protector in Libya in 2011.

[137] Kaim, "Deutsches Interesse versus Bündnisverpflichtung," 183–84. Federal Chancellor Schröder justified the decision (1998) for a German engagement in the NATO campaign against the Federal Republic of Yugoslavia in 1999 with the fact that a German nonparticipation would have caused a disastrous loss of reputation and weight for the Federal Republic of Germany. See Deutscher Bundestag, *Stenografischer Bericht: Plenarprotokoll 13/248* (Bonn: Deutscher Bundestag, October 16, 1998), 23136, accessed January 13, 2014,
http://dipbt.bundestag.de/doc/btp/13/13248.pdf#P.23127.

sharing within the transatlantic and European cooperation.[138] Participation in international military operations, simultaneously, also follows the strategic calculus to preserve and exploit the capacity to act.[139] This participation is an important political capital to self-confidently implement a security policy that roots on national interests as well as to influence multilateral planning and execution.[140] Consequently, even if examples of the last two decades, such as the abstentions from the Gulf War in 1991, the NATO training mission in Iraq in 2004, and the EU operation in Chad/CAR in 2007/2008, suggest that Germany's approach to multilateralism has slightly adjusted toward a "strategic"[141] or flexible "multilateralism by demand,"[142]—stronger incorporating national interests and aspirations for more responsibility—Germany's general foreign and security policy orientation remains multilateral.[143] Germany's dominating concern about the preservation and promotion of its economic strength, however, may additionally explain and contribute to a more selective implementation of multilateralism in the future. As geo-economic power defining national interests increasingly according to economic terms rather than to broader values, Germany may shift from an institutionalized multilateralism toward a more selective form, as bilateral approaches to key economic partner become paramount.[144]

---

[138] Rühle, "In was für einer Welt leben wir?," 19; Federal Ministry of Defense, *White Paper 2006*, 7; Federal Ministry of Defense, *Defense Policy Guidelines*, 6–8; Oppermann, "National Role Conceptions," 504.

[139] For the statement of a former Minister of Defense, see Volker Rühe, "Vorwort: Sicherheitspolitik und Auslandseinsätze," in *Bewährungsproben einer Nation: Die Entsendung der Bundeswehr ins Ausland*, ed. Christoph Schwegmann (Berlin: Duncker & Humblot, 2011), VIII; Roos, "Deutsche Außenpolitik nach der Vereinigung," 27.

[140] Gareis, "Making of Germany's Security and Defense Policy," 71.

[141] Haftendorn, *Deutsche Außenpolitik zwischen Selbstbeschränkung und Selbstbehauptung*, 15.

[142] Baumann, "Multilateralismus," 485.

[143] Daase and Junk, "Strategische Kultur," 156.

[144] Szabo, "Germany's Commercial Realism," 119.

Finally, multilateralism also imposes constraints on Germany's decisions for military engagements. The designation of operational and functional capabilities to the integrated structures within NATO and the EU come automatically with "certain restrictions on national sovereignty and free decision-making."[145] However, these restraints are less today in the institutions of command of forces than as existed, in say, 1980. Once a decision for a multinational military mission has been made, the expectations of allies and Germany's self-imposed commitment as a credible and reliable partner establish high political burdens for failing its obligations and withdrawing its forces. In the same way, the salience of multilateral integration constrains the Bundestag's approval for international military missions, even if, according to a fateful "out of area" and collective security ruling of the German Federal Constitutional Court in 1994, the government needs to secure it with a legislative approval. If not willing to question Germany's treaty obligations, German parliamentarians admit that the Bundestag cannot really refuse its approval.[146] Consequently, no governmental request for a German participation in international military missions has yet been denied.

4. Evolution and Status of Military Engagement

Decisions on participation in military interventions must not only be analyzed in their proper context of changes within the power and security environment, but also within the evolution and status of the country's military engagement itself.[147] The "military legacy" of a

---

[145] Gareis, "Making of Germany's Security and Defense Policy," 71.

[146] Kaim, "Deutsches Interesse versus Bündnisverpflichtung," 182.

[147] For a more comprehensive overview about the history and evolution of the Bundeswehr's out-of-area missions and its consequences, see Federal Ministry of Defense, *The Bundeswehr on Operations: Publication to Mark the 15th Anniversary of the First Parliamentary Mandate for Armed Bundeswehr Missions Abroad* (Berlin: Federal Ministry of Defense, 2009), 50–102; Gareis, "Militärische Beiträge zur Sicherheit," 120–35; Rimscha, "Ein Land tut sich schwer," 65–74; Varwick, "Bundeswehr," 249–56.

nation state comprises many factors. These include the evolution as well as the status of armed forces in law, politics, and society; the political and strategic as well as civil military conception of armed forces; and the modus operandi of using armed forces in international affairs and their capacities. The suite of these factors in their variety not only relate to norms and precepts that characterize a state's foreign and security policy,[148] but also, in turn, such a legacy of war and armies can be expected to affect foreign affairs' behavior and decisions.

Embedded in a much broader framework, therefore, the nature of former or current military engagements, their success or failure, and their costs and implications—human, political, normative, and financial, are expected to affect the decision-making for the participation of national forces in international military interventions as would be the case in any democratic nation alert to the burdens of policy in a violent world marked by the limits of policy amid constrained resources. Learning processes and reorientations[149] influence the view on and the thinking of military means.

At the same time, the calculations for missions abroad relate to personal and societally dominant standards and attitudes toward the use of military force as an instrument of foreign and security policy. In doing so, the evolution and status of a state's military engagement and its strategic culture concerning the perception on role, relevance, and efficacy of the use of military force are coalesced—demonstrating the interdependent relationship between the two factors on the external and internal level. This section focuses on the conception and actual use of the Bundeswehr, whereas the perceptual aspects are elaborated in a following section.

---

[148] Gareis, "Militärische Beiträge zur Sicherheit," 117.
[149] Ibid., 120.

Between 1949 and 1990, the use of military force within the FRG's foreign and security policy had been strongly "hedged" (*eingehegt*)[150]— legally, politically, normatively, and structurally restricted by the realities of defeat in 1945, national division, and the structure of the Cold War in Europe.[151] After the capitulation of the German Reich on May 8, 1945, all four occupation zones were completely demilitarized. Under the external conditions of a deteriorating security situation amid an intensifying East-West conflict on one hand in 1948, and the domestic aspirations for more sovereignty as well as the efforts for reintegrating the state into the Western community, on the other, the two German states were armed, with the foundation of the Bundeswehr in 1955 and the East German People's Army in 1956— despite fierce domestic resistance.[152] The sole *raison d'être* of the new German Armed Forces was however, the national defense in Central Europe within the transatlantic alliance.[153]

Framed by strict legal regulations (such as Basic Law article 87a),[154] a "structural non-aggression capability"[155] of the Bundeswehr, as well as constitutional and civilian values oriented philosophy of the soldiers (*Staatsbürger in Uniform*—citizens in uniform), German politics and society during the Cold War period concurred in refusing the use of the Bundeswehr far beyond Germany's borders—culminating in the tenets of no missions "out-of-area" and

---

[150] Von Krause, *Die Bundeswehr als Instrument deutscher Außenpolitik*, 20, 159.

[151] Ibid., 41–80.

[152] Gareis, "Militärische Beiträge zur Sicherheit," 117–18; Von Krause, *Die Bundeswehr als Instrument deutscher Außenpolitik*, 26.

[153] Von Krause, *Die Bundeswehr als Instrument deutscher Außenpolitik*, 159.

[154] See *Grundgesetz für die Bundesrepublik Deutschland* (Berlin: Bundesministerium für Justiz und Verbraucherschutz, 2014), 24, accessed January 15, 2015, http://www.gesetze-im-internet.de/bundesrecht/gg/gesamt.pdf.

[155] Gareis, "Militärische Beiträge zur Sicherheit," 119; Von Krause, *Die Bundeswehr als Instrument deutscher Außenpolitik*, 45.

"out-of-history."[156] The latter refers to a historically reasoned restriction partially arising from Article VI of the Washington Treaty, but also the West German national interest, which became later known as the "Kohl doctrine"[157] with his public refusal to deploy the Bundeswehr to Yugoslavia in 1991,[158] arguing that no German soldier should be present in a country that had been occupied by the *Wehrmacht*.[159] Nonetheless, until 1990, German soldiers took part in numerous engagements around the globe on a very small scale and subordinate to the forward defense in Central Europe. All deployments, such as the dispatch of a hospital ship to South Vietnam in the middle 1960s, however, included without exception, humanitarian, technical, logistic, or medical support missions, below the level of military missions in the sense of the Basic Law.[160]

Based on disruptive changes in global politics around 1990 that changed the determinants of German security policy, increasing external demands, and a cautiously rising understanding of Germany's international responsibility, the united Germany under Federal Chancellor Helmut Kohl gradually freed the Bundeswehr from the taboo of being used as a means in foreign and security policy—getting access to out-of-area and out-of-history missions *without* loosening its culture of military reticence. Paradigmatic for the struggle of the young united Germany to define its position to military means between the poles of increasing multilateral expectations and a matured military restraint became the Iraq War in 1990/1991. Unable to bring

---

[156] Von Krause, *Die Bundeswehr als Instrument deutscher Außenpolitik*, 159; see also Gareis, "Militärische Beiträge zur Sicherheit," 119.

[157] Wolfram Hilz, "Kontinuität und Wandel deutscher Außenpolitik nach 1990," *Informationen zur politischen Bildung* 304 (November 2009): 41.

[158] See Deutscher Bundestag, *Stenografischer Bericht: Plenarprotokoll 12/60* (Bonn: Dr. Hans Heger, November 27, 1991), 5014, accessed January 15, 2015. http://dipbt.bundestag.de/doc/btp/12/ 12060.pdf.

[159] Von Krause, *Die Bundeswehr als Instrument deutscher Außenpolitik*, 199.

[160] Gareis, "Militärische Beiträge zur Sicherheit," 119–20.

itself to contribute militarily to the coalition forces, the federal government made considerable financial contributions. This decade-long praxis of West Germany was quickly criticized as *"Scheckbuch-Diplomatie"* (checkbook diplomacy).[161]

After Iraq, the German public became more and more familiar with missions abroad of the Bundeswehr. It was a gradual process, however.[162] With mine-detection in the Mediterranean Sea and the Persian Gulf 1990–1991, medical support in Cambodia 1991–1993 (UNTAC), embargo monitoring in the Adriatic Sea 1992–1996, logistic support in Somalia 1993–1994 (UNOSOM II), and the NATO missions in Bosnia-Herzegovina in 1994/1996 (IFOR and SFOR), the focus still remained on Europe and its periphery as well as on peacekeeping operations. Likewise, the numbers of soldiers deployed soldiers did not exceed the limit of 3,000 until the end of Kohl's term of office in 1998.[163] The primary noncombat role of the Bundeswehr gave rise to societally shared and politically enforced image of German soldiers as aid workers in uniform (*Entwicklungshelfer in Uniform*) or an armed technical emergency service (*Technisches Hilfswerk mit Gewehr*).[164]

Since this early phase of international missions after reunification, the scope, quality, and nature of German participations in out-of-area military interventions have changed dramatically—with likewise substantial influences on the perception of the role and significance of the Bundeswehr and its soldiers as a means in international affairs. Beginning with the red-green government of Federal Chancellor Gerhard Schröder and Minister of Foreign Affairs Joschka Fischer,

---

[161] Von Krause, *Die Bundeswehr als Instrument deutscher Außenpolitik*, 168–69; Gareis, "Militärische Beiträge zur Sicherheit," 121.

[162] Von Krause, *Die Bundeswehr als Instrument deutscher Außenpolitik*, 241. See also Ulrike Esther Franke, "A Tale of Stumbling Blocks and Road Bumps: Germany's (Non-)Revolution in Military Affairs," *Comparative Strategy* 31, no. 4 (2012): 360.

[163] Wagner, *Auf dem Weg zu einer 'normalen' Macht?*, 1.

[164] Rimscha, "Ein Land tut sich schwer," 66.

and backed through a ruling of the Federal Constitutional Court in 1994, German soldiers participated not only in more and more out-of-area missions (more than 10,000 at once during the first term of office), but also in combat-operations outside Europe. The broad spectrum of missions included the NATO combat operation in Kosovo 1999 (Allied Forces), peacekeeping mission in Kosovo since 1999 (KFOR), and sea route protection operation in the Mediterranean Sea since 2001 (OAE), but also EU operations in Macedonia 2003 (Concordia), in the Democratic Republic of Congo 2003 (Artemis) and 2006 (EUFOR DR Congo), and in Bosnia-Herzegovina 2004 (EUFOR Althea as successor of SFOR). The affirmation of Germany's unlimited "political and moral solidarity"[165] with the United States after the 9/11 attacks, led the Bundeswehr into the "war against terrorism" and peace-enforcement operations in Afghanistan since 2001 (OEF and ISAF), with approximately 5,000 soldiers at the peak in 2010.

Despite the incremental transformation of the Bundeswehr into "armed forces in mission" with all capabilities engaged abroad, the public and political apprehension concerning the actual role, nature, and significance of its international engagements took many years and remained domestically strongly disputed. Particularly the long-lasting political defensive stance toward the terms war (*Krieg*) and fallen (*Gefallene*) and the attempts to frame the Bundeswehr's Afghan mission as a situation of stabilization and reconstruction rather than as condition of war, followed coherent political calculations in face of a consistently perceived military- and casualty-averse German public.[166] The Kunduz airstrike in September 2009 and rising numbers of fallen

---

[165] Deutscher Bundestag, *Stenografischer Bericht: Plenarprotokoll 14/187* (Berlin: Deutscher Bundestag, September 19, 2001), 18301, accessed January 15, 2015, http://dipbt.bundestag.de/doc/btp/ 14/14187.pdf#P.18301.

[166] Sascha Bleibohm, "On Contemporary War and the German Armed Forces: The Afghan War and its Consequences" (master's thesis, Naval Postgraduate School, 2014), 75–76; Franke, "A Tale of Stumbling Blocks and Road Bumps," 363.

due to the increasingly active involvement of German soldiers in fighting missions against insurgents, however, altered not only the perceptions of governmental actors and the parliamentarians, but also the conception and self-image of the Bundeswehr. Whereas politicians acknowledged the war-conditions and the requirements to project military power "with all necessary means,"[167] the Bundeswehr was transformed in its structure and capacities to a mission-focused professional army, capable and willing of fulfilling complex tasks in a comprehensive security environment.

Although the gradual extension and appreciation of Germany's multilateral out-of-area engagements would make contributions to similar missions more likely, particularly the experiences of fallen soldiers and the controversial discussions about the actual relevance and success of long-lasting, risky, and resource-intensive mission, such as in Afghanistan, feed domestic reservations. These aspects can provoke new shifts in perceptions and attitudes of governmental actors, parliamentarians, and the public toward military operations and constraining decision-making for future participation.

5. Mission Framework

The diversity of international crises and their respective context demands the international community to respond differently to particu-

---

[167] Deutscher Bundestag, *Stenografischer Bericht: Plenarprotokoll 17/11* (Berlin: Deutscher Bundestag, December 16, 2009), 867, accessed January 16, 2015. http://dipbt.bundestag.de/ doc/btp/17/17011.pdf. See also "Afghanistan Einsatz Guttenberg: 'Kriegsähnliche Zustände,'" *Frankfurter Allgemeine Zeitung*, November 3, 2009, http://www.faz.net/aktuell/politik/inland/afghanistan-einsatz-guttenberg-kriegsaehnliche-zustaende-1883496.html; "Afghanistan-Einsatz: Guttenberg hält Bezeichnung 'Krieg' für treffend," *Spiegel Online*, November 15, 2009, http://www.spiegel.de/politik/deutschland/afghanistan-einsatz-guttenberg-haelt-bezeichnung-krieg-fuer-treffend-a-661429.html; "Blitzbesuch der Kanzlerin: Merkel nennt Afghanistan-Einsatz 'Krieg,'" *Spiegel Online*, December 18, 2010, http://www.spiegel.de/politik/ausland/blitzbesuch-der-kanzlerin-merkel-nennt-afghanistan-einsatz-krieg-a-735432.html.

lar challenges as these emerge in fact. Political considerations may include distinct or interconnected diplomatic, economic, and military means in varying intensity and with different durations of actions. Consequently, the framework, characteristic, and scope of a potential German participation in a particular international military mission also shape the decision-making process.

The controversy about the continuing extensions, increasing external demands, and changing nature of German engagements in international military missions throughout the mid-2000s sparked a debate in parliament about adequate criteria for decisions on military engagements. Politicians and scholars who defined these criteria, however, emphasized that they should not be considered as a universal checklist, which may foster a machine-like automatic response in the decision-making process, but rather as guidelines (*Maßstäbe*) to "organize thoughts"[168] and to answer critical questions for each case.[169] The initiatives culminated in the wake of the German abstention from the UNSC resolution concerning Libya in 2011, as the

---

[168] Thomas de Maizière, *Internationale Verantwortung wahrnehmen: Deutschlands Rolle in der Welt von heute, Rede des Bundesministers der Verteidigung, Dr. Thomas de Maizière, bei der Heinrich-Böll-Stiftung am Montag, 25. Februar 2013, in Berlin*, accessed April 1, 2015, http://www.bmvg.de/portal/a/bmvg/!ut/p/c4/NYvBCsIwEET_aDcRFOrNUg R79KL1ImmzhIUmKeu2Xvx4k0Nn4MHwGHxhaXIbB6eck5vxicPE5_ELY9wCR E78URJeI3iS975ByFPCR717gikn0kqlpFwYxGkWWLLoXM0qUgywx8HYrjXW7L G_5njq-2vTHLpbe8clxssfXL-MOg!!/.

[169] Silberhorn, *Deutschlands Interessen*; Institut für Friedensforschung und Sicherheitspolitik an der Universität Hamburg, *Auslandseinsätze der Bundeswehr: Viele Bedingungen müssen erfüllt sein* (Hamburg: Institut für Friedensforschung und Sicherheitspolitik an der Universität Hamburg, 2007), accessed January 20, 2015, http://ifsh.de/pdf/profil/_IFSH_Auslandseinsaetze_der_Bundeswehr_2007.pdf; Jochen Hippler, "Bedingungen, Kriterien und Grenzen militärischer Intervention," *Jochenhippler*, accessed October 10, 2014, http://www.jochenhippler.de/Kriterien_von_Interventionen_Langfassung.pdf; Andreas Schockenhoff, *Kriterien für Auslandseinsätze der Bundeswehr: Orientierungsmaßstab für den jeweiligen Einsatz* (Berlin: CDU/CSU Fraktion im Deutschen Bundestag, September 11, 2006), accessed January 20, 2015, https://www.cducsu.de/presse/texte-und-interviews/kriterien-fuer-auslandseinsaetze-der-bundeswehr.

Green faction of the Bundestag officially requested the German government to develop a catalog of criteria for future out-of-area missions of the Bundeswehr.[170] Although the request ultimately was refused by the Bundestag,[171] the widely agreed guidelines notwithstanding influenced these particular German decisions based on five central categories,[172] hereby, linking elements from the external with the internal system, whereas the relation to German interest and objectives has been already illustrated. Since the relevance of national interests is discussed separately, only the four remaining categories are elaborated in the following.

The first category relates to the legality and the legitimacy of a military mission under the international law. As noted earlier, decisions on deployments of German soldiers generally follow the two key guiding premises of multilateral integration and the strict commitment to international law and the Charter of the United Nations. A ruling of the German Federal Constitutional Court in 1994 held that the German Basic Law legitimizes Germany to actively participate in "systems of mutual collective security," including the em-

---

[170] See Omid Nouripour et al., *Antrag: Prüfkriterien für Auslandseinsätze der Bundeswehr entwickeln—Unterrichtung und Evaluation verbessern* (Berlin: Bundesanzeiger Verlagsgesellschaft, March 16, 2011), accessed January 20, 2015, http://dip21.bundestag.de/dip21/btd/17/050/ 1705099.pdf.

[171] See Deutscher Bundestag, "Beschlussempfehlung und Bericht des Auswärtigen Ausschusses (3. Ausschuss) zu dem Antrag der Abgeordneten Omid Nouripour, Hans-Christian Ströbele, Marieluise Beck, weiterer Abgeordneter und der Fraktion BÜNDNIS 90/DIE GRÜNEN—Drs. 17/5099—Prüfkriterien für Auslandseinsätze der Bundeswehr entwickeln: Unterrichtung und Evaluation verbessern," Drs. 17/8697 (Berlin: Bundesanzeiger Verlagsgesellschaft, February 17, 2012), accessed January 20, 2015, http://dipbt.bundestag.de/dip21/btd/17/086/1708697.pdf.

[172] This study expends the general categorization of Volker Perthes by a category that includes: 1. the availability of military, personal, and financial capabilities and capacities for a mission; 2. the relevance of the German contribution; and 3. the implied costs. See Perthes, "Wie? Wann? Wo? Wie oft?." For more broader approaches, see Mair, "Kriterien für die Beteiligung an Militäreinsätzen," 11–19; For a more recent categorization, see De Maizière, *Internationale Verantwortung wahrnehmen*.

ployment of the Bundeswehr within the framework and according to the rules of these systems.¹⁷³ Subsequently, the UNSC mandate became the predominant domestically imposed and accepted justification for multilateral military actions. The controversial discussions about Germany's participation in the NATO air campaign in Yugoslavia in 1999, or in 2015, with the dispatch of a training mission of Kurdish fighters in Iraq without a UNSC mandate, reflect the outstanding importance for German foreign and security policy.¹⁷⁴ The application of the principle of the "responsibility to protect" as a legitimate extension of the international law, hence, as a legitimate cause for military missions, is also the subject of intense debates in Germany.

The second category refers to the conceptual framework, the prospect of success, and the potential risks of a military mission. Although such strategic dilemmas as the genocide in Rwanda in 1994 or massacres during the war in former Yugoslavia have gradually led to a somewhat greater use of military force as a policy of last resort, Germany continuously prefers to embed military means within an overarching concept of policy grounded in multilateralism and a deep skepticism about the use of force in favor of diplomatic and peaceful means for conflict resolution.¹⁷⁵ The lack of such a political master plan on the model of other democracies, setting clearly defined and achievable objectives that should aim at the roots of an international crisis, is expected to substantially hamper a positive German decision

---

173 Federal Constitutional Court, *BVerfGE 90, 286 = NJW 1994, 2207* (Karlsruhe: 1994).

174 Christian Thiels, "Bundeswehrmission im Nordirak: Dienstreise in den nächsten Krieg?," *Tagesschau*, December 10, 2014, http://www.tagesschau.de/ausland/bundeswehr-irak-107.html. Marie von Mallinckrod, "Zweifel an Verfassungsmäßigkeit: Irak-Einsatz auf wackeligen Füßen," *Tagesschau*, January 15, 2015, http://www.tagesschau.de/ausland/bundeswehr-irak-117.html.

175 Perthes,"Wie? Wann? Wo? Wie oft?," 21; Hippler, "Bedingungen, Kriterien und Grenzen militärischer Intervention," 7; De Maizière, *Internationale Verantwortung wahrnehmen*.

about participation in military missions. Other aspects of feasibility that relate to the higher likelihood of (sustainable) success, such as the anticipated duration of the mission, clearly defined and appropriate rules of engagement, and an existing exit strategy, can have an additional influence.[176]

In light of Germany's experience of war and its effects, risk considerations in conjunction with the nature of a mission also strongly influence decisions on German participation. The extension of Germany's multilateral out-of-area engagements from humanitarian aid and peacekeeping support in Cambodia and Somalia in the early 1990s to the participation in the Afghan ISAF mission since the early 2000s found only grudging and reluctant political acceptance. Such an attitude contrasts with the willingness, say, elsewhere (in the UK and France, for instance, even Denmark today) to send soldiers into combat missions or even war, facing high risks of dead soldiers. Such a willingness evolved only gradually, however, and has always seen a public aversion to the use of force and deaths in action.[177] Likewise, based on the common assumption that missions in Africa are more dangerous than missions in other regions of the world, Germany, like other Western countries, reluctantly contributed to UN peacekeeping operations and other missions in Africa during the last two decades.[178] Overall, reflecting the persistent and predominant German culture of military restraint, contributions of troops in action, which are limited in scope, duration, resources, and risks for soldiers on ground, are most likely to receive broad political and public consent

---

[176] Institut für Friedensforschung und Sicherheitspolitik an der Universität Hamburg, *Auslandseinsätze der Bundeswehr*, 3–4; Mair, "Kriterien für die Beteiligung an Militäreinsätzen," 15.

[177] For the long-lasting avoidance of the notion of "war" within the official political debate see Maybritt Brehm et al., *Armee im Einsatz: 20 Jahre Auslandseinsätze der Bundeswehr* (Hamburg, VSA Verlag, 2012), 164.

[178] Jair van der Lijn and Jane Dundon, *Peacekeepers at Risk: The Lethality of Peace Operations*, (Stockholm: SIPRI, February 2014), 1, accessed January 22, 2015. http://books.sipri.org/files/ misc/SIPRIPB1402.pdf.

when the political conditions are correct and the formation of policy to guide such action is cultivated with care and in detail.

Given the personal, material, and financial limitations of the German Armed Forces, considerations about the availability of national capacities and capabilities for a certain type of mission/task in relation to ongoing commitments, the relevance of Germany's contribution to the overall performance of a mission, and the implied costs,[179] constitute a third guiding category that affects decision-making processes. Particularly through the quantitative and qualitative increase of Bundeswehr engagements in international missions, calculations between what is externally required or relevant and what is domestically available, affordable, and feasible can influence interministerial and parliamentary considerations about the nature, size, and quality of a certain German contribution.

Finally, the relevance and the potential dynamic of a crisis pose the fourth guiding category.[180] Despite the common acceptance to respond to a crisis, assessments of its strategic significance influence the decision-making process for military missions. The more a crisis constitutes a strategic dilemma, hence, has the potential to shock a regional or the international order, the more likely is a political and public consensus on a multilateral reaction, incentivizing and pulling German military contributions to it. In interrelation with the previous category, Germany is likely to support exclusively political efforts or actions of regional organizations, if a crisis is limited in geographic and security terms.

---

[179] De Maizière, *Internationale Verantwortung wahrnehmen.*

[180] Perthes,"Wie? Wann? Wo? Wie oft?," 19–20; Mair, "Kriterien für die Beteiligung an Militäreinsätzen," 15.

C. Determinants on the Internal Level

Within the integrative model for decisions on German military engagement, after reunification, the internal level of German foreign and security policy has become more demanding and less an object of consensus as in the high tide of the Cold War.[181] Because the dividing line between foreign and domestic policy has increasingly blurred and hence, the external and internal levels have interpenetrated each other, the domestic area influences foreign and security policy choices more directly, and the effect of internal determinants within those choices is much stronger. Chief among the interrelated internal factors that relate to a "domestic politicization"[182] of German foreign and security politics, including the decisions on participation in international military missions, are strategic culture and conception of national role, the parliament and political contestation, and the public opinion. This process has also unfolded in the last ten years[183] as the domestic political landscape has changed from its former order, to more parties and a wider ideological divergence of points of view about defense policy with the onset of grand coalition governments amid heightened international crises since September 11, 2001.

---

[181] Collmer, "'All Politics Is Local.'" 201–225; Crossley-Frolick, "Domestic Constraints," 43–75; Oppermann and Höse, "Die innenpolitischen Restriktionen deutscher Außenpolitik," 48–72.

[182] Oppermann, "National Role Conceptions," 509.

[183] For an empirical study that proves that German policy decisions after the end of the Cold War more closely reflect the policy preferences of the constituents can be found in William Davis, "The Public Opinion–Foreign Policy Paradox in Germany: Integrating Domestic and International Levels of Analysis Conditionally," *European Security* 21, no. 3 (2012): 347–69, doi: 10.1080/09662839.2012.655271. One must note that this fact predominantly relates to the condition that policymakers do not consider external threats as being significant.

1. Strategic Culture and Conception of National Role

A state's strategic culture and conception of national role are encompassed as "internal predispositions" with commonly shared norms, values, and attitudes regarding the identity of the state; the state's role within international affairs; and normative preferences for achieving foreign and security objectives.[184] Two major characteristics determine the influence of both conceptions on Germany's foreign and security policy and decision-making regarding the participation in military interventions.[185] First, strategic culture and conceptions of national role frame foreign and security policy through the provision of *collectively* shared, precast orientations, directions, and strategies for the way to behave in face of a problem. Socially constructed and historically grown, both conceptions shape the attitudes and standards of the general public and political elites alike in the way they consider certain policy options as legitimate, feasible, appropriate, and favored, including the role, relevance, and efficacy of the use of military force. Second, as normative frameworks for the perception and interpretation of aspects within and between the external and internal systems, both conceptions influence public opinion and attitudes of key stakeholders while attaching weight to internal and external factors and prioritizing between them in case the two systems come into conflict.[186] Both concepts, therefore, not only can directly affect decisions on military engagements, but also influence decision-makers in

---

[184] Hanns W. Maull, "Außenpolitische Kultur," in *Deutschland-Trendbuch: Fakten und Orientierungen*, ed. Karl-Rudolf Korte and Werner Weidenfeld (Bonn: Bundeszentrale für Politische Bildung, 2001), 648; Oppermann, "National Role Conceptions," 505;

[185] A third characteristic refers to the definition of national interest. See Peters, "Ansätze und Methoden," 822.

[186] Oppermann, "National Role Conceptions," 504–505; Thomas Risse-Kappen, "Public Opinion, Domestic Structure, and Foreign Policy in Liberal Democracies," *World Politics* 43, no. 4 (July 1991): 482; Johnston, "Thinking about Strategic Culture," 46; Longhurst, *Germany and the Use of Force*, 17; Mirow, *Strategic Culture Matters*, 6–7; Berger, *Cultures of Antimilitarism*, 15–19.

mediating between factors in the external and internal systems. This study looks at both characteristics within the decision-making process.[187]

Essentially, both concepts, however, are neither static nor homogenous, and therefore one potential source to explain variations in policy outcomes. Basically shaped through the interactions and tensions between the two systems, strategic culture and national role concept can gradually change, shift, and adapt, as evolutions in the external and internal systems occur. Likewise, facilitated through varying perceptions of consistent or changed guiding paradigms of foreign and security policy, differences between the individual beliefs of key stakeholders concerning the state's role and appropriate behavior in international affairs can occur.

Based on its particular historical and political experiences, the FRG, as any other country, has developed a certain set of norms and axioms of action that characterized its tenets, standards, and preferences for foreign and security affairs.[188] In the case of West and then united Germany (but also the GDR in its time), the country's negative experiences in World Wars I and II had a distinct and widely shared set of norms and values that shaped Germany's strategic culture and the understanding of its role and status in the world. After the war, both Germanies developed an aversion to war with the motto of "never again," while, at the same time, the two states carried a huge military burden in the Cold War confrontation. This experience has resulted in a "culture of restraint" and a self-image of a "civilian power," which aversion to unilateralism and skepticism on the use of armed forces formed following three deeply internalized foreign policy principles: 1) "never alone"—a consequent orientation to the West (*Westorientierung*), an integration into Western institutions, and a

---

[187] Hanrieder, "Compatibility and Consensus," 971; Lantis, *Strategic Dilemmas*, 19; Oppermann, "National Role Conceptions," 505.
[188] Gareis, "Militärische Beiträge zur Sicherheit," 117.

multilateral oriented, coordinated, and implemented foreign policy (European integration, transatlantic partnership, and German-French partnership); 2) "never again"—a commitment to value-oriented foreign policy; and 3) "politics before force"—a skepticism toward military instruments of power as a means to their own end and a constrained use of force in all kinds of international affairs other than national defense.[189]

Consequently, beginning in 1955, the political rather than the military efficacy of the Bundeswehr dominated considerations about the role and relevance of military means in the FRG's foreign and security policy. This generalization especially applied to the formation of domestic consensus in Bonn about foreign and defense policy. The West German armed forces allowed the young state to enter the Western community and to become an integral part of the Western alliance system.[190] As such, the FRG was not a pacifistic state at all, while its population nurtured a strong pacifist or, more properly, antimilitary streak; however, the use of military force was justifiable only to protect its free and democratic order (*freiheitliche und demokratische Grundordnung*) instead of enforcing national interests or of changing a certain political status quo (i.e., a violent reunification of Germany).[191]

Notwithstanding political calculations, the experiences of total defeat, the collapse of state structures, and the ruin of societal values caused fierce resistance among the West German society against Germany's rearmament (*Wiederbewaffnung*) as high refusal rates in the early 1950s demonstrated with the principle of "ohne mich" (without me).[192] Although throughout the Cold War period a "general accep-

---

[189] Longhurst, *Germany and the Use of Force*, 17, 47; Maull, "Germany and the Use of Force," 4–9; Maull, "Deutsche Außenpolitik," 100.

[190] Von Krause, *Die Bundeswehr als Instrument deutscher Außenpolitik*, 26–27, 78–80.

[191] Gareis, "Militärische Beiträge zur Sicherheit," 121.

[192] Von Krause, *Die Bundeswehr als Instrument deutscher Außenpolitik*, 37.

tance of the Bundeswehr"[193] among German citizens arose especially after the Hamburg flood of 1962, the deeply ingrained aversion to all military in the German society remained and matured.[194]

The end of East-West confrontation and the unification of Germany in 1990 brought to the Federal Republic not only full sovereignty through the Two Plus Four Agreement, but also a fundamental transformation of the country's foreign policy and security environment. This change only slowly became clear, while the dictates of domestic reconstruction were foremost in the early 1990s. Although free to change its role in and approach to international affairs, post–Cold War Germany, however, reaffirmed its *raison d'état* with the firm commitment and integration into the Western alliance system which had well served its national interest, the aspiration to intensify the European integration, and the self-imposed limitations of military options—marking a high degree of continuity of Germany's foreign and security policy.[195] Yet the international system from 1990 through 2003 found not perpetual peace, as in Central Europe, but the revival of war as a means of policy.

The developments of this period of peace and war at the same time significantly intensified the "inherent contradictions"[196] within and between Germany's core principles and approaches to foreign and security policy. On the one hand, the two predominant normative imperatives of multilateralism ("never alone") and of reticence in using force ("policy before force") increasingly collided within the decision-making on Germany's participation in military intervention amid a deteriorating global security environment, a consolidating German

---

[193] Philipp Ebert, "Die Geschichte der Wiederbewaffnungsdiskussion in der Bundesrepublik, 1949–1955: Argumente, Alternativen, öffentliche Meinung," study work (Norderstedt, Germany: Grin-Verlag, 2010), 7.

[194] Von Krause, *Die Bundeswehr als Instrument deutscher Außenpolitik*, 80; see Gareis, "Militärische Beiträge zur Sicherheit," 117.

[195] Maull, "Germany and the Use of Force," 9–10.

[196] Ischinger, "Germany after Libya," 46.

unification, and a uniting Europe. On the other, Germany's traditional foreign and security policy tenets became contested with Berlin's growing resocialization to the rigors of (economic) power politics, increasing claims for more international engagement and responsibility,[197] and evolving key actor's attitudes toward the role, relevance, and efficacy of the use of force in international affairs. These complex tensions resulted in—and were reflected by—gradual, shifts of emphasis on certain elements within Germany's strategic culture and self-conception.[198] Consequently, while Germany's policies toward military engagements became not only more self-confident, gradually freeing the Bundeswehr from its customary constitutional and continental restrictions, it was exactly this wave-line like shift of emphasis that resulted in often unexpected ambiguous and ambivalent policy outcomes.[199] This understanding helps to combine the arguments of the two schools of thought concerning "continuation" and "change" in Germany's strategic culture as well as role conception and the respectively evolving impacts on decisions for military engagements.

It is the duality of "change in continuity" and "continuity in change" that condenses this particular phenomenon of German foreign and security policy. Immediately after Germany's reunification in 1990 and 1991 at the time of the Gulf War, then-Federal Chancellor

---

[197] Johannes Varwick, "Neue deutsche Außenpolitik: Kultur der Zurückhaltung versus Kultur des Engagements," *Europäische Sicherheit und Technik* 63, no. 6 (2014) 15–19.

[198] Longhurst, *Germany and the Use of Force*, 147; Overhaus, Harnisch and Katsioulis, "Schlussbetrachtung," 253; Milosevic, "Deutsche Kriegsbeteiligung und—verweigerung," 145–46.

[199] Duffield, "Why Germany Confounds Neorealism," 787–89; Conrad and Stumm, *German Strategic Culture and Institutional Choice*, 63; Von Krause, *Die Bundeswehr als Instrument deutscher Außenpolitik*, 352; Ischinger, "Germany after Libya," 47–51; As diametric examples are often raised Germany's participation within the NATO Operation Allied Forces, in Serbia 1999 and the abstention of a participation in the Iraq War, 2003.

Helmut Kohl (CDU) and then-Foreign Minister Hans-Dietrich Genscher (FDP) stressed Germany's "growing responsibility in the global community,"[200] calling for a change of the Basic Law to allow the Bundeswehr to participate in military missions based on systems of collective security as contained more or less in Article 24 of the Basic Law versus the continental restriction of Article 87a.[201] The change of perception of the Bundeswehr toward a more accepted and justifiable instrument of foreign and security policy, however, only gradually took shape until a climax in 1994; this process did not run smoothly, and has not yet been finished as of this date. In conjunction with personal war experiences, post–Cold War German politicians remained very sensitive in the first years following unity to the decade-long prevailing mood in politics and society widely to refuse the use of military force other than for national defense as in Article 87a of the old model circa 1980.[202] The "culture of (foreign policy) reticence," as characterized by then-Foreign Minister Genscher, remained vivid and fundamental as a thing of consensus.[203]

However, a new generation of leaders came into power, beginning in 1998 with Federal Chancellor Gerhard Schröder, who, unlike his predecessors, was essentially free of direct experience of the world before 1945. These figures adapted what can only be described as a more nationalist interpretation of the lessons of the past which fostered German interests in an altered Europe, and especially a closer relationship to Russia as a revival of a neo-Bismarckian statecraft that

---

[200] Von Krause, *Die Bundeswehr als Instrument deutscher Außenpolitik*, 167–68, 179.

[201] Deutscher Bundestag, *Stenografischer Bericht: Plenarprotokoll 11/228* (Bonn: Dr. Hans Heger, October 4, 1990), 18028, accessed January 20, 2015, http://dipbt.bundestag.de/doc/btp/11/ 11228.pdf#P.18018; Deutscher Bundestag, *Stenografischer Bericht: Plenarprotokoll 12/6* (Bonn: Dr. Hans Heger, January 31, 1991), 137, accessed January 20, 2015, http://dipbt.bundestag.de/doc/btp/12/12006.pdf.

[202] Von Krause, *Die Bundeswehr als Instrument deutscher Außenpolitik*, 241.

[203] Ulrich Roos, Deutsches Außenpolitik: Eine Rekonstruktion der grundlegenden Handlungsregeln (Wiesbaden: VS Verlag für Sozialwissenschaften, 2010), 42.

downplayed Atlanticism. Germany's foreign and security policy implementation in the latter 1990s thus "normalized" along the lines of more self-confidence and a stronger focus on economic and domestic imperatives imposed by globalization and structural determinants in European politics, society and economy. All of it resulted in a rather pragmatic understanding of multilateral commitments and expectations. It also led, however, to the conviction that military capacities are important to "meet international obligations"[204] and that participations in military interventions send a signal to shoulder more responsibility in global security among the other Western powers.[205]

In parallel, the quantitatively and qualitatively changing reality of international deployments and structural reforms gradually transformed the Bundeswehr toward an "Army on Operations."[206] Yet, increasing numbers of German soldiers in military interventions, including those in combat missions in Kosovo in 1999, and abstentions from such participations in multilateral operations as Iraq in 2003 or in Chad/CAR in 2007/2008, raised questions as to what extent the role concept as "civil power" is still valid or had gradually lost its unequivocal determining significance.[207]

The question became even more urgent as political elites slowly began to rethink, against the backdrop of the global security challenges of the twenty-first century, the role, relevance, and efficacy of

---

[204] Federal Ministry of Defense, *Bundeswehr on Operations*, 48.

[205] Germany's claim for a permanent seat in the UNSC underlines the changed perception of its power status, role, and responsibility in the world. See Hilz, "Kontinuität und Wandel deutscher Außenpolitik," 48; Roos, "Deutsche Außenpolitik nach der Vereinigung," 27; Oppermann, "National Role Conceptions," 506–507.

[206] Federal Ministry of Defense, *Bundeswehr on Operations*, 3.

[207] Even the leading proponent of the "civil power" thesis, Hanns W. Maull, acknowledges that evolutions in German foreign and security policy decision suggest that the old role concept has shown serious "wear marks." See Maull, "Deutsche Außenpolitik," 114. See also Roos, "Deutsche Außenpolitik nach der Vereinigung," 27.

the employment of military force in German foreign and security policy. Although a clear preference for civilian solutions remained, military capabilities became increasingly seen as an important complementary (embedded) mean, whose use could be "imperative and indispensable" and therefore should never be "categorically ruled out or merely regarded as a last option when all other approaches have failed."[208]

Such a shifting understanding of the role of the Bundeswehr, however, consistently stays in stark contrast to the public perception of an appropriate use of military force. Contrary to the political elites, the German public in general remains skeptical overall "vis-à-vis military force and its use as a foreign policy instrument,"[209] preferring only limited mission frameworks and averting participation in combat missions.[210]

The government of Chancellor Merkel up to 2011 continued the shift toward a more self-confident implementation of German foreign and security policy.[211] It also cemented the extended role and mission of the Bundeswehr as an instrument for international crisis preven-

---

[208] Federal Ministry of Defense, *Bundeswehr on Operations*, 48.

[209] Franke, "A Tale of Stumbling Blocks and Road Bumps," 363.

[210] Daniel Göler, "Die strategische Kultur der Bundesrepublik: Eine Bestandsaufnahme normativer Vorstellungen über den Einsatz militärischer Mittel," in *Friedensethik und Sicherheitspolitik: Weißbuch 2006 und die EDK-Friedensdenkschrift 2007 in der Diskussion* , ed. Angelika Dörfler-Dierken and Gerd Portugall (Wiesbaden: VS Verlag für Sozialwissenschaften, 2010), 191, 197; Jörg Jacobs, "Germans to the Front?: Attitudes Towards a German Contribution to Worldwide Military Missions," *Journal of Contemporary Central and Eastern Europe* 14, no. 3 (2006): 276–79, doi: 10.1080/09651560601042993; Gerhard Kümmel, "The Winds of Change: The Transition from Armed Forces for Peace to New Missions for the Bundeswehr and its Impact on Civil-Military Relations," *Journal of Strategic Studies* 26, no. 2 (2003): 7–28; Rüdiger Fiebiger and Carsten Pietsch, "Die Deutschen und ihre Streitkräfte," *Aus Politik und Zeitgeschichte* 48 (November 2009): 36–41.

[211] Franz-Josef Meiers, "The German Predicament: The Red Lines of the Security and Defense Policy of the Berlin Republic," *International Politics* 44 (2007): 637–38.

tion and conflict resolution within the Ministry of Defense White Book, 2006, and the Ministry of Defense's *Defense Policy Guidelines*, 2011. At the same time, however, Merkel's government showed a deeply ingrained and continuing aversion to high-risk, high-intensity ground operations as the Afghan campaign struck headlines with growing conflict in the 2010 Kunduz combat. Amplified through the experiences of fallen soldiers and the controversial debate concerning the nature of the ISAF mission in Afghanistan, German foreign and security policy debates and decisions reflected a persistently restrained view on the use of military forces. Merkel's strictly (geo)-economic–orientated *Realpolitik* reinforced the culturally deeply embedded risk-averse attitude, tending to favor a reputation as a stable and reliable economic partner over the commitment as a reliable partner in security affairs.[212]

2. Parliament and Political Contestation

Depending on the domestic political constitution, internal political actors can influence a state's foreign and security policy and decisions. In a parliamentary democracy like in Germany, the constitutional role of the Bundestag as parliament itself and the political contestation between parties within the parliament as well as between the parliament and the government are of particular relevance, as all political factions struggle for public support and governmental responsibility.[213] In political debates within the parliament that precede German foreign and security policy decisions, including those for the deployment of the Bundeswehr, oppositional parties regularly try to question critical decisions of the government and to provide alternatives, to increase their chances for the next elections. The government,

---

[212] Szabo, "Germany's Commercial Realism," 119.

[213] Andreas Hasenclever, "Liberalismus," in *Handbuch der Internationalen Politik*, ed. Carlo Masala, Frank Sauer, and Andreas Wilhelm (Wiesbaden: VS Verlag für Sozialwissenschaften, 2010), 77–101; Oppermann and Höse, "Die innenpolitischen Restriktionen deutscher Außenpolitik," 48–72.

however, seeks to adjust and optimize own actions, to minimize the political contestation by the opposition.[214]

Resting on the German Basic Law, the Bundestag as the highest German legislative body possesses a number of important rights and responsibilities within the framework of foreign and security policy, including parliamentary oversight of executive actions and the exertion of indirect influence, such as budget legislation.[215] A ruling of the German Federal Constitutional Court on July 12, 1994, in which an important change was made to the heretofore primacy of Article 87a concerning the defense mission of the Bundeswehr, however, held that the Bundeswehr is a "parliamentary army" whose armed deployment abroad requires the government to secure the Bundestag's approval. This revision by the constitutional court emerged in the wake of unity, the 1990/1991 Gulf War, and the rise of chaos in the former Yugoslavia as well as the requirements of UN peacekeeping in the 1990s. The subsequent law on parliamentary participation in 2005 cemented the constitutive parliament's right of prior approval and constrained the deployment of German soldiers into international military engagements.[216]

Accordingly, the standard procedure starts with a decision of the Federal Cabinet for a request on approval for the deployment of armed forces, which must be forwarded to the Bundestag in due time before the start of the planned mission. After a first consultation or reading in the full chamber of the Bundestag, the request is further discussed in committees, headed by the committee for foreign affairs

---

[214] Oppelland, "Parteien," 269–71.

[215] For a detailed overview of legally assigned responsibilities see Gareis, "Making of Germany's Security and Defense Policy," 55, 60–61.

[216] Federal Constitutional Court, BVerfGE 90, 286; Bundesministerium der Justiz, *Gesetz über die parlamentarische Beteiligung bei der Entscheidung über den Einsatz bewaffneter Streitkräfte im Ausland (Parlamentsbeteiligungsgesetz)* (Berlin: Bundesministerium der Justiz, 2005), accessed October 31, 2014, http://www.gesetze-im-internet.de/bundesrecht/parlbg/gesamt.pdf.

(*Auswaertiger Ausschuss*). Often as called as the "king committee," it consists of members from all factions of the Bundestag and is one of the few committees with constitutional status.[217] It is in charge of preparing the vote for the governmental requests and giving recommendations for the Bundestag. Before its full plenum decision whether to approve the request, which requires a simple majority, the Bundestag may use further informal means to influence decision-making or the content of the envisioned mandate throughout the process of direct consultation or in interaction with the government.[218]

Despite the significant constitutional changes in procedures for the deployment of the Bundeswehr in missions abroad, five important aspects, however, may mediate the role of the Bundestag and its significance as entire entity within the decision-making process in relation to all political actors.

First, irrespective of the obligation to the role of parliament, the cabinet (that is, the chancellor and the ministers) has retained the primary power to decide *whether* and *how* the Bundeswehr contributes to international military missions. The Bundestag has "only" the option of permitting or preventing its deployment.[219] Furthermore, although having the right to withdraw German Armed Forces from any mission at any time, the Bundestag has no opportunity to bind the government for participation of its own accord.

---

[217] "Was macht eigentlich der Auswärtige Ausschuss?," *Deutscher Bundestag*, accessed February 27, 2015, http://www.bundestag.de/dokumente/textarchiv/2011/34434192_kw21_pa_polenz/205362.

[218] For an overview about parliamentary activities and practical application of the parliament's right of prior approval, see Dieter Wiefelspütz, *Das Parlamentsheer: Der Einsatz bewaffneter deutscher Streitkräfte im Ausland, der konstituive Parlamentsvorbehalt und das Parlamentsbeteiligungsgesetz* (Berlin: Berliner Wissenschafts-Verlag, 2005), 315–40; Von Krause, *Die Bundeswehr als Instrument deutscher Außenpolitik*, 197–98.

[219] Gareis, "Die Organisation deutscher Sicherheitspolitik," 99.

Second, the German parliament is politically and personally closely interlocked with the cabinet and government, intensifying the strong executive power within foreign and security policy. Since the coalition government rests on the simple majority within the Bundestag, party and coalition politics, which are dominated by the party leaders in the executive, make it unlikely that the Bundestag would deny the deployment of German soldiers after the decision has already been made by the cabinet within the systems of collective security.

Moreover, third, there is an unwritten consensus among German politicians that once a decision on multilateral level has been made for Germany's participation in an international military intervention, the German Bundestag cannot really reject it any longer,[220] unless parliament is willing to question Germany's obligations in a general sense of statecraft. In the event, no governmental request for a German participation has been denied to date, a fact that deserves its own prominence in a study of this kind.

Fourth, German politics, including foreign and security policy, have become more volatile through the dynamics of party and coalition politics as the political landscape of Europe in the twenty-first century is, itself, more contentious.[221] Since unification, the composition of the Bundestag has changed from a three-party lineup to first five and now currently four more or less enduring parliamentary groups, representing a more heterogeneous spectrum of foreign policy orientations with diverging attitudes toward the role of military intervention and increasing the contestation between government and opposition parties. The newer "regulars" in parliament include the Green Party (with its own place in the German political spectrum),

---

[220] Kaim, "Deutsches Interesse versus Bündnisverpflichtung," 182.

[221] Rinke, "Die Auslandseinsätze der Bundeswehr im Parteienstreit," 165–75; Rinke, "Parteien," 269–70; Crossley-Frolick, "Domestic Constraints, German Foreign Policy and Post-Conflict Peacebuilding," 58–61; Oppermann, "National Role Conceptions," 508; Oppermann and Höse, "Die innenpolitischen Restriktionen deutscher Außenpolitik," 67–68.

and the LINKE as the hard-left successor to the East German communist party; the latter regularly opposes out-of-area missions of the Bundeswehr as kind of political reflex. The trend of the last decade has been of Socialist-Christian Democratic coalitions, with the gradual disappearance of the old kingmaker, the German liberal party (FDP) whose role in foreign and security policy in the Cold War was pivotal. On the other hand, coalition politics in Germany urge governmental parties to engage in constant consensus building on major foreign policy issues, which imposes pressure on key actors within the decision-making process and does restrain Germany's international affairs, much to the suffering of Germany's critics but likely to the well-being of its citizens.[222]

Fifth, shifting governmental responsibilities also resulted in the pursuance of varying and even inconsistent foreign and security policy preferences toward military interventions. The two red-green coalitions between 1998 and 2005 both freed the military from the old taboos of no to out of area as well as no to actual combat[223] and accentuated a more self-determined international approach for Germany, resulting in Germany's participation in the NATO air campaign in the former Yugoslavia in 1999—and its nonparticipation in Iraq in 2003. Conversely, under the conservative-socialist and conservative-liberal coalitions between 2005 and 2013, the "culture of reticence" was again stronger, allegedly contributing to Berlin's abstention from three EU/NATO operations, all of them in Africa where one can say that the old "out of area" taboo reasserted itself in new

---

[222] Risse-Kappen, "Public Opinion," 488.

[223] Constanze Stelzenmüller, "Mit Gewehr, aber ohne Kompass: Eine Bilanz von vier Jahren rot-grüner Außenpolitik," *Die Zeit*, September 12, 2002, http://pdf.zeit.de/2002/38/Mit Gewehr aber ohne Kompass.pdf; Anna Geis, "Die Zivilmacht Deutschland und die Enttabuisierung des Militärischen," *HSFK Standpunkte* 2 (Frankfurt am Main: Hessische Stiftung Friedens- und Konfliktforschung, 2005).

circumstances.[224] On the other hand, although throughout all German parties a general pacifistic attitude toward military interventions remained, the relatively increased participation of Bundeswehr in out-of-area missions has allegedly led to a familiarization of a more robust German foreign and security policy.[225]

3. Public Opinion

Within the context of the increasing "domestication" of German foreign and security policy and the complex interplay between external and internal factors for German decision-making on participation in military missions, public opinion has an ambivalent but dominant role. In particular, the interaction between public opinion or an attentive public and political elites in the foreign policy-making process is a

---

[224] Coalition contract between CDU/CSU and FDP in 2009. "Wachstum—Bildung—Zusammenhalt: Koalitionsvertrag zwischen CDU, CSU und FDP, 17. Legislaturperiode," *Federal Ministry of Interior*, accessed January 28, 2015, 123, https://www.bmi.bund.de/SharedDocs/Downloads/DE/Ministerium/koalitionsvertrag.pdf?__blob=publicationFile; Deutscher Bundestag, *Schriftliche Fragen: mit den in der Woche vom 4. April 2011 eingegangenen Antworten der Bundesregierung*, 5–9; Brockmeier, "Germany and the Intervention in Libya," 64; Miskimmon, "German Foreign Policy and the Libya Crisis," 403.

[225] Oppelland, "Parteien," 274–77.

subject of vital debate among scholars.[226] Basically, the degree to which public opinion can be a "resource or a restriction"[227] of policy-making, and hence, can promote, contest, and constrain foreign and security policy decisions, depends on four criteria.[228] First, according to Davis, it relates to policy-makers themselves and their perception of an international event as being an external threat (as a strategic dilemma) for German security. The more such an external threat is significant, the more likely policy-makers tend to ignore (pacifistic) public opinion. This conditional phenomenon was particularly salient until 1989. Since the end of the Cold War, however, German state actors decreasingly attributed such events like the Iraq crisis in 2003 as a threat for German security. As a result, within policy calculations,

---

[226] The debate focuses on the question: who follows whom? The two opposing concepts, top-down and bottom-up, provide strength and weaknesses in their argumentation whether either leader or masses follow the other. According to Thomas Risse-Kappen, a simplistic view of either view does not account for the differences in politics. He argues that in particular the domestic structures and coalition-building processes can link the impact of public opinion on the foreign policy of such liberal democracies as Germany, France, or the United States. See Risse-Kappen, "Public Opinion," 484. For a critical analysis of the effect of public opinion on foreign and security policy, in relation to Germany, and with particular focus on security policy see also Biehl and Jacobs, "Öffentliche Meinung und Sicherheitspolitik," in *Deutsche Sicherheitspolitik: Herausforderungen, Akteure und Prozesse*, 2nd ed., ed. Stephan Böckenförde and Sven Bernhard Gareis (Opladen, Germany: Verlag Barbara Buderich, 2014), 265–86; Fabian Endres, Harald Schoen, and Hans Rattinger, "Außen- und Sicherheitspolitik aus der Sicht der Bürger: Theoretische Perspektiven und ein Überblick über den Forschungsstand," in *Sicherheitspolitik und Streitkräfte im Urteil der Bürger: Therorien, Methoden, Befunde,* ed. Heiko Biehl and Harald Schoen (Wiesbaden: VS Springer Fachmedien, 2015), 39–65; Hellmann, Wagner, and Baumann, *Deutsche Außenpolitik*, 179–92.

[227] Biehl and Jacobs, "Öffentliche Meinung und Sicherheitspolitik," 274.

[228] Oppermann and Höse, "Die innenpolitischen Restriktionen deutscher Außenpolitik," 61–67; Davis, "The Public Opinion–Foreign Policy Paradox in Germany," 348, 362–63.

policy-makers gave public opinion much more attention in their own deliberations.[229]

Second, the salience of foreign and security policy issues or of a certain international event within the public opinion, determines the effect to which the electoral power of the general public can impose incentives on political decision-making. This fact means, the higher the significance, importance, and urgency that the general public ascribes to an issue area, the higher the pressure for politicians, and particularly the government, to align their policies in accordance with the popular moods and preferences to avoid any harmful repercussions to their electoral prospects.[230] Foreign and security policy issues, however, continually rank low as priorities in the German public opinion and have done so since unification, if not earlier. Consequently, the economic and internal focus of the German public often draws political attention away from international affairs toward domestic affairs, intensifying the tensions between external expectations and internal constraints.

Conversely, international crises and conflicts that receive extensive media coverage can suddenly attract the public attention and can sensitize public opinion on political decisions as strategic dilemmas. The onset of the war in the former Yugoslavia in 1991; the genocide in Rwanda 1994, the Kosovo War in 1999, and the terrorist attacks on September 11, 2001, not only received above-average attention from the German public, but also sparked fierce public debates about adequate foreign and security policy reactions, including the participation

---

[229] Davis, "The Public Opinion–Foreign Policy Paradox in Germany," 348, 360–63.

[230] Kai Oppermann and Henrike Viehrig, "The Public Salience of Foreign and Security Policy in Britain, Germany, and France," *West European Politics* 32, no. 5 (2009): 926–27; Christopher Wlezien, "On the Salience of Political Issues: The Problem with 'Most Important Problem,'" *Electoral Studies* 24, no. 4 (2005): 556–61.

of the Bundeswehr, putting additional pressure on politicians as external and internal factors clashed.[231]

Institutional opportunities within the political decision-making process constitute the second criterion. Public opinion may "indirectly affect policies by influencing the coalition-building processes among the elites"[232] or even directly with options for a referendum as in, say, Switzerland, where defense policy is a subject of constant public votes. In contrast to other European states, however, the German public only has indirect influence on foreign and security policy behavior through parliamentary elections. This truth means that the greater the relevance of foreign and security policy issues, and hence, the greater the pressure on key stakeholders and other politicians, the closer a decision relates to the next election of the Bundestag and the wider the dissent is between the government and opposition or even among the governmental parties.[233]

Third, and potentially most important—for those who embrace Clausewitz as concerns the political nature of war and the role of politics and group psychology in conflict—public opinion can "matter for state strategy";[234] hence, it can directly influence the making of and decisions within foreign and security policy related to the use of military force. Public opinion and societal groups can affect choices of key decision-makers "by changing policy goals or how goals are prioritized, by narrowing the range of options and/or means to imple-

---

[231] Oppermann and Höse, "Die innenpolitischen Restriktionen deutscher Außenpolitik," 63.

[232] Risse-Kappen, "Public Opinion," 482.

[233] Oppermann and Höse, "Die innenpolitischen Restriktionen deutscher Außenpolitik," 65.

[234] Elizabeth Pond and Hans Kundnani, "Germany's Real Role in the Ukraine Crisis: Caught Between East and West," *Foreign Affairs* (March/April 2015), accessed April 8, 2015, http://www.foreignaffairs.com/articles/143033/elizabeth-pond-and-hans-kundnai/germanys-real-role-in-the-ukraine-crisis.

ment, or by winning symbolic concessions."[235] This fact is particularly relevant for decisions on the deployment of German soldiers in missions abroad—especially outside of Europe.

Given Germany's strategic culture, such decisions have a high political sensitivity. As a consequence, political actors have generally endeavored to seek a broad societal acceptance for security policy decisions and to exclude security policy outside party-political calculations and tactics.[236] Thus, the broader the popular consensus for or against general foreign and security policy behavior and particular measures in relation to certain issue areas, the more it may incentivize or constrain the federal government and the Bundestag because it increases the burden both to decide against it and to mitigate external expectations. Such challenging situations facilitate ambiguity in the face of critical decisions for military interventions. The influence of public opinion on policy decisions, implicated through the awareness of Germany's political elite toward it, is expected to be magnified the closer elections are scheduled and/or the electoral outcome is contested.

Since reunification and the gradual evolution of international missions with Bundeswehr soldiers, the opinion of Germany's citizens toward the Bundeswehr and its diverse tasks has become increasingly ambivalent and divided, with shifting support for certain types of missions. While retaining its general preference of using political rather than military means in international affairs, the German public unquestionably supported the task of national defense. At the same time, the defense within the NATO alliance and peacekeeping missions within the framework of the UN were widely accepted among the German public. Peace-enforcing missions or combat operations, however, remain societally disputed. On the other hand, the evolution of the public opinion toward these types of missions demonstrates

---

[235] Risse-Kappen, "Public Opinion," 482.
[236] Biehl and Jacobs, "Öffentliche Meinung und Sicherheitspolitik," 274.

that the public's attitude follows and reflects international events. Accordingly, the acceptance of combat operations gradually rose from lower than 50 percent until 1994 to more than 70 percent in 2000, a consequence of the Kosovo war in 1999. Since then, however, the acceptance gradually dropped again, despite or even more because of the Bundeswehr engagement in Afghanistan. In 2010, the German public was, again, equally divided about the matter.[237]

The evolution of military engagement has affected public opinion—demonstrating another example of the interlinkage between factors on the external and internal level. The long-lasting, cost- and casualty intensive combat missions in Iraq or Afghanistan have hardened a public that considerably doubts the offensive or preventive use of military. The military means-averse attitude intensified as some missions did not progress as planned, like in Afghanistan, or even had counterproductive effects, like in Iraq. This development may be one additional reason for German citizens to favor military missions that have a supportive character and are embedded in a comprehensive approach that focuses on civil means, to and expect a peaceful evolution.[238]

The general preference of the German public seems to appeal to decision-makers and parliamentarians alike.[239] Federal Chancellor Schröder's refusal to deploy German troops in support of the Iraq operation in 2003 had more to do with his concerns about the pros-

---

[237] Biehl and Jacobs, "Öffentliche Meinung und Sicherheitspolitik," 274–75; Hellmann, Wagner, and Baumann, *Deutsche Außenpolitik*, 186. For the short rise of the approval for combat operations between 1996 and 2001, see Jacobs, "Germans to the Front?," 278.

[238] Biehl and Jacobs, "Öffentliche Meinung und Sicherheitspolitik," 275–76.

[239] Kaim, *Deutschlands Einsatz in Afghanistan*, 9–11; Körber-Stiftung, *Einmischen oder zurückhalten?*, 3–4; Jörn Thießen and Ulrich Plate, "Bundeswehr und Parlament," in *Armee im Einsatz: Grundlagen, Strategien und Ergebnisse einer Beteiligung der Bundeswehr*, ed. Hans J. Gießmann and Armin Wagner (Baden-Baden: Nomos: 2009), 155–56.

pect of success in the upcoming parliamentary elections.²⁴⁰ Given that almost 80 percent of Germans at that time rejected a war in Iraq, and especially Germany's participation in it, Schröder raised this domestic political critique purposefully to set Germany back onto a *Sonderweg* ("special path") for the sake of his own reelection.²⁴¹

The yearlong refusal of key German policy-makers to use officially the term "war" in relation to the operational conditions in Afghanistan, can be partly traced back to the political concerns about the potential lack of a broad public acceptance as well as the to the strategic muddle with which the Afghan operation began and the eventual impact of this fact on the conditions in the years 2009 and 2010.²⁴² In this context, given that a majority of the population openly supports a more self-confident approach of Germany in international affairs (that is, a German national interest) but simultaneously opposes more international engagement,²⁴³ public opinion may

---

[240] Katsioulis, "Deutsche Sicherheitspolitik im Parteiendiskurs," 227–52; Wilfried von Bredow, "Mühevolle Weltpolitik: Deutschland im System internationaler Beziehungen," in *Deutsche Außenpolitik: Sicherheit, Wohlfahrt, Institutionen und Normen*, 2nd ed., ed. Thomas Jäger, Alexander Höse, and Kai Oppermann (Wiesbaden: Springer Fachmedien, 2011), 724.

[241] Johannes Varwick, "Deutsche Sicherheits- und Verteidigunspolitik in der Nordatlantischen Allianz: Die Politik der rot-grünen Bundesregierung, 1998–2003," in *Deutsche Sicherheitspolitik: Eine Bilanz der Regierung Schröder*, ed. Sebastian Harnisch, Christos Katsioulis, and Marco Overhaus (Baden-Baden: Nomos, 2004), 24–25.

[242] Brehm et al., *Armee im Einsatz*, 164.

[243] For the result of a recent opinion poll at the beginning of 2015 see Munich Security Conference, *Munich Security Report 2015: Collapsing Order, Reluctant Guardians?* (Munich: Munich Security Conference, 2015), 11, accessed April 4, 2015, http://www.eventanizer.com/MSC2015/MunichSecurityReport2015.pdf; see also Körber-Stiftung, *Einmischen oder zurückhalten?*, 2–3; Renate Köcher, ed., *Allensbacher Jahrbuch der Demoskopie, 2003–2009* (Berlin: deGruyter, 2009), 33; Collmer, "'All Politics Is Local,'" 208–216. For the evolution of and a more comprehensive overview about the attitude, opinion, and knowledge of the German public toward the Bundeswehr, see Kümmel, "The Winds of Change," 7–28; Fiebiger and Pietsch, "Die Deutschen und ihre Streitkräfte," 36–41; Biehl and Jacobs, "Öffentliche Meinung und Sicherheitspolitik," 270–81.

work as a "domestic catalyst" for an emerging German self-image as a "normal ally," further facilitating ambiguity in the face of critical decisions for military interventions.[244]

D. Determinants on the Actor Level

Domestic political state actors are central in the making of foreign and security policy decisions. Since external and domestic determinants justly gain influence on foreign (and security) policy if they are "grasped and processed by human actors,"[245] individual (and/or collective) policy-makers—those who obtain the authority to decide—act as the binding and mitigating[246] elements between the poles of the external and domestic levels of policy. As these factors influence state actors in their decisions, the major players' personalities, attitudes, perceptions, and preferences also play a decisive role in this process. Thus, apart from their functions in the system, state actors have a "certain leeway"[247] on the policy outcome.[248] Given different attitudes and changing (personal and power) relationships between the individual actors, policy decisions are expected to vary.

In Germany, the formulation and implementation of foreign and security policy is in primary responsibility of the federal cabinet government as executive branch.[249] It maintains diplomatic relations with

---

[244] Oppermann, "National Role Conceptions," 509.

[245] Peters, "Ansätze und Methoden," 827.

[246] Oppermann, "National Role Conceptions," 507.

[247] Hellmann, Wagner, and Baumann, *Deutsche Außenpolitik*, 119.

[248] Hellmann, Wagner, and Baumann, *Deutsche Außenpolitik*, 43–44, 115–16. For a more comprehensive overview about German foreign policy as an outcome of personal leadership, see 124–35.

[249] For a more detailed overview about the distribution of responsibilities between the executive and legislative branches within foreign and security affairs, see Rüdiger Wolfrum, "Grundgesetz und Außenpolitik," in *Handbuch zur deutschen Außenpolitik*, ed. Sigmar Schmidt, Gunther Hellmann, and Reinhard Wolf (Wiesbaden: Verlag für Sozialwissenschaften, 2007), 159.

other states and such international organizations as the UN, NATO, and the EU, and shapes the policies Germany pursues in those organizations. Despite constitutional changes in the praxis for decisions on military engagements, the power to decide whether and how Germany "will participate in collective action[s] ... including [international] military operations," rests with the federal government.[250]

Within the federal government, three actors, and their respective working ministries and subordinate echelons, predominantly design, influence, and implement German foreign and security policy in relation to decisions on missions abroad of the Bundeswehr: the federal chancellor, the minister of foreign affairs, and the minister of defense.[251]

Between those three, and with the disposal of the federal chancellery, the federal chancellor holds the dominant position. This fact is a legacy of the Adenauer cabinet in the first years of the Federal Republic from 1949 to 1955. Article 65 of the Basic Law assigns the federal chancellor, as the highest member of the federal government, the power to determine the general guidelines of (foreign) policy (the so called chancellor principle) and thereby the responsibility for its implementation.[252] The overruling authority of the federal chancellor is constrained through ministerial autonomy, that is, the so called

---

[250] Gareis, "Making of Germany's Security and Defense Policy," 55, 61.

[251] With the intensifying interrelation between foreign and domestic politics, among others based on more complex and new security concerns such as international terrorism, other executive actors, such as the chief of the federal chancellery, the minister of interior, and the minister for development aid, gained increasing significance in designing German foreign and security policy. Unofficial consultation- and decision-preparing bodies outside the Federal Security Council (Bundessicherheitsrat) have become more important since the red-green governments in the mid-1990s. See Oppermann and Höse, "Die innenpolitischen Restriktionen deutscher Außenpolitik," 51–52.

[252] *Grundgesetz für die Bundesrepublik Deutschland*, 17.

cabinet, and coalition principle, with its own checks and balances.[253] Each federal ministry conducts its affairs independently and under its own responsibility. The cabinet principle demands that the federal government settles interministerial differences within the collective discussion and decision-making process. In case of an equality of votes, however, the vote of the federal chancellor as chairman decides. As governments in Germany are generally formed between two parties,[254] party-political differences and the distribution of public offices between the coalition-partners may restrain foreign policy as well.

With the Federal Foreign Office, embassies in other countries and its missions in international organizations, and the ministerial autonomy principle, the minister of foreign affairs has a broad competency for directing and coordinating foreign and security policy. Despite maintaining responsibilities in several key domains of foreign and security policy, the foreign minister's power has been slightly decreased over the last decade, as responsibilities for certain policy subjects have shifted to other parts of the executive as well as the number of personnel dealing with international affairs in other execu-

---

[253] *Grundgesetz für die Bundesrepublik Deutschland*, 50 and 55; Gareis, "Die Organisation deutscher Sicherheitspolitik," 94. For a more detailed overview about the coordinating role of the Federal Chancellery, considered as lynchpin between all principal actors, see Karl-Rudolf Korte, "Bundeskanzleramt," in *Handbuch zur deutschen Außenpolitik*, ed. Sigmar Schmidt, Gunther Hellmann, and Reinhard Wolf (Wiesbaden: Verlag für Sozialwissenschaften, 2007), 203–209.

[254] The only exception from this general rule constitutes the short time between 1960 and 1961, as then–Federal Chancellor Conrad Adenauer briefly ruled his third cabinet only with members of the Christian Democratic Union (CDU) and its Christian-Socialist sister-party (CSU).

tive bodies have exceeded those in the Federal Foreign Office.[255] The foreign minister, however, remains an important actor because the position is traditionally manned by the coalition partner and combined with the role as vice-chancellor, which allows the foreign minister to act as a political counterweight to and contester of the federal chancellor in the decision-making process.[256]

The minister of defense complements the triad of important key stakeholders in relation to foreign and security policy decisions. This role has grown in the last decades since 1990. As commander-in-chief of the armed forces, the defense minister is responsible for the German defense and military policy, including mission, size, and structure of the Bundeswehr, but also the deployment of the Bundeswehr within the framework of international military missions.[257]

Representing Germany in international organizations during specific summits and dealing with general policy guidelines or decisions on particular military operations, all three actors strongly influence German foreign and security policy decisions. Like other decision-makers, they aim to reconcile and balance the two systems so that policies "do not openly contradict either of them."[258] Detailed studies on Germany's participation or nonparticipation in multilateral military operations until 2011—from the Gulf War in 1991, over Yugoslavia in 1999, through Afghanistan in 2001 and Iraq in 2003, to DRC in 2005 and the Gulf of Aden in 2008—reveals that in each case the

---

[255] Oppermann and Höse, "Die innenpolitischen Restriktionen deutscher Außenpolitik," 53–54. Institutional fragmentation and competing interests between executive bodies dealing with international affairs may contribute to tensions in the decision-making process, hence, ambiguous outcomes. See Christoph Weller, "Bundesministerien," in *Handbuch zur deutschen Außenpolitik*, ed. Sigmar Schmidt, Gunther Hellmann, and Reinhard Wolf (Wiesbaden: Verlag für Sozialwissenschaften, 2007), 210.

[256] Milosevic, "Deutsche Kriegsbeteiligung und—verweigerung," 28.

[257] Gareis, "Making of Germany's Security and Defense Policy," 58.

[258] Oppermann, "National Role Conceptions," 504.

then minister of defense significantly influenced the formation and direction of public opinion, the political debate, and ultimately the decision-making itself in a manner that broke with the record of the past from 1955 until 1990.[259] Shifting governmental coalitions brought to these offices personalities with divergent personal beliefs about appropriate German behavior in international affairs and the role of military interventions as political means. Likewise, all of them showed variations in the degree to which their actions were affected either by external or domestic demands and constraints.

Beginning with the federal chancellor and the minister of foreign affairs of the reunification, Helmut Kohl (CDU) and Hans-Dietrich Genscher (FDP), who both claimed a bigger international responsibility for their country, Germany slowly became involved in its first limited military out-of-area mission in Iraq, Cambodia, and Somalia while the conservative interpretation of Article 87a held sway until 1994.[260] Simultaneously, however, Kohl, with reference to historical restrictions of his country, insistently refused a German military engagement in Yugoslavia, a position that became widely known as "Kohl doctrine," but later changed in the wake of dramatic deterioration of the crisis into near genocide in the middle and end of the 1990s.[261] Under the willingly more self-confident leadership of Federal Chancellor Gerhard Schröder (SPD) and Minister of Foreign Affairs Joschka Fischer (Bündnis 90/Die Grünen), rejecting Germany's long-lasting accused "checkbook diplomacy" (as in the Kuwait war of 1990 to 1991), German soldiers deployed in their first combat operation since the end of World War II, as the German government—with support of the majority of the Bundestag—decided to participate

---

[259] Oppermann, "National Role Conceptions," 502–519; Schmitt, "Strategic Users of Culture," 59–81; Wilke, *German Strategic Culture Revisited*, 70–110; Wagner, *Auf dem Weg zu einer 'normalen' Macht?*, 1–3.

[260] Von Krause, *Die Bundeswehr als Instrument deutscher Außenpolitik*, 167–79; Deutscher Bundestag, *Stenografischer Bericht: Plenarprotokoll 11/228*, 18028.

[261] Von Krause, *Die Bundeswehr als Instrument deutscher Außenpolitik*, 199–201.

within the NATO operation Allied Forces against the Federal Republic of Yugoslavia, even without a UNSC mandate.[262] Although continuing the Bundeswehr support to the ISAF mission in Afghanistan after 2002, Federal Chancellor Angela Merkel (CDU), the Ministers of Defense Franz-Josef Jung (CDU) and Karl-Theodor zu Guttenberg (CSU), and particularly Minister of Foreign Affairs Guido Westerwelle (FDP), showed more reservations concerning the need and relevance of military forces as political means,[263] which affected the decision-making processes, such as in the case for the nonparticipation in the EU operation in Chad/CAR in 2007/2008 and the NATO Operation Ocean Shield in the Gulf of Aden in 2008.

---

[262] Martin Wagner, "Normalization in Security Policy?: Deployments of Bundeswehr Forces Abroad in the Era Schröder, 1998–2004," in *Germany's Uncertain Power: Foreign Policy of the Berlin Republic*, ed. Hanns W. Maull (New York: Palgrave Macmillan, 2006), 90; August Pradetto, "The Polity of German Foreign Policy: Changes since Unification," in *Germany's Uncertain Power: Foreign Policy of the Berlin Republic*, ed. Hanns W. Maull (New York: Palgrave Macmillan, 2006), 23; Von Krause, *Die Bundeswehr als Instrument deutscher Außenpolitik*, 252–55, 266–67.

[263] Meiers, "The German Predicament," 623–44.

III. Libya—A "Normal" Special Case: Ambivalent Premises of German Foreign and Security Policy

The Arab Spring of 2011 unleashed a new wave of turmoil in the Middle East that followed the eruption of the US led Iraq war in 2003. The *Götterdämmerung* (Twilight of the Gods) of the Gaddafi regime posed a significant test for the principles of German foreign and defense policy enumerated above. This chapter frames the context and subsequently traces the sequence of events that contributed to the unexpected abstention from the vote for UNSC Resolution 1973 and the nonparticipation in the NATO mission to enforce it. Second, the analysis demonstrates that a complex interplay between elements on all three domains explains the alleged departure from premises of German foreign and security policy. On the macro level this chapter additionally shows, however, that the early German decision for a nonparticipation in an international military intervention also resonated with several continuing tenets of German foreign and security policy—underlying its "normalizing" ambivalent nature, revealed a more direct influence of domestic factors on foreign affairs,

In mid-February 2011, the wave of public resentment that had roiled Tunisia and Egypt only weeks before, spilled over to Libya. As protests against the Gaddafi regime spread around the country, so did violence. Within the first five days of the unrest, an estimated 233 protesters had been killed, rapidly turning the nature of the Libyan revolt from a peaceful uprising to an armed civil conflict.[264] Facing growing protest, the Gaddafi regime confirmed its willingness to suppress the uprising at all costs, echoed by air-strikes against the rebels. On February 22, Gaddafi publicly announced that he would cleanse Libya house by house, killing protesters like rats.[265]

The international community responded comparatively quickly to the crisis. On the same day of Gaddafi's speech, the Arab League and the UNSC denounced the violence employed by the Libyan government.[266] On February 26, the UNSC, including Germany as nonpermanent member, passed unanimously Resolution 1970, condemning the "use of force against civilians," demanding Libyan authorities' "responsibility to protect" its population, and imposing sanctions on Libya.[267] Later that day, Operation Pegasus started, a quickly decided and secretly executed German-British joint military evacuation opera-

---

[264] Brockmeier, "Germany and the Intervention in Libya," 66; Madelene Lindström and Kristina Zetterlund, *Setting the Stage for the Military Intervention in Libya: Decisions Made and Their Implications for the EU and NATO* (Stockholm: Swedish Defense Research Agency, 2012), 13; "Libya: Governments Should Demand End to Unlawful Killings," *Human Rights Watch*, February 20, 2011, http://www.hrw.org/de/news/2011/02/20/libya-governments-should-demand-end-unlawful-killings.

[265] Ian Black, "Libya on Brink as Protests Hit Tripoli," *Guardian*, February 20, 2011, http://www.theguardian.com/world/2011/feb/20/libya-defiant-protesters-feared-dead; Hebah Saleh and Andrew England, "Defiant Gaddafi Vows Fight to Death," *Financial Times*, February 23, 2011, http://www.ft.com/intl/cms/s/0/5b307dd4-3e9d-11e0-9e8f-00144feabdc0.html#axzz3SUtUlhHA; "Libya Protests: Defiant Gaddafi Refuses to Quit," *BBC News*, February 22, 2011, http://www.bbc.co.uk/news/world-middle-east-12544624.

[266] "Security Council Press Statement on Libya," UN Security Council press release, on the United Nations website, updated February 22, 2011, http://www.un.org/press/en/2011/sc10180.doc.htm.

[267] UN Security Council, *UNSC Resolution 1970* (New York: UNSC, February 26, 2011), accessed January 27, 2015, http://www.icc-cpi.int/NR/rdonlyres/081A9013-B03D-4859-9D61-5D0B0F2F5EFA/0/1970Eng.pdf.

tion, in which Bundeswehr soldiers from all services directly conducted or contributed to a successful extraction of some 200 German and other European citizens from southeast Libya.[268] As the violence continuously worsened and the tide turned against the rebels, some European states actively pushed for stronger actions against the Libyan government. Within only a couple of days, the initially reluctant attitude of the international community toward an active role in ending the violence against civilians in Libya reversed, culminating in the UNSC Resolution 1973 on March 17, 2011, which sought to establish a no-fly zone over Libyan airspace.[269]

Germany, unexpectedly, however, abstained from the vote, siding with China, Russia, India, and Brazil. Although not voting against the resolution, Germany's abstention marked a vote against such other NATO and EU allies and partners as France and the UK within the UNSC for the first time. The German government argued later it did so on the assumption that voting in favor of the no-fly zone almost certainly would obligate Germany to join the operation because it was

---

[268] "Die Operation Pegasus," *Bundeswehr*, March 3, 2011, accessed February 2, 2015,
http://www.bundeswehr.de/portal/a/bwde/!ut/p/c4/NUzBCoMwFPujPguDjt0Ud9jYycvmLqXapzzQVt6eE2Qfv3awBBJCQuAJicG9aXRCMbgJHtD2dOo21W0eFVJ4OZQdFc32F2S3w4psPQY7MGFyuOeXtO5jQMkqGISSjuwksloiy5SblTk1ijy0ha4rbYo_9Od4vl3r0phDfakaWOa5_AIEa6xO/; Nico Wingert, "Die Operationen der Bundeswehr im Nirgendwo," *Die Welt*, October 13, 2014, http://www.welt.de/politik/deutschland/article133229488/Die-Operationen-der-Bundeswehr-im-Nirgendwo.html; Miskimmon, "German Foreign Policy and the Libyan Crisis," 395–96.

[269] UN Security Council, *UNSC Resolution 1973* (New York: March 17, 2011), accessed February 2, 2015,
http://www.nato.int/nato_static/assets/pdf/pdf_2011_03/20110927_110311-UNSCR-1973.pdf.

too big to refuse a participation.[270] Indeed, Germany's decision had already been preceded by a withdrawal of German naval assets and Airborne Warning and Control System (AWACS) personnel deployed in the region.[271]

Under U.S. coordination, between March 19 and March 20, French, British and U.S. air- and sea-based military operations started, aiming at preventing further attacks on Libyan citizens and opposition groups, as well as to "degrade the regime's capability to resist the no-fly zone."[272] On March 24, after a weeklong struggle between NATO states about whether and how NATO should play a role in solving the crisis, all members—*including Germany*—agreed, based on the consensus principle within the North Atlantic Council (NAC),

---

[270] Deutscher Bundestag, *Stenografischer Bericht: Plenarprotokoll 17/97* (Berlin: Bundesanzeiger Verlagsgesellschaft, March 18, 2011), 11139, accessed February 3, 2015, http://dipbt.bundestag.de/dip21/btp/17/17097.pdf#P.11137; Nicole Goebel, "Germany Defends Cautious Approach to Libya, Denies Isolation," *Deutsche Welle*, March 23, 2011, http://www.dw.de/germany-defends-cautious-approach-to-libya-denies-isolation/a-14926360; Andreas Rinke, "Eingreifen oder nicht?: Warum sich die Bundesregierung in der Libyen-Frage enthielt," *Internationale Politik* (July/August 2011): 44; Quentin Peel, "Merkel Explains Berlin's Abstention," *Financial Times*, March 18, 2011, http://www.ft.com/intl/cms/s/0/2363c306-51b8-11e0-888e-00144feab49a.html#axzz3SKrTyG7E; Jörg Lau, "Macht mal—ohne uns!," *Die Zeit*, March 24, 2011, http://www.zeit.de/2011/13/Deutschland-Aussenpolitik; Thorsten Jungholt, "Westerwelle rechtfertigt deutschen Libyen-Sonderweg," *Die Welt*, March 20, 2011, http://www.welt.de/politik/deutschland/article12898795/Westerwelle-rechtfertigt-deutschen-Libyen-Sonderweg.html.

[271] Lindström and Zetterlund, *Setting the Stage*, 26; Stelzenmüller, "Germany's Unhappy Abstention From Leadership"; Thorsten Knuf, "Konsequent in die Isolation," *Frankfurter Rundschau*, March 23, 2011, http://www.fr-online.de/aegypten-syrien-revolution/libyen-konsequent-in-die-isolation,7151782,8260742.html.

[272] Bill Gortney, "U.S. Department of Defense News Briefing on Operation Odyssey Dawn," *U.S. Department of Defense*, update March 19, 2011, http://www.defense.gov/transcripts/transcript.aspx?transcriptid=4786; French, British and U.S. military operations started under the different code names of Operation Harmattan (France), Operation Ellamy (UK), and Operation Odyssey Dawn (United States).

that NATO would gradually take over command of the international military intervention. NATO formally assumed its command within Operation Unified Protector on March 31.²⁷³ Germany's official position to not provide military assets to the military intervention remained, even if, however, the Bundeswehr participated "indirectly"—without the approval of the Bundestag—within the mission through its multilateral integration, such as in the commanding Allied Joint Force Command in Naples.²⁷⁴

Despite the operational praxis, however, Germany's abstention from the vote and official nonparticipation in the international military mission in Libya "caused considerable surprise and irritation" among allies and sparked fierce domestic criticism among those repulsed by a coalition of the willing with the Russians and Chinese against the EU and NATO.²⁷⁵ Internationally, speculations about a potential shift from traditional German foreign and security policy toward a "more independent, non-aligned, and mercantilist-driven position" arose, worried about a new German "special path" (*Sonder-*

---

²⁷³ Claire Taylor, "Military Operations in Libya," *Commons Library Standard Note*, SN05099 (London: Library House of Commons, October 21, 2011), 9–10; NATO, "NATO Secretary General's Statement on Libya No-Fly Zone," updated March 25, 2011, http://www.nato.int/cps/en/natolive/news_71763.htm; NATO, "Operation Unified Protector: NATO No-Fly Zone Over Libya Fact Sheet," accessed February 24, 2015, http://www.nato.int/nato_static/assets/pdf/pdf_2011_03/unified-protector-no-fly-zone.pdf.

²⁷⁴ Some 100 German military personnel had contributed to the NATO Operation Unified Protector. Then-Minister of Defense Thomas de Maizière argued that the use of German soldiers within the operation for planning purposes corresponded with NATO standard practices and did not require parliamentary approval. See DPA, "Germany Participated in Libya War without Parliamentary Approval: 100 Germans Involved in NATO Libya Mission," *Global Research*, updated September 11, 2011, http://www.globalresearch.ca/germany-participated-in-libya-war-without-parliamentary-approval/26481; Lothar Rühl, "Deutschland und der Libyenkrieg," *Zeitschrift für Außen- und Sicherheitspolitik* 4 (2011): 567.

²⁷⁵ Brockmeier, "Germany and the Intervention in Libya," 63.

weg).²⁷⁶ Among those who joined the criticism in Germany was former foreign minister Joschka Fischer who after leaving office embraced an Atlanticism of honorable heritage of the Bonn Republic, calling German foreign policy a "farce" and the abstention a "scandalous mistake," through which Germany had demonstrated a "losing touch with reality," and hereby, ultimately had lost its "credibility within the UN and the Middle East."²⁷⁷ These harsh words were echoed by former federal chancellor Helmut Kohl who argued that Germany had lost not only its "compass," but also its reliability in foreign and security affairs.²⁷⁸

A. Context and Framework of the Decision-Making-Process

The knotted developments of security and economy of 2011 within the domestic, European, and international environment framed Berlin's decision-making process. Since 2008, Europe had experienced a multiple crisis of national debts, banks, and economies, which threatened the common currency and the stability of the EU itself. What began as a crisis of the currency became a political crisis and impinged on the security crises after September 11 and also led to a transformed role for Germany in the international system. After several countries, such as Ireland, Portugal, Spain, and particularly Greece, faced serious challenges to manage their national budgets due to macroeconomic performance imbalances, the European Union implemented a variety of financial instruments, such as the European

---

²⁷⁶ Ian Bremmer and Mark Leonard, "U.S.-German Relationship on the Rocks," *Washington Post*, October 8, 2012, http://www.washingtonpost.com/opinions/us-german-relationship-on-the-rocks/2012/10/18/ed6a9f1c-13c2-11e2-be82-c3411b7680a9_story.html; "German Foreign Policy."

²⁷⁷ Fischer, "Deutsche Außenpolitik"; Joschka Fischer, "Außenpolitik: Ein einziges Debakel," interview by Erich Follath and Ralf Neukirch, *Spiegel Online*, August 29, 2011, http://www.spiegel.de/spiegel/a-782871.html.

²⁷⁸ Kohl "'Wir müssen wieder Zuversicht geben,'" 11.

Financial Stability Facility (EFSF) and the European Financial Stabilization Mechanism (EFSM), aimed at preserving financial stability in Europe by providing financial assistance to Eurozone states in difficulty. Germany's economic power and resilience gave it the power to lead the process of dealing with the crisis and to contribute financially on conditions of the members' compliance with austerity measures. Promoted by a particularly Greece-critical media coverage, the German public stood predominantly opposed to any measures that required larger financial burdens from, or risks for, Germany.[279]

As 2010 turned into 2011, politico-societal eruptions occurred in close vicinity to Europe's security environment. Initiated by the "Jasmin"-revolution in Tunisia at the end of 2010, a wave of demonstrations and popular uprisings against long-standing authoritarian regimes hit the Arab world in Northern Africa and the Middle East in early 2011, which would become known as the "Arab Spring." Although different in their underlying economic grievances and social dynamics, all revolts shared the common call for personal dignity, freedom and social justice, and responsive government.[280] In Tunisia and Egypt, these revolts led to a quick overthrow of the respective regimes of Ben Ali and Mubarak, as particularly the army abandoned the former presidents. In Yemen, Libya, and Syria, however, lacking institutional contestation shifted the trajectory of the uprisings toward violence and civil wars of power and resources between governments and rebels.[281]

---

[279] Oppermann, "National Role Conceptions," 511.

[280] Lisa Anderson, "Demystifying the Arab Spring: Parsing the Differences Between Tunisia, Egypt, and Libya," *Foreign Affairs* 90, no. 3 (May-June 2011): 2; Housam Dawisheh, "Trajectories and Outcomes of the 'Arab Spring': Comparing Tunisia, Egypt, Libya, and Syria," *IDE Discussion Paper*, no. 456 (Mihamaku, Japan: Institute for Developing Economies, March 2011), 1.

[281] Dawisheh, "Trajectories and Outcomes of the 'Arab Spring,'" 2, 12; Milosevic, Deutsche Kriegsbeteiligung und—verweigerung," 114.

The views of the European states toward the crises differed considerably. Germany actively supported the transformation processes in the Arab world with diplomatic and financial support along its "policy of alignment with the democratic awakening," arguing that this support would correspond with "German values and German interests alike."[282] This was a position that raised a cheer within the transforming countries, visible during Foreign Minister Westerwelle's visit to the Egyptian capital at the end of February, where he was greeted with chants of "Long live Egypt! Long live Germany!"[283] France and Italy, historically and politically much more strongly tied to the Mediterranean region, however, remained reluctant toward an active engagement into the transformation process. Even more, they initially demanded a stabilizing role of the EU in favor of the ruling regimes, such as Muammar al-Gaddafi's in Libya.[284]

On March 11, 2011, the most serious earthquake of Japan's history and the resulting tsunami caused a nuclear accident at the power plant in Fukushima—a disaster that had been anticipated by antinuclear politics in the Germany since the origin of the Greens in the late 1970s. This tragic event sparked a vigorous debate among parties and within the German general public concerning the security of German nuclear power plants and the future of Germany's energy security, dominating the media coverage. The high level of domestic attention prompted Federal Chancellor Merkel in mid-March 2011 to put the oldest German nuclear power plants temporarily out of operation and

---

[282] Guido Westerwelle, "Regierungserklärung durch Bundesaußenminister Westerwelle vor dem Deutschen Bundestag zum Umbruch in der arabischen Welt," updated March 16, 2011, http://www.auswaertiges-amt.de/DInfoservice/Presse/Reden/2011/110316_BM_BT_arab_Welt.html.

[283] Ibid.; Claudia Ehrenstein, "Westerwelles bewegender Besuch auf dem Tahrir-Platz," *Die Welt*, February 24, 2011, http://www.welt.de/politik/ausland/article12636464/Westerwelles-bewegender-Besuch-auf-dem-Tahrir-Platz.html.

[284] Rinke, "Eingreifen oder nicht?," 45.

to revise a recently developed plan that intended to extend Germany's power plant phase-out until 2036.[285]

As the power-political and security environment before the decision on participation in a military intervention in Libya had changed, so did the international engagement of the Bundeswehr. From Merkel's government takeover in 2005 up to March 2011, the Bundeswehr had either started or had finished several new missions, showing a clear increase of engagement in and around Africa: EUFOR RD Congo (2006), UNIFIL II (Lebanon, since 2006), UMIS (Sudan, 2005–2011), UNAMID (Darfur, since 2008), EU NAVFOR Somalia—Operation Atalanta (since 2008), and EUTM Somalia (since 2010).[286] Most decisively, however, the nature of the Bundeswehr mission in Afghanistan had changed from security building to counterinsurgency. Throughout the years 2007 and 2008, the rising wave of insurgent activities, which had already grasped the rest of Afghanistan, swept into the hitherto comparably calm German area of responsibility in the north of the country—urging political leaders to gradually release their formerly strict defensively oriented operational caveats and risk minimizing approaches for the Bundeswehr soldiers—the latter contrasted to lax rules of engagement for other ISAF contingents involved in frequent combat.[287]

---

[285] Deutscher Bundestag, *Stenografischer Bericht: Plenarprotokoll 17/96* (Berlin: Bundesanzeiger Verlagsgesellschaft, March 17, 2011), 10883–938, accessed February 3, 2015, http://dipbt.bundestag.de/dip21/btp/17/17096.pdf#P.10882; Deutscher Bundestag, "Entschließungsantrag der Fraktionen der CDU/CSU und der FDP zu der Abgabe einer Regierungserklärung durch die Bundeskanzlerin zur Aktuellen Lage in Japan," Drs.17/5048 (Berlin: Bundesanzeiger Verlagsgesellschaft, March 16, 2011), accessed February 3, 2015, http://dipbt.bundestag.de/dip21/btd/17/050/1705048.pdf.

[286] For an overview about out-area-missions and respective contributions of the Bundeswehr as of August 2010, see Aurel Croissant and David Kühn, *Militär und zivile Politik* (München: Oldenbourg, 2011), 90; for a graphical overview about out-area-missions and respective contributions of the Bundeswehr as of 2011, see Appendix.

[287] Bleibohm, "On Contemporary War and the German Armed Forces," 54–56.

Consequently, German soldiers were increasingly confronted with combat situations of guerilla war as well as IED attacks that increased in number and sophistication—with deadly consequences.[288] Whereas in the first six years of the ISAF mission 15 German soldiers died, the number nearly doubled to 23 between 2007 and 2011.[289] Magnified by the incident of a disputed German ordered airstrike in the vicinity of Kunduz in September 2009, which killed more than one hundred Afghan people, the undeniably hostile and lethal reality of the Afghan mission shifted the "German public and political perception of a peacekeeping mission to one of war," changing the entire nature of the German ISAF involvement.[290] Both then-Defense Minister Karl-Theodor zu Guttenberg, whose new vigor and forthrightness brought him fame, and Federal Chancellor Merkel proclaimed that the conflict in Afghanistan and the German fighting within it occur in a "war," breaking long-lasting social and foreign policy taboos.[291]

Finally, domestic events connected to the advent of chaos further framed the German decision-making process. Due to an accusation of plagiarism concerning his dissertation, the formerly glamorous

---

[288] Eric Sangar, "The Weight of the Past(s): The Impact of the Bundeswehr's Use of Historical Experience on Strategy-Making in Afghanistan," *Journal of Strategic Studies* 38, no. 3 (2013): 419.

[289] Andreas Müller, "Todesfälle im Einsatz," *Presse- und Informationsstab BMVg*, updated July 22, 2014, http://www.bundeswehr.de/portal/a/bwde/!ut/p/c4/DcjBDYAgDAXQWVyA3r25hXohRT7YgMUE1ITpJe_2aKdB-ZXITYpyppW2Q2b3Gfd5mAgPTVDT-cxQ-6i3gVMb04pHDYycYeWyEK3cOt1pmX5GIQYT/#par4.

[290] Bleibohm, "On Contemporary War and the German Armed Forces," 78; Michael F. Harsch, "A Reluctant Warrior: The German Engagement in Afghanistan," (Oslo: Peace Research Institute Oslo, 2011): 5, accessed February 4, 2015, http://www.operationspaix.net/DATA/DOCUMENT/6352~v~A_Reluctant_Warrior_The_German_Engagement_in_Afghanistan.pdf.

[291] David P. Auerswald and Stephan M. Saideman, *NATO in Afghanistan: Fighting Together, Fighting Alone* (Princeton, NJ: University Press, 2014), 15; "Blitzbesuch der Kanzlerin."

Defense Minister Guttenberg resigned on March 1 in disgrace, just two weeks before the UNSC vote on Libya. His successor, Thomas de Maizière, was appointed on March 3, with little time to catch up on the speed of change for the deliberations on Libya. In addition, the German political parties faced three important regional elections end of March, including those contested between the conservatives and social-democrats in the federal state of North Rhine-Westphalia and the conservative stronghold of Baden-Wuertemberg. The elections were considered as a crucial test of the governmental coalition between CDU/CSU and the FDP, as the politics of the liberal junior partner had been nationally contested. Consequently, several members of the government, including the federal chancellor and foreign minister, were campaigning throughout the Libyan crisis and the evolving international response to it.

B. Evolution of the International Environment and Germany's Decision-Making-Process

In face of a worsening situation on the ground, the multilateral environment before the UNSC Resolution 1973 and the decision for an international military intervention in Libya was characterized by critical changes in international settings, rapid shifts in national positions, and discordance between members of all important security systems. Simultaneously, Germany's role within and attitude toward the potential solution of the crisis shifted, culminating in an early commitment not to participate in a military intervention and its abstention from the vote for the UNSC Resolution 1973.

1. Acceleration, Germany's Skepticism, and France's Turn-around

Throughout the initial international reaction toward the Libyan crisis, Germany played a considerable role. It strongly supported the efforts to condemn the violence by the Gaddafi regime and even criticized other European states for not joining the common course.[292] UNSC Resolution 1970, which initiated sanctions on the Libyan government and referred the crisis to the International Criminal Court (ICC), resulted in large parts from German diplomatic attempts.[293]

After Resolution 1970 had been passed, however, discussions on further actions started almost immediately. The United Kingdom's Prime Minister David Cameron publicly discussed the "use of military assets" against the violent Libyan regime and announced preparations for a "military no-fly zone."[294] Although emphasizing the requirement of an international mandate as well as a multilateral approach for the implementation of such a decision, London stressed the argument that the international community could not accept the use of military force by Gaddafi against its own population and therefore has the responsibility to protect civilians from the attacks.[295] On the other hand, the federal government was initially willing to explore the changes for a no-fly zone with its partners, but became quickly skeptical toward the idea, which for Germany constituted a military intervention, backed by the equally skeptical position of the United States.[296] In a speech on March 7, Westerwelle underlined Berlin's changed attitude toward a potential solution of the crisis, arguing that

---

[292] Christian Walz, "Merkel verurteilt Gaddafis 'Kriegserklärung,'" *Deutsche Welle*, February 23, 2011, http://www.dw.de/merkel-verurteilt-gaddafis-kriegserkl%C3%A4rung/a-14861369.

[293] Brockmeier, "Germany and the Intervention in Libya," 66.

[294] Joe Murphy and Tom Harper, "David Cameron Proposes Libya No-Fly-Zone and Tells Gaddafi: 'Go Now,'" *London Evening Standard*, February 28, 2011, http://www.standard.co.uk/news/david-cameron-proposes-libya-nofly-zone-and-tells-gaddafi-go-now-6571718.html.

[295] Ibid.

[296] Guido Westerwelle, "Entwicklungen in und um Libyen," interview by Rudolf Geissler, *SWR2*, February 28, 2011, http://www.swr.de/swr2/programm/sendungen/tagesgespraech/-/id=7530064/property=download/nid=660264/7visfy/swr2-tag-esgespraech-20110228.pdf; Rinke, "Eingreifen oder nicht?," 46; Brockmeier, "Germany and the Intervention in Libya," 67.

any further actions beyond sanctions "must be authorized by the UNSC and can only proceed with the approval of partners in the region."[297]

On March 10, a change of course in the French position became evident. Already having had initiated a national military planning process, France's President Nicolas Sarkozy commented for the first time officially in favor of a military intervention, calling for the establishment of a no-fly zone in a joint letter with Prime Minister Cameron. The speed and vehemence of Paris's diplomatic rushing-ahead hit Berlin by surprise. Sarkozy's solo effort one day earlier to recognize the "National Transitional Council" as legitimate representation of the Libyan state, which had neither been coordinated with nor communicated to the German government as well as contradicted standard European policies, notably annoyed Federal Chancellor Merkel. In addition, Berlin questioned the actual motives for the British and French rush for a military intervention, suspecting that the upcoming presidential elections and a desire to score domestically with an active approach in international affairs, was the primary reason for President Sarkozy to end his formerly close relationships with Arab dictators.[298]

2. European Division and Germany's Growing Military Reluctance

At the Euro summit of the heads of state in Brussels and the meeting of the European foreign ministers in Hungary on March 11, it was clear that the European states (and the EU) were unable to define a

---

[297] Federal Foreign Office, "Federal Minister Westerwelle Welcomes Naming of UN Special Envoy to Libya," *Auswaertiges Amt*, updated March 7, 2011, http://www.auswaertiges-amt.de/EN/Infoservice/Presse/Meldungen/2011/110307_VN_Libyen.html.

[298] Brockmeier, "Germany and the Intervention in Libya," 67; Rinke, "Eingreifen oder nicht?," 47; Nicole Koenig, "The EU and the Libyan Crisis: In Quest of Coherence?," *IAI Working Paper* 11, no. 19 (July 2011): 10.

common position concerning their behavior toward the Libyan crisis.[299] Astounded by the French and British compulsion to implement their politics, several East and South-East European countries alongside Germany prevented the incorporation of the notion of a no-fly zone in the official summit declaration.[300] Westerwelle's reaction to the official call for an establishment of a no-fly zone by the Arab League at the UNSC on March 12 revealed for the first time both Germany's growing reluctance toward participation in a military intervention and its efforts to increase the diplomatic burdens to international actions above the level of sanctions. Claiming that "every international military action needs to be authorized by the UN Security Council" and that "a no-fly zone can only be implemented with the active participation of the states of the region," he emphasized simultaneously that "the implementation of a no-fly zone is a military action" and that Germany did not "want to get involved in a civil war in North Africa."[301]

Meanwhile, the situation for the rebels in Libya, however, was deteriorating rapidly during the second week of March. Whereas many external observers had expected a quick fall of the Libyan government based on the initial advances of the rebels, Gaddafi's troops

---

[299] Some analysts argue that the EU has been proven incapable of action in the crisis of Libya. See Jolyon Howorth, *Security and Defense Policy in the European Union*, 2nd ed. (New York: Palgrave Macmillan, 2014), 10; Sally McNamara, "The Crisis in Libya Exposes a Litany of Failed EU Policies," *WebMemo*, no. 3178 (Heritage Foundation, March 4, 2011), accessed February 6, 2015, http://thf_media.s3.amazonaws.com/2011/pdf/wm3178.pdf.

[300] Rinke, "Eingreifen oder nicht?," 48; Milosevic, "Deutsche Kriegsbeteiligung und -verweigerung," 118–19.

[301] "Foreign Minister Westerwelle on Libya," *Permanent Mission of Germany to the United Nations*, updated March 13, 2011, http://www.new-york-un.diplo.de/Vertretung/newyorkvn/en/__pr/press-releases/2011/110313_20Westerwelle_20on_20Libya.html?archive=2990092.

regained the momentum of the offensive and recaptured several cities until March 13, threatening the rebel stronghold of Benghazi.[302]

Encouraged by the worsening conditions on ground, and regardless of Germany's attitude and diplomatic efforts regarding a military intervention, immediately after the call from the Arab League on March 12, French, British, and Lebanese officials in New York had started to draft a UN resolution for a no-fly zone. Following the initial discussions in the UNSC on March 14, the Lebanon delegation distributed a draft version to council members, including Germany, the following day.[303] This document reached Berlin, however, just at the second day of the G8 summit meeting in Paris on March 14 and 15, where the dispute between France as new driving power for a military intervention and Germany as "brakeman" escalated. While France's new Foreign Minister Juppé openly sought support for a no-fly zone, which he got from the United Kingdom and Canada, Westerwelle openly defended Germany's manifest skepticism regarding the success and implications as well as the potential risks and costs of a military interference in Libya. Berlin, crucially, felt vindicated in its position, as U.S. President Barack Obama had shown a cautious approach toward the Libyan crisis and Secretary of Defense Robert Gates expressed considerable concerns about the implementa-

---

[302] Rinke, "Eingreifen oder nicht?," 46.
[303] Brockmeier, "Germany and the Intervention in Libya," 71.

tion and consequences of a no-fly zone, including the potential need for ground troops.[304]

3. U.S. Switch and the Shift toward "All Necessary Means"

Despite the apparent alignment between the German and U.S. position, they differed already substantially by the end of the G8 summit meeting.[305] The skeptical attitude of defense secretary Gates toward a no-fly zone in Libya did not reflect a coherent opinion of the Obama administration. Instead, senior U.S. officials were divided into two camps. Whereas Vice President Joe Biden and top-level Pentagon advisors shared Gates's concerns about the risks and implications of a military intervention for Libya and the region but also for the credibility of the United States, National Security Council (NSC) Senior Director Samantha Power and U.S. ambassador to the UN, Susan Rice, pushed for military actions from the onset of the crisis. Influenced by experiences of failed international responses to the ethnic cleansings in Rwanda and the Balkans during the 1990s, both highlighted the responsibility of the "international community to protect civilian populations from violations of international humanitarian law when states are unwilling or unable to do so."[306]

---

[304] Lena Greiner, "Auf Libyen folgt Syrien?," *Blätter für deutsche und internationale Politik*, no. 7 (2012): 74; David E. Sanger and Thom Shanker, "Gates Warns of Risks of a No-Flight Zone," *New York Times*, March 2, 2011, http://www.nytimes.com/2011/03/03/world/africa/03military.html?pagewanted=all&_r=0; Nicholas Watt, "U.S. Defense Secretary Robert Gates Slams 'Loose Talk' About No-Fly Zones," *Guardian*, March 3, 2011, http://www.theguardian.com/politics/2011/mar/03/robert-gates-dismisses-no-fly-zone; John Barry, "Robert Gates' Fears about Libya," *Daily Beast*, March 8, 2011, http://www.thedailybeast.com/articles/2011/03/09/defense-secretary-robert-gates-fears-about-us-military-action-in-libya.html; Lindström and Zetterlund, *Setting the Stage*, 42.

[305] Brockmeier, "Germany and the Intervention in Libya," 69–70.

[306] Michael Hastings, "Inside Obama's War Room," *Rolling Stone*, October 13, 2011, http://www.rollingstone.com/politics/news/inside-obamas-war-room-20111013.

Most importantly, Secretary of State Hillary Clinton had reversed her initially opposing opinion toward a military intervention, making an unusual break with Defense Minister Robert Gates. In addition, her meetings with Arab leaders in Paris and Cairo on March 14 and 15 revealed that the Arab countries not only supported a no-fly zone but even made serious commitments to actively participate in "military operations against one of their own."[307] Facing the potential threat of "mass atrocity" to civilians in Benghazi but a solution for the credibility problem of a U.S. military intervention in the region, Washington made a crucial change in its stance on the evening of March 15.[308]

Reassured by UN ambassador Susan Rice that the UN would support a broader intervention and with plans for targeted airstrike on the table, President Obama instructed Rice to negotiate a resolution that would authorize not only a no-fly zone, but the use of "all necessary means"[309] to protect civilians in Libya, including NATO strikes against targets on the ground, which he thought to be the only thing "that's going to make a difference."[310] On the same evening, as instructed, the U.S. delegation in New York revised the Lebanese-French-British draft resolution, introduced significant amendments, and coordinated it with their French and British colleagues. Simultaneously, President Obama called French President Sarkozy and UK

---

[307] Helene Cooper and Steven Lee Myers, "Obama Takes Hard Line with Libya after Shift by Clinton," *New York Times*, March 18, 2011, http://www.nytimes.com/2011/03/19/world/africa/19policy.html?pagewanted=all&_r=0.

[308] Hastings, "Inside Obama's War Room"; see also Svenja Sinjen, "Der Preis der Freiheit—Fall Libyen: Was wir neu denken müssen," *Internationale Politik* (May/June 2011): 80.

[309] Ibid.

[310] Brockmeier, "Germany and the Intervention in Libya," 70; Cooper and Myers, "Obama Takes Hard Line."

Prime Minister Cameron to inform them about the shift in the U.S. position.[311]

4. Germany's Misinformed Political Debate and Public Refusal

The German government, however, initially remained uninformed. Only as UN Ambassador Rice called her German colleague Peter Wittig in the late morning on March 16, Berlin learned of Washington's crucial change of mind and the new draft resolution in the later afternoon, local time, on March 16—after Libya-related political meetings in Germany had already been concluded.[312] At first in the morning, the German parliamentary committee for foreign affairs, the most important constitutional instrument to prepare the parliamentarian vote for the approval of the deployment of German forces, met to discuss the situation in Libya. Immediately afterwards, a debate of the German Bundestag took place, in which Foreign Minister Westerwelle gave a governmental declaration concerning the turmoil in the Arab world. Already reflecting the constituting governmental position *against* a German participation in a military intervention in Libya, this speech "made it almost impossible for Westerwelle to turn around and support military measures in Libya the next day, despite the change of circumstances."[313]

Westerwelle raised particular concerns about the potential risks, negative repercussions, and questionable efficiency of a no-fly zone—which equaled for him a military intervention—in Libya. While asking "what happens, if [after having established a no-fly zone] the attacks on the ground continue? Do we then have to fight Gaddafi's tanks from the air? And if this is not enough, do we then have to send ground troops?" he raised questions that the U.S. administration had

---

311 Brockmeier, "Germany and the Intervention in Libya," 71.
312 Ibid.; Greiner, "Auf Libyen folgt Syrien?," 74–75.
313 Brockmeier, "Germany and the Intervention in Libya," 72.

already answered with its amendments to the draft resolution.[314] Consequently, he stated that "the federal government is highly skeptical in regard to a military intervention in the form of a no-fly zone."[315] Westerwelle continued to argue that Germany did not want to and must not become a "war party in a civil war in North Africa," to prevent Germany from a "slippery slope, where on its end then German soldiers are part of a war in Libya."[316] Instead of being inactive, the internationally community should rather use "targeted sanctions, which [would] increase the pressure on Gaddafi."[317]

A poll published by the popular news magazine *Stern* (known for its skeptical editorial stand on defense policy and of U.S. policy, as well) on the same day, supported the manifesting nonparticipatory position of the federal government. Whereas 56 percent of those polled agreed with the establishment of a no-fly zone, in comparison to 70 percent in favor of a trade embargo, 88 percent opposed a direct military engagement of German soldiers in Libya.[318]

The debate following Westerwelle's speech was framed by the common belief that the United States still opposed a military intervention, a respective proposal would be limited to a no-fly zone, a commitment for active engagement by the Arab states did not exist, and a UN resolution was not likely.[319] Whereas Social-Democrat and Green foreign policy experts criticized the governmental policy of having quickly refused instruments of the UN Charter, such as a no-

---

[314] Deutscher Bundestag, *Stenografischer Bericht: Plenarprotokoll 17/95* (Berlin: Bundesanzeiger Verlagsgesellschaft, March 16, 2011), 10816, accessed February 6, 2015, http://dipbt.bundestag.de/dip21/btp/17/17095.pdf#P.10814.

[315] Ibid., 10815.

[316] Ibid., 10815–16.

[317] Ibid., 10816.

[318] "Deutsche wollen sich nicht einmischen," *Stern*, March 16, 2011, http://www.stern.de/politik/ausland/umfrage-zu-unruhen-in-libyen-deutsche-wollen-sich-nicht-einmischen-1664001.html.

[319] Brockmeier, "Germany and the Intervention in Libya," 72.

fly zone, as legitimate means to solve the crisis,[320] Westerwelle's cautious position received broad support by parliamentarians of the governmental coalition as well as from the left-wing party.[321] Foreign policy experts of the governmental coalition, however, contended that in case of an active Arab participation in an intervention, "Germany cannot and will not abdicate its responsibility" and in case of an UNSC Resolution for the establishment of a no-fly zone, "Germany would then have to think again, who could possibly intervene there."[322]

5. UN Negotiations and Merkel's Determination against German Participation

Such a resolution already existed as a draft in New York and was brought into official consultation on March 16, at around noon, local time, under pressure of France and the United Kingdom.[323] Washington had introduced a language that explicitly demanded the "legal

---

[320] See speeches of Rolf Mützenich (SPD) and Frithjof Schmidt (Bündnis90/Grüne), Deutscher Bundestag, *Stenografischer Bericht: Plenarprotokoll 17/95*, 10819, 10825.

[321] See speeches of Andreas Schockenhoff (CDU) or Wolfgang Gehrke (DIE LINKE), Deutscher Bundestag, *Stenografischer Bericht: Plenarprotokoll 17/95*, 10820–23. For the antimilitary intervention position of the LINKE, see also Deutscher Bundestag, "Entschließungsantrag der Abgeordneten Wolfgang Gehrcke, Paul Schäfer, Jan van Aken, Christine Buchholz, Sevim Dagdelen, Dr. Diether Dehm, Nicole Gohlke, Annette Groth, Heike Hänsel, Inge Höger, Andrej Hunko, Harald Koch, Stefan Liebich, Niema Movassat, Thomas Nord, Alexander Ulrich, Kathrin Vogler, Katrin Werner, und die Fraktion DIE LINKE zu der Abgabe einer Regierungserklärung durch den Bundesminister des Auswärtigen: Umbruch in der Arabischen Welt," Drs. 17/5040 (Berlin: Bundesanzeiger Verlagsgesellschaft, March 16, 2011), accessed February 6, 2015,
http://dipbt.bundestag.de/dip21/btd/17/050/1705040.pdf.

[322] See speeches of Rainer Stinner (FDP) and Philipp Missfelder (CDU), Deutscher Bundestag, *Stenografischer Bericht: Plenarprotokoll 17/95*, 10823, 10826.

[323] Brockmeier, "Germany and the Intervention in Libya," 74; Rinke, "Eingreifen oder nicht?," 50.

authority from the UN to use force against Gaddafi's troops and key national security installations"³²⁴ as well as the active participation of the Arab states in a NATO-led air coalition. Both developments caused fierce debates between the members of the council. As the German Ambassador Wittig informed Westerwelle after the end of the consultation in New York at 7 p.m., it was clear, however, that neither Russia nor China would use its veto to a block a UNSC resolution, which vote was expected to take place the following day.³²⁵

While after the first information from New York officials in the Foreign Office were still debating how Germany should vote as a nonpermanent member in the upcoming resolution, allegedly excluding a "no"-option from the onset as unrealistic,³²⁶ the federal chancellor had already made up her mind regarding the German stance toward the Libyan case—*against* German participation in a potential international military intervention in Libya. In an interview on March 16, which was published the following day, she expressed her skepticism toward a military interventions and argued that "as Federal Chancellor, she could not lead [Germany] in a mission with an extremely uncertain end."³²⁷ In case the minimal preconditions for such an intervention would have existed, namely a UNSC resolution and an active engagement of the Arab League, two aspects from which

---

³²⁴ Colum Lynch, "Amb. Rice: Leading From Behind? That's 'Whacked,'" *Foreign Policy*, October 31, 2011, http://foreignpolicy.com/2011/10/31/amb-rice-leading-from-behind-thats-whacked/.

³²⁵ Greiner, "Auf Libyen folgt Syrien?," 75.

³²⁶ Rinke, "Eingreifen oder nicht?," 50; Brockmeier, "Germany and the Intervention in Libya," 79.

³²⁷ Angela Merkel, "Kanzlerin Angela Merkel kündigt Überprüfung aller Atomkraftwerke an," interview by Werner Kolhoff und Hagen Strauß, *Saarbrücker Zeitung*, March 17, 2011, http://www.saarbruecker-zeitung.de/nachrichten/berliner_buero/art182516,3679553,5#; "Saarbrücker Zeitung: Merkel lehnt deutsche Beteiligung an Militäreinsatz in Libyen ab," *Presseportal*, March 16, 2011, http://www.presseportal.de/pm/57706/2009198/saarbr-cker-zeitung-merkel-lehnt-deutsche-beteiligung-an-milit-reinsatz-in-libyen-ab; Rinke, "Eingreifen oder nicht?," 50.

Federal Chancellor Merkel believed that they were still undecided, she made clear that even then "this still does not mean, that Germany will … participate."328

6. From Nonparticipation to Abstention

On the morning of March 17, German and Libyan time, Gaddafi publicly threatened the rebels, announcing that "his armed forces were coming to their capital Benghazi tonight and would not show any mercy."329 Members of the international community in favor of an intervention understood the urgency to act swiftly before Benghazi would be lost. In the meantime in Germany, Foreign Minister Westerwelle reaffirmed in a radio interview his strong position against the notion that Germany would become part of a "permanent civil war" in Libya and that "German soldiers will be involved" in such a prolonged war. He explicitly excluded the opportunity that the "German Air Force bombs Libyan anti-aircraft positions."330 The entire morning, however, was dominated by the governmental declaration of Federal Chancellor Merkel and the parliamentarian debate regarding the energy turnaround in Germany after the nuclear catastrophe in Fukushima.331

On the sidelines of the debate, Westerwelle spoke frequently with the faction leaders in the Bundestag, getting the impression that all of them shared the governmental skepticism regarding a military inter-

---

328 "Saarbrücker Zeitung."

329 "Gaddafi Tells Benghazi His Army Is Coming Tonight," *Reuters*, March 17, 2011,
http://uk.reuters.com/article/2011/03/17/libya-gaddafi-address-idUKLDE72G2E920110317.

330 Guido Westerwelle, "Zur aktuellen Lage in Libyen," interview by Christoph Heinemann, *Deutschlandfunk*, March 17, 2011, http://www.auswaertiges-amt.de/DE/Infoservice/Presse/Interviews/2011/110317_BM_DLF.html.

331 See Deutscher Bundestag, *Stenografischer Bericht: Plenarprotokoll 17/96*, 10883–938.

vention.³³² Not earlier than 2 p.m., German time—as negotiations at working level had already resumed in New York—diplomats and advisors of the Foreign Office got the opportunity to discuss Germany's further course of action with Foreign Minister Westerwelle.³³³ The focus of the short meeting was on a politically acceptable justification for the *definite* nonparticipation of the Bundeswehr in a military intervention in Libya.³³⁴ Central issues and questions concerning Germany's alliance solidarity, the price to pay for a German nonparticipation, and the protection of civilians were addressed. Proponents of an abstention argued that a "yes" vote without participating would be politically unsustainable and could be even more damaging for Germany's reputation in the alliance, if Germany did not provide its available military capacities as required for the enforcement of the no-fly zone. Only a few diplomats, including Wittig, advocated a conditioned "yes" vote—a common German political praxis within the UN—as they feared the consequences of a potential German isolation from its Western allies.³³⁵

The formal decision to abstain from the vote was finalized not later than the second meeting of the group in the evening on March 17. Until then, three important evolutions occurred. First, during the day it became clear that, even if still not fully certain, there was a sufficient majority within the UNSC to pass the vote without Germany's approval. Portugal, also initially skeptical toward the proposal of a no-fly zone, had decided to vote "yes," even if it intended not to partici-

---

332 Rinke, "Eingreifen oder nicht?," 51.

333 Participants of the meeting were Foreign Minister Guido Westerwelle; his Head of Office, Thomas Bagger; the director general of the UN division in the foreign office, Michael Freiherr von Ungern-Sternberg; the deputy director general for the Middle East and North Africa, Andreas Michaelis; political director Emily Haber; and State Secretary for Europe Wolf-Ruthart Born. UN Ambassador Peter Wittig was cut in from New York. Greiner, "Auf Libyen folgt Syrien?," 75–76.

334 Ibid.

335 Brockmeier, "Germany and the Intervention in Libya," 77–78; Greiner, "Auf Libyen folgt Syrien?," 76.

pate in the military intervention. At the same time, under pressure from U.S. Ambassador Rice, the African states showed the willingness to vote for the resolution. Second, Federal Chancellor Merkel, Foreign Minister Westerwelle, and Defense Minister de Maizière had already internally agreed to endorse an abstention from the vote, based on their common decision that Germany would not participate with soldiers or with equipment in a military intervention in Libya. Yet in a call with Prime Minister Cameron, Federal Chancellor Merkel reassured her counterpart flexibility for the unlikely case that the passing of the resolution would ultimately depend on German support. Third, to mitigate potential concerns about Germany's alliance solidarity, Defense Minister de Maizière offered in a call with NATO General Secretary Anders Fogh Rasmussen German military air crews for the AWACS-mission in Afghanistan, which offer he accepted.[336]

Late attempts by British and U.S. officials to shift the German government's opinion proved unsuccessful. Federal Chancellor Merkel did not take a call from U.S. President Obama, trying to explain to her the change of the American position. An offer by the British Foreign Minister Hague shortly before the vote to exclude the notions of ground troops and occupation force in the resolution, was refused by Westerwelle with a reference to an already existing unbearable threat throughout the enforcement of a no-fly zone.[337]

Eventually, as the vote for UNSC Resolution 1973 took place around midnight German time, UN Ambassador Wittig raised his hand for abstention. In a statement immediately after the passage of the resolution, Westerwelle justified Germany's course:

> When the resolution was put to vote, Germany abstained. The resolution contains significantly tougher

---

[336] Brockmeier, "Germany and the Intervention in Libya," 79–80; Greiner, "Auf Libyen folgt Syrien?," 76; Rinke, "Eingreifen oder nicht?," 51–52.

[337] Brockmeier, "Germany and the Intervention in Libya," 80–81; Rinke, "Eingreifen oder nicht?," 51–52; Greiner, "Auf Libyen folgt Syrien?," 76.

international sanctions against the Gaddafi regime. We welcome and support this, as we ourselves had pushed in this direction. We are still very skeptical, however, about the option of a military intervention in Libya, also contained in the resolution. We see considerable risks in this. Therefore we cannot subscribe to this part of the resolution. German soldiers will not participate in a military action in Libya.[338]

C. Analysis of the Relevance and Interplay of Determinants for the German Decision for Nonparticipation

As the sequence of events demonstrates, days before the final decision to abstain from the vote, the German government was trapped in an apparently unsolvable dilemma.[339] On one hand, it could act according to the expectations of its allies and partners and participate in the military intervention, but face enormous domestic pressure and potential political backfire from an opposing German public in the upcoming elections. This problem was hardly unique to 2011, and has existed in other forms as far back as the foundation of the FRG in 1949. On the other hand, Merkel, Westerwelle, and de Maizière could act accordingly to their substantial doubts about the viability of a military operation in Libya and eschew a German contribution to it, but risk a break with premises of own foreign and security policy. The early predetermination of the German government against a military participation, which ultimately shaped the logical foundation for an abstention from the vote against UNSC Resolution 1973, rested on a

---

[338] "Federal Foreign Minister Westerwelle on the Libya Resolution of the UN Security Council," *Permanent Mission of Germany to the United Nations*, updated March 17, 2011,
http://www.new-york-un.diplo.de/Vertretung/newyorkvn/en/ pr/press-releases/2011/110317 20Westerwelle 20on 20Libya.html.
[339] Rinke, "Eingreifen oder nicht?," 51.

complex interplay between overlapping, contradicting, and mutually reinforcing impulses and constraints on all three levels, exemplarily revealing the mutually dependent and interpenetrated linkage between the domains in the formation of policy for military intervention not only on the continent of Africa, but elsewhere.

1. Determinants on the External Level

In contrast to some studies,[340] this study posits that the external system cannot be neglected in explaining Germany's decision for a nonparticipation in the military intervention in Libya. Instead, as demonstrated in the following, external factors either did not create the "normal" level of impulse for, or disincentivized the German government from a German military contribution in Operation Unified Protector. Consequently, the specific qualities of the external system redirected the attention to, magnified, and fueled domestic concerns as well as actor-related traits that favored a nonparticipation.

a. Power and Security Environment

The conditions and evolutions of the power and security environment in Europe and Africa in 2011 affected Germany's decision for a nonparticipation in the military intervention considerably, as many of the discrete elements reduced the salience of Libyan crisis as a "strategic dilemma," and hence, disincentivized or distracted the general public and the politicians from taking a more positive stance toward a

---

[340] In his study on German participation or refusal to international military missions, Milosevic argues that Germany's power and interest in the international system as well as its multilateral integration had only low influence on the decision for the nonparticipation in the NATO operation in Libya. Like Oppermann, however, he neglects the disincentivizing quality of many external factors that gave room to the preponderance of domestic and actor-related factors. See Milosevic, "Deutsche Kriegsbeteiligung und—verweigerung," 143–44; Oppermann, "National Role Conceptions," 513–14.

German military contribution.³⁴¹ The Eurozone and financial crisis dominated the headlines and mass attention in Germany in 2010 and 2011, overshadowing the public and political discourse and keeping the federal government preoccupied with the "interests of German taxpayers" as well as highly occupied with the mitigation of the crisis' potential strategic ramifications for Germany's role in Europe.³⁴² The emphasis on the primacy of the German taxpayer has been a legacy of the past 20 and more years of national reconstruction in unification, and more recently, in the imperative to preserve European unity as the basis of German national interests of prosperity and security.

The federal government's primary focus on strengthening Germany's economic power base in face of a challenging environment limited the appeal of the Libyan crisis as a direct threat to Germany's security. As a result, it gradually reinforced a geo-economically dominated attitude, reluctant to actively shape the international response to the crisis and to become involved in another costly and risky international military commitment as it had been going in the wrong direction in Afghanistan during the past year.³⁴³ Framed and increasingly internationally criticized by this declining disposition for (military) engagement, Germany, as a nonpermanent member in the UNSC, lacked the opportunity and willingness to use its political leverage to influence the design of UNSC Resolution 1973.³⁴⁴ Instead, as part of the triad of western European powers, Germany's international restraint and lack of alternatives indirectly affirmed France's and Brit-

---

341 Brockmeier, "Germany and the Intervention in Libya," 77; Lindström and Zetterlund, *Setting the Stage*, 27–28; Milosevic, "Deutsche Kriegsbeteiligung und—verweigerung," 126.

342 Deutscher Bundestag, *Stenografischer Bericht: Plenarprotokoll 17/99* (Berlin: Bundesanzeiger Verlagsgesellschaft, March 24, 2011), 11256, accessed February 6, 2015, http://dipbt.bundestag.de/doc/btp/17/17099.pdf; Oppermann, "National Role Conceptions," 511; Miskimmon, "German Foreign Policy and the Libya Crisis," 406.

343 Miskimmon, "German Foreign Policy and the Libya Crisis," 402, 404.

344 Milosevic, "Deutsche Kriegsbeteiligung und—verweigerung," 135–36.

ain's active and forceful course (where few or no inhibitions operate about the African continent and the need to use military force, following the model of Suez or Algeria in the 1950s), which in turn reinforced the federal government's sentiments toward the potential implications of a military intervention.

The military engagement–averse conditions intensified throughout the crucial phase of a shifting international perception for a more active role in Libya, as German politicians, including the federal government, were completely focused on discussions about Germany's energy security policy, resulting from the nuclear accident in Fukushima on March 11—a primacy of domestic politics of a particular kind. Since Merkel's coalition had just prolonged the operational lives of the country's nuclear power plants, many of them in Baden-Wuerttemberg, against the opposition of the Social Democrats and Green parties in the autumn of 2010, the federal government feared an "anti-nuclear backlash" in the upcoming regional elections where the CDU was on the losing side in what had traditionally been an old bastion of West German Christian Democracy. While having lost one of its key projects and facing broad criticism after reversing its stance on nuclear energy, the federal government therefore was under enormous pressure to "get Libya right" in terms of electoral politics, sensitizing Merkel and Westerwelle for public concerns and disincentivizing both from becoming involved in a mounting unpopular crisis management commitment.[345]

b. *National Interests and Strategies*

National interests that related to the region itself, the protection of human rights, and the security dimension of Germany's foreign and security policy, were mainly disregarded in the decision about Germany's involvement in the international military intervention in Libya.

---

[345] Ischinger, "Germany after Libya," 50; Miskimmon, "German Foreign Policy and the Libya Crisis," 404.

Instead, "interests" related to economic concerns, domestic short-term calculations,[346] and considerations regarding the potential impacts of a military intervention framed and dominated the decision-making process, promoting nonparticipation. Germany's White Paper 2006 identified unresolved regional conflicts in the European periphery and resulting uncontrolled migration as two of the key challenges and risks, as they have the potential to result in civil wars, destabilize entire regions, affect the security of the international community, and particularly threaten the "European area of stability"—Germany's overriding security concern.[347] The evolution of the armed civil conflict in Libya thus had all qualities to negatively affect this stability—directly and indirectly. Furthermore, Gaddafi's declaration of war against his own people clearly constituted a serious violation of human rights.

Throughout the political debates and in public announcements until the decision for nonparticipation and abstention from the vote on UNSC Resolution 1973, however, the federal government failed to highlight the steadily worsening humanitarian crisis in Libya and its potential to strike at European, and respectively, German security interests.[348] Instead, Federal Chancellor Angela Merkel argued in her interview on March 16 that, in contrast to the fight against international terrorism in Afghanistan, Germany's security was not threatened in Libya, and thus a (military) intervention would not be justified.[349] Moreover, Westerwelle repeatedly attempted to raise the

---

[346] Klaus-Dieter Frankenberger and Hanns W. Maull, "'Gimme a Break': Germany Takes Time Out from a Complex World," *Deutsche Aussenpolitik*, updated March 24, 2011, http://www.deutsche-aussenpolitik.de/digest/op-ed_inhalt_59.php.

[347] Federal Ministry of Defense, *White Paper 2006*, 17–20.

[348] Former Foreign Minister Joschka Fischer argued similarly, claiming that the "southern Mediterranean coast directly belongs to the security zone of the EU. It would be naïve to argue that the most populous and economic strongest European state could and may remain on the sidelines." Joschka Fischer, "Deutsche Außenpolitik."

[349] Merkel, "Kanzlerin Angela Merkel."

threshold for an international involvement and publicly affirmed that Germany is "incapable to eradicate injustice all over the world,"[350] a statement that was echoed by Defense Minister Thomas de Maizière one day after the abstention.[351] This position suggests that key German stakeholders even willingly refused to pursue clearly affected national interests in accordance with the UN Charter, as they stood in contrast to other policy considerations.

In contrast, with the initial enthusiasm about the Arab Spring that operated at this moment in 2011, Westerwelle frequently emphasized that the public upheavals and democratic movements, particularly in Tunisia and Egypt, corresponded to Germany's "values and interests alike," which needed to be diplomatically and financially supported and even "protected" against the potentially negative spillover effects of an external intervention in Libya.[352] This overall ambivalent position remained, although the Maghreb region had successively gained relevance for German foreign and security policy in relation to three aspects: 1) the increased significance of energy security, as Libya and Algeria ranked at the beginning of 2011 as Germany's fourth and eighth biggest oil suppliers respectively; 2) the containment of migration, as the region had become an important transit hub of migrant

---

[350] Guido Westerwelle, "Regierungserklärung durch Bundesminister Westerwelle vor dem Deutschen Bundestag zur aktuellen Entwicklung in Libyen (UN-Resolution)," updated March 18, 2011, http://www.auswaertiges-amt.de/DE/Infoservice/Presse/Reden/2011/110318_BM_Regierungserkl%C3%A4rung_Libyen.html.

[351] "Statt in Libyen fliegt Deutschland in Afghanistan," *Handelsblatt*, March 18, 2011, http://www.handelsblatt.com/politik/deutschland/awacs-aufklaerer-statt-in-libyen-fliegt-deutschland-in-afghanistan/3966958.html.

[352] Deutscher Bundestag, *Stenografischer Bericht: Plenarprotokoll 17/95*, 10815, 10817. For the public statements of Foreign Minister Westerwelle from February until March 2011 see also Westerwelle, "Entwicklungen in und um Libyen"; Deutscher Bundestag, *Stenografischer Bericht, Plenarprotokoll 17/97*, 11117–39.

movements to Europe; and 3) the fight against terrorism and organized crime, with the rise and spread of al Qaida in the Maghreb.³⁵³

Despite the increased significance of the entire North African region for German foreign and security policy, in early 2011, Germany still lacked an overall strategic concept that determined and coordinated policies for that particular area, demonstrating Germany's continuing problems to define and understand its relations with, and particular its interests in, the African continent.³⁵⁴ On the other side, Westerwelle's permanent reference to the responsibility of the Arab world to be part of the solution for the crisis, could also be understood as Germany's approach to promote Africa's political "self-reliance," formulated early in 2000.³⁵⁵ While uncertain about the implications of a strong Western influence in Africa and of the potential repercussions of a military engagement, the motto "African solutions

---

³⁵³ Isabelle Wehrenfels, "Maghreb," in *Deutsche Nah-, Mittelost- und Nordafrikapolitik—SWP Studie* S15, ed. Guido Steinberg (Berlin: German Institute for International and Security Affairs, May 2009), 7–11; Stefan Angenendt, "Migration," in *Deutsche Nah-, Mittelost- und Nordafrikapolitik—SWP Studie* S15, ed. Guido Steinberg (Berlin: German Institute for International and Security Affairs, May 2009), 46.

³⁵⁴ Guido Steinberg, "Schlussfolgerungen: Deutsche Politik gegenüber dem Nahen und Mittleren Osten und Nord-Afrika," in *Deutsche Nah-, Mittelost- und Nordafrikapolitik—SWP Studie* S15, ed. Guido Steinberg (Berlin: German Institute for International and Security Affairs, May 2009), 77. It existed only as a concept by the Federal Ministry for Economic Cooperation and Development. See Bundesministerium für wirtschaftliche Zusammenarbeit und Entwicklung (BMZ), *Grundlagen, Schwerpunkte und Perspektiven der deutschen Entwicklungspolitik mit der Region Nahost/Nordafrika-BMZ Konzepte* 156 (Berlin: BMZ, 2008), accessed March 11, 2015, http://www.bmz.de/de/mediathek/publikationen/reihen/strategiepapiere/konzept156.pdf.

³⁵⁵ Helga Gräfin Strachwitz, "Außenpolitisches Regionalkonzept für Afrika," in Afrika zu Beginn des 21. Jahrhunderts: Herausforderungen und Entwicklungspotenziale—Handlungsoptionen für eine strategische Entwicklungspolitik, Dokumentation des Afrika-Tages des BMZ und DIE am 3. Mai 2001, ed. Deutsches Institut für Entwicklungspolitik (Bonn: Deutsches Institut für Entwicklungspolitik, 2001), 11.

for African problems" could additionally justify Germany's overall reticent stance.

Lacking or disregarding clearly articulated German national and European security interests in Libya, but being mainly concerned with economic and domestic challenges, the German government, however, was both hampered and reluctant to follow the shifting international attitude for a forceful international engagement—an old, familiar problem. Consequently, while indirectly criticizing France and Italy for "having paid court to Gaddafi in the past," Defense Minister de Maizière posited that the federal government "would not see any duty for Germany" to remove the Libyan ruler. Even if supporting the efforts of the international community, the federal government would "reserve the right in the German interest, to say [Germany] will be not involved this time."[356] He missed to explain further, where Germany's interests for a nonparticipation rested—contributing to the notion that only decision-makers decide what national interests are.[357]

    c. Multilateral Integration

Germany's external expectations finally proved insufficiently powerful to overrule domestic and operational concerns in favor of a military participation.[358] The push of events overwhelmed an initially reluctant cabinet. This fact led to rapidly changing but continuously discordant positions in the multilateral environment, which exceeded the capabilities of the German decision-making process.[359] Thus

---

[356] "Statt in Libyen fliegt Deutschland in Afghanistan."

[357] Friedrich Kratochwill, "On the Notion of 'Interests' in International Relations," *International* Organization 36, no. 1 (1982): 2, http://dx.doi.org/10.1017/ S0020818300004768.

[358] Rinke, "Eingreifen oder nicht?," 51; Oppermann, "National Role Conceptions," 514.

[359] Lindström and Zetterlund, *Setting the Stage*, 27; Brockmeier, "Germany and the Intervention in Libya," 64–66.

arose crucial German misinterpretations,[360] misassumptions, and miscalculations in the case of Libya and the intervention. All of these factors facilitated an early predisposition of the German government to eschew participation, letting the federal government falsely assume to act, at least, partly according to its premises of *Westorientierung* (orientation to the West) and "alliance solidarity." Such policy considerably hampered, however, also a redirection of the German position in support of a (Western-heavy) multilateral engagement as the conditions rapidly changed—resulting in harsh criticism from within and without as concerns Germany's reputation as a credible and reliable multilateral partner.

Relativizing the initially harsh domestic criticism aimed at the federal government due to Germany's isolation amid its most important Western allies, Germany did not stand alone within NATO and the EU with its skeptical position regarding a military intervention, which in turn had increased the incentives for a decision against a national military contribution. Instead, deeper and rather unusual dissents among the members characterized the internal conditions of both institutions, weakening their adhesive and centripetal effects on a Germany participation.[361]

Whereas past security disputes in Brussels, especially Iraq in 2002 and 2003 had often been fought between Anglo-Saxon and Eastern European states and parts of Western Europe under the common German-French lead, the case of Libya split both institutions between the old Western core of NATO with France and East European states with Germany. In particular, the gradual "disillusionment" of

---

[360] Wolfgang Seibel, "Libyen, das Prinzip der Schutzverantwortung und Deutschlands Stimmenthaltung im UN-Sicherheitsrat bei der Abstimmung über Resolution 1973 am 17. März 2011," *Die Friedens-Warte* 88, no. 1-2 (2013): 107–108.

[361] Nikolas Busse, "Europas neue Risse," *Frankfurter Allgemeines Zeitung*, March 23, 2011, http://www.faz.net/aktuell/politik/ausland/naher-osten/einsatz-gegen-gaddafi-europas-neue-risse-1611274-p2.html?printPagedArticle=true#pageIndex_2; Koenig, "The EU and the Libyan Crisis," 3, 11, 13.

Eastern European states, such as Poland, Romania, Bulgaria, and Czech Republic, concerning the implications of their contributions to Western interventions and France's unilateral actions deprived the EU of a common, more active, and more robust response to the Libyan crisis. Likewise in NATO, Turkey's reticence to a possible Western intervention in a Muslim country and opposition to a potential French leadership of a coalition of the willing, France's reluctance to involve the alliance, and the United States' long-lasting skeptical position raised considerable political tensions among its members and hampered coherent actions, even if the alliance internally prepared operational plans for Libya.[362] Thus, the EU and NATO's internal incoherence strengthened Germany's risk- and intervention-averse stance, disincentivizing German participation.

Magnified by sincere suspicions about the real motives of France and the United Kingdom and by the lack of up to date information, all these factors led the federal government and the majority of the Bundestag falsely to believe, first, that an UNSC resolution on a military intervention in Libya was unlikely to be initiated, and second, that even if achievable, the French-British-Lebanese proposal for a no-fly zone would fail against the opposition of the United States as well as the potential veto of Russia and China.[363] Within the context of questions regarding Germany's alliance solidarity, such evidence as Westerwelle's governmental declaration and Merkel's interview on March 16, suggests that it is precisely the misassumption about the enduring agreement of the U.S. side with Germany's general skepticism about intervention, which facilitated and promoted an early pre-

---

[362] Busse, "Europas neue Risse"; Rinke, "Eingreifen oder nicht?," 48; International Institute for Strategic Studies, "War in Libya: Europe's Confused Response," *Strategic Comments* 17, no. 18 (April 2011): 2, accessed April 2, 2015, http://www.tandfonline.com/doi/pdf/10.1080/13567888.2011.596314; Sally McNamara, "Crisis in Libya," 1; Howorth, *Security and Defense Policy*, 10.

[363] Seibel, "Libyen," 107; Brockmeier, "Germany and the Intervention in Libya," 72; Christian Hacke, "Deutschland und der Libyen Konflikt: Zivilmacht ohne Zivilcourage," *Aus Politik und Zeitgeschichte* 61, no. 39 (September 2011): 52.

disposition of the federal government against a German military involvement in Libya—believing it would still act in concert with its most important transatlantic ally.

This misinformation-based misperception of the international constellation also supports the notion that the federal government miscalculated the consequences of an abstention from the vote for UNSC Resolution 1973, resulting in an underestimation of the resulting damage to Germany's reputation as a reliable multilateral partner. While weighing between potential foreign and domestic policy costs and benefits, the government in Berlin believed it could politically afford its military intervention–skeptical attitude against the positions of other allies with the support of a U.S. stance of reticence in this case, as well as domestically score in advance of two important regional elections.[364]

Despite protests to the contrary that the German abstention "should not be confused with neutrality" and that Germany "share[s] the goals of the resolution unreservedly," once determined, the federal government felt unable to reverse its overall reticent position in face of rapidly changed circumstances—even if such a stance would violate its solidarity with its biggest allies and partners.[365] It believed and argued that a vote for the resolution "without subsequent military contributions would not [only] have been inconsistent," but also impossible to sustain. As "the largest European member of NATO" and with its available military capabilities precisely to enforce the no-fly zone, Germany would be deprived of the opportunity to decide whether it wanted to send troops. Rather, Berlin could deal only with

---

[364] Seibel, "Libyen," 108–109.

[365] Deutscher Bundestag, *Stenografischer Bericht: Plenarprotokoll 17/99*, 11251; Peel, "Merkel Explains Berlin's Abstention." See also Gunther Hellmann, "Berlins Große Politik im Fall Libyen," *WeltTrends* 19, no. 80 (2011): 19–22.

the question of how many soldiers to send.³⁶⁶ The conviction prevailed that such a position would have a higher potential to damage Germany's multilateral reputation.³⁶⁷ Consequently, the federal government adhered to its attitude that "[it] cannot send German soldiers to Libya, because the others do it."³⁶⁸

d. Evolution of Military Engagement

German public outcry about the casualties of the ISAF mission in Afghanistan both nourished a public opinion that stood increasingly opposed to any further foreign engagements of the Bundeswehr, particularly in combat operations, and strongly magnified governmental concerns about potential backlash toward a military intervention in Libya—all of them facilitating a refusal to deploy forces.³⁶⁹ All new missions of the Bundeswehr starting from Merkel's government takeover in 2005 up to Libya had a clear humanitarian or peace-supporting mandate, with a partial exception of combatting piracy within the EU NAVFOR Somalia—Operation Atalanta, and thus, broadly corresponded with the general risk aversion and military restraint that dominates domestic politics and the thinking of political elites.

The ongoing mission in Afghanistan with its escalation after 2008, however, had an unprecedented negative influence on the perception

---

³⁶⁶ Guido Westerwelle, "Wir sind nicht isoliert," interview by Damir Fras, *Frankfurter Rundschau*, April 14, 2011, http://www.fr-online.de/politik/interview-mit-westerwelle--wir-sind-nicht-isoliert-,1472596,8341026.html. See also Goebel, "Germany Defends Cautious Approach;" Rinke, "Eingreifen oder nicht?," 52. Lothar Rühl argues that Germany could have provided personal and material capacities without being directly involved in airstrike operations. See Rühl, "Deutschland und der Libyenkrieg," 567, 570.

³⁶⁷ Greiner, "Auf Libyen folgt Syrien?," 76.

³⁶⁸ Busse, "Europas neue Risse."

³⁶⁹ Ischinger, "Germany after Libya," 55–56; Milosevic, "Deutsche Kriegsbeteiligung und—verweigerung," 126.

of the government, the parliamentarians, and the public regarding the role and relevance of military forces as an instrument of foreign policy. The limited NATO operation in Kosovo in 1999 had created the impression that an "intervention could be efficient and successful, with low risks and costs."[370] The international engagement in Afghanistan, conversely, had proven the opposite because of the strategic problems of the U.S.-led global war on terror and the security realities of Southwestern Asia as they have stood for two centuries. Despite enormous personal, material, and financial efforts amid and in parallel to NATO ISAF and U.S.-led Operation Enduring Freedom, such as political reforms and development assistance, the security situation in Afghanistan had worsened since 2008 into an insurgency on a broad scale and more or less on the pattern of the resistance to the British and the Soviets in earlier times.

As the publicly and politically perceived nature of the Bundeswehr engagement shifted from a "peacekeeping mission to one of war," [371] so did the political and public assessment of the mission. This development, in and of itself, represented the climax of the evolution of German security and military policy as it had progressed from 1990 to 2011. Even if Federal Chancellor Merkel and Defense Minister de Maizière argued later in 2011 that "military means cannot and must be excluded as ultimo ratio"[372] as well as that "the use of military force can be a political means to prevent or to contain worse violence,"[373] the Bundeswehr mission in Afghanistan became broadly

---

[370] Ischinger, "Germany after Libya," 55–56.

[371] Bleibohm, "On Contemporary War and the German Armed Forces," 78.

[372] Merkel, *Deutschland weiß um seine Verantwortung in der Welt*.

[373] Thomas de Maizière, *Rede des Bundesministers der Verteidigung anlässlich der 8. Handelsblatt Konferenz am 25. Oktober 2011 in Berlin*, accessed March 12, 2015, http://www.bmvg.de/portal/a/bmvg/!ut/p/c4/NY3BCsIwEET_KGmQovVmK YKHXrxovYQ0WdKFJimbbQXx422FzsC7vIGRL7k2mgW9YUzRjPIpO4vn_i36s HgRMGJmIJyD8JDtgHZg0H-3ADGgQz9Hn_ehzoCsVVWWgocUTNYOdDD4 QSCQj-3OgbApAm9kiIwrPRlOJKZEPG5mJlqNQCe7QjV1oYo96ntqu2tZH45V c6vvcgrh8gO9ubH1/.

seen by its critics and its supporters, too, as a "risky, long, and costly enterprise with [questionable] benefits."[374] A study conducted by the German Marshall Fund of the United States in mid-2011 revealed the intensifying public opposition to the mission, as 51 percent of the respondents demanded that Germany should withdraw all troops from Afghanistan and 19 percent wanted that Germany should at least reduce its troops there.[375]

Most importantly, the unexpected evolutions and implications of the Bundeswehr engagement in Afghanistan considerably influenced political thinking in Berlin regarding the calculus and implicit criteria for using military force as foreign policy tool—strengthening a risk-averse position toward a German participation in the military intervention in Libya. Accordingly, Westerwelle publicly stated on March 10, 2011, that it is imperative for him to ensure that "we as Germans will not be drawn carelessly in war, from which we then cannot escape for many years."[376] His reticent attitude was echoed one day later by Defense Minister de Mazière arguing that avoiding unpersuasive and unenforceable tasks requires that "military actions have to be thought through to the end."[377]

  e. Mission Framework

Framed and magnified by the "Afghanistan experience," mission-related concerns about the lack of an overall strategic concept, shortfalls in the planning, potential costs of an intervention, and risks for

---

[374] Ischinger, "Germany after Libya," 56.

[375] Zsolt Nyiri and Ben Veater-Fuchs, "Transatlantic Trends 2011: Key Findings," The German Marshall Fund of the United States, accessed March 12, 2015, http://www.gmfus.org/publications/transatlantic-trends-2011; Lindström and Zetterlund, *Setting the Stage*, 28.

[376] "De Mazière kritisiert militärische Drohungen," *Frankfurter Allgemeine Zeitung*, March 11, 2011, http://www.faz.net/aktuell/politik/ausland/naher-osten/libyen-de-maiziere-kritisiert-militaerische-drohungen-1611689.html.

[377] "De Mazière kritisiert militärische Drohungen."

German soldiers, significantly influenced German key stakeholders to opt for Germany's nonparticipation in 2011 as they trumped considerations of a legitimate cause for a military invention in North Africa. While arguing along its general preference of political solutions over military means, the federal government assumed a deeply skeptical and critical position toward a no-fly zone over Libya early in the decision-making process. Worried about the French and British motives for the initiative and with a sense of having been excluded from Franco-British diplomacy, Merkel, Westerwelle, and de Maizière sincerely questioned whether such an intervention had been "one hundred percent thought through" regarding the goals, appropriate means, potential consequences, and conditions for ending the mission—all vital criteria for German decisions on participation in military interventions.[378]

With the accusation that the French-British plan lacked a coherent strategy, the federal government doubted that "a no-fly zone or similar military engagement from the air could be successful [and effective] in protecting civilians."[379] Instead, the German side feared that such an inadequate military intervention could even worsen the situation, lead to more violence and civilian casualties, and finally "weaken the entire democratic movement in Northern Africa."[380] Even more

---

[378] Thomas de Maizière, "We Will Not Get Involved in Syria," interview by Ralf Beste and Dirk Kurbjuweit, *Spiegel Online*, June 20, 2011, http://www.spiegel.de/international/germany/spiegel-interview-with-defense-minister-de-maiziere-we-will-not-get-involved-in-syria-a-769339.html; Hannes Vogel, "Antwort auf Libyen-Resolution: Deutschland verrät die Freiheit und seine Verbündeten," *Handelsblatt*, March 18, 2011, http://www.handelsblatt.com/politik/international/antwort-auf-libyen-resolution-deutschland-verraet-die-freiheit-und-seine-verbuendeten/3964624-all.html; Miskimmon, "German Foreign Policy and the Libyan Crisis," 397.

[379] Brockmeier, "Germany and the Intervention in Libya," 67; Deutscher Bundestag, *Stenografischer Bericht: Plenarprotokoll 17/95*, 10815.

[380] Deutscher Bundestag, *Stenografischer Bericht: Plenarprotokoll 17/95*, 10815; Deutscher Bundestag, *Stenografischer Bericht: Plenarprotokoll 17/97*, 11138. See also Sinjen, "Der Preis der Freiheit—Fall Libyen," 82.

problematic for the federal government, a military intervention from the air, once proven unsuccessful, could potentially cause a "slippery slope," of mission creep, dragging Western states into a prolonged Libyan civil war, which would require an intervention with ground troops.[381] With Federal Chancellor Merkel being "unable to lead [Germany] into a mission with uncertain end,"[382] and Foreign Minister Westerwelle being unwilling for German soldiers to become "part of a war in Libya, a permanent civil war in Libya,"[383] the federal government internally decided not later than March 16, 2011, after having weighed "both considerable foreign policy and military threats and risks"[384] against potential benefits, that Germany would not take part with the Bundeswehr in a military intervention in Libya. All public statements made clear that the federal government's sensitivity toward the risks and consequences of an *engagement,* rather than about the risks and consequences of a *nonengagement* loomed as more crucial for the decision against a participation of German soldiers in the mission.

This fact would also explain why the German government disregarded legitimate and value-based causes that have justified—and even required—participation in a more robust answer to the Libyan crisis. As recently as the end of 2010, Foreign Minister Westerwelle publicly had stated that the "protection of human rights is a cornerstone of German foreign policy" and only with "the respect of human rights, permanent peace and economic development can flour-

---

[381] Deutscher Bundestag, *Stenografischer Bericht: Plenarprotokoll 17/95,* 10816; Westerwelle, "Zur aktuellen Lage in Libyen"; Severin Weiland, "FDP-Chef Westerwelle: Der Außenseiterminister," *Spiegel Online,* March 23, 2011, http://www.spiegel.de/politik/deutschland/fdp-chef-westerwelle-der-aussenseiterminister-a-752269.html; Harald Müller, "Ein Desaster: Deutschland und der Fall Libyen," *HSFK Standpunkte,* no. 2 (2011): 6.

[382] "Saarbrücker Zeitung"; Hellmann, "Berlins Große Politik im Fall Libyen," 21.

[383] Westerwelle, "Zur aktuellen Lage in Libyen"; Deutscher Bundestag, *Stenografischer Bericht: Plenarprotokoll 17/95,* 10816.

[384] Deutscher Bundestag, *Stenografischer Bericht: Plenarprotokoll 17/97,* 11139.

ish."[385] Gaddafi's open declaration of war against his own people clearly violated these ideals and thus formed a reasonable and justifiable basis to intervene in the humanitarian framework of a "responsibility to protect" the Libyan civilian population against the arbitrariness of its own government. With the mandate of the UNSC and the support of the Arab League, the political, legal, and moral preconditions for a German military engagement in Libya were even more pressing than in the case of the Kosovo in 1998 and 1999.[386] Yet, whereas some scholars doubt whether the German government clearly understood the humanitarian and peace enforcement concept of a "responsibility to protect" and its significance to the situation in Libya,[387] the weight of the mission framework–related concerns, domestic politics calculations, and cultural facets decisively reduced their importance during the decision-making process.

2. Determinants on the Internal Level

Factors in the internal system significantly influenced the national and collective security decision to refuse to participate with German soldiers in the international military operation in Libya. Within the extended, interpenetrated three-level logic of (German) foreign and security policy, the insufficient and even disincentivizing nature of external factors magnified the impact of domestically-motivated actor-related short-term calculations, considerations to domestic accep-

---

[385] Federal Foreign Office, "Außenminister Westerwelle: Schutz der Menschenrechte ist Grundpfeiler deutscher Außenpolitik," *Auswaertiges Amt*, updated December 12, 2010, http://www.auswaertiges-amt.de/DE/Infoservice/Presse/Meldungen/2010/101210-BM-Tag_der_MR.html.

[386] Milosevic, "Deutsche Kriegsbeteiligung und—verweigerung," 117; Hacke, "Deutschland und der Libyen Konflikt," 51.

[387] Seibel, "Libyen," 106–110.

tance,[388] and certain elements of Germany's strategic cultural as well as role conception on the decision-making process. The Libyan case not only supports the notion of an increased "domestic politicization"[389] of German foreign policy, but also illustrates to what extent the salience of other aspects, including foreign policy aims and principles, allow internal factors to unfold their influence on the decision.

a. Strategic Culture and Conception of National Role

Germany's foreign policy strategic culture and its conception of its national role significantly influenced the decision for nonparticipation; however, beside the impact of a more self-confident attitude of members of the federal government in 2011, the effect overwhelmingly relates to the over-emphasis on the nonviolent and civil premise "politics before force" and the related "culture of (military) restraint,"[390] as both superposed all other cultural and role conceptual subcomponents of a "civil power" and deprived them of their salience. As elucidated in the last section, the nature of the Libyan crisis in 2011 and the conditions of the international response completely corresponded with to these two conceptual tenets of German foreign and security policy.

First, "never again," as the protection of the Libyan population within the framework of a "responsibility to protect" would have been consistent with Germany's national interests, value-based approach, and normative self-image. Second, "never alone," as the unanimous vote of its Western allies for UNSC Resolution 1973 and

---

[388] Frankenberger and Maull, "'Gimme a Break'"; Seibel, "Libyen," 105; Stelzenmüller, "Germany's Unhappy Abstention From Leadership." For the speech of Rolf Mützenich in the Bundestag after the governmental declaration by Foreign Minister Guido Westerwelle see Deutscher Bundestag, *Stenografischer Bericht: Plenarprotokoll 17/97*, 11140.

[389] Oppermann, "National Role Conceptions," 509.

[390] Maull, "Außenpolitische Entscheidungsprozesse in Krisenzeiten," 36.

its implementation through a NATO operation would have been consistent with the multilateral premise of German foreign and security policy.[391] Yet, fueled by the Afghan experience in 2008 to 2010 and a particular domestic political constellation of contested coalitions, Berlin was sincerely concerned about the risks and implications of an international military intervention, through which Germany could have become a "war party" in potentially long-lasting violent conflict in Libya. This fear magnified the inherent risk-averse stance in international affairs in the body politic and elites as well as the reticent attitude toward the use of military force in general as the overwhelming "lesson of history," even when certain facts of the moment suggested that no such lesson really existed at all. Both elements of political culture, role concept, and diplomatic practice won primacy over all other subcomponents within the governmental decision-making process—including alliance solidarity, which has played a lesser role in the recent past than in the worst days of the Cold War at which time such solidarity was more essential. Germany's favor of "political (and economic) before military means," resulting in the abstention from the vote for UNSC Resolution 1973 and nonparticipation in the multilateral military intervention, therefore, simultaneously corresponded with, and contradicted, core tenets of German foreign and security policy—demonstrating its continuing ambivalent nature.

The publicly displayed determination of the federal government to defend Germany's national stance against international positions,[392] hereby arguing and acting against such key allies as France and the United Kingdom, further supports to the notion that Merkel, Westerwelle, and de Maizière had developed, during the years of their

---

[391] Maull, "Deutsche Außenpolitik," 100, 111; Milosevic, "Deutsche Kriegsbeteiligung und—verweigerung," 120, 122; Hacke, "Deutschland und der Libyen Konflikt," 53.

[392] For example, Westerwelle repeatedly claimed to "protect" Germany against the consequences of a "quick reflex" calling for military intervention. Westerwelle, "Zur aktuellen Lage in Libyen."

common government, of a self-confident attitude toward and a nuanced image of Germany's role in international affairs in the midst of a tumultuous international system that has grown multipolar and been beset with overlaying crises. In particular, Germany's economic-based strengthened power position amid the financial and economic crisis after 2008 backed this more self-assured appearance and partly "solipsistic mindset."[393] This environment facilitated an inward-looking early predisposition to refuse the use of military force as a solution for the crisis in Libya—even against potential external resistance, which, in the event, was greater than the stakeholders of such German policy initially conceived in the heat of crisis. Although limited through the misassumptions about the conditions in the international environment and the miscalculations about the implications of Germany's foreign policy decisions, a matured national role conception, with less emphasis on the premises of a "civilian power," may additionally explain why the federal government could partly subordinate long-term foreign policy interests and goals under short-term domestic political considerations.[394]

b. Parliament and Political Contestation

Domestic political motives and considerations, such as the party politics of the FDP in crisis, upcoming regional elections in which the health of the coalition was at risk, strained cohesion of the coalition in the face of a deteriorating party landscape, and uncertain parliamentary support also played a significant role for the decision for nonparticipation[395]—supporting the notion that "[German] politics is

---

[393] Jürgen Habermas, "Germany's Mindset Has Become Solipsistic," *Guardian*, June 11, 2010, http://www.theguardian.com/commentisfree/2010/jun/11/germany-normality-self-absorption.

[394] Heinrich August Winkler, "Politik ohne Projekt: Gedanken über Deutschland, Libyen und Europa," *Internationale Politik* 5 (September/Oktober 2011): 28–37.

[395] Maull, "Deutsche Außenpolitik," 112; Hellmann, "Berlins Große Politik im Fall Libyen," 21; Milosevic, "Deutsche Kriegsbeteiligung und—verweigerung," 124–25.

local."³⁹⁶ This generalization also applies to defense policy since 2001, if not since 1949 and 1950. In the wake of the Libyan crisis, the federal government stood under enormous domestic pressure. Intensified by a strong opposition within the Bundestag toward the government's handling of the Eurozone crisis with the rise of populism on the right and a revival of extreme left agitation, the conservative-liberal coalition's fragile status mainly reverted to the weakness of the Liberal junior partner.

The FDP's intraparty division and tough stance toward solutions of the European financial crisis had backfired after 2008 in the face of a rising anticapitalistic tide in politics generally. Consequently, it experienced a dramatic collapse of its poll ratings, down to 3 percent in voter's rate in December 2010, and a stunning loss of 80 percent of its supporters in less than one year.³⁹⁷ Party leader, vice-chancellor, and Foreign Minister Westerwelle was threatened with losing both his party leadership and his cabinet position depending on the outcomes of the upcoming regional elections particularly in Baden-Wuertemberg and North Rhine-Westphalia where the politics of non-establishment-parties became strongly felt in turn.³⁹⁸ Facing a skeptical German general public, the prospect of taking advantage of the crisis in Libya to "reverse the party's political fortunes"³⁹⁹ by promoting a stance of refusal toward the military intervention in general, and toward an involvement of the Bundeswehr in particular, was reasonably high. Even if the decision for abstaining from the vote for UNSC Resolution 1973 remains disputed whether or not it was a result of an "intra-coalition compromise," to the extent that Federal Chancellor

---

³⁹⁶ Collmer, "'All Politics Is Local,'" 201.
³⁹⁷ See "Umfrage: FDP rasselt auf tiefsten Wert seit fast 15 Jahren," *Spiegel Online*, December 21, 2010, http://www.spiegel.de/politik/deutschland/umfrage-fdp-rasselt-auf-tiefsten-wert-seit-fast-15-jahren-a-735797.html; Oppermann, "National Role Conceptions," 511; Brockmeier, "Germany and the Intervention in Libya," 74.
³⁹⁸ Ischinger, "Germany after Libya," 49.
³⁹⁹ Oppermann, "National Role Conception," 515.

Merkel may have convinced Foreign Minister Westerwelle to refrain from his intention to vote even for "no" in the UNSC,[400] the decision to not participate was unanimously made between the members of the federal government.

Two additional aspects regarding the Bundestag facilitated and contributed to the decision. First, between the eruption of the crisis in mid-February and the UNSC Resolution 1973 on March 17, 2011, only two parliamentary debates over the topic Libya took place in the Bundestag. In a *aktuelle Stunde* ("current hour"—debate on matters of topical interests) on February 24, all parties condemned the violence of the Gaddafi regime and encouraged the government to continue both its support for the democratic movements in the Arab world and its approach to answer the crisis with a determined position as well as with political pressure and economic sanctions.[401] Despite critical developments in Libya and in the multilateral environment, it lasted until the morning on March 17, 2011, that a second parliamentary discussion of the topic took place—thus constraining the influence of the Bundestag on the decision-making of the federal govern-

---

[400] German media reported, with reference to an article of Lothar Rühl (a former defense-ministry official) that the abstention from the vote for UNSC Resolution 1973 was a "coalition compromise." He claimed that on the morning of 17 March 2011, Westerwelle still wanted to vote against the resolution in New York. Merkel, however, succeeded in wresting an abstention from him during a meeting later in the afternoon of the same day. The government immediately denied this illustration of the situation as being "completely wrong" and "totally fabricated." Lothar Rühl, "Militärisch erfolgreich, politisch konfus: Die Alliierten über Libyen," *Frankfurter Allgemeine Zeitung*, March 22, 2011, http://www.faz.net/aktuell/politik/militaerisch-erfolgreich-politisch-konfus-1606092.html?printPagedArticle=true%20-%20pageIndex_2; Severin Weiland and Philipp Wittrock, "Libyen-Enthaltung in der Uno: Wie es zu dem deutschen Jein kam," *Spiegel Online*, March 23, 2011, http://www.spiegel.de/politik/deutschland/libyen-enthaltung-in-der-uno-wie-es-zu-dem-deutschen-jein-kam-a-752676.html.

[401] Deutscher Bundestag, *Stenografischer Bericht: Plenarprotokoll 17/93* (Berlin: Bundesanzeiger Verlagsgesellschaft, February 24, 2011), 10468–71, accessed February 10, 2015, http://dipbt.bundestag.de/dip21/btp/17/17093.pdf#P.10468.

ment. Instead, on the sidelines of a debate about no longer germane events, Westerwelle became convinced that the government's skeptical position about military involvement in Libya was shared by the opposition parties.[402] Yet, not only during this last debate, but also in the first debate on March 18, 2011, one day after Germany's abstention from the vote in New York, facts on the ground revealed that the federal government faced bipartisan resistance—even from within the coalition—to its refusal to participate militarily in North Africa.[403] Politicians from all parties, except from DIE LINKE, continued to criticize the federal government's approach of having connected the behavior in the vote for UNSC Resolution 1973 with the question of a participation of the Bundeswehr—hereby violating Germany's reputation as reliable and trustworthy ally and partner. Instead, many argued that Germany should have voted "yes" and opted for a limited military footprint within the NATO mission.[404]

Second, although it is not clear whether Merkel, Westerwelle, and de Maizière had sensed this broader bipartisan resistance to an abstention and complete nonparticipation, a contributing factor for the decision of the federal government may have been its reluctance to request a mandate for German participation in a military intervention from the Bundestag. Given the serious concerns in Berlin regarding the risks and implications of a military operation in Libya, and in the face of a deeply averse German public, the federal government could have simply avoided asking the Bundestag for a mandate of an inter-

---

[402] Brockmeier, "Germany and the Intervention in Libya," 76; Rinke, "Eingreifen oder nicht?," 51.

[403] For the speeches of Rolf Mützenich (SPD) and Frithjof Schmidt (Bündnis90/Grüne) on March 17, 2011, see Deutscher Bundestag, *Stenografischer Bericht: Plenarprotokoll 17/95*, 10819, 10825. For the speeches of Rolf Mützenich (SPD) and Ruprecht Polenz (CDU) on March 18, 2011 see Deutscher Bundestag, *Stenografischer Bericht: Plenarprotokoll 17/97*, 11139–45.

[404] Jungholt, "Westerwelle rechtfertigt deutschen Libyen-Sonderweg"; Matthias Lohre, "Die Grünen zu Libyen: Krieg ja, aber ohne uns," *TAZ*, March 21, 2011, http://www.taz.de/!67775/.

vention which it did not believe in.[405] A contested result or an outright failure not only could have negatively affected the outcome of the upcoming regional elections, but also have further weakened the vulnerable governing coalition.

c. Public Opinion

Between the poles of foreign policy expectations and domestic constraints, German public opinion had a significant influence on the governmental decision for nonparticipation, suggesting that "more than ever, voter's sentiment dictated policy,"[406] however, seemingly not for the abstention from the vote in the UNSC. Accordingly, opinion polls and the news media coverage revealed a rather ambivalent domestic attitude, distinguishing between the international response to the crisis in Libya itself and Germany's role within it. Whereas the dispersion of pro- and contra-arguments concerning an international military intervention was relatively equally represented in German articles in the weeks before the resolution in New York,[407] the poll of the magazine *Stern*, conducted between March 10 and 11 and published on March 16, clearly demonstrated a broad public resentment against any German military participation in Libya.[408]

While the focus of the public and media attention shifted in the week before the resolution toward the nuclear accident in Fukushima, Japan, the worsening conditions for the Libyan population turned the public opinion in favor of an international engagement; however, the

---

[405] Brockmeier, "Germany and the Intervention in Libya," 76.

[406] Ischinger, "Germany after Libya," 49.

[407] Jessica Bucher, "Domestic Politics, News Media, and Humanitarian Intervention: Why France and Germany Diverged over Libya," *European Security* 22, no. 4 (2013): 534.

[408] "Umfrage zu Unruhen in Libyen," *Stern*, March 16, 2011, http://www.stern.de/politik/ausland/umfrage-zu-unruhen-in-libyen-deutsche-wollen-sich-nicht-einmischen-1664001.html.

deep skepticism among the news media and within the German public toward a German military engagement in Libya remained in place. This attitude expressed deep concerns about becoming involved as a warring party. This fact reflects the specific nature of Germany's dominant culture of reticence, which generally opposes military force as an appropriate means in international affairs, but particularly refuses the involvement of German soldiers especially in what has long been an area taboo from anything other than adventure tourism. In such a constellation, and having German national concerns about the success of a military engagement in Libya as well as facing two important regional elections, the federal government acted in what it believed to be with its electorate when deciding against a German contribution, aiming at limiting potential electoral repercussions. Although supported by polls after the abstention from the vote for UNSC Resolution 1973, showing that two-thirds of the German public were in favor of Germany's nonparticipation while 60 percent supported the NATO mission,[409] the short-term domestic calculus to take advantage from a restrained position did not pay off for the governing coalition. Westerwelle's FDP lost control over Baden-Wuertemberg to the first Green party–led regional government in Germany.

3. Determinants on the Actor Level

Whereas all three important key actors in the federal government unanimously advocated Germany's refusal for a military intervention in Libya,[410] it was Foreign Minister Westerwelle who predominantly framed and influenced the governmental decision-making process,

---

[409] "Krieg gegen Libyen: Über 60 Prozent der Deutschen befürworten den Angriff, Aber: Große Mehrheit lehnt Beteiligung der Bundeswehr ab," *Bild*, March 20, 2011,
http://www.bild.de/politik/2011/libyen-krise/aber-mehrheit-lehnt-beteiligung-ab-16933388.bild.html.

[410] Brockmeier, "Germany and the Intervention in Libya," 78.

giving short-term domestic political considerations and personal preferences primacy over long-term policy goals and external expectations. Federal Chancellor Angela Merkel assumed a rather cautious stance to the Libyan crisis, widely leaving the design and the communication of Germany's foreign policy orientation to Foreign Minister Westerwelle as part of the customs of cabinet practice as well as the dynamics of coalition government in the FRG.

Despite her power to determine the general guidelines of foreign policy (chancellor principle), two reasons may explain her approach. First, as head of government, Merkel was heavily involved in dealing with the consequences of the Eurozone crisis, the implications of the nuclear accident in Japan—all of which loomed large in domestic politics—and the preparation for the upcoming regional elections, simply limiting her ability to focus on other foreign policy issues. Second, given the FDP's growing weakness in the wake of the Euro crisis and the backlash, a lead of a publicly accepted German foreign policy toward Libya by Westerwelle could strengthen both the Foreign Minister and his party, helping to improve the electoral outcome in the regional elections and consolidating the fragile coalition.[411]

Regardless of whether Merkel really urged Westerwelle to disregard a potential "no" vote, she was getting publicly more involved the more it became clear that Westerwelle's exaggerated approached could threaten Germany's alliance policy. While defending—because unable (or unwilling) to reverse—Germany's decision to not take part in military measures as reasons for the abstention in the vote, it was Merkel who firstly publicly attempted to calm the waves and opt for foreign policy "damage control." She stated that Germany would nevertheless "share the goals of the resolution unreservedly," arguing that Germany's "abstention should not be confused with neutral-

---

[411] Milosevic, "Deutsche Kriegsbeteiligung und—verweigerung," 128.

ity."[412] This position may also reflect Federal Chancellor Merkel's deeply rooted pragmatic approach—her very own version of *Realpolitik* in the Berlin Republic—always aiming for the achievable rather than the desirable.[413]

Her resilience to criticism about a violation of Germany's Western orientation and alliance solidarity may also have its roots in the rationally nuanced adjustments of her basic positions. Although emphasizing the traditional concept of multilateralism, *Westorientierung*, transatlantic partnership, and value-orientation as core tenets of German foreign and security policy, Merkel underlined in her speech at the 47th security conference in Munich in February 2011 as well "that NATO alone, the transatlantic partnership alone," are insufficient to solve the major conflicts. Instead, "the [Western states] need partners worldwide … because this [is] a multipolar world."[414] Looking hereby as a geo-economic oriented state at emerging countries and important trading partners, such as Russia and China, Merkel did not change her decision as it became clear that Germany would side along these states in the vote for UNSC Resolution 1973—against all its Western NATO allies.

Foreign Minister Westerwelle dominantly influenced Germany's decision against a participation of the Bundeswehr in the military intervention in Libya and to abstain from the vote. He had already publicly interrelated a no-fly zone with a potentially broader military intervention early in the management of the international crisis, arguing

---

[412] Deutscher Bundestag, *Stenografischer Bericht: Plenarprotokoll 17/99*, 11251; Peel, "Merkel Explains Berlin's Abstention."

[413] Dietmar Riemer, "Merkels Realpolitik setzt Putin unter Druck," *Tagesschau*, February 11, 2015, http://www.tagesschau.de/kommentar/merkel-ukraine-105.html.

[414] Angela Merkel, *Rede der Bundeskanzlerin auf der 47. Münchner Sicherheitskonferenz* (Munich: February 5, 2011), accessed August 4, 2014, http://www.bundesregierung.de/ContentArchiv/DE/Archiv17/Reden/2011/02/2011-02-05-bkin-m%C3%BC-si-ko.htm; Merkel, *Deutschland weiß um seine Verantwortung in der Welt*.

that "nobody should cherish the illusion that [a no-fly zone] is just putting up a traffic sign. To enforce a flying ban, the Libyan air defense has to be military neutralized first."[415] Hence, it was Westerwelle's framing of the risky and unforeseeable implications of a military intervention in Libya as well as categorical refusal of any German military contribution to it that narrowed Germany's opportunity to act and finally maneuvered it in a foreign policy dead end, impossible to reverse direction as the conditions had changed. Simultaneously, his risk-averse and German nonparticipation stance dominated the political and public discourse, intensifying the skeptical attitude of the German public to arms and policy.

Four factors chiefly explain his stance. First, Westerwelle saw himself normatively anchored in a "tradition of restraint, what concerns military missions."[416] Consequently, military force always constituted for him an ultima ratio that should be used only after having exploited all other political means. Westerwelle's repeated claims that he personally, and not the German Bundestag, would do everything to keep Germany from becoming a warring party in a civil war in Libya, and German soldiers involved in it, reflected his deeply internalized attitude that the "culture of military restraint [is] a constant of German foreign policy."[417] Even as Gaddafi publicly threatened ultimate violence against his people, Westerwelle, therefore, still believed that the sanction policy of the international community "was not exhausted" and should be continued.[418] Second, facing upcoming regional elections and simultaneously pressure through declining popu-

---

[415] Westerwelle, "Regierungserklärung durch Bundesaußenminister Westerwelle."

[416] Guido Westerwelle, "Gaddafi muss weg-ohne Frage," interview by Ralf Neukirch, Erich Follath, and Georg Mascolo, *Spiegel Online*, March 21, 2011, http://magazin.spiegel.de/EpubDelivery/spiegel/pdf/77531597.

[417] Hans Monath, "Westerwelle und de Maizière: Zwei für Krieg und Frieden," *Der Tagesspiegel*, May 21, 2011.

[418] See Deutscher Bundestag, *Stenografischer Bericht: Plenarprotokoll 17/95*, 10815; Deutscher Bundestag, *Stenografischer Bericht: Plenarprotokoll 17/97*, 11138.

lar ratings for the FDP, Westerwelle had considerable domestic incentives to take advantage of the intervention-weary mood of the German public by demonstrating a determined, antimilitary stance. Third, Westerwelle's loosened normative and institutional ties to the transatlantic alliance explain why he adhered to a completely participation-averse attitude, even as the circumstances changed, willingly taking chances on a weakened German reputation within NATO and the EU in favor of domestic considerations and violating his own high expectations to the protection of human rights.[419] Finally, being relatively inexperienced in the foreign policy field, Westerwelle might not have fully comprehended the potential implications of voting against Germany's Western allies. Linking abstention as a logical consequence of nonparticipation narrowed his view for political alternatives.[420]

As former head of the Office of the Federal Chancellor and Minister for Interior, Defense Minister de Maizière was considered as a close confidante of Federal Chancellor Merkel. Although his appointment to the post limited his role among the federal government in the decision-making process for nonparticipation, he clearly supported Merkel's and Westerwelle's restraint. It was he who warned on March 10, 2011—before any public statement from Merkel—that all military actions "must be thought through to the end" and that the international community should take care not to get involved in something, "from what one is not convinced afterwards, and what one is unable to enforce."[421]

---

[419] Ralf Beste et al., "Friede den Zeltpalästen," *Der Spiegel*, no. 13 (2011): 24, http://magazin.spiegel.de/EpubDelivery/spiegel/pdf/77745550; Heinrich August Winkler, "Gehört Deutschland noch zum Westen?," interview by Richard Herzinger and Claus Christian Malzahn, *Die Welt*, June 6, 2011, http://www.welt.de/politik/ausland/article13426251/Gehoert-Deutschland-noch-zum-Westen.html.
[420] Brockmeier, "Germany and the Intervention in Libya," 78; Lindström and Zetterlund, *Setting the Stage*, 27.
[421] "De Maizière kritisiert militärische Drohungen."

D. Conclusion—Libya: The Ambivalence in a German *Sonderfall*

The analysis of the decision-making process for the nonparticipation of the Bundeswehr in the international military intervention in Libya as well as the abstention vote may well demonstrate how the mutual interplay and inherent tensions between imperatives of the two systems and the impact of state actors while mediating between them affected a rather unexpected outcome. To understand the astonishment of Germany's allies and subsequent domestic and international criticism concerning the federal government's decisions compels one to consider the broader external setting in which the decision took place as well as what it finally related to. First, the crisis in Libya related to German security interests as it gradually gained the potential to destabilize an entire region close to the European sphere of security. Likewise, from a legal and normative perspective, it constituted a clear case of state failure to fulfil its responsibility to protect its own people.

Consequently, an international engagement according to the principle of a "responsibility to protect (R2P)" would have had at least the same level of legitimation than the military intervention in Kosovo in 1999. Second, in contrast to the Kosovo case, however, Germany could have justified its military engagement based on the UN Charter with a resolution of the UNSC. Finally, Germany's most important Western allies not only unanimously voted for UNSC Resolution 1973, but also participated in its enforcement. Consequently, shaping the overall nature of the external pole in the two-level system, these factors created sufficient incentives and reasons to drive the federal government to a decision in favor of a participation of the Bundeswehr in the military intervention. Such a decision would have been in accordance with the German key foreign and security policy principles of "never again" and "never alone."

The opposite decision was a consequence both of a complex confluence between several, mutually related factors on all three dimensions and the particular circumstances of the Libyan crisis as well as the international response. Other dominant events in the external environment, doubts about French and British motives, the late and surprising shift by the United States, the negative Afghan war experiences of the Bundeswehr, and deep concerns about the risks and consequences of a military involvement in Libya all reduced the salience of the abovementioned imperatives in favor of German military participation, and instead redirected the attention to and magnified domestic politics considerations as well as basic positions that favored nonparticipation—facilitated by critical misinterpretations and misassumptions about the consequences. In particular, Germany's inherent risk-averse stance in international affairs and its "culture of military reticence" regarding the international involvement of the Bundeswehr ("politics before force") became the predominant normative background in which the federal government's decision took place. The upcoming elections, the weakness of the FDP, and a German military participation–averse public, reinforced the federal government, and at its forefront Foreign Minister Westerwelle, to firmly pursue its intervention-skeptical course.

The particular circumstances of the Libyan case and the unfolding of events and factors in relation to the decision-making process, therefore, lead to three major conclusions. First, both aspects relativize the generalized argument made by some analysts that "international expectations of alliance solidarity no longer rank as the predominant driving force in German foreign policy"[422] and as a crucial

---

[422] Oppermann, "National Role Conceptions," 514. For the argument that the multilateral orientation of the FRG's foreign and security policy is not determined anymore by a reflex-like acception of international responsibilities, see Franz-Josef Meiers, "Von der Scheckbuchdiplomatie zur Verteidigung am Hindukusch: Die Rolle der Bundeswehr bei multinationalen Auslandseinsätzen, 1990–2009," *Zeitschrift für Außen- und Sicherheitspolitik* 3, no. 2 (2010): 218.

factor "within the calculation of national interests."[423] Even if impossible to prove the counterfactual, but a more transparent communication by France and the United Kingdom regarding the goals and scope of their plans for establishing a no-fly zone, a better inclusion of Germany within the diplomatic preparation for UNSC Resolution 1973, and an early information by U.S. senior officials regarding a shift in their attitude toward a military intervention in Libya, could have decisively put more weight to the multilateral impulses, hence, incentivized the federal government to side with its allies and opt for a (limited) participation. This assumption is supported by the fact that, although Berlin defended its decision for nonparticipation, the federal government was immediately endeavored to relativize its resolution-averse stance and most importantly, to underline its unaltered multilateral commitment by indirectly supporting the NATO mission in Libya. While increasing its involvement in surveillance flights over Afghanistan, Germany helped to free up NATO AWACS capacities for enforcing the no-fly zone over Libya, and hereby, as Defense Minister de Maizière claimed, send a "political sign of our solidarity with the alliance."[424]

Second, the case demonstrates that, at this particular stage, German foreign and security policy *continued* "to be driven by inherent contradictions"[425] between its traditional core principles and between external and internal imperatives, causing *ambiguous* and *ambivalent* policy-decision outcomes depending on the salience of either side. On one hand, Germany still adhered to the tenets of *Westorientierung*,

---

[423] Hellmann, "Berlins Große Politik im Fall Libyen," 21.

[424] "Germany's Libya Contribution: Schmid Merkel Cabinet Approves AWACS for Afghanistan," *Spiegel Online*, March 23, 2011, http://www.spiegel.de/international/world/germany-s-libya-contribution-merkel-cabinet-approves-awacs-for-afghanistan-a-752709.html; "Statt in Libyen fliegt Deutschland in Afghanistan."

[425] Ischinger, "Germany after Libya," 46; Gareis, "Die Organisation deutscher Sicherheitspolitik," 106.

multilateralism, and value orientation as backbones of its foreign and security policy. On the other, simultaneously, Germany remained deeply bound to a general risk-averse position in international affairs, a culture of military restraint, and domestic politics considerations.

This attitude has repeatedly led to criticism of "responsibility gap(s)" where Germany missed opportunities to "support its declared policy objectives and its allies ... by taking concrete actions."[426] Accordingly, the Libyan decisions would add another example after Chad in 2008 and Ivory Coast in 2010 and 2011, notably all of them on the African continent. Moreover, Germany's reticence resulted in a dominant tendency to self-restrict its policy toolbox, excluding the use of force (for combat-like tasks) almost categorically, and in a specific sensitivity toward domestic demands. The more Germany's multilateral institutions became involved in international military interventions, however, the imperatives of multilateral commitments and military restraint conflicted as they provided diametric impulses. Supported by personal preferences and attitudes (including role concepts) of governmental key actors—who were compelled to mediate between the different impulses—domestic policy considerations, risk aversion, and military reticence were given primacy over multilateral imperatives (both external expectations and internal commitments), facilitating the decision for nonparticipation in the military intervention in Libya.

Finally, the characteristics of all influences on the decision-making process suggests that the decision for nonparticipation in the NATO operation in Libya, despite the existence of justifiable reasons, a UNSC resolution, and an international mission to implement it, constituted a "normal" special case (*Sonderfall*) rather than a first step on a German special path (*Sonderweg*) by considerably departing from premises of German foreign and security policy. Instead, it is more a proof of Germany's *normalizing* ambivalence in decisions for a partici-

---

[426] Major and Mölling, *German Defense Policy in 2014*, 7.

pation of the Bundeswehr in military interventions. Pending on the specific context and the salience of certain factors and premises, the policy outcomes are expected to vary.

IV. Mali—A Standard Case: Germany's Return to Consistent Patterns of Decisions for Military Engagement

This chapter frames the context and subsequently traces the sequence of events that contributed to the decisions of *whether* and *how* German forces should participate in EUTM Mali, contribute to AFISMA, and support to France in 2013, that is, two years after the Libyan debacle. Second, the analysis suggests that a complex interplay between factors on all three domains, and particularly tensions between the external and internal domains, explain not only Germany's decisions in favor of the Bundeswehr engagements in Mali, but also its reluctance to get involved more actively and with "robust" capacities, that is, military force. Finally, this chapter shows that the Mali case marked a return to consistent patterns of German foreign and security policy decisions for international military engagements as interpreted above. While increasingly willing to assume more responsibility and to fulfill its multilateral commitments, Germany remained bound to its risk-averse position in international affairs, a hesitancy within the decision-making process, a position of military restraint, and the leading role of domestic politics considerations.

Both the crisis and the international reaction in Mali 2012 and 2013 are in many ways directly connected to the crisis and international reaction in Libya in 2011. The support of the NATO air campaign paved the way for the Libyan opposition to overthrow the Gaddafi regime in October 2011, hence, for further disorder that spread southward.

By then, ethnic Tuaregs from the Sahel region, whom the Libyan dictator had long used as mercenaries, had already deserted. They fled into neighboring countries as they feared reprisals from the new authorities.⁴²⁷ Embedded in the long-lasting struggle of the disenfranchised Tuareg ethnicity to achieve the territorial and cultural autonomy of the Azawad,⁴²⁸ this influx of manpower, arms, and equipment into Mali fueled the separatist ambitions of the Tuareg population, leading to the creation of the National Movement for the Liberation of the Azawad (MNLA)⁴²⁹ in October 2011. It also worsened the intensifying power-struggle in the northern parts of the country and facilitated the emergence and spread of Islamist groups throughout the poorly governed region.⁴³⁰

By the end of 2011, not only had al Qaeda in the Islamic Maghreb (AQIM) extended its presence in northern Mali, but also Ansar al-

---

⁴²⁷ Bernhard Schmid, *Die Mali-Intervention: Befreiungskrieg, Aufstandsbekämpfung oder neokolonialer Feldzug?* (Münster, Germany: Unrast, 2014), 29–30; Denis M. Tull and Wolfram Lacher, "Die Folgen des Libyen-Konfliktes für Afrika: Gräben zwischen der AU und dem Westen, Destabilisierung der Sahelzone," *SWP Studie S8* (Berlin: German Institute for International and Security Affairs, March 2012): 2; Wolfram Lacher and Denis M. Tull, "Mali: Jenseits von Terrorismusbekämpfung," *SWP-Aktuell* 9 (Berlin: German Institute for International and Security Affairs, February 2013), 1–3; Martin Pabst, "Staatliche Schwäche begünstigt Dschihadisten: Neuer Risikoraum Sahelzone," *Sicherheit und Frieden* 31, no. 1 (2013): 6; Rachel Dicke, "The European Union Training Mission in Mali: A Case Study," *CIRR* 20, no. 71 (2014): 97, doi:10.2478/cirr-2014-0010; Rajan Meno, "The French Mess in Mali and Libya," *Atlantic Council*, January 24, 2013, http://www.atlanticcouncil.org/blogs/new-atlanticist/the-french-mess-in-mali-and-libya.

⁴²⁸ In the Berber language, Azawad figuratively describes an extreme plain, desertlike area that encompassed a big portion of the northern part of Mali. Interestingly, although they populate a much larger territory, reaching from south Algeria, over southwest Libya as well as west and center Niger, to the northern parts of Burkina Faso and Nigeria, the Tuaregs have striven for autonomy and independence, particularly in Mali. See the National Pact between the Malian government and the United Movement and Fronts of Azawad (MFUA) in April 1992. Robin-Edward Poulton and Ibrahim ag Youssouf, *La paix de Tombouctou: Gestion démocratique, développement et construction africaine de la paix* (New York: United Nations Institute for Disarmament Research, 1999), 68–72.

⁴²⁹ In French: *Mouvement national de libération de l'Azawad (MNLA)*.

⁴³⁰ Tull and Lacher, "Die Folgen des Libyen-Konfliktes für Afrika," 2; Dicke, "The European Union Training Mission in Mali," 97.

Dine, a militant Islamist group seeking to impose Sharia law across Mali, and the Movement for Unity and Jihad in West Africa (MUJWA),[431] a black African–led radical Islamist splinter-group from AQIM seeking to establish a caliphate in West Africa were gaining influence in the region.[432] Aligning itself with those groups, on January 17, 2012, the MNLA made its first attack on Malian Armed Forces near Menaka, marking the outbreak of the violent crisis in northern Mali.[433] Within only a few weeks, the already weak governmental control of the Malian North collapsed, as Malian armed units, trained and equipped by the United States, "either fled or Tuareg soldiers and commanders defected to the insurgents."[434] Reports about massacres of some 85 unarmed soldiers and civilians on January 18, 2012, near Aguelhok[435] and accusations about an insufficient approach against the rebellion caused public uproar in the capital Bamako, culminating in a military coup d'état on March 22, 2012, under the lead of U.S.-trained Captain Amadou Sanogo.

The political chaos in the capital of the "poster child of democracy"[436] in Africa fueled the offensive of the armed groups. After

---

[431] In French, *Mouvement pour l'Unicité et le Jihad en Afrique de l'Ouest (MUJAO)*.

[432] Pabst, "Staatliche Schwäche begünstigt Dschihadisten," 6–7; Tull and Lacher, "Die Folgen des Libyen-Konfliktes für Afrika," 2. See also Zachary Laub and Jonathan Masters, "Al Qaeda in the Islamic Maghreb (AQIM)," *Council on Foreign Relations*, updated March 27, 2015, http://www.cfr.org/terrorist-organizations-and-networks/al-qaeda-islamic-maghreb-aqim/p12717.

[433] Schmid, *Die Mali-Intervention*, 29.

[434] Meno, "The French Mess in Mali and Libya."

[435] It is still disputed whether the MNLA or allied radical Islamist groups were responsible for massacre of unarmed and defenseless soldiers and civilians. Although the MNLA claims innocence, more recent research inquiries argue that the MNLA most likely bears responsibility for it. See Schmid, *Die Mali-Intervention*, 33–34; Laurant Touchard, "Aguelhok: Qui es responsable du massacre?," *MaliActu*, October 23, 2013, http://maliactu.info/nord-mali/aguelhok-qui-est-responsable-du-massacre.

[436] Sergei Boeke and Antonin Tisseron, "Mali's Long Road Ahead," *The RUSI Journal* 159, no. 5 (2014): 32, doi:10.1080/03071847.2014.969942.

having seized control over vast areas in northern Mali until early April 2012, the alliance between the MNLA and the Islamist groups, however, gradually disintegrated, finally resulting in the expulsion of secular-nationalist Tuareg forces from all major northern cities by mid-2012 and the establishment of a Sharia-based state.[437] By the late summer of 2012, Mali was de facto divided, with the Islamists and the Malian military settling into a phony war.[438] Recognizing a demarcation line between northern and southern Mali for almost half a year, with more than 1,000 troops and 200 vehicles on January 10, 2013, the Islamist groups occupied the small town of Konna, south of this line—but only 500 kilometers northeast of Bamako.[439]

Fearing a further advance toward the capital, the Malian interim government appealed to France, the long-term dominant power in the region with its own imperial tradition and finally, a strategic culture and civil-military relations that brooked little or no hesitancy to use force with troops stationed nearby for immediate help; Paris responded on January 11, 2013, by launching Operation Serval. After the initial engagement of Special Forces Aviation Units, France quickly deployed some 4,000 troops to Mali, successful blocking a potential advance of the Islamist groups to the south and expelling them from all major cities in the North until February 2013.[440] Hereby, African troops from a growing African-led International Support Mission in Mali (AFISMA), authorized by the UNSC Resolution 2085 on December 20, 2012, and reaching some 6,000 troops by

---

[437] Boeke and Tisseron, "Mali's Long Road Ahead," 32; Schmid, *Die Mali-Intervention*, 33–34; Pabst, "Staatliche Schwäche begünstigt Dschihadisten," 6.

[438] Michael Shurkin, *France's War in Mali: Lessons for an Expeditionary Army* (Santa Monica, CA: RAND Corporation, 2014), 6.

[439] Meno, "The French Mess in Mali and Libya."

[440] Olivier Tramond and Philippe Seigneu, "Operation Serval: Another Beau Geste of France in Sub-Saharan Africa?," *Military Review* 94, no. 6 (November/December 2014): 76-82; Shurkin, *France's War in Mali*, 13–25. For a chronological overview about the events of Operation Serval, see also Jan Kraak, "Opération Serval," *Air International* 84, no. 3 (2013): 74–79.

March 2013, supported France's combat efforts and gradually took over the responsibility for helping Mali to "restore the authority of the State of Mali over its entire national territory, to uphold the unity and territorial integrity of Mali, and to reduce the threat posed by terrorist organizations and associated groups."[441]

In parallel, based on UNSC resolutions and a direct appeal from Malian authorities, the EU decided to launch its Training Mission in Mali (EUTM Mali).[442] Initially planned for a 15-month period, the mission started with approximately 500 European personnel from 23 nations in April 2013. Located with its headquarters and an advisory task force in Bamako as well as with some 250 military instructors in Koulikoro, 60 kilometers northeast of the Malian capital, EUTM Mali continues to help restore the capacities of the Malian Defense and Security Forces and to help Mali to regain and maintain its territorial integrity and internal stability.[443]

Throughout the evolution of the crisis and despite the backing of France's intervention in Mali, the German government constantly refused to get directly involved into any form of a combat operation

---

[441] UN Security Council, *UNSC Resolution 2085* (New York: December 20, 2012), 4, accessed February 12, 2015, http://www.globalr2p.org/media/files/sres2085-on-mali.pdf.

[442] Council of the European Union, *Council Conclusions on Mali, 3222nd Foreign Affairs Council Meeting* (Brussels: Council of the European Union Press Office, February 18, 2013), accessed February 12, 2015, http://www.consilium.europa.eu/uedocs/cms_data/docs/pressdata/EN/foraff/135522.pdf; Council of the European Union, *Council Conclusions on Mali, 3217th Foreign Affairs Council Meeting* (Brussels: Council of the European Union Press Office, January 17, 2013), accessed February 12, 2015, http://www.consilium.europa.eu/uedocs/cms_data/docs/pressdata/EN/foraff/134756.pdf.

[443] Dicke, "The European Union Training Mission in Mali," 98–99; Nicholas Fiorenza, "EU Launces Training Mission for Mali," *Aviation Week*, February 18, 2013, http://aviationweek.com/blog/eu-launches-training-mission-mali; Derek E. Mix, *The European Union: Foreign and Security Policy* (Washington: Congressional Research Service, April 2013), 13.

with its troops in Mali. Instead, the federal government stressed the need for a political solution to the crisis and offered logistic, medical, and humanitarian support.[444] Consequently, in mid-January 2013, the federal government decided, more or less in a familiar pattern of the nonlinear approach, to *indirectly* support France's engagement in Mali, by deploying up to three transport aircraft of the vastly overcommitted German air force to Dakar, Senegal, helping to transport troops and materiel from AFISMA forces. The engagement, however, ruled out actively supporting French forces and air operations in the northern battle zone.[445] On February 28, 2012, framed by further decisions within EU, another French appeal, and the federal government's requests, the German Bundestag gave finally its approval that Germany would contribute to both EUTM Mali and AFISMA with up to 330 soldiers, including 40 engineer trainers, 40 medical personnel, and air-

---

[444] "Mali-Mission: Westerwelle schließt Entsendung von Kampftruppen aus," *Spiegel Online*, October 23, 2012, http://www.spiegel.de/politik/ausland/westerwelle-schliesst-entsendung-deutscher-kampftruppen-nach-mali-aus-a-862978.html; "De Maizière schließt Kampfeinsatz aus," *Süddeutsche*, November 19, 2012, http://www.sueddeutsche.de/politik/bundeswehr-in-mali-de-maizire-schliesst-kampfeinsatz-aus-1.1527416; Charles Hawley, "The World from Berlin: French mission in Mali 'is not without risk,'" *Spiegel Online*, January 14, 2013, http://www.spiegel.de/international/world/germany-offers-support-to-france-in-mali-as-commentators-warn-of-risk-a-877401.html.

[445] Thorsten Jungholt,"Paris ruft—doch Berlin schickt nur zwei Flieger," *Die Welt*, January 16, 2013, http://www.welt.de/politik/deutschland/article112818164/Paris-ruft-doch-Berlin-schickt-nur-zwei-Flieger.html; Dominic Johnson, "Bundesregierung beschließt Mali-Einsatz: Deutsche in den Sand gesetzt," *TAZ*, February 19, 2013, http://www.taz.de/!111377/.

transport and air-refueling capacities—the latter were allowed to operate throughout all of Mali to directly support French forces.[446]

A. Context and Framework of the Decision-Making-Process

Various developments within the international, European, and domestic, environment framed Berlin's decision-making process on a military engagement in Mali. Internationally, three major dominant factors of policy were determining. First, the internationally community became increasingly concerned about and focused on Syria, as the public uprising against the Assad regime, which had started in March 2011, turned into a bloody and brutally fought civil war with nearly 15,000 casualties after 12 months of fighting, resulting from a state declaration of war against the rebellion in June 2011. In 2012, the conflict became protracted, as both sides proved unable to achieve a decisive momentum, the opposition splintered, the country

---

[446] Antrag der Bundesregierung, "Entsendung bewaffneter deutscher Streitkräfte zur Beteiligung an der EU-geführten militärischen Ausbildungsmission EUTM Mali auf Grundlage des Ersuchens der Regierung von Mali sowie der Beschlüsse 2013/34/GASP des Rates der Europäischen Union (EU) vom 17. Januar 2013 und vom 18. Februar 2013 in Verbindung mit den Resolutionen 2071 (2012) und 2085 (2012) des Sicherheitsrates der Vereinten Nationen," Drs. 17/12367 (Berlin: Bundesanzeiger Verlagsgesellschaft, February 19, 2013), accessed February 15, 2015, http://dipbt.bundestag.de/ dip21/btd/17/123/1712367.pdf; Antrag der Bundesregierung, "Entsendung bewaffneter deutscher Streitkräfte zur Unterstützung der Internationalen Unterstützungsmission in Mali unter afrikanischer Führung (AFISMA) auf Grundlage der Resolution 2085 (2012) des Sicherheitsrates der Vereinten Nationen," Drs. 17/1 12368 (Berlin: Bundesanzeiger Verlagsgesellschaft, February 19, 2013), http://dipbt.bundestag.de/dip21/btd/17/123/1712368.pdf; Deutscher Bundestag, *Stenografischer Bericht: Plenarprotokoll 17/225* (Berlin: Bundesanzeiger Verlagsgesellschaft, February 28, 2013), 27959–71, 27974–79, accessed February 15, 2015, http://dipbt.bundestag.de/ dip21/btp/17/17215.pdf; "Breite Zustimmung für Mali-Einsatz der Bundeswehr," *Deutscher Bundestag*, accessed February 15, 2015, http://www.bundestag.de/dokumente/textarchiv/2013/43167387_kw09_de_mali/211134.

experienced an enormous influx of foreign fighters, and extremist groups entered or emerged throughout the fight.[447] The views, on how to react to the crisis differed considerably. While France's newly inaugurated President Francois Hollande argued in May 2012 that a military intervention could not be excluded, the German federal government, endeavored to close ranks with its Western allies after the abstention from the Libyan vote—especially with the United States—stood skeptical toward such an approach, intending to "prevent a military wildfire spreading across the entire region."[448]

These concerns about a "highly dangerous situation" in the Middle East became magnified, second, with an escalation of the Palestinian-Israeli conflict in October and November 2012.[449] As a result of an increase in rockets attacks by the Hamas throughout the second half of 2012, Israel responded with air strikes against targets in Gaza, causing civilian casualties and evoking the threat of a potential ground

---

[447] Fouad Ajami, *The Syrian Rebellion* (Stanford, CA: Hoover Institution Press, 2012), 10; Jonathan Spyer, "Syrian Regime Strategy and the Syrian Civil War," *Rubincenter*, updated November 14, 2012, http://www.rubincenter.org/2012/11/syrian-regime-strategy-and-the-syrian-civil-war/; Nikolaos Van Dam, "How to Solve or Not to Solve the Syrian Crisis?," *Orient—Deutsche Zeitschrift für Politik und Wirtschaft des Orients Orient* 53, no. 3 (2012): 31–37.

[448] Michael Steiniger, "Military Intervention in Syria? Germany Pushes Back Hard on French Warning," *Christian Science Monitor*, May 31, 2012, http://www.csmonitor.com/World/Europe/2012/0531/Military-intervention-in-Syria-Germany-pushes-back-hard-on-French-warning; Veit Medick and Severin Weiland, "Frankreichs Syrien-Vorstoß: Hollande irritiert Berlin," *Spiegel Online*, May 30, 2012, http://www.spiegel.de/politik/deutschland/deutschland-lehnt-militaerische-intervention-in-syrien-ab-a-835956.html.

[449] Thorsten Jungholt, "'Der ganzen Region droht die Eskalation,'" *Die Welt*, November 19, 2012, http://www.welt.de/politik/ausland/article111289917/Der-ganzen-Region-droht-die-Eskalation.html.

offensive.[450] Third, the most decisive influence on the international power and security framework, however, had the announcement of the United States in January 2012 to "necessarily rebalance" the geographic priorities of its security and defense policy from the Transatlantic "toward the Asia-Pacific region."[451] Notwithstanding an "enduring strategic relevance of the transatlantic partnership," Europe and Germany would have to accept the reality that their "security concerns (may) no longer remain the top U.S. priority," requiring them to better coordinate their policies and boost their capacities required to achieve own security interests.[452]

In the European theater, the Eurozone crisis continued to dominate the political domain with ever more destructive effects that gradually went beyond the familiar confines of the stock markets and central banks to the hearts and minds of the citizens of the EU. After being initially reluctant, Germany stepped into leadership at the end

---

[450] "Krise in Nahost: Merkel macht Hamas für Gewalt verantwortlich," *Spiegel Online*, November 16, 2012, http://www.spiegel.de/politik/ausland/nahost-merkel-macht-hamas-fuer-gewalt-verantwortlich-a-867638.html; "Gaza Rockets Land near Jerusalem as Fears of Ground Offensive Grow," *Guardian*, November 17, 2012, http://www.theguardian.com/world/2012/nov/17/gaza-attacks-israeli-reserve-troops.

[451] Department of Defense, *Sustaining U.S. Global Leadership: Priorities for 21st Century Defense* (Washington, DC: Department of Defense, January 2012), 2, accessed February 2, 2015, http://www.defense.gov/news/Defense_Strategic_Guidance.pdf; Catherine Dale and Pat Towell, *In Brief: Assessing the January 2012 Defense Strategic Guidance (DSG)* (Washington, DC: Congressional Research Service, August 13, 2013), accessed February 21, 2015, http://fas.org/sgp/crs/natsec/R42146.pdf.

[452] Niels Annen and Marius Müller-Henning, *Report from the 1st FES Tiergartenconference 2012—A Fundamental Geostrategic Shift?: Consequences of U.S. Rebalancing towards the Asia-Pacific Region for Regional and Global Security Policy* (Berlin: Friedrich-Ebert-Stiftung, September 2012), 5, accessed March 5, 2015, http://www.fes.de/gpol/pdf/20121218-FES_Tiergarten_report_final.pdf; Karl Kaiser and Manuel Munitz, "Global Europe: Europe, too, Needs an Asian 'Pivot,'" *Europe's World*, updated June 1, 2013, http://europesworld.org/2013/06/01/europe-too-needs-an-asian-pivot/#.VSVGqvmG8XQ.

of 2011 and assumed responsibility for the European crisis management to protect the union's politico-economic stability. The Euro crisis brought about the consolidation of German power in Europe, as the global order of states further adjusted in the twenty-first century. In this process, no one was more surprised than the Germans themselves.

Against the resistance of, and partly at the price of Southern Europe, Germany enforced a comprehensive strategy, combining an austerity policy through fiscal consolidation of the Eurozone (fiscal compact in January 2012) and budgetary ceilings in all Euro member states with a permanent fiscal rescue mechanism (European Financial Stability Facility) and banking regulations. Such policy, itself, arose from strictures of domestic politics as well as political culture, but was fated also to have a variety of unintended results in the realm of power. As a result, although widely criticized for its rigorous stance—culminating in South European media attempts to match Merkel's Germany with the Huns of yore or even with the Nazis[453]—until end of 2012, Germany came out of the crisis as the uncontested European leader, strong economically and dominating the narrative for a crisis resolution.[454] Such power, however, for the reasons examined in this study was not without its contradictions, which were again to be put to the test in Africa.

---

[453] Jakob Augstein, "The Return of the Ugly Germans: Merkel Is Leading the Country into Isolation," *Spiegel Online*, December 8, 2011, http://www.spiegel.de/international/europe/the-return-of-the-ugly-germans-merkel-is-leading-the-country-into-isolation-a-802591.html; "Per la Bild la satira non esiste: 'Alla Merkel attacco malign,'" *Libero*, August 8, 2011, http://www.liberoquotidiano.it/news/esteri/799538/Per-la-Bild-la-satira-non.html; Clemens Wergin, "Der Zorn der Südländer auf Deutschland," *Die Welt*, August 20, 2012, http://www.welt.de/debatte/article108701761/Der-Zorn-der-Suedlaender-auf-Deutschland.html; Kundnani, "Germany as a Geo-Economic Power," 30–31.

[454] Ulrike Guérot, "Merkel's European and Foreign Policy Legacy on the Eve of the German Elections: European Hegemon or Global Player?," *Polish Quarterly of International Affairs*, no. 2 (2013): 21–22.

The international engagement of the Bundeswehr and its context also had changed in the past two years from Libya. Established at the Afghanistan Conference in Bonn, December 2011, and formally decided on the NATO Summit in Chicago, May 2012, the international community agreed upon the full transition of the security responsibility toward Afghan authorities by the end of 2014, hereby, terminating the Afghan ISAF mission.[455] Alongside other partners, Germany, after ending its largest, most contested, and costly international military engagement in the history of the FRG, pledged that Afghanistan would not be abandoned and promised a "clear and reliable commitment to a long-term engagement for the next decade beyond 2014."[456]

Since its fiercely debated nonparticipation in the NATO operation in Libya, Germany also had become engaged in new international military missions. Beside contributions to an UN peacekeeping mission in South Sudan (UNMISS, since July 2011), required through the founding of an independent South Sudan state, and an EU-capacity building mission to fight piracy off the coast of Somalia (EUCAP

---

[455] *Conference Conclusions—Afghanistan and the International Community: From Transition to the Transformation Decade* (Bonn: The International Afghanistan Conference, December 5, 2012), 3, accessed February 25, 2015,
http://eeas.europa.eu/afghanistan/docs/2011_11_conclusions_bonn_en.pdf;
NATO, *Chicago Summit Declaration Issued by the Heads of State and Government Participating in the Meeting of the North Atlantic Council in Chicago on 20 May 2012* (Brussels: NATO, 2012), updated August 1, 2012,
http://www.nato.int/cps/en/natolive/official_texts_87593.htm.

[456] Guido Westerwelle, *Rede des Bundesministers des Auswärtigen, Dr. Guido Westerwelle, MdB, Afghanistan-Konferenz Eröffnung, am 05. Dezember 2011, in Bonn*, accessed February 26, 2015, http://www.auswaertiges-amt.de/cae/servlet/contentblob/602938/publicationFile/162593/Germany.pdf; Angela Merkel, *Rede von Bundeskanzlerin Angela Merkel anlässlich der Eröffnung der Internationalen Afghanistan-Konferenz, am 05. Dezember 2011, in Bonn*, accessed February 26, 2015, http://www.bundesregierung.de/ContentArchiv/DE/Archiv17/Reden/2011/12/2011-12-05-merkel-afgh-konf.html.

Nestor, since August 2012),[457] Germany deployed, based on Turkey's request and a NAC decision, several Patriot air-defense systems and some 300 Bundeswehr soldiers to the country, helping to strengthen NATO air defense against potential attacks from Syrian soil (Operation Active Fence, since December 2012).[458]

Finally, domestic evolutions informed Germany's decision-making process. Between 2011 and 2012, Germany issued four new strategic documents that underlined Germany's unchanged foreign and security policy principles, such as its commitment to multilateralism and its concept of comprehensive approach, its evolving conception of its international role in the world of power, and its stance toward the African continent. These documents included the new *Defense Policy Guidelines* (May 2011); the "Concept of the Federal Government for Africa"[459] (June 2011)—the first integrated Africa policy document of the Federal Republic;[460] the governmental concept "Shaping

---

[457] Antrag der Bundesregierung, "Beteiligung bewaffneter deutscher Streitkräfte an der von den Vereinten Nationen geführten Friedensmission in Südsudan," Drs.17/6449 (Berlin: Bundesanzeiger Verlagsgesellschaft, July 6, 2011), accessed February 26, 2015, http://dipbt.bundestag.de/doc/btd/17/064/1706449.pdf. For the vote of the German parliament, see Deutscher Bundestag, *Stenografischer Bericht: Plenarprotokoll 17/121* (Berlin: Bundesanzeiger Verlagsgesellschaft, July 8, 2011), 14313–15, accessed February 26, 2015, http://dipbt.bundestag.de/dip21/btp/17/17121.pdf#P.14290.

[458] Antrag der Bundesregierung, "Entsendung bewaffneter deutscher Streitkräfte zur Verstärkung der integrierten Luftverteidigung der NATO auf Ersuchen der Türkei und auf Grundlage des Rechts auf kollektive Selbstverteidigung Artikel 51 der Charta der Vereinten Nationen sowie des Beschlusses des Nordatlantikrates vom 4. Dezember 2012)," Drs. 17/11783 (Berlin: Bundesanzeiger Verlagsgesellschaft, December 6, 2012), accessed February 26, 2015, http://dip21.bundestag.de/dip21/btd/17/117/1711783.pdf. For the vote of the German parliament, see Deutscher Bundestag, *Stenografischer Bericht: Plenarprotokoll 17/215* (Berlin: Bundesanzeiger Verlagsgesellschaft, December 12, 2012), 26565–67, accessed February 26, 2015, http://dipbt.bundestag.de/dip21/ btp/17/17215.pdf.

[459] Bundesregierung, *Deutschland und Afrika*.

[460] Ulf Engel, "The G8 and Germany's Africa Policy: A Case of Hegemonic Mainstreaming," *Global Governance* 18, no. 4 (October-December 2012): 474.

Globalization—Extending Partnerships—Sharing Responsibility"[461] (February 2012) that primarily defined Germany's new global order policy and relation to emerging "shaping powers;" and the "Interagency Guidelines for a Coherent Policy of the Federal Government toward Fragile States"[462] (September 2012). Moreover, already having suspended conscription after 45 years as of July 2011, Germany continues to significantly reform the Bundeswehr.

As direct consequences of discrepancies between Germany's level of ambition and actual available forces for international missions as well as the Eurozone crisis–related reductions of the defense budget, the federal government decided to reduce the size of the Bundeswehr down to 185,000 soldiers and restructure the entire organization.[463] Finally, German political parties faced parliamentary elections in September 2013, an event that particularly gained external attention, speculating about continuity or shifts in Germany's future stance toward the Eurozone crisis.[464]

---

[461] Bundesregierung, *Globalisierung gestalten*.

[462] Auswärtiges Amt, Bundesministerium der Verteidigung, and Bundesministerium für wirtschaftliche Zusammenarbeit, *Für eine kohärente Politik der Bundesregierung gegenüber fragilen Staaten: Ressortübergreifende Leitlinien* (Berlin: BMZ, September 2012), 4, accessed March 4, 2015,
http://www.auswaertiges-amt.de/cae/servlet/contentblob/626452/publication File/171897/120919_Leitlinien_Fragile_Staaten.pdf.

[463] Von Krause, Die Bundeswehr als Instrument deutscher Außenpolitik, 326–37; Thomas De Maizière, Unser Auftrag ist Ausgangspunkt und Ziel der Neuausrichtung: Rede des Bundesministers der Verteidigung, Dr. Thomas de Maizière, anlässlich der Bundeswehrtagung am Montag, 22. Oktober 2012, in Strausberg (Berlin: Federal Ministry of Defence, 2012), 38.

[464] Ryszarda Formuszewicz, "Waiting for Germany's European Choices," *Polish Quarterly of International Affairs*, no. 2 (2013): 5–10.

B. Evolution of the International Environment and Germany's Decision-Making-Process

In the face of a continuously deteriorating situation in Sub-Saharan Africa, the international community indeed recognized the potential threat emanating from a loss of state control over vast areas in Northern Mali. The leaders of the powers, however, only slowly developed a position that considered an active external interference into the crisis, supporting the Malian state in reestablishing constitutional order, regaining territorial control, and building capacities. This particularly restrained the Western stance and set the context for Germany's decision-making process. Consequently, while willing to assume Germany's international responsibility and acknowledging the potential impacts of the Malian crisis on European, and hence, German security, the federal government exercised restraint and caution in deciding *whether* and *how* German troops would operate in Mali. Early on, the Berlin government refused any participation of German soldiers in combat operations in the West African country; emphasized the primary responsibility of regional organizations to respond to the crisis; and exclusively considered noncombat alternatives, such as training, medical help, and logistic support, as suitable policy options.

At the same time, Germany's political elite continued to focus on a necessary political process to both address the underlying root causes of the conflict and help Mali to reestablish its constitutional order.[465] In contrast to its apparently well defined (restrained) stance, the federal government did not encourage a political debate about Germany's strategic approach to the crisis, which would incorporate and

---

[465] See speech by Foreign Minister Westerwelle in the German parliament on February 20, 2013; Federal Foreign Office, "Rede von Außenminister Westerwelle im Deutschen Bundestag zum Mali-Einsatz der Bundeswehr, 20. Februar 2013," *Auswaertiges Amt*, updated February 28, 2013, http://www.auswaertiges-amt.de/sid_6BF78E917193A5DC0ABED7A7814B221A/DE/Infoservice/Presse/Reden/2013/130220-BM-BT-Mali-Rede.html?nn=352220.

coordinate a broader set of policy tools according to Germany's "networked security" philosophy. Likewise, the actual German contributions to EUTM Mali and AFISMA also remained vague for a long time. Germany's challenges concerning the decisions for participation in international military engagements in Mali eventually culminated with the onset of Operation Serval at the beginning of 2013. France's actions magnified the permanent tensions within Germany's foreign and security policy, dragging the federal government between external expectations, its own aspirations, and internal constraints.

1. Coup d'état, Deteriorating Security Situation, and Slowly Evolving International Response

Although the violent crisis in Northern Mali had broken out already at the beginning of 2012, the country gained considerable international, and Germany's, attention just with the military coup d'état in Bamako between March 21 and 22, forcing then-President Touré out of office. In concert with the international community, Germany condemned the "illegitimate to take-over of power," claiming that the "constitutional rule and order must be re-installed immediately," and suspended its bilateral aid and support.[466] The unstable political situation in Mali's capital accelerated the offensive of the rebel and jihadist groups, allowing them to take over large swathes of Mali's north within two weeks after the coup, culminating in the MNLA's declara-

---

[466] "Putschisten übernehmen Macht in Mali," *Zeit Online*, March 22, 2012, http://pdf.zeit.de/politik/ausland/2012-03/mali-putsch.pdf; "Security Council Press Statement on Mali," UN Security Council press release SC/10590-AFR/2359, *United Nations*, updated March 22, 2012, http://www.un.org/press/en/2012/sc10590.doc.htm; Antwort der Bundesregierung auf die Kleine Anfrage der Abgeordneten Jan van Aken, Niema Movassat, Christine Buchholz, weiterer Abgeordneter und der Fraktion DIE LINKE, "Aktuelle Situation in Mali und die geplante EU-Ausbildungsmission malischer Streitkräfte," Drs.17/11542 (Berlin: Bundesanzeiger Verlagsgesellschaft, November 20, 2012) 4, accessed March 2, 2015, http://dip21.bundestag.de/ dip21/btd/17/115/1711542.pdf; Schmid, *Die Mali-Intervention*, 41.

tion of an independent Azawad on April 6, 2012.[467] Despite serious concerns about the "rapidly deteriorating humanitarian situation"[468] as well as the implications of the tense security and political situation in Mali, the international community left the initial response to crisis to the African states and organizations.

Consequently, it was the West African economic organization ECOWAS that, after an unanswered 72 hour ultimatum, imposed severe financial and economic sanctions against Mali at the beginning of April. Cut off from all external sources, the military junta around Captain Sanogo on April 6 signed a framework agreement for the restoration of constitutional order in Mali, stepped down, and handed over the power to a transitional government under the lead of interim president Traoré, the then-President of the Malian Parliament.[469] While ECOWAS had already started with initial planning for a potential deployment of its troops toward Mali, Western countries, such as

---

[467] Paige McClanahan, "Mali's Humanitarian Crisis May Worsen if Intervention Calls Heeded, UN Warned," *Guardian*, September 27, 2012, http://www.theguardian.com/global-development/2012/sep/27/mali-humanitarian-crisis-worsen-intervention-un; Schmid, *Die Mali-Intervention*, 31, 42; Pabst, "Staatliche Schwäche begünstigt Dschihadisten," 6.

[468] "Security Council Press Statement on Mali," UN Security Council press release, SC/10603-AFR/2370, on the United Nations website, updated April 10, 2012, http://www.un.org/press/en/2012/sc10603.doc.htm.

[469] "ECOWAS Imposes Sanctions on Mali," *Voice of America*, April 1, 2012, http://www.voanews.com/content/west-african-leaders-impose-sanctions-on-mali-145801255/180314.html; "West African ECOWAS Leaders Impose Mali Sanctions," *BBC News*, April 3, 2012, http://www.bbc.com/news/world-africa-17591322; AFP, "West African Leaders Lift All Sanctions Imposed on Mali," *Al Arabia News*, updated April 8, 2012, http://english.alarabiya.net/articles/2012/04/08/206220.html; "Security Council Press Statement on Mali," April 10, 2012; Schmid, *Die Mali-Intervention*, 45–46.

France and Germany, refused any military engagement in the country, calling for "waiving violence"[470] and a "political solution."[471]

The worsening situation in Mali, however, gradually changed the international perception. By mid-2012, Islamist groups had expelled MNLA from nearly all major cities in northern Mali and imposed a strict Sharia law. At the same time, the political situation in South Mali had deteriorated, and the humanitarian crisis across the country had also deepened. Hundreds of thousands of people fled from the fights and the brutality of the jihadist rule in the North, their sensitive situation worsened by a countrywide food shortage.[472] As a consequence of the continuously deteriorating situation in Mali, ECOWAS and the AU jointly requested a mandate of the UNSC, authorizing "the deployment of an ECOWAS stabilization force in order to ensure the protection of Malian State institutions and assist in upholding the territorial integrity of Mali and in combating terrorism."[473]

---

[470] "Außenminister Westerwelle verurteilt Gewalt gegen Zivilbevölkerung in Mali," *Artikel-Presse*, April 4, 2012, http://www.artikel-presse.de/ausenminister-westerwelle-verurteilt-gewalt-gegen-zivilbevolkerung-in-mali.html.

[471] French Foreign Minister Alain Juppé declared on April 5, 2012 that the deployment of French troops to Mali would be "totally unrealistic." Instead, a "political solution" is required. Le Monde, AFP, and Reuters, "Mali: Réunion de la Cédéao pour envisager une intervention," *Le Monde Afrique*, April 5, 2012, http://www.lemonde.fr/afrique/article/2012/04/05/mali-reunion-de-la-cedeao-pour-envisager-une-intervention_1681185_3212.html#9QevkTdt4hUh5Wau.99; Schmid, *Die Mali-Intervention*, 44.

[472] Simone Haysom, "Security and Humanitarian Crisis in Mali: The Role of Regional Organizations," *HPG Working Paper* (London: Humanitarian Policy Group, March 2014), 2, 6, accessed March 4, 2015, http://www.odi.org/sites/odi.org.uk/files/odi-assets/publications-opinion-files/8829.pdf; Schmid, *Die Mali-Intervention*, 49–51.

[473] "Security Council Press Statement on Mali," UN Security Council press release SC/10676-AFR/2407, on the United Nations website, updated June 18, 2012, http://www.un.org/press/en/2012/sc10676.doc.htm; Schmid, *Die Mali-Intervention*, 47; Pabst, "Staatliche Schwäche begünstigt Dschihadisten," 6.

In response, the UNSC, including Germany as nonpermanent member, issued the French-drafted Resolution 2056 on July 5, which officially condemned the coup d'état in March and endorsed the (West) African political efforts to support the restoration of state authority throughout Mali, but stopped short of backing the military intervention until further details had been provided.[474]

2. France's Push, the International Struggle toward a Military Engagement, and Germany's Quest for Participation

Around the same time, France's stance concerning the response toward the Malian crisis started to shift. In mid-July 2012, Foreign Minister Juppé argued that "at one moment or another there will probably be the use of force (in northern Mali)," noting that such an intervention "would be African-led but supported by international forces." France could not lead a military intervention because "its colonial past in the country would complicate matters."[475]

The direct appeal of Mali's interim president both to ECOWAS and to the UN in September 2012, asking for troops and for authorizing a military intervention against the jihadist groups, facilitated the international efforts in support of a military response to the destabi-

---

[474] UN Security Council, *UNSC Resolution 2056* (New York: July 5, 2012), 3–4, accessed March 2, 2015, http://www.un.org/en/ga/search/view_doc.asp?symbol=S/RES/2056(2012); McClanahan, "Mali's Humanitarian Crisis"; Louis Charbonneau, "UN Ready to Consider ECOWAS Request to Back Mali Force," *Reuters*, June 19, 2012, http://in.reuters.com/article/2012/06/18/africa-mali-un-idINL1E8HI84X20120618.

[475] John Irish and David Lewis, "Military Intervention in Mali 'Probable': French Foreign Minister," Reuters, July 12, 2012, http://www.reuters.com/article/2012/07/12/us-france-mali-idUSBRE86B0XS20120712.

lizing situation and the spread of terrorism in northern Mali.[476] Considering the crisis in Mali as "a risk for the international community as a whole," it was, however, France's new president, Francois Hollande, who urged an immediate response as a "dictate of the moment."[477] During a high-level UN meeting on the Sahel on September 26, he called the UNSC to approve a resolution for an African military intervention in Mali "as quickly as possible."[478] Considering Mali as a "powder keg that the international community cannot afford to ignore,"[479] U.S. Secretary of State Hillary Clinton echoed Hollande's critical assessment of the crisis in Mali. Yet, even if "the chaos and violence in Mali ... (did) threaten to undermine the stability of the entire region," she called for a more cautious approach, favoring a

---

[476] Mathieu Bonkoungou, Bate Felix, and Jackie Frank, "Mali Requests Military Assistance to Free North: France." *Reuters*, September 4, 2012, http://www.reuters.com/article/2012/09/05/us-mali-ecowas-troops-idUSBRE88403120120905; Ashley S. Boyle, *Mali: A Timeline and Factsheet*, (Washington, DC: American Security Project, November 2012), 3, accessed March 4, 2015, http://americansecurityproject.org/ASP%20Reports/Ref%200099%20-%20Mali%20-%20timeline%20and%20factsheet.pdf; "Mali bittet UN um Militäreinsatz gegen Islamisten," *Die Welt*, September 25, 2012, http://www.welt.de/politik/ausland/article109438915/Mali-bittet-UN-um-Militaereinsatz-gegen-Islamisten.html; Anne Gearan, "UN Security Council Will Be Asked to Approve Force to Confront Al-Qaeda in Mali," *Washington Post*, October 3, 2012, http://www.washingtonpost.com/world/national-security/un-security-council-will-be-asked-to-approve-force-to-confront-al-qaeda-in-mali/2012/10/03/3836405e-0d6b-11e2-a310-2363842b7057_story.html.

[477] Francois Hollande, S*peech by M. Francois Hollande, President of the Republic at the High-Level Meeting on Sahel, September 26, 2012* (New York: Embassy of France in Washington DC, September 27, 2012), http://www.ambafrance-us.org/spip.php?article3911; Ron Depasquale, "France's Hollande Urges Intervention in Mali to Root Out Islamists," *The Star*, September 26, 2012, http://www.thestar.com/news/world/2012/09/26/frances_hollande_urges_intervention_in_mali_to_root_out_islamists.html.

[478] Hollande, *Speech by M. Francois Hollande*.

[479] "Clinton at UN Secretary General Meeting on Sahel," *U.S. Department of State*, updated September 26, 2012, http://iipdigital.usembassy.gov/st/english/texttrans/2012/09/20120926136634.html#axzz3Wwc7rKI0.

political solution, the preparation for elections, and the training of Malian forces.[480]

On October 12, the UNSC passed at France's urging Resolution 2071, asking the African organizations and other interested parties within 45 days to provide detailed plans for an international military intervention according to Chapter VII of the UN Charter.[481] The adaptation of the resolution provoked the group Mouvement pour l'Unicité et le Jihad en Afrique de l'Ouest (MUJAO) to threaten France with the murder of four hostages and attacks on her citizens in West Africa.[482]

On October 15, in response to the UNSC resolution, a letter from Mali's interim president, and a request by ECOWAS, the Foreign Affairs Council (FAC) of the EU decided to support the international efforts by starting the "planning of a possible CSDP military operation," relating to the "reorganization and training of the Malian defense forces."[483] Other military options, such as a direct combat support, however, were not further pursued.[484] While France and the

---

[480] "Clinton at UN Secretary General Meeting on Sahel."

[481] UN Security Council, *UNSC Resolution 2071* (New York: October 12, 2012), 3–4, accessed March 2, 2015, http://www.un.org/ga/search/view_doc.asp?symbol=S/RES/2071(2012); Boyle, *Mali*, 3.

[482] "Al Qaida–Linked Islamists in Mali Threaten French Citizens after UN Move," *Guardian*, October 13, 2012, http://www.theguardian.com/world/2012/oct/13/al-qaida-islamists-mali-french-citizens-un.

[483] Council of the European Union, *Press Release 3191st Council Meeting Foreign Affairs* (Brussels: Council of the European Union Press Office, October 15, 2012), 9, accessed March 5, 2015, http://www.consilium.europa.eu/uedocs/cms_data/docs/pressdata/EN/foraff/132896.pdf.

[484] There are no further sources available, explaining to what extent the EU considered plans for accompanying Malian troops in battle, as claimed by one Western diplomat. See "European Union Drawing Up Plans for Military Intervention in Mali," *London Evening Post*, October 16, 2012, http://www.thelondoneveningpost.com/european-union-drawing-up-plans-for-military-intervention-in-mali/.

United States had officially ruled out any direct military intervention in Mali, but offered support of an African-led operation, both states sought to lobby a military intervention in northern Mali, as questions about ECOWAS-capabilities to ensure sufficient forces for a military intervention arose.[485]

Germany, on the other hand, needed until the end of October to announce a tentative position concerning its engagement in an international response to the crisis in Mali. In a speech at a convention of civilian and military top staff personnel of the Bundeswehr near Berlin on October 22, Federal Chancellor Merkel announced Germany's general willingness to participate in a "training and support mission for Mali," however, only if the "preconditions are clarified and in place."[486] Foreign Minister Westerwelle immediately refused the deployment of German combat troops and arms deliveries to the country. Instead, Germany would see Africa's primary responsibility in responding to the crisis and could offer logistic, technical, and financial support.[487] While echoing Westerwelle's military intervention-averse stance, Defense Minister de Maizière made clear that the federal government was still "evaluating potential task" of German soldiers in a training mission in Mali and whether such a contribution

---

[485] Anne Gearan, "U.S. Pushes Algeria to Support Military Intervention in Mali," *Washington Post*, October 29, 2012, http://www.washingtonpost.com/world/us-pushes-algeria-to-support-military-intervention-in-mali/2012/10/29/fee8df44-21a3-11e2-92f8-7f9c4daf276a_story.html; Pabst, "Staatliche Schwäche begünstigt Dschihadisten," 11.
[486] Merkel, *Rede von Bundeskanzlerin Angela Merkel anlässlich der Tagung des zivilen und militärischen Spitzenpersonals der Bundeswehr.*
[487] "Mali-Mission."

would need the approval of the German Bundestag.[488] Notwithstanding Germany's overall cautious attitude, during a visit to Mali on November 1, Foreign Minister Westerwelle underlined the "significance of Mali's stability for Europe's security," pledging "German solidarity" and to increase Germany's humanitarian support.[489]

Between November and December 2012, the African and European responses toward Mali assumed shape. On November 13, following a series of meetings between African, European, and UN military planners as well as in response to the tasks set by UNSC Resolution 2071, the AU backed an ECOWAS plan to deploy 3,300 ground forces to Mali. These forces should support the Malian state in expelling armed Islamist and terrorist groups from the North and in reestablishing territorial integrity and stability throughout the country.[490] One week later, on November 19, the EU foreign and defense ministers met in Brussels to discuss EU's High Representative (HR) Catherine Ashton's draft of a crisis management concept for a possible

---

[488] "De Maizière erwägt Einsatz ohne Bundestagsmandat," *Die Welt*, November 3, 2012, http://www.welt.de/politik/deutschland/article110587708/De-Maiziere-erwaegt-Einsatz-ohne-Bundestagsmandat.html; "De Maizière erwägt Einsatz in Mali," *Spiegel Online*, November 3, 2012, http://www.spiegel.de/politik/deutschland/verteidigungsminister-de-maiziere-erwaegt-bundeswehr-einsatz-in-mali-a-865123.html.

[489] "Westerwelle Pledges German Solidarity With Mali," *Deutsche Welle*, November 1, 2012, http://www.dw.de/westerwelle-pledges-german-solidarity-with-mali/a-16348029.

[490] Boyle, Mali, 3–4; Tiemoko Diallo, "Military Planners Prepare for War in Mali," Reuters, November 6, 2012, http://www.reuters.com/article/2012/11/06/us-mali-crisis-idUSBRE8A50UO20121106; "West Africa Bloc ECOWAS Agrees to Deploy Troops to Mali," *BBC News*, November 11, 2012, http://www.bbc.com/news/world-africa-20292797; "Mali Crisis: African Union Backs Plan to Deploy Troops," *BBC News*, November 13, 2012, http://www.bbc.com/news/world-africa-20315423.

CSDP operation for reorganizing and training the Malian Armed Forces.[491]

Following this meeting, Defense Minister de Maizière reemphasized Germany's position that the "crystal clear" distinction between the envisioned combat operation of the Africans and the EU training mission, constitute a "precondition for a German participation to such a mission."[492] With the approval of the Crisis Management Concept (CMC) for a CSDP military mission to provide military training and advice to the Malian Armed Forces through the FAC on December 10, 2012, the EU-internal preconditions for a European engagement in Mali were established, allowing for the start of detailed planning and negotiations for the national contributions to the mission.[493] The EU efforts got additional backing with a letter from Mali's interim president toward the EU's HR Ashton on December 24, directly asking for the help of the EUTM Mali for his country.[494]

---

[491] Council of the European Union, *Press Release 3199th Council Meeting Foreign Affairs* (Brussels: Council of the European Union Press Office, November 19, 2012), 9–11, accessed March 5, 2015, http://www.consilium.europa.eu/uedocs/cms_data/docs/pressdata/en/foraff/133604.pdf.

[492] Federal Ministry of Defense, "EU berät über Militäreinsatz in Mali," *BMVg*, updated November 21, 2012, http://www.bmvg.de/portal/a/bmvg/!ut/p/c4/NYtNC8IwEET_UTYRoerNUhBBL1603tI0pKv5YrutF3-8ycEZeId5DDyhNOoVnWZMUXt4QG_wMHzEEFYnXmmhsooZzWRpsshzTh4Z33Cv19EKk6LlSraRsdCR5kQiJ2JfzUJUjMAReqm6Vir5j_ruN83petk12-7c3iCHcPwByVzcGQ!!/; Jungholt, "Der ganzen Region droht die Eskalation."'

[493] Council of the European Union, *Council Conclusions on Mali, 3209th Foreign Affairs Council Meeting* (Brussels: Council of the European Union Press Office, December 10, 2012), accessed March 6, 2015, http://www.consilium.europa.eu/uedocs/cms_data/docs/pressdata/EN/foraff/134144.pdf.

[494] See Council of the European Union, "Council Decision 2013/34/CFSP of 17 January 2013 on a European Union Military Mission to Contribute to the Training of the Malian Armed Forces (EUTM Mali)," *Official Journal of the European Union* 14 (January 18, 2013): 19, accessed March 6, 2015, http://eur-lex.europa.eu/LexUriServ/LexUriServ.do?uri=OJ:L:2013:014:0019:0021:EN:PDF.

In parallel, France further pushed toward the international community to approve a quick start of a military intervention in Mali. Defense Minister Le Drian claimed that in Mali "our own security [would be] at stake" and if "we do not move swiftly, then there will gradually emerge a terrorist state."[495] Consequently, France, with support of the United States, the United Kingdom, Morocco, and Togo, drafted UNSC Resolution 2085, which the UNSC finally passed on December 20, 2012.[496] The German UN ambassador Wittig described the decision as an "important step" that would complement the efforts for a political solution of the crisis.[497] The resolution authorized the African-Led International Support Mission in Mali (AFISMA)[498] for an initial period for one year to take "all necessary measures" to support the Malian authorities in regaining territorial control and in "reducing the threat posed by terrorist organizations."[499]

Yet, while the resolution also urged to finalize a political roadmap and to call for elections before April 2013, it did not set a start of the intervention.[500] The restraint might have resulted from the ongoing skepticism about the plans and capacities of the ECOWAS to effectively implement and sustain the envisioned combat mission in north-

---

[495] "Kampf gegen Islamisten: Sicherheitsrat genehmigt Militäreinsatz in Mali," *Spiegel Online*, December 20, 2012, http://www.spiegel.de/politik/ausland/uno-sicherheitsrat-genehmigt-militaereinsatz-in-mali-gegen-islamisten-a-874218.html.

[496] UN Security Council, *UNSC Resolution 2085*.

[497] "Kampf gegen Islamisten."

[498] In French: *Mission international de soutien au Mali sous conduite africaine (MISMA)*.

[499] UN Security Council, *UNSC Resolution 2085*, 4.

[500] UN Security Council, *UNSC Resolution 2085*, 3–4.

ern Mali.⁵⁰¹ Accordingly, military experts assumed that because of the required preparation time and climate conditions, the mission could not start earlier than autumn 2013, almost nine months after the UNSC decision.⁵⁰²

3. Operation Serval and Germany's Ambivalent Position to Support

With the beginning of 2013, the security situation in Mali changed, urging France to respond militarily, accelerating the start of the AFISMA operation, and leaving Germany struggling to find a coherent answer to the shifting dynamics. Until the end of 2012, jihadist and terrorist groups, such as Ansar al-Dine, MUJAO, and AQIM, had constrained their actions on the vast northern territory of the country. After retreating from peace talks and revoking a truce, AQIM and MUJAO-reinforced Ansar al-Dine troops overstepped the fictive demarcation line and captured the small town of Konna from the Malian Armed Forces on January 10, 2013.⁵⁰³ In a response to an urgent call by Mali's interim president directly to Paris on the same day, France's President Hollande launched Operation Serval on January 11, arguing that "the very existence of the Malian state" is at

---

⁵⁰¹ According to Pabst, the UNSC should have repeatedly postponed the authorization of the AFISMA mission because of the insufficient operational plans. See Pabst, "Staatliche Schwäche begünstigt Dschihadisten," 11. Beginning January 2013, AU Chairman Thomas Boni Yayi called for NATO troops in support of the African mission. See "NATO Forces Needed in Mali, Says AU's Thomas Boni Yayi," *BBC News*, January 9, 2013, http://www.bbc.com/news/world-africa-20957063.

⁵⁰² Lacher and Tull, "Mali: Jenseits von Terrorismusbekämpfung," 5; Pabst, "Staatliche Schwäche begünstigt Dschihadisten," 10; "Kampf gegen Islamisten."

⁵⁰³ Meno, "The French Mess in Mali and Libya"; Tramond and Seigneu, "Operation Serval," 78–79.

stake.[504] The lacking readiness of the ECOWAS-forces to immediately answer to the crisis, the potential threat for thousands of French citizens in South Mali, and the threat that a later intervention could be decisively hampered through the seizure of the Sévaré airport near Konna by the jihadists, might have triggered the shift in France's stance to avoid a direct, unilateral engagement in its former colony.[505]

While the EU pledged to accelerate its planning and preparation process for the deployment of the EUTM to Mali[506] as well as the announcement from the United States and the United Kingdom of "unspecific support" for the French intervention apart from "boots on the ground,"[507] Germany remained cautious and restrained toward its potential engagement in Mali within the first days after France's intervention. On one hand, Defense Minister de Maizière publicly stated that the immediate action of France "was decisive, correct and deserves … (Germany's) support."[508] At the same time, however, he and Foreign Minister Westerwelle made clear that "the deployment of

---

[504] Edward Cody, "France's Hollande Sends Troops to Mali," *Washington Post*, January 11, 2013, http://www.washingtonpost.com/world/africa/frances-hollande-sends-troops-to-mali/2013/01/11/21be77ae-5c0f-11e2-9fa9-5fbdc9530eb9_story.html.

[505] "Africa: Mali," Security Council Report, January 31, 2013, http://www.securitycouncilreport.org/monthly-forecast/2013-02/mali_4.php; Schmid, *Die Mali-Intervention*, 74–75; Shurkin, *France's War in Mali*, 9; Cody, "France's Hollande Sends Troops to Mali."

[506] "Statement by EU High Representative Catherine Ashton on the Situation in Mali," *EEAS*, January 11, 2013, accessed March 7, 2015, http://www.consilium.europa.eu/uedocs/cms_Data/docs/pressdata/EN/foraff/134646.pdf.

[507] Simon Tisdall, "France's Lonely Intervention in Mali," *Guardian*, January 14, 2013, http://www.theguardian.com/commentisfree/2013/jan/14/france-lonely-intervention-mali.

[508] Bernd Gräßler, "Germany Backs French Intervention in Mali," *Deutsche Welle*, January 14, 2013, http://www.dw.de/germany-backs-french-intervention-in-mali/a-16520834; Hawley, "The World from Berlin."

German combat troops is not up for debate."[509] Instead, without a specified French request, the German cabinet had decided to start talks with France to clarify opportunities to support France's military engagement "short of sending combat troops, for example in the political, logistics, humanitarian, and medical fields."[510]

Yet Defense Minister de Maizière immediately lowered the expectations, emphasizing that such support would raise "complex political, legal, and technical questions."[511] On the other hand, the federal government stressed that the decision for a German contribution to EUTM Mali had not been made. Given the ongoing planning process in Brussels, the decision "whether and how Germany will participate, will be … (made) when the plans are complete" and "when a political consensus about the engagement of the international community in Mali" had been found.[512]

While intensifying its troop deployment to Mali, France sent a direct request for help to Germany on January 15, causing a political debate about the appropriateness of Germany's response and raising questions in Paris about Berlin's solidarity. In a joint statement after the celebrations of the 50th anniversary of the Elysée Treaty between Germany and France on January 16, Defense Minister de Maizière

---

[509] Thomas de Maizière, "Mali durch Ausbildungsmission nachhaltig stabilisieren," interview by Dirk-Oliver Heckmann, Deutschlandfunk, January 14, 2013, http://www.deutschlandfunk.de/de-maiziere-mali-durch-ausbildungsmission-nachhaltig.694.de.html?dram:article_id=234115; Tisdall, "France's Lonely Intervention in Mali."

[510] "Germany Considers Options to Aid Mali Intervention," *Deutsche Welle*, January 14, 2013, http://www.dw.de/germany-considers-options-to-aid-mali-intervention/a-16520168-.

[511] De Maizière, "Mali durch Ausbildungsmission nachhaltig stabilisieren."

[512] "Berlin sichert Paris Unterstützung zu," *Deutsche Welle*, January 14, 2013, http://www.dw.de/berlin-sichert-paris-unterst%C3%BCtzung-zu/a-16519121; "Operation Serval: SPD fordert deutsche Beteiligung an Mali-Einsatz," *Die Welt*, January 14, 2013, http://www.welt.de/politik/ausland/article112743916/SPD-fordert-deutsche-Beteiligung-an-Mali-Einsatz.html.

and Foreign Minister Westerwelle announced that their country would provide two airplanes to transport the 3,300 activated ECOWAS troops to Bamako. Germany, hence, would not directly support the French intervention in Mali. It could, however, immediately respond because the logistical support would not require the approval of the Bundestag.[513] While Federal Chancellor Merkel defended the decision with reference to Germany's other international military commitments,[514] the restrained and conditioned help sparked a bipartisan debate, reflecting Germany's politically instable stance toward a military engagement in Mali.

Between mid- and end-January 2013, the international efforts concerning Mali intensified, paralleled by the deployment of German soldiers and equipment in support of AFISMA and ongoing discussion about additional German contributions. After the launch of AFISMA on January 19 and the gradual buildup of its forces in Mali, Nigerian and Chadian troops in particular supported France's efforts in fighting jihadist and terrorist groups, allowing them to expel the groups from Timbuktu and Gao until the end of the month.[515] In an emergency meeting of the EU FAC on January 17—as frequently requested by German Foreign Minister Westerwelle[516]—the EU established the CSDP mission EUTM Mali, creating the legal basis for the mission. The decision by the Council of the European Union not only named the French general François Lecointre as mission commander, but also requested him to accelerate the preparations already in place since December 2012 to ensure the launch of the envisioned

---

[513] Jungholt, "Paris ruft."

[514] Ibid.

[515] Tramond and Seigneu, "Operation Serval," 80–82; Shurkin, *France's War in Mali*, 13–21.

[516] See Thorsten Jungholt and Karsten Kammholz, "Bundesregierung sucht noch eine Strategie für Mali," *Die Welt*, January 15, 2013, http://www.welt.de/politik/deutschland/article112764631/Bundesregierung-sucht-noch-eine-Strategie-fuer-Mali.html.

15-month mission in Mali not later than mid-February.[517] As a consequence of the EU decision, Defense Minister de Maizière announced that federal government would soon submit a request to the Bundestag, asking for approval to contribute to the missions with nearly 30 soldiers to the expected pool of 250 European trainers.[518] In parallel, Germany deployed up to three Transall airplanes and some 75 personnel to Dakar, Senegal, supporting the deployment of AFISMA-forces.[519]

4. From Indirect Support to Decisions on Contribution to EUTM Mali and AFISMA

Framed by developments in the European environment, Germany settled to formal decisions on, and parliamentary approvals for, the participation of armed German soldiers to EUTM Mali and AFISMA until end of February 2013. Following an additional French request at the end of January 2013, the federal government had already announced a potential extension of its Mali-related engagement toward AFISMA, offering the provision of air-refueling capacities for French warplanes. Since such a task would come close the "mission-threshold" as determined by the Federal Court, Defense Minister de Maizière declared to ask the Bundestag for approval, combining the

---

[517] Council of the European Union, "Council Decision 2013/34/CFSP of 17 January 2013"; Council of the European Union, *Council Conclusions on Mali, 3217th Foreign Affairs Council Meeting*; Dicke, "The European Union Training Mission in Mali," 98.

[518] "De Maizière gegen Lammert: CDU zofft sich wegen deutschen Mali-Einsatzes," *Spiegel Online*, January 19, 2013, http://www.spiegel.de/politik/ausland/mali-einsatz-de-maiziere-gegen-lammerts-forderung-a-878517.html.

[519] Johnson, "Bundesregierung beschließt Mali-Einsatz."

request with those for the EUTM Mali.[520] During the Munich Security Conference at the beginning of February, however, a politically strained climate between Paris and Berlin became public. French foreign policy expert François Heisbourg expressed his displeasure about the federal government's continuing stance to only provide two transport airplanes and to refuse a direct support to France. While Foreign Minister Westerwelle evasively pointed to Germany's other international military engagements, such as in Afghanistan, Defense Minister de Maizière tried to calm down the bilateral tensions. He underlined that the German cabinet would soon decide for the EUTM Mali and AFISMA mandates, offering to fill "more or less 40 (EUTM trainer) positions" and to ensure the provision of air-refueling capacities directly to France.[521]

Despite the alleged bilateral tensions and Germany's approach favoring political measures, the international and domestic political setting further pushed Germany to engage in military missions in Mali. With the approval of the mission plan and the rules of engage-

---

[520] "Deutsche Stiefel für die Mission in Mali," *Die Welt*, January 27, 2013, http://www.welt.de/politik/ausland/article113158983/Deutsche-Stiefel-fuer-die-Mission-in-Mali.html; "De Maizière will Mali-Einsatz ausweiten: Mandat für Luftbetankung gesucht," *TAZ*, January 31, 2013, http://www.taz.de/!110120/; Christoph Hickmann and Caroline Ischinger, "Deutschland will Hilfe für Mali-Einsatz ausweiten," *Süddeutsche*, January 31, 2013, http://www.sueddeutsche.de/politik/krisengebiet-in-westafrika-deutschland-will-hilfe-fuer-mali-einsatz-ausweiten-1.1587730.

[521] Thorsten Jungholt, "Deutscher Mali-Beitrag sorgt für Ärger bei Franzosen," *Die Welt*, February 3, 2013, http://www.welt.de/politik/ausland/article113350416/Deutscher-Mali-Beitrag-sorgt-fuer-Aerger-bei-Franzosen.html.

ment for the mission, the EU launched EUTM Mali through a Council decision on February 18 with immediate effect.[522]

One day later, the German cabinet finally decided to participate with up to 330 soldiers to the international engagement in Mali, submitting two 12-month-long mandates for approval by the Bundestag.[523] The first mandate foresaw the deployment of up to 180 German soldiers for EUTM Mali, including some 40 engineer trainers, 40 medical staff, a national support element, and headquarters personnel. At the same time, the mandate forbade German EUTM personnel to participate in training efforts to the benefit of AFISMA, to accompany Malian forces in combat operations (mentoring), or to directly support AFISMA and Malian Armed Forces operations.[524]

The second mandate allowed up to 150 German soldiers to support to AFISMA and French operations in the entire Malian territory by providing air-transport and air-refueling capacities.[525] After a first reading in the Bundestag on February 20 had already showed biparti-

---

[522] Council of the European Union, "Council Decision 2013/87/CFSP of 18 February 2013 on the Launch of a European Union Military Mission to Contribute to the Training of the Malian Armed Forces (EUTM Mali)," *Official Journal of the European Union* L46 (February 18, 2013): 27, accessed March 10, 2015, http://www.defensa.gob.es/Galerias/areasTematicas/misiones/fichero/UE-2013-87-EUTM-Mali.pdf; Council of the European Union, *Council Conclusions on Mali, 3222nd Foreign Affairs Council Meeting.*

[523] "Kabinett beschließt Mali-Einsatz der Bundeswehr," *Zeit Online*, February 19, 2013, http://www.zeit.de/politik/ausland/2013-02/mali-einsatz-bundeswehr-soldaten-mandat; "Regierung will 330 Soldaten nach Mali schicken," *Die Welt*, February 18, 2013, http://www.welt.de/politik/deutschland/article113733174/Regie-rung-will-330-Soldaten-nach-Mali-schicken.html.

[524] Antrag der Bundesregierung, "Entsendung bewaffneter deutscher Streitkräfte zur Beteiligung an der EU-geführten militärischen Ausbildungsmission EUTM Mali."

[525] Antrag der Bundesregierung, "Entsendung bewaffneter deutscher Streitkräfte zur Unterstützung der Internationalen Unterstützungsmission in Mali unter afrikanischer Führung (AFISMA)."

san support for the proposed mandates, with only DIE LINKE announcing its refusal,[526] on February 27 the Bundestag's committee for foreign affairs also gave its recommendation to approve the government's requests.[527] The legal national preconditions for the participation of German soldiers within EUTM Mali and in support of AFISMA were eventually set as the Bundestag simultaneously approved both mandates with broad majorities.[528]

---

[526] "Regierung wirbt um Zustimmung für Mali-Einsatz," *Deutscher Bundestag*, accessed March 11, 2015, http://www.bundestag.de/dokumente/textarchiv/2013/43100677_kw09_sp_mali/211048.

[527] Deutscher Bundestag, "Beschlussempfehlung und Bericht des Auswärtigen Ausschusses (3. Ausschuss) zu dem Antrag der Bundesregierung—Drucksache 17/12367—Entsendung bewaffneter deutscher Streitkräfte zur Beteiligung an der EU-geführten militärischen Ausbildungsmission EUTM Mali auf Grundlage des Ersuchens der Regierung von Mali sowie der Beschlüsse 2013/34/GASP des Rates der Europäischen Union (EU) vom 17. Januar 2013 und vom 18. Februar 2013 in Verbindung mit den Resolutionen 2071 (2012) und 2085 (2012) des Sicherheitsrates der Vereinten Nationen," Drs. 17/12520 (Berlin: Bundesanzeiger Verlagsgesellschaft, February 27, 2013), 1–3, accessed March 11, 2015, http://dipbt.bundestag.de/dip21/btd/17/125/1712520.pdf; Deutscher Bundestag, "Beschlussempfehlung und Bericht des Auswärtigen Ausschusses (3. Ausschuss) zu dem Antrag der Bundesregierung—Drucksache 17/12368—Entsendung bewaffneter deutscher Streitkräfte zur Unterstützung der Internationalen Unterstützungsmission in Mali unter afrikanischer Führung (AFISMA) auf Grundlage der Resolution 2085 (2012) des Sicherheitsrates der Vereinten Nationen," Drs. 17/12522 (Berlin: Bundesanzeiger Verlagsgesellschaft, February 27, 2013), 1–3, accessed January 20, 2015, http://dipbt.bundestag.de/dip21/btd/17/125/1712522.pdf.

[528] "Breite Zustimmung für Mali-Einsatz der Bundeswehr"; "Namentliche Abstimmungen: Bundeswehreinsatz in Mali," *Deutscher Bundestag*, updated February 28, 2013, http://www.bundestag.de/bundestag/plenum/abstimmung/grafik/?id=210.

C. Analysis of Relevance and Interplay of Determinants for the German Decisions for Participation in and Contributions to the Military Missions in Mali

Germany's decision-making process toward the participation in, and the contribution to, military missions in Mali was characterized by an overall risk-minimizing, precarious, restrained,[529] and partly reactive approach concerning the use of the Bundeswehr. All of this resulted, as demonstrated in the following, from multiple impulses and constraints on the external and internal levels, complex contradictions and reinforcements between single factors within and across the different levels, and the challenges for key German stakeholders to mitigate between the ambivalent imperatives.

1. Determinants on the External Level

The external system itself provided an ambivalent context for Germany's decisions for participation in EUTM Mali and contribution to AFISMA. On one hand, aspirations for a power-political reintegration after the backlash from the nonparticipation in Libya, shifts in Germany's global self-image, perceived implications of the Malian crisis on German security, multilateral consensus for a modest military engagement in Mali, and a mission framework that set distinct and limited objectives and tasks for the forces involved, *pulled* the federal government to decide for, and the Bundestag to approve, a participation of German soldiers.

On the other, evolutions in the power and security environment, strategic approaches in the region, an overall hesitant international community, and existing international commitments, disincentivized

---

[529] Katarina Engelberg argues that Germany had proved reluctant to a new EU military involvement in Mali. See Katarina Engelberg, *The EU and Military Operations: A Comparative Analysis* (New York: Routledge, 2014), 172.

Germany from assuming a more active role within the international crisis response and from contributing with "robust" capacities. Within the interlocked three-level framework of German foreign and security policy, the latter factors on the external level, therefore, mutually reinforced Germany's overarching domestically motivated hesitancy and risk-averse stance—politically and publicly—toward the use of military force.

a. Power and Security Environment

The power and security environment affected Germany's decisions for the participation in, and contribution to, the military interventions in Mali considerably. Discrete conditions and evolutions, however, provided ambivalent impulses, simultaneously pulling Germany toward and disincentivizing it from an active (military) engagement within the international crisis response. Important among the pulling factors was Germany's aspiration to compensate for its (power)-political isolation after the abstention in the UNSC vote on Libya as well as its categorical refusal to participate in the subsequent military intervention in the country in 2011. Both the vote and the nonparticipation had not only undermined Germany's credibility as reliable partner, but also had "revealed immediate and long-term political costs" for Germany's status in international affairs and within multilateral institutions.[530]

---

[530] Major and Mölling, *German Defense Policy in 2014*, 7; "Reformulation of Germany's foreign policy towards active military engagements"; Klose and Polenz, "Wahre Werte, falsche Freunde," 22; Steiniger, "Military Intervention in Syria?" Some German policymakers feared that Germany's hope for gaining a permanent seat on the UNSC had been seriously damaged through its behavior amid the international crisis resolution. See Eve Bower, "Germany's Libya Policy Reveals a Nation in Transition," *Deutsche Welle*, September 12, 2011, http://www.dw.de/germanys-libya-policy-reveals-a-nation-in-transition/a-15367751.

In the aftermath of the disputed Libyan decisions, key German stakeholders sought to strengthen Germany's political position. Federal Chancellor Merkel posited in September 2011 that Germany would "know its responsibility in the world" and that its interests and values would even "oblige ... (Germany) to assume responsibility."[531] Federal Chancellor Merkel's remark reflected a stance that she and Defense Minister de Maizière publicly reaffirmed and reemphasized amid the worsening security situation in Mali in the autumn of 2012, presenting the prospect of Germany's support for the weakened country.[532]

Berlin's attempts of (power)-political recovery coincided with Germany's new "global governance"-approach, adopted with the governmental "New Players Concept" in February 2012,[533] suggesting the interpenetration and interrelation between the factors of power consideration, national strategies, and conceptions of national role. With this concept, Germany acknowledged the massive power shifts in international politics over the recent decades toward the emerging powers of Brazil, Russia, India, China and South Africa (BRICS). Within an increasingly globalized, interdependent, and multipolar world, Germany sought to define its policy and interaction premises in relation to the new global actors.[534] Hereby, Germany aimed to pursue politics actively, coherently, and within multilateral institutions.[535] Although the document avoided direct association of the idea of a "shaping power" with Germany, the conceptual criteria,

---

[531] Merkel, *Deutschland weiß um seine Verantwortung in der Welt.*

[532] Merkel, *Rede von Bundeskanzlerin Angela Merkel anlässlich der Tagung des zivilen und militärischen Spitzenpersonals der Bundeswehr*; De Maizière, *Unser Auftrag ist Ausgangspunkt und Ziel der Neuausrichtung*, 2, 12–13.

[533] Bundesregierung, *Globalisierung gestalten*, 9–53.

[534] See Jörg Binding and Lukas Kudlimay, "Deutschland: Neue Wege in der Internationalen Zusammenarbeit," *GIGA Focus*, no. 7 (Hamburg: German Institute of Global and Area Studies, 2013), 2; Kappel, "Global Power Shifts," 341–42.

[535] Bundesregierung, *Globalisierung gestalten*, 6–11.

such as economic strength and an importance in designing regional approaches, suggest an evolving understanding of Germany's (power)-political status in international affairs.[536]

Two aspects might have further facilitated the resocialization and reorientation of Germany's global power politics. First, Germany's opening to new actors followed directly after the US announcement in early 2012 to "rebalance" to the Asia-Pacific region. It had forced European states to expand their global networks and to improve their capacities in pursuing their (common) interests more efficiently. Second, Germany became even embroiled in a more active exercise of its power. In an internationally recognized speech in Berlin at the end of November 2011, Poland's Foreign Minister Radek Sikorski made an urgent call to Germany as "Europe's indispensable nation" that it "may not fail to lead." Instead of fearing German power, he claimed that he began "to fear German inactivity." This was a historically unprecedented appeal that was backed during the Munich Security Conference in 2012 by even Israel's deputy foreign minister.[537]

In contrast to these pulling conditions, the deteriorating Syrian civil war and the sparking Gaza conflict repeatedly reduced the salience of the Malian crisis as an immanent security threat for Europe and Germany, despite opposing claims. The fact that the Malian crisis was only of secondary importance during the 49th security conference in Munich at the beginning of February, just two weeks after the

---

[536] Sandschneider concludes comparably. See Eberhard Sandschneider, "Deutsche Außenpolitik: Eine Gestaltungsmacht in der Kontinuitätsfalle," *Aus Politik und Zeitgeschichte* 62, no. 10 (März 2012): 6–7.

[537] Radek Sikorski, *Poland and the Future of the European Union: Speech by the Foreign Minister of Poland Radek Sikorski at a Debate at the German Association for Foreign Policy* (Berlin: Deutsche Gesellschaft für Auswärtige Politik e.V., November, 28 2011), accessed March 6, 2015, https://dgap.org/sites/default/files/event_downloads/radoslaw_sikorski_poland_and_the_future_of_the_eu_0.pdf; Sandschneider, "Deutsche Außenpolitik," 6.

launch of the French intervention, supports that assumption.[538] Above all, it was Germany's continuing focus on strengthening its economic power base by solving the Eurozone crisis that distracted key German stakeholders from pursuing a more active policy toward Mali within international institutions. Interlinked with other external and internal factors, as demonstrated below, it disincentivized state actors from considering a robust, costly, and risky German military contribution.

b. National Interests and Strategies

Closely interlocked with the security environment, national interests and strategies often had contrasting influence on the decision-making process toward German military engagement in Mali. On one hand, European and German security interests drew the political and public attention toward the Malian crisis and gave reason for a participation of the Bundeswehr. On the other hand, strategic guidelines related to the region, however, disincentivized Germany from assuming a more active role in the crisis management and from contributing more "robustly."

Throughout the public statements and political debates until the decisions for participation in EUTM Mali and contribution to AFISMA, the federal government and German parliamentarians repeatedly stressed the significance of the steadily worsening security, humanitarian, and human rights situation in Northern Mali and its potential to both indirectly and directly implicate commonly shared European, and thus, German security interests. As early as October 2012, Foreign Minister Westerwelle echoed a common conclusion of the EU FAC, arguing that a collapse of North Mali and the emer-

---

[538] An important aspect was that the French Foreign Minister and Defense Minister had canceled their participation on short notice and accompanied France's President Hollande on a visit to Mali. Jungholt, "Deutscher Mali-Beitrag sorgt für Ärger bei Franzosen."

gence of terrorist schools would not only "threaten Mali, the region, the North African states, but also threaten ... (the people) in Europe."[539] The danger for Europe's security posed by state collapse, safe havens for terrorists, and strongholds for organized crime "on Europe's doorstep"[540] thus became the main theme in the line of argument of European and German politicians to *justify* an external engagement in the West African country.[541]

Germany's decisions to help to mitigate commonly shared security concerns through the participation in EUTM Mali and contribution to AFISMA militarily, therefore laid, as Defense Minister de Maizière pinpointed in March 2013, "in African interest, in European interest, and therefore also in German interest."[542] While asking for the Bundestag's approval for the two Bundeswehr mandates, Foreign

---

[539] Cited in "Mali-Mission." The EU was concerned about the serious political and security situation in Mali which posed, according to the FAC, "an immediate threat to the Sahel region and those living there, who are already suffering from an acute food crisis, as well as to West and North Africa and to Europe." Council of the European Union, *Press Release 3191st Council Meeting Foreign Affairs*, 7.

[540] Foreign Minister Westerwelle cited in Gräßler, "Germany Backs French Intervention in Mali."

[541] For the European perspective See Council of the European Union, *Council Conclusions on Mali, 3209th Foreign Affairs Council Meeting*, 1. For a bi-partisan perspective in the German Bundestag see Deutscher Bundestag, *Stenografischer Bericht: Plenarprotokoll 17/221*, 27457-68.

[542] Cited in Simone Meyer, "'Das, was wir tun, liegt im deutschen Interesse,'" *Die Welt*, March 18, 2013, http://www.welt.de/politik/ausland/article114527292/Das-was-wir-tun-liegt-im-deutschen-Interesse.html. Both mandates as requested by the German federal government explicitly stress the implications of the Malian crisis for Europe's and Germany's security. They justify Germany's military engagement based on the efforts to contribute to the reinstallation of Mali's territorial integrity and improvement of institutional capacities as preconditions to internal, and hence, regional stability. See Antrag der Bundesregierung, "Entsendung bewaffneter deutscher Streitkräfte zur Beteiligung an der EU-geführten militärischen Ausbildungsmission EUTM Mali," 4–6; Antrag der Bundesregierung, "Entsendung bewaffneter deutscher Streitkräfte zur Unterstützung der Internationalen Unterstützungsmission in Mali unter afrikanischer Führung (AFISMA)," 4–5.

Minister Westerwelle even indirectly resorted in his speech on February 20, 2013, to the famous statement of former Defense Minister Peter Struck that "the security of the Federal Republic of Germany is defended even at the Hindu Kush."[543] Referring to threats posed by the spread of terrorism in Mali, he claimed that Germany's engagement is required to *defend* "our freedom, our open society, and the way of life in Europe."[544]

Despite affected national interests, however, Germany, alongside its European allies and partners, remained hesitant and restrained in getting too actively and too strongly involved in a military response to the Malian crisis. Whenever the federal government underlined the implications of the crisis in Mali for the region, Europe, and Germany's security, it simultaneously stressed the primary responsibility of the African states and regional organizations to respond to it, particularly in the context of envisioned combat operations. Defense Minister de Maizière and Foreign Minister Westerwelle unison justified Germany's step back from the first line in the international response by arguing that "Germany could not solve the Mali crisis alone" and that external (European) actors had "only a limited influence" on the long-term development in Mali.[545] Instead, Germany and its European counterparts should better "enable the Africans"

---

[543] Federal Ministry of Defense, "Pressekonferenz am 5. Dezember 2002 mit Bundesminister Dr. Peter Struck zur Weiterentwicklung der Bundeswehr," *BMVg*, updated December 5, 2013, http://www.bmvg.de/portal/a/bmvg/!ut/p/c4/NY3BCsIwEET_KGkOFetNUUEPetR6KWmypItNUjabevHjTYXOwBzmDYx8yeKgZ3SaMQY9yqdsDe76j-j97ITHgImBMHvhIJkBzcDQ_dkMxIAWXQ4urcMuAXKnmroWliYoTWLK5i0fy5MFYWIAXpIhMJZ0pDmSmCLxuJBMVIhAK9tKHQ-Vqlap72bbXk9NqS63811O3u9_-L2Ycw!!/.

[544] Federal Foreign Office, "Rede von Außenminister Westerwelle im Deutschen Bundestag zum Mali-Einsatz der Bundeswehr."

[545] Deutscher Bundestag, *Stenografischer Bericht: Plenarprotokoll 17/221*, 27457, 27469.

through training and logistic support so that they can provide "their own contribution to a stabilization of the Malian North."[546]

Consequently, Germany's decisions for modest military contributions to Mali were not only related to factors on the internal level, such as Germany's risk aversion, culture of military reticence, and sensitivity to an intervention-reluctant public, but also were affected by traditional foreign and security policy guidelines for the African continent as amplified by several newly issued strategic concepts, such as the "Interagency Guidelines for a Coherent Policy of the Federal Government toward Fragile States"[547] and the "Concept of the Federal Government for Africa."[548] As first comprehensive governmental strategy for Africa, the 2011 concept manifested Germany's historically rooted restrained approach to the neighboring continent, up front stating that given "a *realistic* assessment of the continent," Germany's Africa Policy bears in mind that "the people in Africa are primarily responsible for their continent"[549]—with a particular focus on security affairs.[550] The national mandates for EUTM Mali and AFISMA directly reflect the federal government's strategic emphasis to favor "African (local) solutions," to "strengthen African self-reliance," and to "do no harm" to African politics,[551] justifying the responsible but limited level of Germany's military engagement in Mali.

---

[546] Federal Foreign Office, "Rede von Außenminister Westerwelle im Deutschen Bundestag zum Mali-Einsatz der Bundeswehr."

[547] Auswärtiges Amt, Bundesministerium der Verteidigung, and Bundesministerium für wirtschaftliche Zusammenarbeit, *Für eine kohärente Politik der Bundesregierung gegenüber fragilen Staaten*.

[548] Bundesregierung, *Deutschland und Afrika*.

[549] Bundesregierung, *Deutschland und Afrika*, 5, emphasis by the author.

[550] Ibid., 12.

[551] Ibid., 17, 19; Auswärtiges Amt, Bundesministerium der Verteidigung, and Bundesministerium für wirtschaftliche Zusammenarbeit, *Für eine kohärente Politik der Bundesregierung gegenüber fragilen Staaten*, 4–5.

c. *Multilateral Integration*

Germany's multilateral integration also had a significant but ambivalent influence on the decisions both *whether* and *how* Germany should engage militarily in Mali. Of particular importance for Berlin's decision-making process throughout the evolving crisis management were Paris's role and the French-German relationship. Based on its tradition, history, and relationships as a former colonial power in the entire Sahel region, France had a strategic interest in Mali.[552] These interests explain Paris's continuing attempts to bring the worsening security situation in North Mali into the focus of the international community and to push it for a more active and more immediate response. Simultaneously, France, however, eschewed unilateral actions, a behavior that had alienated many European partners, including Germany, in the Libyan case.[553] Instead, Paris particularly endeavored to closely involve Berlin as early as possible within the intergovernmental consultation process.[554] Long before the European Union confirmed its plans for a training mission in Mali, both capitals already "stood in close contact regarding potential solutions for the crisis," as the federal government officially confirmed in November 2012.[555]

Paris's inclusive and transparent approach facilitated Merkel's early assured German disposition "to contribute to a supporting mission in

---

[552] Katrin Sold, "Frankreichs Werk und Europas Beitrag," *The European*, February 2, 2013, http://www.theeuropean.de/katrin-sold/5850-europaeischer-einsatz-in-mali; Gräßler, "Germany Backs French Intervention in Mali."

[553] Busse, "Europas neue Risse"; Howorth, *Security and Defense Policy*, 138–39.

[554] Katrin Sold, "Krise in Mali: Frankreich treibt internationalen Einsatz voran," *Deutsche Gesellschaft für Außen- und Sicherheitspolitik* (dgap), updated November 15, 2012, https://dgap.org/de/article/22762/print.

[555] The close consultation also included the American government. Antwort der Bundesregierung auf die Kleine Anfrage der Abgeordneten Jan van Aken, "Aktuelle Situation in Mali," 11.

Mali, as long as the preconditions therefore would be clarified."[556] The revitalized strong German-French relationship also explains why Berlin gave "its full support" to Paris's intervention in Mali in January 2013 and why it immediately announced plans to investigate how to best assist to France's efforts.[557] Although once again ruling out the deployment of German combat troops, the federal government underlined its solidarity with France, publicly declaring that it "did not want to 'leave France alone in this difficult hour.'"[558]

Berlin's solidarity stance toward Paris transformed to the multilateral level and magnified Germany's aspiration to side with its allies and partners because the imperatives gradually evolved, particularly on the European level, which set the conditions for a modest engagement of European soldiers in Mali. The notable interrelation between decisions in Brussels and Berlin suggest that as soon as a consensus among European states was manifested in favor of a training and advisory mission in Mali, and the more the preconditions for such a mission were set, the more Germany's hesitancy to commit itself to participate with German troops in the mission was reduced.

In interrelation with Germany's strategic culture and general risk aversion, conversely, the multilateral environment also nourished Berlin's temporizing stance and promoted its predisposition to contribute exclusively with noncombat capacities. Based on the persistent institutional, political, and military instability in Bamako after the outbreak of the Malian crisis, international actors, apart from African

---

[556] Merkel, *Rede von Bundeskanzlerin Angela Merkel anlässlich der Tagung des zivilen und militärischen Spitzenpersonals der Bundeswehr.*
[557] Gräßler, "Germany Backs French Intervention in Mali"; "Germany Considers Options."
[558] Hawley, "The World from Berlin."

regional organizations and later France, had assumed "a wait-and-see attitude"[559] for a long time.

The reactive, cautious, and restrained approach was particularly evident within the EU. First, although acknowledging the implications of an instable Malian North for its own security, the EU attributed the primary responsibility in the crisis response to African hands, considering itself exclusively in a supportive role.[560] Second, by mainly focusing on a political solution in Mali, European states persistently refused a deployment of their combat forces, nationally or on the EU level (Battle Groups), into the country.[561] Even in the wake of France's intervention in January 2013, the European community remained unwilling to send "boots on the ground"[562] in support of one of their partners. Finally, the planning of the EU for a contribution to the crisis was considerably slow and constrained. Already having begun to "study" the opportunities of training the Malian Army in July 2012[563] and to specifically plan for such a mission in October 2012,[564] the EU had no preconditions set in place after six months of

---

[559] International Crisis Group, *Mali: The Need for Determined and Coordinated International Action*, Policy Briefing—Africa Briefing, no. 90 (Brussels: ICG, September 24, 2012), 6, http://www.crisisgroup.org/~/media/Files/africa/west-africa/mali/b090-mali-the-need-for-determined-and-coordinated-international-action-english.pdf.

[560] Council of the European Union, *Press Release 3191st Council Meeting Foreign Affairs*, 8–9.

[561] Engelberg, *The EU and Military Operations*, 172–73; Gräßler, "Germany Backs French Intervention in Mali"; Howorth, *Security and Defense Policy*, 84.

[562] Tisdall, "France's Lonely Intervention in Mali."

[563] Council of the European Union, *Council Conclusions on Mali, 3138th Foreign Affairs Council Meeting* (Brussels: Council of the European Union Press Office, July 23, 2012), 15, accessed March 14, 2015, http://www.consilium.europa.eu/uedocs/cms_data/docs/pressdata/EN/foraff/134144.pdf; Howorth, *Security and Defense Policy*, 167.

[564] Council of the European Union, *Press Release 3191st Council Meeting Foreign Affairs*, 9; see also Dicke, "The European Union Training Mission in Mali," 98.

preparation, as France launched its intervention.[565] At the same time, the envisioned mission area was constrained in the safe Malian south, deliberately reducing the threat for European soldiers. All aspects suggest to have been related to the EU's persistent challenge in committing itself to Africa.[566]

The EU's overall hesitancy and reticence allowed the federal government from the onset of the international crisis management to defer, to satisfy domestic concerns, and to rule out the participation of Bundeswehr soldiers in combat operations in Mali without fearing to violate its solidarity with or to isolate itself from its allies and partners. The cautious stance of the United States[567] as well as the early announcement of the African regional organizations that they would assume some responsibility in the fight against the jihadist groups in northern Mali, additionally promoted Berlin's convenient position.

d. Evolution of Military Engagement

Experiences made during the military engagement in Afghanistan and the status of Germany's military commitments considerably influenced the political thinking in Berlin. The calculus for using military force in Mali and considerations about to what extent Germany

---

[565] Michael Gahler, "Kein Konflikt der Anderen," *The European,* February 7, 2013, http://www.theeuropean.de/michael-gahler/5831-deutsches-engagement-in-mali.

[566] Roy H. Ginsberg and Susan E. Penska, *The European Union in Global Security: The Politics of Impacts* (New York: Palgrave Macmillan, 2014), 66–67.

[567] Apart from considering a military intervention as too risky, thus, favoring a political solution in Mali, the United States had also recalibrated its approach to the EU-NATO relations, additionally explaining its reticence. As a direct consequence from its geostrategic rebalance efforts since 2011, the United States requested European states to take a stronger lead in operations close to the European theater. The approach of stepping back in the second line has become known as "leading from behind." Howorth, *Security and Defense Policy,* 139; Ken Dilanian, "Obama Administration Weighs Intervention in Mali," *Los Angeles Times Blog* (blog), July 27, 2012, http://latimesblogs.latimes.com/world_now/2012/07/obama-administration-weighs-intervention-in-mali.html; Tisdall, "France's Lonely Intervention in Mali."

should contribute adequately chiefly caused the effects. Amid the preparation for transferring the responsibility for the security of Afghanistan from international toward national forces, Berlin had identified two critical lessons[568] that dominated its strategic narrative toward Mali. Both lessons suggest to have additionally nourished Germany's cultural and strategic foreign and security policy preferences, and hence, incentivized Berlin to opt for a limited participation in Mali.

First, Foreign Minister Westerwelle's conceded at the Afghanistan Conference in Bonn end of 2011 that, despite the long-lasting efforts and heavy losses in Afghanistan, "there is no military solution, there can be only a political solution,"[569] precisely reflecting one pillar of Berlin's approach toward Mali one year later. Second, Afghanistan also had demonstrated to Berlin's political elite the importance of encouraging regional leadership, strengthening regional security architectures, and qualifying local security forces.[570] Consequently, whenever the question for Germany's contribution to Mali arose, both the federal government and German parliamentarians consistently justified Germany's (and Europe's) hesitant stance and limited engagement with Africa's primary responsibility in solving the Malian cri-

---

[568] The defense-political spokesperson of the SPD, Rainer Arnold, had raised a third lesson from Afghanistan, which, however, stood in contrast to Berlin's hesitant approach. He argued that it is fatal (for the international community) to wait and allow Islamist extremists to take control of a state and, thereby, establish safe havens for terrorists. Deutscher Bundestag. *Stenografischer Bericht: Plenarprotokoll 17/221*, 27458.

[569] Westerwelle, *Rede des Bundesministers des Auswärtigen, Dr. Guido Westerwelle, MdB, Afghanistan-Konferenz Eröffnung*.

[570] "De Maizière erwägt Einsatz in Mali;" Thomas de Maizière, "Wir haben aus Afghanistan gelernt," interview by Sueddeutsche Zeitung, *Bundesregierung*, updated November 5, 2012, http://www.bundesregierung.de/ContentArchiv/DE/Archiv 17/Interview/2012/11/2012-11-05-de-maiziere-sz.html; Deutscher Bundestag. *Stenografischer Bericht: Plenarprotokoll 17/221*, 27458; Federal Foreign Office, "Rede von Außenminister Westerwelle im Deutschen Bundestag zum Mali-Einsatz der Bundeswehr."

sis[571]—clearly reflecting Germany's preferred strategic approach to the region. Moreover, the lesson should also have promoted Germany's early declaration of willingness and final decision to participate in a training mission for the Malian Army and to logistically support AFISMA.

On the other hand, Germany's ongoing and evolving military engagements in international missions also served Berlin as a justification for its limited and only indirect support for France's Operation Serval between January and February 2013. Interlocked with the factor of multilateral integration, it helped Berlin to mitigate external and domestic criticism, to stress shared responsibilities between allies and partners, and to maintain Germany's comparably minimalistic approach. In a direct reaction to the domestic criticism concerning the appropriateness of Germany's support to France's intervention in Mali, Federal Chancellor Merkel posited that "each country ... must determine its capacity to contribute without endangering the safety of its soldiers involved in other missions."[572] Merkel, and a few days later also de Maizière, referred pointedly to Germany's ongoing involvement in Afghanistan, in the Balkans, and to the recent deployment of German Patriot systems to Turkey, three missions in which France was any longer not active.

At the same time, Merkel argued that the provision of two transport airplanes, which should support the deployment of AFISMA forces to Mali, would equal the contributions from other European

---

[571] De Maizière, "Wir haben aus Afghanistan gelernt;" Deutscher Bundestag, *Stenografischer Bericht: Plenarprotokoll 17/221*, 27458.

[572] Matthias Gebauer and Philipp Wittrock, "Germany's Mali Predicament: Trapped between France and War," *Spiegel Online*, January 17, 2013, http://www.spiegel.de/international/world/french-mission-in-mali-puts-germany-in-a-tight-spot-a-878187-druck.html.

states, such as the United Kingdom and Denmark.⁵⁷³ While Berlin's arguments were true, however, the gradual reduction of Bundeswehr soldiers in international military missions starting in mid-2012⁵⁷⁴ had freed capacities, both in the Army and the Air Force,⁵⁷⁵ which would have allowed Germany to support France, AFISMA, and finally EUTM Mali more substantially.

Finally, Berlin's decision for a participation in EUTM Mali with engineer training capacities also must be attributed to the fact that Germany and Mali had maintained military relationships for 40 years. Within the framework of an equipment support program for foreign forces, since 2007, Germany had even provided Mali with decommissioned materiel, most related to river-crossing capacities. Between 2009 and 2012, the Bundeswehr repeatedly trained Malian forces in Bapho, 140 kilometers northeast of Bamako, in river-crossing skills, the only capabilities that Mali offered as a contribution to ECOWAS' readiness forces.⁵⁷⁶

---

⁵⁷³ De Maizière, "Mali durch Ausbildungsmission nachhaltig stabilisieren"; "De Maizière gegen Lammert"; Gebauer and Wittrock, "Germany's Mali Predicament"; Jungholt, "Paris ruft."

⁵⁷⁴ Whereas approximately 6,500 German soldiers were deployed on international missions as of September 27, 2012, the number had declined to some 5,800 soldiers as of February 14, 2013. See de Maizière, *Unser Auftrag ist Ausgangspunkt und Ziel der Neuausrichtung*, 1; De Maizière, *Internationale Verantwortung wahrnehmen*.

⁵⁷⁵ It is argued that up to five airplanes would have been available, two of them equipped with the rare capacities for strategic airlift for medical evacuation (StratAirMedEvac). Jungholt, "Paris ruft."

⁵⁷⁶ Hauke Friedrichs, "Die Bundeswehr ist längst in Mali," *Zeit Online*, October 29, 2012, http://www.zeit.de/politik/deutschland/2012-10/bundeswehr-mali-einsatz-ausbildung. Although the author only mentions a period between November 2009 and January 2010, internal sources from the German Ministry of Defense confirm that the Bundeswehr maintained a small, permanent advisor team in Bapho until early 2013. The team not only trained Malian engineers in river crossing skills but also created and implemented a comprehensive apprenticeship system. For more details on the advisor team and the close military relationship between the two countries see Ronald Rogge, "Hand in Hand für Mali," *Y: Magazin für die Bundeswehr* 13, no. 6/7 (2013): 44–51.

e. Mission Framework

Magnified by strategic approaches and the Afghan lessons, Germany's decisions to militarily engage in Mali significantly resorted to vital criteria of the mission framework in relation to the use of military force, epitomizing Germany's foreign and security policy preferences. With the UNSC Resolutions 2071 and 2085, the decisions of the European and EU Foreign Affairs Council, and the two Bundestag mandates, Germany's overarching legal and legitimate framework for the engagement of the Bundeswehr in international military actions in Mali was successfully set up. Critically, the international mandates carefully differentiated between the training and (support for) the combat tasks, a precondition that the federal government had persistently attached to the participation of German soldiers[577] and actively enforced within the multilateral negotiations.[578]

The separation of the mandates allowed federal government to "dose"[579] the national contributions to EUTM Mali, AFISMA, and France based on calculation between what was externally required and what was domestically available and affordable. Consequently, it enabled Berlin to condition each of its contributions according to vital policy preferences (risk aversion) and domestic constraints (public opinion), but without offending multilateral sentiments.

Closely interlocked with legitimate, interest-related, and value-based causes, the simultaneously broadly incorporated and limited

---

[577] Antwort der Bundesregierung auf die Kleine Anfrage der Abgeordneten Jan van Aken, "Aktuelle Situation in Mali"; "De Maizière schließt Kampfeinsatz aus"; Federal Ministry of Defense, "EU berät über Militäreinsatz in Mali."

[578] De Maizière, "Mali durch Ausbildungsmission nachhaltig stabilisieren."

[579] Rainer Stinner, the foreign policy speaker of the FDP (from the junior-partner in the coalition), claimed in his speech before the Bundestag before the vote for the EUTM Mali and AFISMA mandates that Germany would accurately dose its contributions to Mali. Deutscher Bundestag, *Stenografischer Bericht: Plenarprotokoll 17/225*, 27959.

designed conceptual frameworks for EUTM Mali and AFISMA are suggested to have eased Germany's decision to opt for a contribution with German soldiers. Essentially, all international military efforts were embedded within, and hence subordinated to, a comprehensive approach that aimed at reestablishing the rule of law, reconciling between the different parties, and guaranteeing stability in Mali.[580] The priority of such an overarching master plan for peaceful conflict resolution, initiated with the approval of the political roadmap by the Malian parliament on January 30, 2013, explicitly corresponded with Berlin's lessons learned from Afghanistan and the conviction that the political process, and not military means, was vital to sustainably solve the crisis in Mali.[581]

Reflecting Germany's persistent culture of military restraint and risk aversion, the limitations set by European and national plans concerning objectives, duration, required resources, and risks for soldiers on ground for EUTM Mali[582] suggest to additionally have increased the likelihood to decide for, and approve, the participation of Bundeswehr soldiers in this mission. Despite the provision of the second or third largest contingent to the mission during the first mandate up to April 2014, however, it should be noted that Germany did not offer capacities for infantry training or force protection, both

---

[580] Antrag der Bundesregierung, "Entsendung bewaffneter deutscher Streitkräfte zur Beteiligung an der EU-geführten militärischen Ausbildungsmission EUTM Mali," 5; Antrag der Bundesregierung, "Entsendung bewaffneter deutscher Streitkräfte zur Unterstützung der Internationalen Unterstützungsmission in Mali unter afrikanischer Führung (AFISMA)," 5; UN Security Council, "UNSC Resolution 2071," 3; UN Security Council, *UNSC Resolution 2085*, 2–5;

[581] For the arguments of Defense Minister de Maizière and Foreign Minister Westerwelle see Deutscher Bundestag, *Stenografischer Bericht: Plenarprotokoll 17/221*, 27455 and 27459–60.

[582] Regarding the limitations for the contributions of Bundeswehr soldiers to AFISMA as set by the national mandate see Julian Junk, "Vom Gestaltungsunwillen einer 'Gestaltungsmacht:' Ein Kommentar zur deutschen Malipolitik," *Sicherheit und Frieden* 32, no. 2 (2014): 95.

implying a much more combat-related footprint. Instead, Germany provided engineer training and medical capacities,[583] acknowledging that the latter included with the construction of a military hospital in Koulikoro the most cost-intensive national contribution to the mission. Notwithstanding these efforts, it also reflected to a certain extent Germany's persistent military restraint.

In contrast to the supportive elements of the mission frameworks for Berlin's positive decision, insecurities about the implications of a military intervention in Mali and about the questions regarding to what extent Germany's participation is reasonable, feasible, and appropriate, suggest to have influenced Berlin's decision-making process repeatedly. The federal government's long-lasting caution to commit itself to Bundeswehr participation in Mali and to clearly define its actual contribution most evidently underlined those aspects.[584] Particularly Defense Minister de Maizière persistently emphasized the necessity to "first clarify what could be a task for us (the Bundeswehr) and what ... (the Bundeswehr) needs to fulfill it," before even considering to ask the Bundestag for approval.[585]

2. Determinants on the Internal Level

Determinants on the internal level simultaneously posed diametrical incentives for the decision-makers in Berlin whether and how Germany should embark on military engagements in Mali. On the one hand, Germany's culturally embedded military restrained and risk-averse stance, electoral considerations, and public sentiments, influ-

---

[583] Antrag der Bundesregierung, "Entsendung bewaffneter deutscher Streitkräfte zur Beteiligung an der EU-geführten militärischen Ausbildungsmission EUTM Mali," 1–3.

[584] For public statements of Federal Chancellor Merkel and Defense Minister de Maizière, see Merkel, *Rede von Bundeskanzlerin Angela Merkel anlässlich der Tagung des zivilen und militärischen Spitzenpersonals der Bundeswehr*; "De Maizière erwägt Einsatz ohne Bundestagsmandat."

[585] De Maizière, "Mali durch Ausbildungsmission nachhaltig stabilisieren."

enced the federal government to rule out any German involvement in combat operations early on, to call for a comprehensive approach toward Mali, and to remain cautious in defining Germany's actual contribution. On the other, strongly felt multilateral commitments that were magnified by the power-political backlash from the nonparticipation in Libya, an evolving national self-image, a further "normalizing" understanding of the use of military force, and bipartisan parliamentary consensus, outweighed intervention-related resentments and *pushed* the federal government to decide for, and the Bundestag to approve, an engagement of German soldiers. The ambivalent domestic setting also helps to explain why Germany indeed declared its solidarity with France after the launch of Operation Serval, but deferred to support its partner directly and/or more substantially. Within the interpenetrated three-level framework of (German) foreign and security policy, the external level magnified the ambivalent conditions on the domestic level, urging key German stakeholders to balance between them.

a. *Strategic Culture and Conception of National Role*

Germany's foreign policy strategic culture and role concept had significant but ambivalent influences on the Bundeswehr engagement in Mali. Strongly felt multilateral commitments ("never alone"), amplified by nuanced shifts in standards of Germany's self-image and role, decisively promoted the decisions to participate in EUTM Mali, to contribute to AFISMA, and to (indirectly) support France. Conversely, Germany's premise of reticence in using force—including a general risk aversion and the preference of "politics before force"—found expression in Berlin's aversion toward combat operations, temporizing attitude, focus on a political process, and reasoning for its indirect support to France.

Between 2011 and 2012, one could note a gradual and cautious rethinking among the German political elite concerning the Germany's international role.[586] Although the process was primarily based on a reflection of Germany's long-lasting manifested economic power and permanent external demands for more German engagement in international affairs, Germany's abstention from the UNSC vote on Libya, however, particularly promoted the evolution. Not later than two months after the heavily disputed decision, Defense Minister de Maizière publicly argued that Germany "as rich country in the world, as potent country," should ask itself "whether … (Germany) has to make a contribution, as other states too, if that corresponds with the international responsibility" and even if "national interests are not immediately threatened."[587] Such a nuanced conception of Germany role in the world, appealing for a more active and responsible approach while maintaining vital principles of German foreign and security policy, was not only echoed by Federal Chancellor Merkel,[588] but also found its way in new strategic documents. Whereas the *Defense Policy Guidelines* in 2011 posited Germany as "an active member of the international community,"[589] the "New Players Concept" considered Germany even as a power with aspirations to shape "global governance."[590]

Without making any bid for German leadership, Germany's shifting self-image (particularly among the political elites), therefore, constituted a further step toward a still modest emancipation from Germany's historically rooted self-restraint. Some of its supportive effect on the decision for the deployment of German troops to Mali was surely reinforced through a changing perception of the role and effi-

---

[586] Sandschneider, "Deutsche Außenpolitik," 6.

[587] Thomas de Maizière, "Neuausrichtung der Bundeswehr entschieden," interview by Tom Buhrow, *ARD Tagesthemen*, May 18, 2011, https://tsarchive.wordpress.com/2011/05/19/bundeswehrreform166/.

[588] Merkel, *Rede von Bundeskanzlerin Angela Merkel anlässlich der Tagung des zivilen und militärischen Spitzenpersonals der Bundeswehr.*

[589] Federal Ministry of Defense, *Defense Policy Guidelines*, 3.

[590] Bundesregierung, *Globalisierung gestalten*, 9–11.

cacy of force within international affairs by some key German stakeholders, such as Merkel and de Maizière.[591] As demonstrated in actor-level section, the use of military means gradually became understood still as one foreign and security policy instrument among others, but one that is important and indispensable, and that should not be categorically ruled out any more.

Concerning the decisions on Mali, Germany's heightened sense for responsibility suggest to have been manifested in a stronger awareness of its commitments within multilateral organizations, thus amplifying Germany's multilateral-oriented foreign policy principle ("never alone"). Given a hesitant and cautious international environment, it was most notably Germany's determination to act accordingly to its own obligations of *Westorientierung* (orientation to the West), alliance solidarity, and conflict resolution within multilateral frameworks that steered the federal government to commit itself early for, and to finally decide in favor of, a (modest) military participation.

Sensitized by the harsh international criticism in 2011, Berlin *deliberately* strove to "make up for its hurried and categorical refusal to participate in the international operation in Libya."[592] It first became obvious with Merkel's early (but conditioned) announcement end of October 2012 that Germany was willing to participate in a "support mission for Mali"[593] although no plans for such a mission had been initiated up to this moment. The Federal Chancellor's public pledge stood in stark contrast to Berlin's characteristic restraint in international (and military) affairs. Later, Berlin's immediate declaration of solidarity with France after the launch of Operation Serval[594] and

---

[591] De Maizière, *Rede des Bundesministers der Verteidigung anlässlich der 8. Handelsblatt Konferenz am 25. Oktober 2011 in Berlin*; Merkel, *Rede von Bundeskanzlerin Angela Merkel anlässlich der Tagung des zivilen und militärischen Spitzenpersonals der Bundeswehr*.

[592] Gebauer and Wittrock, "Germany's Mali Predicament."

[593] Merkel, *Rede von Bundeskanzlerin Angela Merkel anlässlich der Tagung des zivilen und militärischen Spitzenpersonals der Bundeswehr*.

[594] Gräßler, "Germany Backs French Intervention in Mali."

Westerwelle's appeal toward the Bundestag parliamentarian at the end of February 2013, positing that Germany "must neither abandon the Africans nor the French,"[595] clearly reflected the aspiration "to be seen (once again) as a reliable partner"[596] and the willingness to avoid the appearance of choosing a "special path" (*Sonderweg*) as in the Libyan case.[597] This assumption remained valid, even if Defense Minister de Maizière still argued in November 2012 that soldiers never could be deployed only based on alliance solidarity.[598]

In contrast to the elements in favor of a German engagement in Mali, several culturally-conceptual qualities suggest to have disincentivized Berlin from a more active stance and a more robust contribution. First, Germany's foreign and security policy key premise of "politics before force" took a dominant role in Berlin's narrative on Mali. Closely interlinked with the Afghan lessons and the criteria-related claim for an overarching, comprehensive master plan, Berlin persistently emphasized that the "political process had priority within … (Germany's) efforts."[599] Already in a common public statement with the UN special envoy for the Sahel region Romano Prodi in October 2012, Westerwelle declared that Germany would "seek a political solution of the conflict, not a military intervention."[600] The condition that "it cannot give a simple military solution (in Mali)" but "vital for the conflict solution in Mali is the political process," consti-

---

[595] Federal Foreign Office, "Rede von Außenminister Westerwelle im Deutschen Bundestag zum Mali-Einsatz der Bundeswehr."

[596] Gebauer and Wittrock, "Germany's Mali Predicament."

[597] Rolf Mützenich, "Der ungewollte Krieg," *The European*, February 2, 2013, http://www.theeuropean.de/rolf-muetzenich/5820-deutsche-beteiligung-bei-mali-intervention.

[598] De Maizière, "Wir haben aus Afghanistan gelernt;" "De Maizière erwägt Einsatz ohne Bundestagsmandat."

[599] Federal Foreign Office, "Rede von Außenminister Westerwelle im Deutschen Bundestag zum Mali-Einsatz der Bundeswehr."

[600] Cited in "Mali-Mission."

tuted an important cultural-normative framework for Berlin's justification to opt for the deployment of Bundeswehr soldiers to EUTM Mali and in support of AFISMA in February 2013. Both national mandates made crystal clear that German military contributions would be subordinated to a broadly designed support of the political process.[601]

It also might be the "politics dominance" in German thinking that gave Berlin further reason to favor an indirect support to the crisis resolution. Interlocked with the conceptual basis to call for regional approaches, Berlin found satisfaction[602] in the situation to "only" provide secondary-tier support either for the Malian state by training Malian forces or indirectly for France by logistically supporting the AFISMA operation.

Second, Berlin's cautious and hesitant attitude toward Mali also can be interpreted as an expression of Germany's domestically motivated "politic of restraint."[603] Although early presenting the prospect of German Bundeswehr soldiers in a potential EU training mission in Mali, Berlin struggled to define a consistent and unified governmental vision about the scope and scale of the Bundeswehr contribution.[604] Clearly related to a persistently complicated security and power situa-

---

[601] Antrag der Bundesregierung, "Entsendung bewaffneter deutscher Streitkräfte zur Beteiligung an der EU-geführten militärischen Ausbildungsmission EUTM Mali," 5; Antrag der Bundesregierung, "Entsendung bewaffneter deutscher Streitkräfte zur Unterstützung der Internationalen Unterstützungsmission in Mali unter afrikanischer Führung (AFISMA)," 5; For the bipartisan emphasis on political means see Deutscher Bundestag, *Stenografischer Bericht: Plenarprotokoll 17/221*, 2758, 27460, 27463–64.

[602] Federal Foreign Office, "Rede von Außenminister Westerwelle im Deutschen Bundestag zum Mali-Einsatz der Bundeswehr."

[603] Bernhard Rinke, "Auslandseinsätze der Bundeswehr zwischen Bündnisverpflichtungen und einer außenpolitischen Kultur der Zurückhaltung," *Politik Unterrichten* 1 (2014): 31.

[604] Junk, "Vom Gestaltungsunwillen einer 'Gestaltungsmacht,'" 91; Mützenich, "Der ungewollte Krieg."

tion in Northern Mali and Bamako—dragging the federal government between the poles of immediate intervention and absence as Defense Minister de Maizière admitted[605]—Berlin took a wait-and-see-attitude and did not develop any particular ambitions to bring the planning forward.[606] On February 13, 2013, many weeks after the EU-internal approval of a training mission in the country, the Bundeswehr was allowed to send a fact-finding team to Mali to reconnoiter and assess the conditions for Germany's training contributions.[607]

Finally, a deeply ingrained risk aversion also influenced the decision-making toward the use of military force in Mali. Apart from the categorical refusal to become involved in combat operations, the attitude was most evident with Berlin's reluctance to support France's Operation Serval more actively and more substantially. Experiences in Afghanistan or Iraq had shown that supposedly time and capacity limited operations can change their nature, enmeshing the participants in prolonged and intensive wars. Berlin, therefore, might have feared that "if the French meet more resistance from the Islamists than expected, Paris could request additional urgent military support from its partners."[608] Once too strongly committed and too actively engaged, the federal government would have faced serious challenges to balance between its categorical refusal to become directly involved in combat operations and its declared (unlimited) solidarity with France. Consequently, to solve the dilemma, Berlin quickly opted for

---

[605] See de Maizière, "Mali durch Ausbildungsmission nachhaltig stabilisieren."

[606] Jungholt and Kammholz, "Bundesregierung sucht noch eine Strategie für Mali"; Omid Nouripour, "Vorbeugen ist besser als Heilen," *The European*, February 16, 2013, http://www.theeuropean.de/omid-nouripour/5861-klare-ziele-fuer-mali.

[607] Matthias Gebauer, "Geplante EU-Trainingsmission: Bundeswehr schickt Erkundungsteam nach Mali," *Spiegel Online*, February 13, 2013, http://www.spiegel.de/politik/ausland/eu-trainingsmission-bundeswehr-schickt-erkundungsteam-nach-mali-a-883236.html.

[608] Gebauer and Wittrock, "Germany's Mali Predicament."

an indirect support for France, allowing both to keep its face and to avoid negative consequences.

b. *Parliament and Political Contestation*

Even if the federal government's decisions to categorically rule out combat operations in Mali and to only indirectly support France's Operation Serval raised bipartisan parliamentary criticism, the sequence of events suggest that the Bundestag did not contest the federal government's stance. Instead, such domestic political motives and considerations as the upcoming parliamentary elections in the autumn of 2013[609] and a broad public refusal of German involvement in combat operations in Mali seem to have broadly *streamlined* Germany's political elite—the federal government *and* all major parties in the Bundestag—in favor of a multilateral-incentivized Bundeswehr engagement in Mali, but under the clear conditions of a domestically justifiable limited scale. Thus, the decisions lend further support to the notion that German foreign and security policy toward Mali took place between the poles of external and internal imperatives.

Until the start of France's intervention, Mali and Germany's potential engagement in the country did not constitute an issue of an (intensive) political or public discourse.[610] Only the left-wing party DIE LINKE questioned the federal government in an inquiry (*Anfrage*) end of October 2012 about Germany's assessment of the security situation in the country, plans for and implications of international efforts, and considerations toward an engagement of the Bundeswehr.[611] The federal government's repeated public assurance

---

[609] For the claim of a relation between the elections and the decision-making claim, see Gebauer and Wittrock, "Germany's Mali Predicament"; Mützenich, "Der ungewollte Krieg."
[610] Junk, "Vom Gestaltungsunwillen einer 'Gestaltungsmacht,'" 91, 94.
[611] Antwort der Bundesregierung auf die Kleine Anfrage der Abgeordneten Jan van Aken, "Aktuelle Situation in Mali."

in the last quarter of 2012 that a decision for a Bundeswehr engagement had not been made at all because several preconditions, such as the separation of mandates, still had to be set up and the tasks for German soldiers to be clarified,[612] may explain the stillness in Germany's political landscape. By implication, the calm domestic political environment could have facilitated and amplified the federal government's temporizing and cautious stance.

The situation, however, changed with the federal government's decision mid-January 2013 to send two airplanes for the deployment of ECOWAS forces to Mali in an indirect support to France's efforts—splitting the Bundestag across factions. Surprisingly, the harshest criticism came out of Federal Chancellor Merkel's CDU. Bundestag President Norbert Lammert's argument that the deployment of two transport airplanes is "surely not enough" and could only be understood as "an initial demonstrative signal that … Germany would not position oneself as in the case of Libya,"[613] was echoed by the chairman of the Foreign Affairs Committee, Rudolf Polenz, who claimed that even if "the current help of Germany for Mali is correct," it should not be constrained by the previous commitments.[614] Andreas Schockenhoff, deputy parliamentary floor leader of the CDU, intensified their criticism, saying that "Germany should not rule out any form of participation" in the military operation in Mali.[615] Referring to Europe's Common Foreign and Security Policy (CFSP), SPD defense-policy spokesperson Rainer Arnold

---

[612] De Maizière, "Wir haben aus Afghanistan gelernt"; "De Maizière erwägt Einsatz ohne Bundestagsmandat"; "De Maizière schließt Kampfeinsatz aus."

[613] "Lammert findet deutsches Mali-Engagement zu gering," *Die Welt*, January 19, 2013, http://www.welt.de/politik/deutschland/article112901467/Lammert-findet-deutsches-Mali-Engagement-zu-gering.html.

[614] "De Maizière gegen Lammert."

[615] Ralf Neukirch and Gordon Repinski, "Germany abroad: 'Mealy-mouthed' foreign policy angers allies," *Spiegel Online*, January 22, 2013, http://www.spiegel.de/international/germany/german-approach-to-crisis-regions-frustrates-allies-a-878717.html.

joined the choir of critics, arguing that a support for France should not be "reflexively refused."[616] In contrast, both SDP party leader Sigmar Gabriel and chancellor candidate Peer Steinbrück underlined their party's unwillingness to support a more substantial engagement of the Bundeswehr in Mali, refusing any contribution of the Bundeswehr in combat operations in Mali.[617]

The public, partisan criticism—particularly the claims made by Polenz and Schockenhoff—suggest that the federal government either insufficiently or did not at all coordinate its decision with the party leaders and important parliamentary institutions. The fact that the logistical support constituted a deployment below the "mission-threshold,"[618] could explain the federal government's behavior. While being indecisive about the success of France's intervention in Mali, the federal government, however, also could have decided not to support France with more or robust capacities, exactly to avoid asking the Bundestag for approval of a mandate which it did not believe in and which risky consequences it feared. A contested or even failed result could have negatively affected the outcomes in the upcoming parliamentary elections for the governmental coalition.

In contrast to the criticism related to its support of France, the federal government was basically politically uncontested regarding the planned participation of Bundeswehr soldiers in EUTM Mali and their support to AFISMA. Consequently, after the parliamentary consultation process, both mandates found the Bundestag's approval on February 28, 2013.[619] The approval signified a broad political consen-

---

[616] "SPD-Politiker fordert deutsche Hilfe für Mali," *Zeit Online*, January 13, 2013, http://www.zeit.de/politik/ausland/2013-01/mali-frankreich-deutschland.

[617] "De Maizière gegen Lammert."

[618] "De Maizière will Mali-Einsatz ausweiten."

[619] Deutscher Bundestag, *Stenografischer Bericht: Plenarprotokoll 17/225*, 27959–71 and 27974–79.

sus concerning the national position that Germany should engage militarily in Mali, but only in a limited, modest, or indirect way.

 c. *Public Opinion*

Between the poles of external and internal imperatives, sentiments toward the public opinion are suggested to have had a considerable influence on Germany's decisions for both whether and how the Bundeswehr should engage in Mali. The argument that German foreign and security policy toward Mali had been "increasingly responsive to domestic pressures—or 'domesticated,'"[620] can be made as Berlin's political elite admitted the dependent relationship between German contributions to international military missions and public approval. In a speech at the Third Forum for Defense Policy in Coblenz on January 19, 2013, Defense Minister de Maizière had explicitly expressed that "military missions without the approval of the general public will not be sustainable."[621] Drawing a comparison with a rubber band, whereby nobody could precisely determine the point of ripping when stretched, de Maizière underlined the need of German politics to "create an understanding for the public concerning the international situation and Germany's role" as well as to "justify missions well and realistic."[622]

---

[620] Pond and Kundnani, "Germany's Real Role in the Ukraine Crisis."

[621] Thomas Wiegold, "Gegen Einsatz in Mali?: Die de-Maizière-Exegeten," *Augengeradeaus* (blog), January 20, 2013, http://augengeradeaus.net/2013/01/gegen-einsatz-in-mali-die-de-maiziere-exegeten/.

[622] Ibid.; "Koblenzer Forum zur Verteidigungspolitik: Lehren aus dem Afghanistan-Einsatz," *BMVg*, updated January 21, 2013, http://www.bmvg.de/portal/a/bmvg/!ut/p/c4/NYu7DsIwEAT_yGdHCGQ6ojR0KA2EznEs5yB-6HIJDR-PXbArTbGjhSeURrOjN4wpmgUeMFg8jx8xht2LV9qorGJFOzuaHfKa04KMb7jX6-SETdFxJbvI-WOjJcCKRE_FSzUZUjMAJBqm6Vir5j_rqw1HfTo1uumvbQw7h8gO5hIXC/.

By implication, de Maizière's remarks implied both a strong sensitivity and dependency of German politics to the extent the public agrees with *whether* and *how* Germany should engage militarily—especially in a year with parliamentary elections. Several polls conducted between mid- and end-January 2013,[623] asking for the public opinion regarding Germany's support to France, therefore, gave political elites in Berlin the opportunity to assess the general mood of German citizens concerning forms and scale of German military engagement in Mali just a few weeks before the vote in the Bundestag. Unsurprisingly, all poll results reinforced the federal government's categorical refusal of a participation of Bundeswehr soldiers in combat operations in Mali, as only a minority of the respondents favored this option. Instead, while only some 25 percent ruled out any engagement of the Bundeswehr in Mali, a clear majority of the respondents supported Germany's logistic and medical help for French troops. Given the limited and modest nature of the Bundeswehr mandates for EUTM Mali and AFISMA, the broad parliamentary approval for both mandates clearly corresponded with the public opinion, suggesting to have influenced, or at least facilitated, the calculations of Germany's politicians.

3. Determinants on the Actor Level

In the process of mediating between imperatives on the external and internal level, key German stakeholders and their characterizing attitudes and preferences suggest to have significantly influenced the policy outcomes concerning the Bundeswehr engagement in Mali. All

---

[623] "Lammert findet deutsches Mali-Engagement zu gering"; "Mali: Mehrheit für logistische und medizinische Unterstützung durch Deutschland," *Infratest Dimap*, accessed April 12, 2015, http://www.infratest-dimap.de/umfragen-analysen/bundesweit/umfragen/aktuell/mali-mehrheit-fuer-logistische-und-medizinische-unterstuetzung-durch-deutschland-fdp-mehrheit-f/; "Umfrage: Unterstützung für deutschen Beitrag bei Militäreinsatz in Mali," *Zeit Online*, January 25, 2013, http://www.zeit.de/news/2013-01/25/deutschland-umfrage-unterstuetzung-fuer-deutschen-beitrag-bei-militaereinsatz-in-mali-25131218.

three essential key actors in the federal government shared a restrained stance toward a deployment of German troops into combat operations in Mali, accentuated Germany's interests in a safe and stable Mali, and emphasized their willingness to support the crisis response in the West African country with modest capacities as well as within a comprehensive approach under a regional lead.[624] The federal government's final decisions to participate in EUTM Mali, to provide indirect help for France, and to contribute to AFISMA, however, seemed to most notably resort to Federal Chancellor Merkel and Defense Minster de Maizière's shared attitudes and positions. Both underlined Germany's aspiration to assume multilateral responsibility and had further "normalized" their *understanding* of the role of military force as a subordinately and cautiously used but necessary instrument of German foreign and security policy (in Mali). In doing so, they outranked Foreign Minister Westerwelle in his culturally-preferred military-averse stance. This was possible because of two major reasons. First, Foreign Minister Westerwelle's authority in designing and enforcing German foreign policy—internationally and domestically—had been decisively weakened by his harshly criticized attitude amid the Libyan decision.[625] Second, Merkel and de Maizière were closely connected for years, most recently since 2005 as Merkel appointed

---

[624] See Federal Foreign Office, "Rede von Außenminister Westerwelle im Deutschen Bundestag zum Mali-Einsatz der Bundeswehr"; Merkel, *Rede von Bundeskanzlerin Angela Merkel anlässlich der Tagung des zivilen und militärischen Spitzenpersonals der Bundeswehr*; Neukirch and Repinski, "Germany abroad"; Thomas de Maizière, *Rede des Ministers zu den Mali Mandaten im Bundestag, BMVg*, updated Febuary 20, 2013, http://www.bmvg.de/portal/a/bmvg/!ut/p/c4/NYvBCsIwEET_aDdBFPVmKY I38aLtRdJmCQtNUtZtvfjxJofOwIPhMdhjaXIrB6eck5vwhd3I5ELQ1wDRE78UR JeIniS97ZByFPCZ717gjEn0kqlpFwYxGkWmLPoVM0iUgywx87YtjHWbLG _0_5w7e92d2xvzQPnGC9_YO2o_g!!/.

[625] The claim for Westerwelle's suffered authority had been made by Monath after the abstention from the UNSC vote on Libya in May 2011 and was reinforced by Neukirch and Repinski in relation to Germany's reaction on France's launch of Operation Serval in January 2013. See Monath, "Westerwelle und de Maizière"; Neukirch and Repinski, "Germany abroad."

the then-head of office of the Saxon chancellery (*Staatskanzlei*) in Dresden as federal minister of the chancellery in Berlin.

Both politicians shared general views on Germany's role, German foreign and security policy, and a rational approach to politics. After Federal Chancellor Merkel's general endorsement of a limited German military engagement, however, Foreign Minister Westerwelle and Defense Minister de Maizière most notably communicated Germany's foreign and security policy orientation toward Mali and shaped the political-public opinion.

Although Federal Chancellor Merkel maintained a rather modest stance within the federal government's reaction to the Malian crisis, it was her exceptional early (and conditioned) statement on October 22, 2012, declaring Germany's willingness to participate in a "support mission for Mali,"[626] that predisposed and framed the federal government's principal attitude concerning the questions of *whether* and *how* Germany should militarily engage in Mali. The fact that many public statements of Westerwelle and de Maizière after Merkel's announcement often focused on aspects of *how* or *how not* rather than *whether* (or *why*) Germany should embark in international military missions in Mali suggest that the Federal Chancellor had used her influence (chancellor principle) in determining the general guidelines of German foreign and security policy in favor of such an engagement.

Intensified by the lack of any civilian or military plans for Mali at the moment of her statement, Merkel's rushing ahead, however, decisively contrasted her typical "cautious, step-by-step approach."[627] Given Merkel's immediate attempts for political "damage control" after the highly criticized abstention from the vote on Libya,[628] her advance is suggested to be significantly related to a sensitivity of

---

[626] Merkel, *Rede von Bundeskanzlerin Angela Merkel anlässlich der Tagung des zivilen und militärischen Spitzenpersonals der Bundeswehr.*
[627] Pond and Kundnani, "Germany's Real Role in the Ukraine Crisis."
[628] See section III C 3.

avoiding another political isolation of Germany regarding the engagement of Bundeswehr soldiers in a foreign military mission.[629] While mitigating between external and internal imperatives, Merkel, therefore, seemed to have given Germany's long-term policy goals (multilateral integration), national interests,[630] and conceptual policy standards ("never alone") a (conditioned) preponderance over a domestically justifiable and culturally-ingrained aversion of using military means.

In this case, a mélange of several mutually reinforcing foreign and security policy attitudes and preferences incentivized Federal Chancellor Merkel's positive stance toward a Bundeswehr engagement in Mali. It included her deeply rooted pragmatic approach (*Realpolitik*),[631] a shifting national self-image with an increased sense for Germany's international responsibility,[632] and preference for multilaterally coordinated and implemented crisis resolution.[633]

Most importantly, Merkel's evolved personal orientation concerning the relevance and efficacy of the use of force in international affairs is suggested to have influenced the intra-governmental decision-making process. Already in 2011, the Federal Chancellor had publicly acknowledged that "military means cannot and must be excluded as

---

[629] Robert Birnbaum, "Deutscher Einsatz in Mali: Merkel und Westerwelle marschieren voran," *Der Tagesspiegel*, October 24, 2012, http://www.tagesspiegel.de/meinung/deutscher-einsatz-in-mali-merkel-und-westerwelle-marschieren-voran/7290224.html.

[630] For statements regarding the implications of a spreading international terrorism in Northern Mali for European and German security, see Angela Merkel, *Rede von Bundeskanzlerin Angela Merkel anlässlich der Tagung des zivilen und militärischen Spitzenpersonals der Bundeswehr* ; "Merkel rechtfertigt deutsche Militärhilfe in Mali," *Süddeutsche*, January 16, 2013, http://www.sueddeutsche.de/politik/krieg-gegen-rebellen-merkel-rechtfertigt-deutsche-militaerhilfe-in-mali-1.1574329.

[631] Riemer, "Merkels Realpolitik."

[632] Merkel, *Deutschland weiß um seine Verantwortung in der Welt.*

[633] Merkel, *Rede von Bundeskanzlerin Angela Merkel anlässlich der Tagung des zivilen und militärischen Spitzenpersonals der Bundeswehr.*

ultima ratio"[634] and "the use of the Bundeswehr is just an instrument, but even a very important and indispensable (one)."[635] This attribution of a more nuanced, rational, and balanced—a "normalizing"—role for the Bundeswehr within German foreign and security policy could have facilitated Merkel's generally positive stance toward an active but limited engagement of German soldiers in Mali, and hence, guided the federal government's decision-making process.

While some of her other policy preferences, such as the "networked approach"[636] and the inclusion as well as the strengthening of regional actors,[637] also found expression in the federal government's approach toward Mali, Merkel's relationship with France's President Hollande[638] is suggested to have also helped to coordinate between Paris's requests and Berlin's ability to support Operation Serval.

Foreign Minister Westerwelle and Defense Minister de Maizière had a complex and distinct influence on the federal government's decision-making process. On one hand, Westerwelle's and de Maizière's positions toward the question *how* Germany should engage in Mali widely concurred in terms of substance.[639] Both ministers opposed the deployment of German troops for ground combat operations, considered African actors as being primary responsible to act, and favored (German) modest military engagements that should

---

[634] Merkel, *Deutschland weiß um seine Verantwortung in der Welt*.

[635] Merkel, *Rede von Bundeskanzlerin Angela Merkel anlässlich der Tagung des zivilen und militärischen Spitzenpersonals der Bundeswehr*.

[636] Merkel, *Rede von Bundeskanzlerin Angela Merkel anlässlich der Tagung des zivilen und militärischen Spitzenpersonals der Bundeswehr*.

[637] Konstantin Von Hammerstein et al., "German Weapons for the World: How the Merkel Doctrine Is Changing Berlin Policy," *Spiegel Online*, December 3, 2012, http://www.spiegel.de/international/germany/german-weapons-exports-on-the-rise-as-merkel-doctrine-takes-hold-a-870596.html.

[638] "Merkel rechtfertigt deutsche Militärhilfe in Mali."

[639] Neukirch and Repinski, "Germany abroad."

empower local/regional actors for sustainable self-help.[640] On the other, however, the foreign minister and the defense minister differed significantly regarding their attitudes toward the preconditions of Germany's involvement, Germany's multilateral responsibility, the role of military force in international affairs, and the respectively felt requirement of a modest Bundeswehr engagement in Mali. Consequently, with contrasting perspectives and tones, Westerwelle and de Maizière mainly determined the design and communication of Germany's foreign and security policy orientation on *how* or *how not* Germany should engage militarily, but also influenced to a certain extent the decisions on *whether* Germany should be involved in Mali at all.

Like the Federal Chancellor, a mélange of several mutually reinforcing policy orientations and personal attitudes of Defense Minister de Maizière's indicate to have affected the federal government's decision for, and the public support toward, an active but modest Bundeswehr engagement in Mali. First, holding the view that "Germany should not overestimate ... but also not underestimate (itself),"[641] and that "Germany must meet its security-policy requirements,"[642] de Maizière even actively supported a changing German self-conception,[643] calling for a more confident assumption of Germany's (shared) responsibility in international affairs with all available means.

Second, de Maizière's characterizing constructive approach in seeking feasible, affordable, and implementable solutions suggest to have eased the opportunities for Germany to define its military contributions to Mali in coordination with its partners. Without pushing ahead or committing Germany hastily, de Maizière always pointed out

---

[640] "De Maizière erwägt Einsatz ohne Bundestagsmandat"; "De Maizière schließt Kampfeinsatz aus"; De Maizière, *Rede des Ministers zu den Mali Mandaten*; Federal Foreign Office, "Rede von Außenminister Westerwelle im Deutschen Bundestag zum Mali-Einsatz der Bundeswehr"; "Mali-Mission."

[641] De Maizière, *Internationale Verantwortung wahrnehmen.*

[642] Monath, "Westerwelle und de Maizière."

[643] De Maizière, *Internationale Verantwortung wahrnehmen.*

what Germany is willing and capable to do and what preconditions must be fulfilled.[644] In doing so and because of his notable media presence, the German defense minister might have had crucial influence on the public opinion—broadly supporting an active but restrained engagement of German soldiers in Mali—which facilitated, in turn, the approval of the German Bundestag. In addition, it is likely that de Maizière's status outranked Federal Minister Westerwelle's general risk-averse stance in providing with two airplanes, which was considered to be at least indirect support to France's Operation Serval.[645]

Most importantly, de Maizière's matured personal orientation toward the role and efficacy of the use of force in international affairs likely contributed to the federal government's decision in favor of a Bundeswehr engagement in Mali. In step with Federal Chancellor Merkel, de Maizière had acknowledged already in 2011 that "the use of military force can be a political mean to prevent or to contain worse violence."[646] While sharing Germany's policy preference to embed military means in a comprehensive approach, de Maizière, in contrast to Foreign Minister Westerwelle, therefore, critically considered to always condemn military interventions in conflicts and to only call for political solutions. Calling for a case-by-case assessment of whether the use of military force is needed, affordable, and feasible, de Maizière simultaneously highlighted that the politics also incur blame if it decides against a military intervention, as happened in Rwanda or in the Balkans.[647] Given the implications of an instable and insecure Mali for Europe and Germany's security as well as the multilateral imperatives, this more rational and balanced understand-

---

[644] "De Maizière schließt Kampfeinsatz aus"; Neukirch and Repinski, "Germany abroad."
[645] Jungholt, "Paris ruft."
[646] De Maizière, *Rede des Bundesministers der Verteidigung anlässlich der 8. Handelsblatt Konferenz am 25. Oktober 2011 in Berlin.*
[647] De Maizière, *Internationale Verantwortung wahrnehmen.*

ing of the role of the Bundeswehr within German foreign and security policy is suggested to have led de Maizière to pursue a positive approach toward an active but modest deployment of German soldiers in Mali.

Foreign Minister Westerwelle's role in Berlin's decision-making on Mali, in contrast, was rather ambivalent. While the federal chancellor and the defense minister agreed on his persistent focus on a political solution of the crisis in Mali, as repeatedly highlighted in the national mandates for EUTM Mali and AFISMA, he proved to be ineffective in enforcing his deeply ingrained attitude "of restraint, what concerns military missions"[648] within the Mali case.[649] Even if the actual engagement of the Bundeswehr in Mali remained exclusively limited on training and logistical support, a crucial aspect that corresponded with and might even relate to Westerwelle's preference of a "culture of military restraint [as] a constant of German foreign policy,"[650] the engagements themselves suggest, however, that Westerwelle had only a minor influence on the decision whether German soldiers should be deployed.

Westerwelle's limited role among the three key stakeholders is owed chiefly to his weakened authority after the diplomatic debacle over Libya. Foreign Minister Westerwelle had decisively lost credibility[651] on both the domestic and international stage because of his overemphasized and often nonreflective reference to a guiding "culture of military restraint," tending to ignore Germany's international responsibility. Merkel and de Maizière distancing themselves—only slightly and modestly—from a politically tarnished foreign minister

---

[648] Westerwelle, "Gaddafi muss weg."

[649] Gebauer and Wittrock, "Germany's Mali Predicament"; "Germany Abroad"; Monath, "Westerwelle und de Maizière."

[650] Monath, "Westerwelle und de Maizière."

[651] Gebauer and Wittrock, "Germany's Mali Predicament"; "Germany Abroad"; Monath, "Westerwelle und de Maizière."

and his strong refusal of military force in an election year may also have contributed to Westerwelle's reduced influence within the decision-making process on Mali.

It became particularly apparent especially amid the tense situation concerning the question of whether and how Germany should support France's intervention in Mali. Although Westerwelle kept arguing that the "deployment of German combat troops is not an option" and even affronted France at the same time in emphasizing that "Germans are highly involved in Afghanistan, where the French are hardly involved at all,"[652] only a few days later, Germany sent two airplanes to support France's efforts—even if indirectly.

D. Conclusion: Mali—A German "Standard" Case

The analysis of the decision-making processes for the closely inter-linked decisions on *whether* and *how* the Bundeswehr participates in EUTM, contributes to AFISMA, and supports France in Mali has demonstrated that the policy outcome rests on a complex interplay between determinants on the external and internal level as well as the role of state actors in mediating in-between them.

The decisions for the Bundeswehr engagements in Mali are chiefly a result of vital, mutually reinforcing pull and push factors on all three levels that outweighed domestic or personal resentment concerning the use of military force. Shifting self-perceptions of Germany's international responsibility and broad political willingness to fulfil bi- and multilateral commitments, particularly after the power-political backlash from the nonparticipation in Libya, reinforced Germany's cultural-conceptual principle to implement foreign and security politics within multilateral frameworks ("never alone"). Since these multi-

---

[652] Cited in Neukirch and Repinski, "Germany abroad." For Westerwelle's general refusal of German particiaption in combat operations in Mali, see Jungholt, "Paris ruft"; Jungholt and Kammholz, "Bundesregierung sucht noch eine Strategie für Mali"; "Mali-Mission"; Neukirch and Repinski, "Germany abroad."

lateral frameworks provided conditions that corresponded with German foreign and security policy preferences, such as a comprehensive legitimate foundation; shared interests in a more secure and stable Mali; a strong consensus to intervene militarily but under the primary responsibility of regional actors and embedded in an approach that prioritized political means; and a mission framework that imposed limited risks, objectives, and capacity requirements, all of these factors incentivized the federal government, and at its forefront the federal chancellor and the defense minister, to finally decide that German soldiers should participate in EUTM Mali and contribute to AFISMA. Widely sharing the federal government's view on the due necessity to modestly support international military efforts in Mali, German parliamentarians not only approved the federal government's decisions, but also contributed to their genesis.

Conversely, the mélange between other external and internal factors, including evolutions in the power and security environment, strategic approaches, an overall hesitant international environment, a remaining instable security situation in all of Mali, and domestic calculations about ongoing military commitments, elections, and public opinion, determined the political considerations on *how* or *how not* Germany should be engaged militarily in Mali. All of these factors corresponded with and mutually reinforced Germany's persistently salient restraint in using military force, risk-avoiding stance, and considerations of domestic politics. They disincentivized Germany from assuming a more active role within the international crisis response and from contributing with "robust" military capacities. As a result, almost always alongside all other Western states except later France, early on Germany ruled out the deployment of combat troops into the West African country, used the reference to the responsibility of regional actors as pretext for its wait-and-see attitude as well as modest engagement, and remained cautious in defining its actual contributions below the level of combat forces. Between the poles of external expectations, emerging aspirations, internal constraints, and personal preferences, the salience of these factors also explains Berlin's challenges to quickly find suitable and affordable policy options in response to Paris's requests for support of Operation Serval.

The unfolding of events and factors in relation to the decision-making processes for Germany's military engagements in Mali lead to five major conclusions. First, the Malian case demonstrates that the shifts of Germany's self-conception after the political debacle around Libya as well as the "normalizing" understanding of the role and relevance of force in international affairs did not result in significant changes in the fundamental attitudes and principles of Germany's foreign and security policy. On the one hand, Germany's self-image of its statecraft as that of a "shaping power," as understood among Germany's political elites, and its increased sense of responsibility, therefore, were more related to the willingness to share responsibility in common efforts for international stability and security as well as to cooperate more closely with traditional and new partners. At the same time, Germany carried the burden of the shaping of global governance.[653] Hence, both aspects strengthened Germany's axiom of policy that exemplifies multilateralism.

On the other hand, more responsibility and the normalizing understanding of the military force's role were not metonymic—and should not be confused—with an increased willingness of German politicians simply to deploy more German troops abroad. Little prospect exists of a more robust German footprint in international military missions because of the factors analyzed in this study. Instead, such tenets as a restrained foreign and security policy approach, particularly when it comes to the use of military means, have remained valid in the case under review.

Second, the Malian case also demonstrates that all shifts did not affect Germany's long-term thinking on, and Germany's restrained approach toward, Africa. Particularly when it comes to security con-

---

[653] Bundesregierung, *Globalisierung gestalten*, 6–11.

cerns and military engagements on the African continent, Germany continued to point out the primary responsibility of local and regional actors in dealing with the crisis.[654] Despite all documented interests in the region and the situationally pronounced security implications of the crisis in Mali, German politicians refused a stronger engagement in the country (including the participation in combat operations), and instead, called for an active role of, and robust mandate for, the AU and ECOWAS. With this restrained stance, German and European attitudes perfectly matched. Because even if Africa had been the focus of CSDP operations since 2003, the actual European (CSDP) engagement on the continent continued to be "under-resourced and under-funded, especially in the light of scope and scale of the needs."[655]

Closely interlinked with the former aspect, third, the decisions of whether and how Germany should engage militarily in Mali reflects Germany's continuing paradigm to implement its foreign and security policy through and with multilateral institutions—even if "national interests are not directly concerned."[656] In doing so, the Mali case does not provide any evidence to support the claim, as raised by some scholars in relation to the German abstentions in Iraq in 2003 and in Libya in 2011,[657] that multilateral institutions have lost their significance on setting the framework for organizing and implementing German foreign and security policy in general, and on determining German decisions for the use of military force. Instead, it shows that German Africa policy is generally a multilaterally—predominantly on European level—embedded and effectuated policy.

---

[654] See Bundesregierung, *Deutschland und Afrika*, 5; Auswärtiges Amt, Bundesministerium der Verteidigung, and Bundesministerium für wirtschaftliche Zusammenarbeit, *Für eine kohärente Politik der Bundesregierung gegenüber fragilen Staaten*, 5.
[655] Ginsberg and Penska, *European Union in Global Security*, 67.
[656] Ginsberg and Penska, *European Union in Global Security*, 67.
[657] Baumann, "Multilateralismus," 481–85; Milosevic, "Deutsche Kriegsbeteiligung und—verweigerung," 143–44; Oppermann, "National Role Conceptions," 513–14.

Fourth, most importantly, Germany's decisions on Mali underline that the question of how German soldiers will be engaged in a military mission continues to significantly affect the political willingness to decide, and the public willingness to support, whether the Bundeswehr should be deployed at all. Between the poles of Germany's commitment as a reliable ally and partner and the unchanging reservations about the efficacy, success, and costs of foreign military interventions, particularly in war or war-like scenarios, the very limited framework for participation in EUTM Mali and the contribution to AFISMA in terms of objectives, risks, troops, and resources, therefore, definitely eased Berlin's decision in favor of the engagement.

Despite Germany's persistent premise of multilaterally implemented foreign and security policy, multilateral imperatives do not necessarily narrow down the federal government's freedom of action while weighing and deciding whether or not Germany should be involved in international military missions, as the concept of the "multilateralism trap"[658] posit. Instead, Berlin's categorical ruling out of German combat troops and focus on a political solution in Mali suggest that in a hypothetical case of a "robust" European mission in the country, Germany was likely to decide not to participate and would rather convince its partners to contribute with noncombat military means.

Finally, the nature of the decision-making process, the impacts of each single factor on the decision, and the interrelated effects between all determinants on the policy outcomes suggest that Germany's military engagements in Mali constitute a "standard case," and hence, mark a return to consistent patterns of German foreign and security policy on decisions for *whether* and *how* Germany should engage in international military missions. The "return" relates to Berlin's reemphasis on multilaterally framed and implemented decisions for

---

[658] Kaim, "Deutsches Interesse versus Bündnisverpflichtung"; Gießmann and Wagner, "Auslandseinsätze der Bundeswehr," 7.

the use of force and to its intensified awareness of multilateral commitments. As such, the Mali case may be considered as a return to Germany's predictability in international affairs—a departure from former Federal Chancellor Schröder or Foreign Minister Westerwelle's *Sonderweg* ("special path"). While being increasingly willing to share international responsibility, Germany, however, maintained its historical-normative risk-averse attitude, a hesitance within the decision-making process, a position of military restraint, and its focus on domestic politics. Consequently, with reinvigorated multilateral imperatives, the characterizing "inherent contradictions"[659] of Germany's foreign and security policy have even increased around the decisions on Mali. Germany's rather expected policy outcome, therefore, can be traced back, beside many other factors, to the federal government's capacity to mitigate between the poles of external and internal imperatives and constraints.

---

[659] Ischinger, "Germany after Libya," 46; Gareis, "Die Organisation deutscher Sicherheitspolitik," 106.

V. Germany: A Responsible and Restrained "Shaping Power"

The policy outcomes in the two recent case studies of Libya and Mali lead to four important conclusions related to German foreign and security policy and the use of force. First, even if Germany's multilateralism has become more contingent, pragmatic, instrumental, or selective over the last decade with the spread of security crises around Europe and on the continent of Africa,[660] both cases demonstrate that an effective multilateralism—the paradigm of "never alone"—is not only "a must" for Germany's foreign and security policy "because of ... [Germany's] history and geostrategic location,"[661] but also remains a key principle in German strategic thought.[662] Even the Libyan case supports this argument as the rash decision of the federal government in 2011 to support indirectly the Libyan intervention, following the harsh international criticism of German inaction, can be understood as a clear sign of Berlin's effort to be a credible multilateral partner as has been the case for decades. Specifically, Germany

---

[660] Baumann, "The Transformation of German Multilateralism," 1–26; Kundnani, "Germany as a Geo-Economic Power," 35; Oppermann, "National Role Conceptions," 507; Roos, "Deutsche Außenpolitik nach der Vereinigung," 33–34; Regina Karp, "The New German Foreign Policy Consensus," *Washington Quarterly* 29, no. 1 (Winter 2005-2006): 68.

[661] "US-Sicherheitsstrategie und ihre Auswirkungen auf Europa, Rede von Kerstin Müller, Staatsministerin im Auswärtigen Amt, auf der 4. Außenpolitischen Jahrestagung der Heinrich-Böll-Stiftung, Berlin, 13.11.2003," *Auswaertiges Amt*, updated November 19, 2003,
http://presseservice.pressrelations.de/standard/result_main.cfm?aktion=jour_pm&r=140036&quelle=0&pfach=1&n_firmanr_=109207&sektor=pm&detail=1.

[662] See Gauck, *Germany's Role in the World*, 6–7; German Institute for International and Security Affairs, and German Marshall Fund of the United States, *Neue Macht— Neue Verantwortung*, 5–6; Mützenich, "Gemeinsame Erklärungen reichen nicht aus!"; Von der Leyen, *Rede der Bundesministerin der Verteidigung anlässlich der 50. Münchner Sicherheitskonferenz*, 3–4.

will seek the dialog and cooperation of the UN, NATO, and EU and continue to organize and implement foreign and security policy through and within these multilateral institutions.[663] In relation to Germany's Africa policy, this fact becomes even more important, as the new federal government political guidelines of May 2014 regarding Africa explicitly stated, that German Africa policy is, and will remain, predominantly embedded in an EU-framework.[664] The refugee crisis since the spring of 2015 can only be expected to add further impetus to such policy.

Second, in contrast to the argument that the binding power of NATO (and the EU) on German foreign and security policy has decreased, this study concludes that Germany will even need a closer integration into, and cooperation within, multilateral collective security and collective defense institutions. This fact is true if Germany wants to gain influence among the other powers and beyond[665] and to assume a more responsible and a more decisive approach to international affairs—particularly when the use of military means is concerned amid worsening crises. Given the closely intertwined institutional frameworks in NATO and EU and the reduction of national military capacities across Europe in the wake of demographic as well as economic straits, the mutual dependencies among European states for planning, coordinating, and conducting military operations have increased.[666] Being evermore dependent on multilateral institutions to pursue its (foreign and) security policy, hence, Germany is unable to sustain a position that is blind to the external expectations of the

---

[663] Federal Ministry of Defense, *Bundeswehr on Operations*, 45–46; Federal Ministry of Defense, *Defense Policy Guidelines*, 5–6.

[664] Bundesregierung, *Afrikapolitische Leitlinien der Bundesregierung*, 12.

[665] Gauck, Germany's *Role in the World*, 6–7.

[666] Claudia Major and Christian Mölling, "Die europäische Armee kommt," *Neue Züricher Zeitung*, April 29, 2015, http://www.nzz.ch/meinung/debatte/die-europaeische-armee-kommt-1.18531717.

European and world powers with which it must exist in order to maintain an effective statecraft.

Yet, third, the "relevance of domestic priorities and societal debates on [German] foreign [and security] decision-making processes"[667] has further increased as the international environment has slid into crisis and as the world economy has also reinforced German power amid a public mind that celebrates Swiss ideals as the leading lights of statecraft. Affected by the turmoil of the digital and social media cosmos, German policy-makers orientate their calculations to the shifts and twists of domestic considerations[668] and constraints—particularly public opinion[669]—when mitigating between the poles of external and internal imperatives. Thus, German politics is, as in many other states, first and foremost "local,"[670] and "voters' sentiments" affect policies.[671] This feature of domestic politics of the last two decades today stands in very sharp contrast to a deepening security crisis in the Middle East, Africa and now in Eastern Europe.

Finally, fourth, despite the shifts of emphasis between normative axioms and the calls for "more substantial" German contributions to international crisis resolution,[672] the "culture of (military) restraint" remains the most influential imperative for German foreign and secu-

---

[667] Von Bredow, "Mühevolle Weltpolitik," 724.

[668] Helga Haftendorn, "Deutschlands Rückkehr in die Weltpolitik," *Politische Studien* 60, no. 425 (2009): 53.

[669] On January 19, 2013, Defense Minister de Maizière had explicitly expressed that "military missions without the approval of the general public will not be sustainable." See Wiegold, "Gegen Einsatz in Mali?"

[670] Collmer, "'All Politics Is Local,'" 201.

[671] Ischinger, "Germany after Libya," 49.

[672] Nünlist, "Mehr Verantwortung?, 3; see also Gauck, *Germany's Role in the World*, 4; German Institute for International and Security Affairs, and German Marshall Fund of the United States. *Neue Macht—Neue Verantwortung*, 5–6; Mützenich, "Gemeinsame Erklärungen reichen nicht aus!"

rity policy with its strong grounding in domestic politics.⁶⁷³ Such restraint dominates both the public stance toward the missions abroad of the Bundeswehr and the strategic calculations within political decision-making. As a result, military contributions to such noncombat missions as humanitarian aid, training support, or peacekeeping/enforcing operations—*limited* and calculable over all categories—will most likely constitute Germany's foreign and security policy touchstone on the use of military force between what is (mainly) externally required versus politically desired and indispensable, militarily affordable and feasible, and domestically justifiable. These steps constitute the measures of judgment for the political efficacy of German military involvement abroad that will find the broadest acceptance among politicians and the German public, as recently confirmed by several public polls.⁶⁷⁴ Consequently, despite the "normalizing" of the role, relevance, and efficacy of the use of military force in German foreign and security policy thinking,⁶⁷⁵ a German "aversion to

---

⁶⁷³ Franke, "A Tale of Stumbling Blocks and Road Bumps," 363; Kundnani, "Germany as a Geo-Economic Power," 32–37; Milosevic, "Deutsche Kriegsbeteiligung und—verweigerung," 146; Von Krause, *Die Afghanistaneinsätze der Bundeswehr*, 282.

⁶⁷⁴ In May 2014, almost 90 percent of the respondents to a public poll of the Körber Foundation agreed that the deployment of German armed forces in mission abroad is justified, when "there is a direct threat to peace and security in Europe." See Munich Security Conference, *Munich Security Report 2015*, 11; "Mehrheit der Deutschen lehnt Auslandseinsätze ab," *Zeit Online*, December 28, 2014, http://www.zeit.de/politik/deutschland/2014-12/umfrage-deutsche-ablehnung-internationale-bundeswehr-einsaetze. A survey from the Pew Research Center at the end of February 2015 confirms the predominant attitude among German citizens against a more active role of Germany in international affairs. Instead, almost 70 percent of all respondents said that Germany should limit its military role. Pew Research Center, *Germany and the United States: Reliable Allies-But Disagreements on Russia, Global Leadership, and Trade* (Washington, DC: Pew Research Center, May 7, 2015), 10, accessed March 25, 2015, http://www.pewglobal.org/files/2015/05/Pew-Research-Center-U.S.-Germany-Report-FINAL-FOR-WEB.pdf.

⁶⁷⁵ Von Krause, *Die Bundeswehr als Instrument deutscher Außenpolitik*, 362.

involvement in war-fighting"[676] remains, which raises the threshold for sending the Bundeswehr into combat operations in comparison with, say, the UK and France.

Germany's abstention from the vote on the UNSC Resolution 1973 and from the international military mission in Libya in 2011 marked a critical turning point in contemporary German foreign and security policy. Throughout the next almost three years, as this study shows, not only had the federal government kept emphasizing Germany's commitment for an active and responsible role in international affairs, but also Germany's self-image among the political (and societal) elites had gradually shifted as a result. This process culminated at the 50th Munich Security Conference, beginning in 2014 at a time of deepening international crisis.

Such statements by high-level states official that Germany should take "more resolute steps to uphold and help shape the [world] order" and "must ... be ready to do more to guarantee the security that others have provided it with for decades"[677] and that it should engage in foreign and security affairs "earlier, more decisively, and more substantially,"[678] "rattled German self-certainties"[679] that have determined the Federal Republic of Germany's orientation and stance in international affairs since 1949.

A.   Germany's International Role in Action

Given the far-reaching experience of Germany's internationally and domestically criticized abstention in Libya, the question remains: how does German military engagement in Africa after Libya (and particularly since the beginning of 2014), correspond with—and how can it

---

[676] Franke, "A Tale of Stumbling Blocks and Road Bumps," 363.
[677] Gauck, Germany's Role in the World, 4.
[678] Steinmeier, *Rede des Außenministers anlässlich der 50. Münchner Sicherheitskonferenz.*
[679] Joffe, "Friedensarbeit 2.0."

be understood in relation to—Berlin's stance for more responsibility in international affairs?

A brief look at the evolution of German military presence in Africa up to 2015 unveils an ambivalent outcome—active, but modest. Apart from the ongoing participation in the EU operation for protection of humanitarian aid and antipiracy operations at the Horn of Africa (NAVFOR ATALANTA) and in UN peace support missions in Sudan (UNAMID), German military personnel were engaged in up to six new missions on the African continent since 2011, with four of these six missions still active. These include: a) UN peace support mission in South Sudan (since July 2011); b) EU training mission (EUTM) and the UN Stabilization Mission (MINUSMA) in Mali (since February 2013); c) UN Monitoring Mission in West Sahara (MINURSO, since October 2013); and d) EU training mission in Somalia (reestablished in April 2014).

Germany's contribution to the EU peacekeeping mission in the Central African Republic (EUFOR RCA) ended in February 2015, shortly before the mission itself was closed after 11 months on March 23, 2015.[680] In April 2015, Germany also ended its three-year military contribution to the civilian-led EU maritime capacity building mission in Somalia (EUCAP Nestor).[681]

The comparably large number of missions, however, does not correspond with numerous deployments of German soldiers within those missions. As of the end April 2015, only 200 Bundeswehr sol-

---

[680] "Closing Ceremony of EUFOR RCA"; "Zentralafrikanische Republik—EUFOR RCA (European Union Force République Centrafricaine)," *BMVg*, updated April 1, 2015, http://www.einsatz.bundeswehr.de/portal/a/einsatzbw/!ut/p/c4/04_SB8K8xLLM9MSSzPy8xBz9CP3I5EyrpHK9pPKU1PjUzLzixJIqIDcxKT21ODkjJ7-4ODUPKpFaUpWql1qall9UlJyoX5DtqAgAvelJGg!!/.

[681] "Die EU-geführte zivile Mission am Horn von Afrika"; "What is EUCAP Nestor?," *European Union External Action Service*, accessed May 6, 2015, http://www.eucap-nestor.eu/en/mission/general_overview/what_is_eucap_nestor_online.

diers took part in these newly approved missions. Even together with the contributions to EUFOR ATALANTA (311) and UNAMID (9), these numbers clearly rank below the soldiers deployed in Afghanistan (Resolute Support, 832), Kosovo (KFOR, 676), and Turkey (Active Fence, 257).[682]

Germany's ambivalence toward crisis resolution in Africa, its willingness to participate more actively while simultaneously being restrained in actual contributions (hereby, primarily limiting risks for its own soldiers), became particularly evident in three instances in the first half of 2014.

First, against the backdrop of changes in the EUTM Mali mission as well as increased security policy challenges on the African continent, the federal government sought to adapt Germany's contributions to the mission in a "suitable" manner in preparation of the required new national mandate.[683] As a consequence, Berlin raised the upper limit set by the parliamentary mandate from 180 to 250 soldiers. Even if Berlin's new approach has led to qualitative improvements of German contributions to the mission, for example through the participation of Bundeswehr soldiers in infantry and logistic training[684] as well as the through the takeover of several staff-functions (Germany took over the lead of EUTM Mali in August 2015 for the

---

[682] For more details, see Appendix.

[683] Antrag der Bundesregierung, "Fortsetzung der Beteiligung bewaffneter deutscher Streitkräfte zur Beteiligung an der EU-geführten militärischen Ausbildungsmission EUTM Mali auf Grundlage des Ersuchens der Regierung von Mali sowie der Beschlüsse 2013/34/GASP des Rates der Europäischen Union (EU) vom 17. Januar 2013 und vom 18. Februar 2013 in Verbindung mit den Resolutionen 2071 (2012) und 2085 (2012) des Sicherheitsrates der Vereinten Nationen," 5.

[684] "Erneuter Ausbildungsstart in Mali," *BMVg*, updated January 27, 2015, http://www.einsatz.bundeswehr.de/portal/a/einsatzbw/!ut/p/c4/LYvBCoMwEE T_KGvaQrW3ipdCe-nF6qWsZpGlMZG4VpBfBNwBgZmHgMtRDv88oDC3qG FFzQ9X7pVdauhN7GbUbZY8SMLWbtPJBtBnc6GVO8dSUohJxxzCCg- qMkHsYksIUSi2ECT6arU51O2S_-Ke563j0NxrG7lE6ZxvP4BtoW_uQ!!/.

next 10 months),[685] the quantitative changes came off rather short. Under the limitations set by the European force generation process, there are now some 50–60 more German soldiers deployed to the West African country than those deployed in the period between 2013 and 2014.[686] In addition to that, a direct support to the Malian Armed Forces and MINUSMA, which would expose German (and all other European) soldiers to the threats in northern part of Mali, is still excluded.

Second, in case of Germany's participation to MINUSMA (the UN follow-up operation to AFISMA), technical limitations of the German Transall airplanes but also German operational caveats had led the UN to refuse the resumption of Germany's support in the summer of 2014. As a result, less than 10 German soldiers out of the previous 130 soldiers are now part of the mission.[687]

Third, amid the debates about Europe's reaction to the crisis in the Central African Republic, Germany (again) early and categorically ruled out the deployment of German combat troops.[688] Instead, Foreign Minister Frank Walter Steinmeier argued that Germany should

---

[685] Christoph B. Schiltz, "Bundeswehr wird EU-Ausbildungsmission leiten," *Die Welt*, May 7, 2015, http://www.welt.de/politik/ausland/article140591706/Bundeswehr-wird-EU-Ausbildungsmission-leiten.html.

[686] One must note that the EU, as any other multilateral organization, relies on a strong multilateral foundation for their missions. Given both political and operational requirements, hence, throughout the force generation process the EU seeks to integrate as much as possible states into the force posture of a mission. Consequently, even if offering to provide a variety of assets, a single state's opportunities to finally fill the positions or to increase its national contributions are limited.

[687] See Appendix. See also Thomas Wiegold, "Bundeswehr weltweit: 17 Einsätze, von einem bis 1.600," *Augengeradeaus* (blog), October 20, 2014, http://augengeradeaus.net/2014/10/bundeswehr-weltweit-17-einsaetze-von-einem-bis-1-600-soldaten/.

[688] Denis M. Tull, *Deutsche Afrikapolitik: Ein Beitrag zu einer überfälligen Debatte* (Berlin: Friedrich-Ebert-Stiftung, February 2014), 1.

instead focus on the EU training mission in Mali.[689] This position clearly corresponds, as this study argues, with Germany's (increasing) preference for noncombat operations in Africa and elsewhere. Eventually, Germany decided in April 2014 to contribute up to 80 German soldiers to the very narrowly designed EU peacekeeping operation in the Central African state.[690] While Germany provided civil air transport and in case of an emergency, air medevac capabilities, de facto, however, less than 10 German soldiers were engaged in staff functions in the Force Headquarters (FHQ) in Bangui (CAR) and in the Operational Headquarters (OHQ) in Larissa (Greece).

B. Responsiveness and Responsibility

In essence, the instances of German military engagement in Africa after Libya may not constitute the "substantial shift" as some observers had expected particularly after the statements at the Munich Security Conference at the beginning of 2014.[691] Their ambivalent pos-

---

[689] "Steinmeier gegen Einsatz deutscher Kampftruppen," *Die Welt*, January 20, 2014, http://www.welt.de/politik/deutschland/article124022914/Steinmeier-gegen-Einsatz-deutscher-Kampftruppen.html.

[690] Antrag der Bundesregierung "Entsendung bewaffneter deutscher Streitkräfte zur Beteiligung an der Europäischen Überbrückungsmission in der Zentralafrikanischen Republik (EUFOR RCA) auf Grundlage der Beschlüsse 2014/73/GASP sowie 2014/183/GASP des Rates der Europäischen Union vom 10. Februar 2014 und vom 1. April 2014 in Verbindung mit den Resolutionen 2127 (2013) und 2134 (2014) des Sicherheitsrates der Vereinten Nationen vom 5. Dezember 2013 und vom 28. Januar 2014," Drs. 18/1081 (Berlin: Bundesanzeiger Verlagsgesellschaft, April 8, 2014), accessed March 26, 2015, http://dipbt.bundestag.de/dip21/btd/18/010/1801081.pdf; Deutscher Bundestag, *Stenografischer Bericht: Plenarprotokoll 18/30* (Berlin: Bundesanzeiger Verlagsgesellschaft, April 10, 2014), 2535–38, accessed March 26, 2015, http://dipbt.bundestag.de/dip21/btp/18/18030.pdf.

[691] Sabine Matthay, "Raus aus Afghanistan, rein nach Afrika? *Deutschlandradio*, February 19, 2014, http://www.deutschlandradiokultur.de/sicherheitspolitik-raus-aus-afghanistan-rein-nach-afrika.1005.de.html?dram:article_id=277510; Mützenich, "Gemeinsame Erklärungen reichen nicht aus!"; Tull, *Deutsche Afrikapolitik*, 1.

ture—active but modest—however, corresponds with Germany's understanding of a (more) active and responsible approach in international affairs, particularly in relation to Africa and the use of military force. Such a policy plays out among three interrelated premises of contemporary German foreign and security policy (in Africa): "empower others," "being responsible," and "being restrained."

First, in the course of the last decade, "Africa has become gradually but steadily part of the routine foreign and security policy business"[692] of Germany. The fact that Berlin "takes Africa [more and more] seriously"[693] relates to the increasing relevance of the African continent for Germany (and Europe) in terms of chances and challenges as strategically acknowledged with the two governmental concepts in 2011 and in 2014.[694] Under the comprehensive and networked approach of Germany's Africa policy—embedded in an EU framework[695]—the primary aim of Germany's security policy engagement in Africa, however, *remains* to strengthen "African self-reliance through the empowerment of African partners for successful

---

[692] Tull, *Deutsche Afrikapolitik*, 1; Corina Schuhkraft, "Die Afrikapolitik Deutschlands—Von der 'freundlichen Vernachlässigung' hin zu einem stärkeren Engagement," in *Die Afrikapolitik der Europäischen Union: Neue Ansätze und Perspektiven*, ed. Gisela Müller-Brandeck-Bocquet et al. (Würzburg: Barbara Budrich, 2007), 195–220; Ulrich Golaszinski, *Subsahara-Afrika: Die Wiederentdeckung eines Kontinentes* (Berlin: Friedrich-Ebert-Stiftung, 2007), 7–10. For the critical argument that Germany continues to face challenges to face up to, and to assure itself of its objectives and interests in the African continent, see Robert Kappel, "Deutsche Afrikapolitik: Uneinig und Inkohärent," *Internationale Politik und Gesellschaft*, March 17, 2014, http://www.ipg-journal.de/kolumne/artikel/deutsche-afrikapolitik-uneinig-und-inkohaerent-317/; Mair and Tull, *Deutsche Afrikapolitik*, 34–46; Steinberg, "Schlussfolgerungen," 77.

[693] Speech by Roderich Kiesewetter in Deutscher Bundestag, *Stenografischer Bericht: Plenarprotokoll 18/30*, 2532.

[694] Bundesregierung, *Deutschland und Afrika*, 5–16; Bundesregierung, *Afrikapolitische Leitlinien der Bundesregierung*, 1–4.

[695] Bundesregierung, *Afrikapolitische Leitlinien der Bundesregierung*, 12–13.

crisis prevention and effective crisis reaction."[696] In doing so, Germany's preference of "African solutions for African problems" coalesces with an overarching tenet of German foreign and security policy that seeks to "make others fit to assume responsibility for security in their own regions."[697]

Consequently, Germany's deployments in, and emphasized focus on, the EU training missions in Mali and Somalia not only clearly reflect Berlin's security policy premise of "empower others," but also constitute the level of (military) engagement that is considered as being responsible, and hence, as (mainly) externally required, politically desired and indispensable, militarily affordable and feasible, and domestically justifiable. Apart from not being politically intended and supported in society, therefore, a more substantial German military engagement in Africa, particularly if it comes to combat operations, cannot be reasonably expected by commentators on world affairs. With a clear focus on EU frameworks and a restrained stance toward the use of military means, Berlin's security policy in Africa also reflects and continues Germany's two axioms of foreign and security policy. Thus, Germany's general thinking and action concerning security affairs in relation to the African continent will not shift considerably in the near future, if no significant threat emerges and if there is no change in the multilateral environment, particularly a strong consensus among the EU member states, that acknowledges the need for a more active policy and a more substantial engagement on the

---

[696] Bundesregierung, *Afrikapolitische Leitlinien der Bundesregierung*, 14; Dagmar Dehner, Ulrike Scheffer, and Michael Schmidt, "Was mehr deutsche Soldaten in Afrika ausrichten können," *Der Tagesspiegel*, January 28, 2014,
http://www.tagesspiegel.de/politik/auslandseinsaetze-der-bundeswehr-was-mehr-deutsche-soldaten-in-afrika-ausrichten-koennten/9392336.html.

[697] Ursula von der Leyen, *Speech by the Federal Minister of Defense, Dr. Ursula von der Leyen, on the Occasion of the 51st Munich Security Conference* (Munich: NATO, February 6, 2015), 3, accessed April 2, 2015,
https://www.securityconference.de/fileadmin/MSC_/2015/Freitag/150206-2015_Rede_vdL_MSC_Englisch-1_Kopie_.pdf.

African continent. The advent of the refugee crisis in the Mediterranean will pose a test to this generalization, for certain, but the weight of policy analyzed in this study cannot be made to vanish in a day or a week.

Second, Germany's aspiration to "shoulder greater responsibility, to make contributions, [and] to take actions"[698] should neither be confused with a unilateral or dominant stance in international affairs nor be misunderstood with an increased likelihood to deploy more soldiers abroad or with the greater acceptance of "tough military actions," as high-level German politicians and parliamentarians have repeatedly emphasized.[699] Instead, "being [more] responsible" implies three major considerations. It means, at first, to better share responsibility.[700] Such a sharing of responsibility in collective security and collective defense encompasses a means to help shape global governance and to influence international (security) affairs through a deepened cooperation with traditional and new partners and allies.[701] Beyond doubts about such policies, such statecraft includes the principle not to "refrain from anything"[702] or "to sight tight,"[703] but to act if deemed indispensable by makers of policy, to adhere to the commitments made among partners, and to be aware of the consequences of

---

[698] Von der Leyen, Speech by the Federal Minister of Defense, 2–3.

[699] Gauck, *Germany's Role in the World*, 6; Mützenich, "Gemeinsame Erklärungen reichen nicht aus!"; Von der Leyen, *Speech by the Federal Minister of Defense*, 3.

[700] Gauck, *Germany's Role in the World*, 7. See also De Maizière, *Internationale Verantwortung wahrnehmen*; Von der Leyen, *Speech by the Federal Minister of Defense*, 3.

[701] Bundesregierung, *Globalisierung gestalten*, 6–11; German Institute for International and Security Affairs, and German Marshall Fund of the United States, *Neue Macht—Neue Verantwortung*, 9, 14–15.

[702] Steinmeier, *Rede des Außenministers anlässlich der 50. Münchner Sicherheitskonferenz*.

[703] Von der Leyen, *Rede der Bundesministerin der Verteidigung anlässlich der 50. Münchner Sicherheitskonferenz*, 5.

inactivity on Germany's standing in the international system[704] and upon the human ideals that underlie German statecraft in Europe and beyond. The fact that Germany has actively contributed, on a larger and smaller scale, to all major EU CSDP military missions in Africa after Libya or to the international efforts in combating the Ebola epidemic in West Africa reflects this one facet of a heightened sense of responsibility that has arisen out of the cases examined here in this study.

In addition, based on "more [German] power and influence,"[705] "being responsible" also means for Germany to be ready and capable to lead, an unaccustomed role that is nonetheless made necessary for the changing international system and its crisis laden multipolarity. The type of leadership Germany is prepared to exercise, however, is not to storm ahead or to dictate the multilateral decision-making process as done by others or as done in the past by another generation of Germans. Instead, it stands for leading among and through the close cooperation with others, by enabling "others with less resources to make their vital contributions as equal partners," and by having "the will and capacity to act."[706] Germany's nuanced understanding of leadership in policy and security has found expression in Defense Minister Ursula von der Leyen's motto of "leadership from the center,"[707] raised at the 51st Munich Security conference in February 2015—a play on German international and domestic politics of

---

[704] Foreign Minister Frank-Walter Steinmeier emphasized in his closing remarks to the conference "Review 2014 – Thinking Foreign Policy Broader" that Germany shoulders responsibility for its actions and non-actions alike. See Steinmeier, Frank-Walter, *Schlussrede von Außenminister Frank-Walter Steinmeier anlässlich der Konferenz 'Review 2014 - Außenpolitik Weiter Denken,*' May 20, 2014, accessed August 8, 2015, http://www.auswaertiges-amt.de/DE/Infoservice/Presse/Reden/2014/140520-BM_Review2014_Abschlussrede.html.

[705] German Institute for International and Security Affairs, and German Marshall Fund of the United States, *Neue Macht—Neue Verantwortung*, 2.

[706] Von der Leyen, *Speech by the Federal Minister of Defense*, 3, 5.

[707] Von der Leyen, *Speech by the Federal Minister of Defense*.

the geographical center, but also an ideological center at the same time. Germany's close embedment in the planning processes for the EU missions in Africa and the envisioned takeover of the lead of EUTM-Mali beginning in August 2015 can be taken as evidence for such a commitment to lead within the ranks of others and not from atop the structure. Clearly, Berlin's current efforts to bring the Bundeswehr armaments and equipment into shape after decades of underinvestment or hard service in distant climes also underlines Germany's appreciation that responsibility and leadership undoubtedly need resources of power to ensure that feasible deeds in support of policy can follow good intentions that echo well in public opinion.

"Being responsible" also means that Germany seeks to actively prevent crises in Africa and elsewhere and always encounter them with all instruments of politics, instead focusing on a single means that is blind to actual conflict.[708] In doing so, Germany continues to promote a comprehensive and networked approach, in which military means *can*—but not must—play a necessary role—as Berlin has emphasized for the crisis resolution in Mali.

C. German Restraint

Interconnected with Germany's strategic understanding of "being responsible" is the tenet of "being restrained." While such a policy of checks and balances matters for Germany's general appearance in international affairs, it mainly relates to the use of military force. In the face of a persistently evolving security environment over the last two decades, Germany's understanding of the role, relevance, and efficacy of military means has "normalized." Instead of either the categorical ruling out of *any* use of military force (not only in war or war-like scenarios) or merely regarding it exclusively as a last resort

---

[708] Mützenich, "Gemeinsame Erklärungen reichen nicht aus!"; Bell et al., "Früher, entschiedener und substanzieller?," 6.

when all other options have failed,[709] military means now possess a more rational, constructive, and balanced role within Germany's foreign and security policy thought. Defense Minister de Maizière's statements in February 2013 pinpointed this emerging realism. While acknowledging that the military is not a sole solution for new threats and conflicts, he argued that

> the military but can contribute to permanent stability and security, sometimes and in particular situations even the only one. And the politics sometimes can only be successful with the help of the military. We need sometime both: military means, to establish security, and political means, to maintain security and foster peace. There is no development without security and no security without development.[710]

At the same time, the Bundeswehr has conceptually and structurally evolved over the last two decades as an "armed forces on operations," which is to say, a force that can be deployed by its nation, like other NATO armies, engaged in operations in the field far from home that may or may not include combat on a limited scale.

While all reasonable observers of policy came increasingly to acknowledge the potential benefits (and risks) of military means in international affairs, neither the aspirations for more responsibility nor a normalizing understanding of the role of military force imply a wholesale dissolution in Germany of boundaries and constraints in actually using military force. Thus, these developments did not lead—and will not lead—to a "militarization" of German foreign and security policy, as some German critics of the recent past have postulated otherwise with an exaggeration that is also typical of war and peace in

---

[709] Federal Ministry of Defense, *Bundeswehr on Operations*, 48.

[710] De Maizière, *Internationale Verantwortung wahrnehmen*.

German domestic politics.[711] Such a shift would manifest itself in a stronger focus on military force as a favorable means in crisis resolution, an acceptance of greater risks and consequences of deploying German soldiers, and an increase in deployments of German troops abroad or in a more robust posture in international military missions. Nowhere in the real world of Germany in 2015 do such phenomena even remotely exist.

Conversely, Germany's normative imperative of "being restrained" concerning the use of force, grounded in the "lessons of the past," the political desire to avoid risks, the preference for comprehensive approaches to crisis resolution, and the public skepticism toward military means remained widely intact. Thus, Germany adheres to principles of employing military means on a proportional scale, for clearly defined purposes, and under the conditions they are "imperative and indispensable."[712] The premise of "being restrained" found expression in Germany's military engagement in Africa since 2011 through the refusal of participations in combat operations (Libya, Mali, and Central African Republic), the struggle to define actual military contributions, the preference of civilian instruments, the focus on missions with limited employments of military means, and the overall modest German military presence throughout the missions.

D. Reflections

Clearly, the mixed and ambivalent outcomes of German military engagement in Africa since 2011 add one piece to the much larger picture of Germany's ongoing struggle to "flesh out the details"[713] of

---

[711] Jacob Augstein, "S.P.O.N.-Im Zweifel links: Das Gerede vom Krieg," *Spiegel Online*, February 2, 2014, http://www.spiegel.de/politik/deutschland/jakob-augstein-ueber-den-einsatz-von-soldaten-der-bundeswehr-im-ausland-a-950725.html.

[712] Federal Ministry of Defense, *Bundeswehr on Operations*, 48.

[713] Major and Mölling, German Defense Policy in 2014, 27.

what taking greater responsibility as well as contributing to international affairs earlier, more decisively, and more substantially, entails for the different policy areas but particularly for the use of military force as an instrument of German foreign and security policy. Until then, the simultaneous salience of the two principles of "being responsible" and "being restrained" is expected to repeatedly create tensions, and hence, challenges for state actors to find a balance between what is externally (mainly) required versus what is politically desired and indispensable, militarily affordable and feasible, and domestically justifiable.

Yet, in contemporary German strategic thinking on the use of military force, neither is "being restrained" metonymic with "refrain from anything," nor is "being responsible" the same as "willing to do everything." Germany can be responsible *and* restrained at the same time—without dissolving boundaries or overemphasizing normative constraints. Instead, both premises must be understood as two sides of the same coin, mutually dependent, characterizing the dual nature of contemporary German foreign and security policy—particularly in relation to the use of military force—as Defense Minister Ursula von der Leyen echoed in February 2015 a statement of then-Defense Minister Thomas de Maizière in May 2011:[714]

> Germany is virtually condemned to play an increasingly important part. Well, this is true. With a sense of proportion. With the courage to act, but with humility in action. Committed to our security interests, our humanitarian obligation and our historic responsibility.[715]

---

[714] De Maizière, "Neuausrichtung der Bundeswehr entschieden."
[715] Von der Leyen, *Speech by the Federal Minister of Defense*, 6.

Eventually, in foreseeable future, Germany will remain a responsible and restrained shaping power—for the good reasons of both of these ideals of statecraft when measured against the dangers of neglecting such principles in the past and present.

Appendix

Overview of out-of-area missions and respective contributions of the Bundeswehr, as of 2011.[716]

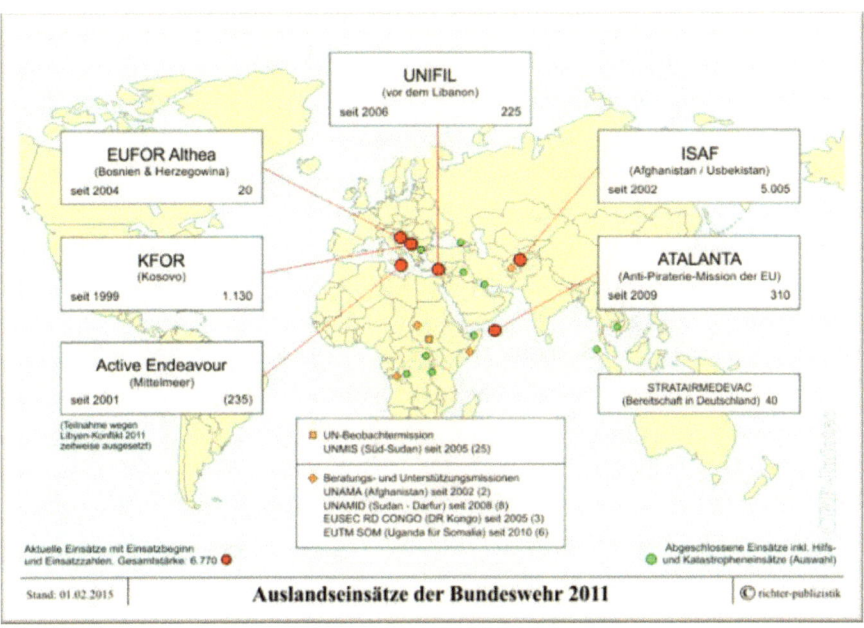

---

[716] "Auslandseinsätze der Bundeswehr 2011," *CRP-Infotec*, updated February 23, 2015, http://www.crp-infotec.de/05sipo/bundeswehr/grafs/mil_ausland_2011.gif.

Overview of out-of-area missions and respective contributions of the Bundeswehr, as of March 7, 2013.[717]

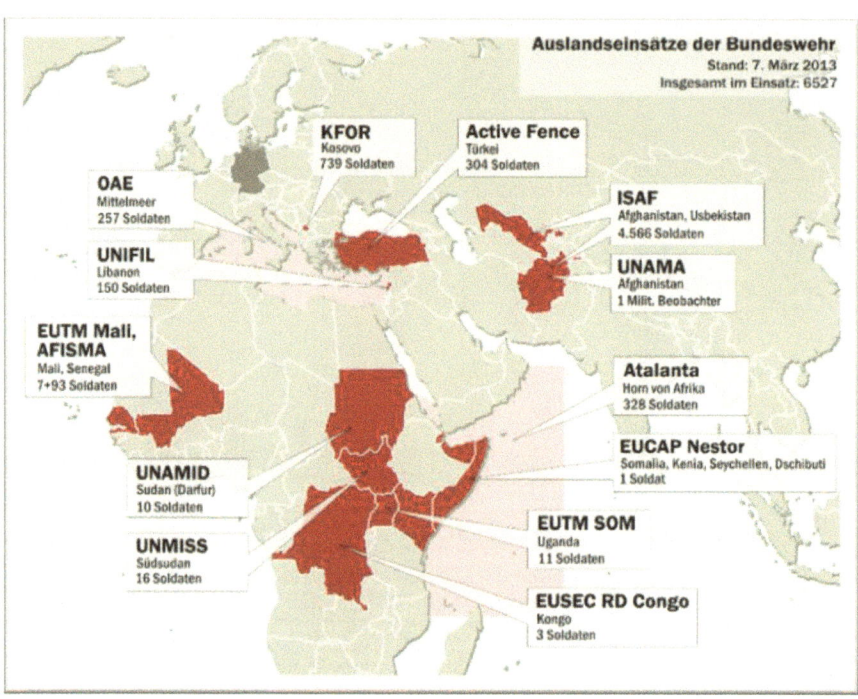

---

[717] "Auslandseinsätze der Bundeswehr: Stand 7. März 2013," *Wikipedia*, accessed January 5, 2015, http://de.wikipedia.org/wiki/Deutsche_Beteiligung_am_Krieg_in_Afghanistan#/media/File:Auslandseins%C3%A4tze_der_Bundeswehr.2013-03-07.svg.

Overview of out-of-area missions and respective contributions of the Bundeswehr, as of February 1, 2015.[718]

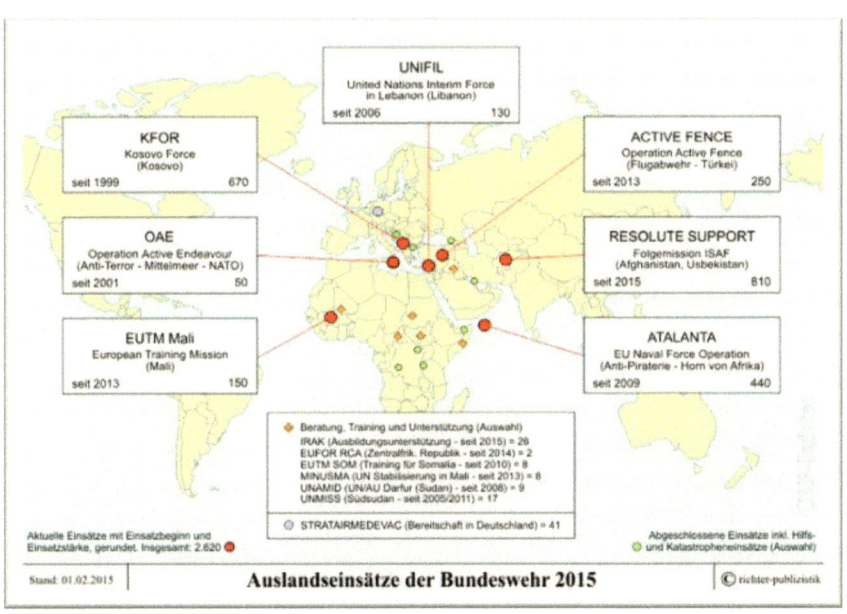

---

[718] "Auslandseinsätze der Bundeswehr 2015," *CRP-Infotec*, updated February 23, 2015, http://www.crp-infotec.de/05sipo/bundeswehr/grafs/mil_ausland_aktuell.gif.

Overview of out-of-area missions and respective contributions of the Bundeswehr, as of May 18, 2015.[719]

Strength of the German Mission Contingents

Mission	Area	Strength
Resolute Support	Afghanistan, Uzbekistan	839
KFOR	Kosovo	697
Active Fence	Turkey	254
UMISS	South Sudan	16
UNAMID	Sudan	9
Operation Active Endeavour (OAE)	Mediterranean Sea	184
UNFIL	Lebanon	144
EUTM Mali	Mali	162
MINUSMA	Senegal, Mali	8
Atalanta	Horn of Africa	305
EUTM SOM	Somalia	8
Training Support Iraq	Iraq	80

---

[719] "Einsatzzahlen."

Further Missions and Support

Mission	Area	Strength
UNAMA	Afghanistan	3
STRATAIRMEDIVAC	Germany	41
MINURSO	West Sahara	4

Total of German soldiers engaged in missions abroad	2756

List of References

Titles are freely translated by the author as a guide for non–German-speaking readers; these translations should not be taken to bind a formal translator.

Abenheim, Donald, and Carolyn Halladay. "Stability in Flux: Policy, Strategy, and Institutions in Germany." In *The Routledge Handbook of Civil-Military Relations*, edited by Thomas C. Bruneau and Florina Cristiana Matei, 304–317. New York: Routledge, 2013.

"Afghanistan Einsatz Guttenberg: 'Kriegsähnliche Zustände' [Afghanistan Mission Guttenberg: 'Warlike conditions']." *Frankfurter Allgemeine Zeitung*, November 3, 2009. http://www.faz.net/aktuell/politik/inland/afghanistan-einsatz-guttenberg-kriegsaehnliche-zustaende-1883496.html.

"Afghanistan-Einsatz: Guttenberg hält Bezeichnung 'Krieg' für treffend [Afghanistan Mission: Guttenberg considers term 'war' as appropriate]." *Spiegel Online*, November 15, 2009. http://www.spiegel.de/politik/deutschland/afghanistan-einsatz-guttenberg-haelt-bezeichnung-krieg-fuer-treffend-a-661429.html.

AFP. "West African Leaders Lift All Sanctions Imposed on Mali." *Al Arabia News*, Updated April 8, 2012. http://english.alarabiya.net/articles/2012/04/08/206220.html.

"Africa: Mali." Security Council Report, January 31, 2013. http://www.securitycouncilreport.org/monthly-forecast/2013-02/mali_4.php.

"Africa Rising: A Hopeful Continent." *Economist*, March 2, 2013. http://www.economist.com/news/special-report/21572377-african-lives-have-already-greatly-improved-over-past-decade-says-oliver-august.

Ajami, Fouad. *The Syrian Rebellion*. Stanford, CA: Hoover Institution Press, 2012.

"Al Qaida–Linked Islamists in Mali Threaten French Citizens after UN Move." *Guardian*, October 13, 2012. http://www.theguardian.com/world/2012/oct/13/al-qaida-islamists-mali-french-citizens-un.

Anderson, Lisa. "Demystifying the Arab Spring: Parsing the Differences between Tunisia, Egypt, and Libya." *Foreign Affairs* 90, no. 3 (May-June 2011): 2–7.

Angenendt, Stefan. "Migration." In *Deutsche Nah-, Mittelost- und Nordafrikapolitik—SWP Studie* [German Near-, Middle East, and North Africa Policy—SWP Study] S15, edited by Guido Steinberg, 41–50. Berlin: German Institute for International and Security Affairs, May 2009.

Annen, Niels. "Eine Militarisierung unserer Außenpolitik findet nicht statt [A militarization of our foreign policy does not take place]." *Internationale Politik und Gesellschaft* [International policy and society], September 14, 2014. http://www.ipg-journal.de/schwerpunkt-des-monats/interventionen/artikel/detail/eine-militarisierung-unserer-aussenpolitik-findet-nicht-statt-587/.

Annen, Niels, and Marius Müller-Henning. *Report from the 1st FES Tiergartenconference 2012—A Fundamental Geostrategic Shift?: Consequences of U.S. Rebalancing towards the Asia-Pacific Region for Regional and Global Security Policy*. Berlin: Friedrich-Ebert-Stiftung, September 2012. Accessed March 5, 2015 http://www.fes.de/gpol/pdf/20121218_FES_Tiergarten_report_final.pdf.

Antrag der Bundesregierung. "Beteiligung bewaffneter deutscher Streitkräfte an der von den Vereinten Nationen geführten Friedensmission in Südsudan [Participation of German Armed Forces in the UN-led peace mission in South Sudan]." Drs.17/6449. Berlin: Bundesanzeiger Verlagsgesellschaft, July 6, 2011. Accessed February 26, 2015. http://dipbt.bundestag.de/doc/btd/17/064/1706449.pdf.

Antrag der Bundesregierung. "Entsendung bewaffneter deutscher Streitkräfte zur Verstärkung der integrierten Luftverteidigung der NATO auf Ersuchen der Türkei und auf Grundlage des Rechts auf kollektive Selbstverteidigung Artikel 51 der Charta der Vereinten Nationen sowie des Beschlusses des Nordatlantikrates vom 4. Dezember 2012) [Deployment of German Armed Forces in reinforcement of the NATO Integrated Air Defense at the request of Turkey and on the basis of the right for collective self-defense article 51 of the UN Charter as well as the NATO Council Decision on December 4, 2012)]." Drs. 17/11783. Berlin: Bundesanzeiger Verlagsgesellschaft, December 6, 2012. Accessed February 26, 2015. http://dip21.bundestag.de/dip21/btd/17/117/ 1711783.pdf.

———. "Entsendung bewaffneter deutscher Streitkräfte zur Beteiligung an der EU-geführten militärischen Ausbildungsmission EUTM Mali auf Grundlage des Ersuchens der Regierung von Mali sowie der Beschlüsse 2013/34/GASP des Rates der Europäischen Union (EU) vom 17. Januar 2013 und vom 18. Februar2013 in Verbindung mit den Resolutionen 2071 (2012) und 2085 (2012) des Sicherheitsrates der Vereinten Nationen [Deployment of German Armed Forces for participation in the EU-led military training mission (EUTM) Mali at the request of the Malian government as well as the EU council decisions 2013/34/CFSP on January 17, 2013, and February 18, 2013, in connection with UN Resolutions 2071 (2012) and 2985 (2012)]." Drs. 17/12367. Berlin: Bundesanzeiger Verlagsgesellschaft, February 19, 2013. Accessed February 15, 2015. http://dipbt.bundestag.de/dip21/ btd/17/123/1712367.pdf.

Antrag der Bundesregierung. "Entsendung bewaffneter deutscher Streitkräfte zur Unterstützung der Internationalen Unterstützungsmission in Mali unter afrikanischer Führung (AFISMA) auf Grundlage der Resolution 2085 (2012) des Sicherheitsrates der Vereinten Nationen [Deployment of German armed forces in support of the international support mission under African Lead (AFISMA) on the basis of UNSC Resolution 2085 (2012)]." Drs. 17/1 12368. Berlin: Bundesanzeiger Verlagsgesellschaft, February 19, 2013.
http://dipbt.bundestag.de/dip21/btd/17/123/1712368.pdf.

———. "Entsendung bewaffneter deutscher Streitkräfte zur Beteiligung an der Europäischen Überbrückungsmission in der Zentralafrikanischen Republik (EUFOR RCA) auf Grundlage der Beschlüsse 2014/73/GASP sowie 2014/183/GASP des Rates der Europäischen Union vom 10. Februar 2014 und vom 1. April 2014 in Verbindung mit den Resolutionen 2127 (2013) und 2134 (2014) des Sicherheitsrates der Vereinten Nationen vom 5. Dezember 2013 und vom 28. Januar 2014 [Deployment of German armed forces for participation in a European Bridging mission in the Central African Republic (EUFOR RCA) on the basis of the EU Council Decisions 2014/73/CFSP as well as 2014/183/CFSP on February 10, 2014, and April 1, 2014, in connection with the UNSC Resolutions 2127 (2013) and 2134 (2014) on December 5, 2013 and January 28, 2014]." Drs. 18/1081. Berlin: Bundesanzeiger Verlagsgesellschaft, April 8, 2014. Accessed March 26, 2015.
http://dipbt.bundestag.de/dip21/btd/18/010/1801081.pdf.

Antrag der Bundesregierung. "Fortsetzung der Beteiligung bewaffneter deutscher Streitkräfte zur Beteiligung an der EU-geführten militärischen Ausbildungsmission EUTM Mali auf Grundlage des Ersuchens der Regierung von Mali sowie der Beschlüsse 2013/34/GASP des Rates der Europäischen Union (EU) vom 17. Januar 2013 und vom 18. Februar 2013 in Verbindung mit den Resolutionen 2071 (2012) und 2085 (2012) des Sicherheitsrates der Vereinten Nationen [Continuation of the participation of German armed forces in the EU-led military training mission (EUTM) Mali on the basis of the request by the Malian government as well as the EU Council Decisions 2013/34/CFSP on January 17, 2013, and February 18, 2013, in Connection with the UN Resolutions 2071 (2012) and 2985 (2012)]." Drs. 18/437. Berlin: Bundesanzeiger Verlagsgesellschaft, February 2, 2014).
http://dipbt.bundestag.de/dip21/btd/18/004/1800437.pdf.

Antwort der Bundesregierung auf die Kleine Anfrage der Abgeordneten Jan van Aken, Niema Movassat, Christine Buchholz, weiterer Abgeordneter und der Fraktion DIE LINKE. "Aktuelle Situation in Mali und die geplante EU-Ausbildungsmission malischer Streitkräfte [Current situation in Mali and the planned EU training mission for Malian armed forces]." Drs.17/11542. Berlin: Bundesanzeiger Verlagsgesellschaft, November 20, 2012. Accessed March 2, 2015.
http://dip21.bundestag.de/dip21/btd/17/115/1711542.pdf.

Auerswald, David P., and Stephan M. Saideman. *NATO in Afghanistan: Fighting Together, Fighting Alone*. Princeton, NJ: University Press, 2014.

Augstein, Jacob. "S.P.O.N.-Im Zweifel links: Das Gerede vom Krieg [S.P.O.N.-In case of doubt, left: The Talk about War]." *Spiegel Online*, February 2, 2014.
http://www.spiegel.de/politik/deutschland/jakob-augstein-ueber-den-einsatz-von-soldaten-der-bundeswehr-im-ausland-a-950725.html.

Augstein, Jacob. "The Return of the Ugly Germans: Merkel Is Leading the Country into Isolation." *Spiegel Online*, December 8, 2011. http://www.spiegel.de/international/europe/the-return-of-the-ugly-germans-merkel-is-leading-the-country-into-isolation-a-802591.html.

"Auslandseinsätze der Bundeswehr 2011 [Mission Abroad of the Bundeswehr 2015]." *CRP-Infotec*. Updated February 23, 2015. http://www.crp-infotec.de/05sipo/bundeswehr/grafs/mil_ausland_2011.gif.

"Auslandseinsätze der Bundeswehr 2015 [Mission Abroad of the Bundeswehr 2015]." *CRP-Infotec*. Updated February 23, 2015. http://www.crp-infotec.de/05sipo/bundeswehr/grafs/mil_ausland_aktuell.gif.

"Auslandseinsätze der Bundeswehr: Stand 7. März 2013 [Mission Abroad of the Bundeswehr: As of March 7, 2013]." *Wikipedia*. Accessed January 5, 2015. http://de.wikipedia.org/wiki/Deutsche_Beteiligung_am_Krieg_in_Afghanistan#/media/File:Auslandseins%C3%A4tze_der_Bundeswehr.2013-03-07.svg.

Auswärtiges Amt, Bundesministerium der Verteidigung, and Bundesministerium für wirtschaftliche Zusammenarbeit. *Für eine kohärente Politik der Bundesregierung gegenüber fragilen Staaten: Ressortübergreifende Leitlinien* [For a coherent policy of the federal government toward fragile states: Interministerial guidelines]. Berlin: BMZ, September 2012. Accessed March 4, 2015. http://www.auswaertiges-amt.de/cae/servlet/contentblob/626452/publicationFile/171897/120919_Leitlinien_Fragile_Staaten.pdf.

"Außenminister Westerwelle verurteilt Gewalt gegen Zivilbevölkerung in Mali [Foreign Minister Westerwelle condemns violence against civilians in Mali]." *Artikel-Presse*, April 4, 2012. http://www.artikel-presse.de/ausenminister-westerwelle-verurteilt-gewalt-gegen-zivilbevolkerung-in-mali.html.

Barry, John. "Robert Gates' Fears about Libya." *Daily Beast*. March 8, 2011. http://www.thedailybeast.com/articles/2011/03/09/defense-secretary-robert-gates-fears-about-us-military-action-in-libya.html.

Baumann, Rainer. "Deutschland als Zentralmacht [Germany as a central power]." In *Handbuch zur deutschen Außenpolitik* [Handbook for German foreign policy], edited by Sigmar Schmidt, Gunther Hellmann, and Reinhard Wolf, 62–72. Wiesbaden: Verlag für Sozialwissenschaften, 2007.

Baumann, Rainer. "Multilateralismus: Die Wandelung eines vermeintlichen Kontinuitätselements der deutschen Außenpolitik [Multilateralism: The transition of an alledged continuing element of German foreign policy]." In *Deutsche Außenpolitik: Sicherheit, Wohlfahrt, Institutionen und Normen* [German foreign policy: Security, welfare, institutions, and norms], 2nd ed. Edited by Thomas Jäger, Alexander Höse, and Kai Oppermann, 468–87. Wiesbaden: Springer Fachmedien, 2011.

Baumann, Rainer. "The Transformation of German Multilateralism: Changes in the Foreign-Policy Discourse since Unification," *German Politics and Society* 20, no. 4 (Winter 2002): 1–26.

Baumann, Rainer, and Gunther Hellmann. "Germany and the Use of Force: 'Total War,' the 'Culture of Restraint,' and the Quest for Normality." *German Politics* 10, no. 1 (April 2001): 61–82.

Bell, Arvid, Matthias Dembinski, Thorsten Gromes, and Berthold Meyer. "Früher, entschiedener und substanzieller?: Engagiertes außenpolitisches Handeln und militärische Zurückhaltung sind kein Widerspruch [Earlier, more decisive, and more substantial?: Dedicated foreign policy action and military restraint do not contradict each other]." *HSFK Standpunkte* 1. Frankfurt am Main: Hessische Stiftung Friedens- und Konfliktforschung, 2014.

Berger, Thomas U. *Cultures of Antimilitarism: National Security in Germany and Japan*. Baltimore: John Hopkins University Press, 1998.

"Berlin sichert Paris Unterstützung zu [Berlin guarantees support to Paris]." *Deutsche Welle*, January 14, 2013. http://www.dw.de/berlin-sichert-paris-unterst%C3%BCtzung-zu/a-16519121.

Bertelsmann Stiftung, ed. *Gut, aber nicht gut genug: Das neue sicherheitspolitische Weißbuch der Bundesrepublik Deutschland* [Good, but not good enough: The new security political white paper of the German Federal Republic]. Gütersloh, Germany: Bertelsmann Stiftung, 2006. Accessed September 21, 2014. http://www.fundacionbertelsmann.org/cps/rde/xbcr/SID-1503D609-1DA671C6/bst/Analyse_Weissbuch.pdf.

Beste, Ralf, Ulrike Demmer, Dirk Kurbjuweit, Ralf Neukirch, Christina Schmidt, and Christoph Schult. "Friede den Zeltpalästen [Peace for the Palaces of Tents]." *Der Spiegel*, no. 13 (2011): 23–25. Accessed March 14, 2011. http://magazin.spiegel.de/EpubDelivery/spiegel/pdf/77745550.

Biehl, Heiko, and Jörg Jacobs. "Öffentliche Meinung und Sicherheitspolitik [Public opinion and security policy]." In *Deutsche Sicherheitspolitik: Herausforderungen, Akteure und Prozesse* [German security policy: Challenges, actors, and processes]. 2nd ed. Edited by Stephan Böckenförde and Sven Bernhard Gareis, 265–86. Opladen, Germany: Verlag Barbara Buderich, 2014.

Binding, Jörg, and Lukas Kudlimay. "Deutschland: Neue Wege in der Internationalen Zusammenarbeit [Germany: New ways in international cooperation]." *GIGA Focus*, no. 7. Hamburg: German Institute of Global and Area Studies, 2013.

Birnbaum, Robert. "Deutscher Einsatz in Mali: Merkel und Westerwelle marschieren voran [German mission in Mali: Merkel and Westerwelle are marching ahead]." *Der Tagesspiegel*, October 24, 2012. http://www.tagesspiegel.de/meinung/deutscher-einsatz-in-mali-merkel-und-westerwelle-marschieren-voran/7290224.html.

Black, Ian. "Libya on Brink as Protests Hit Tripoli." *Guardian*, February 20, 2011. http://www.theguardian.com/world/2011/feb/20/libya-defiant-protesters-feared-dead.

Bleibohm, Sascha. "On Contemporary War and the German Armed Forces: The Afghan War and its Consequences." Master's thesis, Naval Postgraduate School, 2014.

"Blitzbesuch der Kanzlerin: Merkel nennt Afghanistan-Einsatz 'Krieg' [Brief visit of the chancellor: Merkel calls Afghan mission a 'war']." *Spiegel Online*, December 18, 2010. http://www.spiegel.de/politik/ausland/blitzbesuch-der-kanzlerin-merkel-nennt-afghanistan-einsatz-krieg-a-735432.html.

Boeke, Sergei, and Antonin Tisseron. "Mali's Long Road Ahead." *RUSI Journal* 159, no. 5 (2014): 32–40. doi:10.1080/03071847.2014.969942.

Bonkoungou, Mathieu, Bate Felix, and Jackie Frank. "Mali Requests Military Assistance to Free North: France." *Reuters*, September 4, 2012. http://www.reuters.com/article/2012/09/05/us-mali-ecowas-troops-idUSBRE88403120120905.

Bosold, David, and Christian Achrainer. "Die normativen Grundlagen deutscher Außenpolitik [The Normative Principles of German Foreign Policy]." In *Deutsche Außenpolitik: Sicherheit, Wohlfahrt, Institutionen und Normen* [German foreign policy: Security, welfare, institutions, and norms], 2nd ed. Edited by Thomas Jäger, Alexander Höse, and Kai Oppermann, 444–67. Wiesbaden: Springer Fachmedien, 2011.

Bower, Eve. "Germany's Libya Policy Reveals a Nation in Transition." *Deutsche Welle*, September 12, 2011. http://www.dw.de/germanys-libya-policy-reveals-a-nation-in-transition/a-15367751.

Boyle, Ashley S. *Mali: A Timeline and Factsheet*. Washington, DC: American Security Project, November 2012. Accessed March 4, 2015. http://americansecurityproject.org/ASP%20Reports/Ref%200099%20-%20Mali%20-%20timeline%20and%20factsheet.pdf.

"Breite Zustimmung für Mali-Einsatz der Bundeswehr [Broad approval for Mali mission of the Bundeswehr]." *Deutscher Bundestag.* Accessed February 15, 2015. http://www.bundestag.de/dokumente/textarchiv/2013/43167 387_kw09_de_mali/211134.

Brehm, Maybritt, Christian Koch, Werner Ruf, and Peter Strutynski. *Armee im Einsatz: 20 Jahre Auslandseinsätze der Bundeswehr* [Armed forces on a mission: 20 years of missions abroad of the Bundeswehr]. Hamburg, VSA Verlag, 2012.

Bremmer, Ian, and Mark Leonard. "U.S.-German Relationship on the Rocks." *Washington Post*, October 8, 2012. http://www.washingtonpost.com/opinions/us-german-relationship-on-the-rocks/2012/10/18/ed6a9f1c-13c2-11e2-be82-c3411b7680a9_story.html.

Brockmeier, Sarah. "Germany and the Intervention in Libya." *Survival: Global Politics and Strategy* 55, no. 6 (2013), 63–90.

Brummer, Klaus. *Die Innenpolitik der Außenpolitik: Die Große Koalition, 'Governmental Politics' und Auslandseinsätze der Bundeswehr* [The domestic policy of the foreign policy: The grand coalition, "governmental politics," and missions abroad of the Bundeswehr]. Wiesbaden: Springer VS, 2013.

Bruns, Malte, Tobias Bunde, Astrid Irgang, Lena Kilee, Verena Lepper, Berend Lindern, Georg Matthes, Nele Matz-Lück, Timo Noetzel, and Imke-Frederike Tiemann. "Die strategische Kultur der deutschen Sicherheitspolitik: Brauchen wir eine nationale Sicherheitsstrategie? [The strategic culture of the German security policy: Do we need a national security strategy?]." *Policy Brief—Globale Fragen* [*Policy brief—Global questions*]. Berlin: Stiftung Neue Verantwortung, August 2009.

Bucher, Jessica. "Domestic Politics, News Media, and Humanitarian Intervention: Why France and Germany Diverged over Libya." *European Security* 22, no. 4 (2013): 524–39.

Bundesministerium der Justiz. *Gesetz über die parlamentarische Beteiligung bei der Entscheidung über den Einsatz bewaffneter Streitkräfte im Ausland (Parlamentsbeteiligungsgesetz)* [Law on the parliamentary participation within the decision to use military armed forces abroad (Parliamentary Participation Act)]. Berlin: Bundesministerium der Justiz, 2005. Accessed October 31, 2014. http://www.gesetze-im-internet.de/bundesrecht/parlbg/ gesamt.pdf.

Bundesministerium für wirtschaftliche Zusammenarbeit und Entwicklung (BMZ). *Grundlagen, Schwerpunkte und Perspektiven der deutschen Entwicklungspolitik mit der Region Nahost/Nordafrika-BMZ Konzepte* [Principles, point of main efforts, and perspectives of the German development policy in the Near East region] 156. Berlin: BMZ, 2008. Accessed March 11, 2015. http://www.bmz.de/de/mediathek/publikationen/reihen/strategiepapiere/konzept156.pdf.

———. *Übersektorales Konzept zur Krisenprävention, Konfliktbearbeitung und Friedensförderung in der deutschen Entwicklungszusammenarbeit: Eine Strategie zur Friedensentwicklung* [Over sectoral concept for crisis prevention, conflict management, and peace promotion in German development cooperation: A strategy for peace building]. Berlin: BMZ, June 2005. Accessed October 11, 2014. http://www.bmz.de/de/zentrales_downloadarchiv/themen_un d_schwerpunkte/frieden/krisenpraevention.pdf.

Bundesregierung. *Afrikapolitische Leitlinien der Bundesregierung* [Federal Government Policy Guidelines for Africa]. Berlin: Bundesregierung, 2014. Accessed August 7, 2014. http://www.monrovia.diplo.de/contentblob/4246600/Daten/ 4317323/Afrika_Leitlinien_Engl.pdf.

———. *Aktionsplan "Zivile Krisenprävention, Konfliktlösung und Friedenskonsolidierung* [Action plan 'Civil Crisis Prevention, Conflict Resolution, and Peace Consolidation']." Berlin: May 12, 2004. Accessed October 11, 2014. http://www.auswaertiges-amt.de/cae/servlet/contentblob/ 384230/publicationFile/4345/Aktionsplan-De.pdf.

Bundesregierung. *Deutschland und Afrika: Konzept der Bundesregierung* [Germany and Africa: Concept of the federal government]. Berlin: Ministry of Foreign Affairs, June 2011. Accessed August 7, 2014. http://www.auswaertiges-amt.de/cae/servlet/contentblob/581096/publicationFile/155321/110615-Afrika-Konzept-download.pdf.

———. "Gesamtkonzept der Bundesregierung: 'Zivile Krisenprävention, Konfliktlösung und Friedenskonsolidierung [Overall concept of the federal government: 'Civil Crisis Prevention, Conflict Resolution, and Peace Consolidation']." In *Aktionsplan 'Zivile Krisenprävention, Konfliktlösung und Friedenskonsolidierung'* [Action Plan 'Civil Crisis Prevention, Conflict Resolution, and Peace Consolidation']." Berlin: Bundesregierung, May 12, 2004, XVI–XVII. Accessed October 11, 2014. http://www.auswaertiges-amt.de/cae/servlet/contentblob/384230/publicationFile/4345/Aktionsplan-De.pdf.

———. *Globalisierung gestalten—Partnerschaften ausbauen—Verantwortung teilen* [Shape globalization—Expand partnerships—Share responsibility]. Berlin: Auswärtiges Amt, 2012. Accessed January 15, 2015. https://www.auswaertiges-amt.de/cae/servlet/contentblob/608384/publicationFile/169965/Gestaltungsmaechte-konzept.pdf.

———. *Krisenprävention als gemeinsame Aufgabe: 2. Bericht der Bundesregierung über die Umsetzung des Aktionsplans "Zivile Krisenprävention, Konfliktlösung und Friedenskonsolidierung," Berichtszeitraum Mai 2006 bis April 2008* [Crisis prevention as joint task: 2nd report of the federal government over the implementation of the Action Plan 'Civil Crisis Prevention, Conflict Resolution, and Peace Consolidation,' Report period May 2006 to April 2008]. Berlin: Bundesregierung, July 16, 2008. Accessed October 11, 2014. http://www.auswaertiges-amt.de/cae/servlet/contentblob/384192/publicationFile/4340/Aktionsplan-Bericht2-de.pdf.

Busch, Andreas, and Roman Goldbach. "Die Stellung Deutschlands in der Weltwirtschaft [Germany's position in the world economy]." In *Deutsche Außenpolitik: Sicherheit, Wohlfahrt, Institutionen und Normen* [German foreign policy: Security, welfare, institutions, and norms]. 2nd ed. Edited by Thomas Jäger, Alexander Höse, and Kai Oppermann, 275–95. Wiesbaden: Springer Fachmedien, 2011.

Busse, Nikolas. "Europas neue Risse [Europe's new rifts]." *Frankfurter Allgemeines Zeitung*, March 23, 2011.
http://www.faz.net/aktuell/politik/ausland/naher-osten/einsatz-gegen-gaddafi-europas-neue-risse-1611274-p2.html?printPagedArticle=true#pageIndex_2.

Cantir, Cristian, and Juliet Kaarbo. "Contested Roles and Domestic Politics: Reflection on Role Theory in Foreign Policy Analysis and IR Theory." *Foreign Policy Analysis* 8 (2012): 5–24.

Charbonneau, Louis. "UN Ready to Consider ECOWAS Request to Back Mali Force." *Reuters*, June 19, 2012.
http://in.reuters.com/article/2012/06/18/africa-mali-un-idINL1E8HI84X20120618.

Chiari, Bernhard, and Magnus Pahl. *Auslandseinsätze der Bundeswehr: Wegweiser zur Geschichte* [Missions abroad of the Bundeswehr: Historical guidebook]. Paderborn, Germany: Schöningh, 2010.

Clement, Rolf. "Die neue Bundeswehr als Instrument deutscher Außenpolitik [The new Bundeswehr as an instrument of German foreign policy]." *Aus Politik und Zeitgeschichte* [From politics and contemporary history] B11 (2004): 40–46.

"Clinton at UN Secretary General Meeting on Sahel." *U.S. Department of State*. Updated September 26, 2012.
http://iipdigital.usembassy.gov/st/english/texttrans/2012/09/20120926136634.html#axzz3Wwc7rKI0.

"Closing Ceremony of EUFOR RCA." *European Union External Action Service*. Updated March 23, 2015.
http://www.eeas.europa.eu/csdp/missions-and-operations/eufor-rca/news/archives/20150323_en.htm.

Cody, Edward. "France's Hollande Sends Troops to Mali." *Washington Post*, January 11, 2013. http://www.washingtonpost.com/world/africa/frances-hollande-sends-troops-to-mali/2013/01/11/21be77ae-5c0f-11e2-9fa9-5fbdc9530eb9_story.html.

Collier, David. "Understanding Process Tracing." *Political Science and Politics* 44, no. 4 (2011): 823–30.

Collmer, Sabine. "'All Politics Is Local': Deutsche Sicherheits- und Verteididungspolitik im Spiegel der Öffentlichen Meinung ['All politics is local': German security and defense policy as reflected in public opinion]." In *Deutsche Sicherheitspolitik: Eine Bilanz der Regierung Schröder* [German security policy: A record of the Schröder government], edited by Sebastian Harnisch, Christos Katsioulis, and Marco Overhaus, 201–225. Baden-Baden, Germany: Nomos, 2004.

Conference Conclusions—Afghanistan and the International Community: From Transition to the Transformation Decade. Bonn: The International Afghanistan Conference, December 5, 2012. Accessed February 25, 2015. http://eeas.europa.eu/afghanistan/docs/2011_11_conclusions_bonn_en.pdf.

Conrad, Björn, and Mario Stumm. *German Strategic Culture and Institutional Choice: Transatlanticism and/or Europeanism?* Trierer Arbeitspapiere zur Internationalen Politik. Trier, Germany: Lehrstuhl für Außenpolitik und Internationale Beziehungen, 2004.

Cooper, Helene, and Steven Lee Myers. "Obama Takes Hard Line with Libya after Shift by Clinton." *New York Times*, March 18, 2011. http://www.nytimes.com/2011/03/19/world/africa/19policy.html?pagewanted=all&_r=0.

Council of the European Union. *Council Conclusions on Mali, 3138th Foreign Affairs Council Meeting*. Brussels: Council of the European Union Press Office, July 23, 2012. Accessed March 14, 2015. http://www.consilium.europa.eu/uedocs/cms_data/docs/pressdata/EN/foraff/134144.pdf.

Council of the European Union. *Council Conclusions on Mali, 3209th Foreign Affairs Council Meeting.* Brussels: Council of the European Union Press Office, December 10, 2012. Accessed March 6, 2015. http://www.consilium.europa.eu/uedocs/cms_data/docs/pressdata/EN/foraff/134144.pdf.

———. *Council Conclusions on Mali, 3217th Foreign Affairs Council Meeting.* Brussels: Council of the European Union Press Office, January 17, 2013. Accessed February 12, 2015. http://www.consilium.europa.eu/uedocs/cms_data/docs/pressdata/EN/foraff/134756.pdf.

———. *Council Conclusions on Mali, 3222nd Foreign Affairs Council Meeting.* Brussels: Council of the European Union Press Office, February 18, 2013. Accessed February 12, 2015. http://www.consilium.europa.eu/uedocs/cms_data/docs/pressdata/EN/foraff/135522.pdf.

———. "Council Decision 2013/34/CFSP of 17 January 2013 on a European Union Military Mission to Contribute to the Training of the Malian Armed Forces (EUTM Mali)." *Official Journal of the European Union* 14 (January 18, 2013): 19–21. Accessed March 6, 2015. http://eur-lex.europa.eu/LexUriServ/LexUriServ.do?uri=OJ:L:2013:014:0019:0021:EN:PDF.

———. "Council Decision 2013/87/CFSP of 18 February 2013 on the Launch of a European Union Military Mission to Contribute to the Training of the Malian Armed Forces (EUTM Mali)." *Official Journal of the European Union* L46 (February 18, 2013): 27. Accessed March 10, 2015. http://www.defensa.gob.es/Galerias/areasTematicas/misiones/fichero/UE-2013-87-EUTM-Mali.pdf.

———. *Press Release 3191st Council Meeting Foreign Affairs.* Brussels: Council of the European Union Press Office, October 15, 2012. Accessed March 5, 2015. http://www.consilium.europa.eu/uedocs/cms_data/docs/pressdata/EN/foraff/132896.pdf.

Council of the European Union. *Press Release 3199th Council Meeting Foreign Affairs*. Brussels: Council of the European Union Press Office, November 19, 2012. Accessed March 5, 2015. http://www.consilium.europa.eu/uedocs/cms_data/docs/pressdata/en/foraff/133604.pdf.

Croissant, Aurel, and David Kühn. *Militär und zivile Politik* [Military and civil policy]. München: Oldenbourg, 2011.

Crossley-Frolick, Katy A. "Domestic Constraints, German Foreign Policy and Post-Conflict Peacebuilding." *German Politics and Society* 31, no. 3 (Autumn 2013): 43–75.

"CDSP Map: Mission Chart." ISIS Europe. Updated October 2014. http://www.csdpmap.eu/mission-chart.

"CSDP Note: Overview Ongoing CSDP Missions." International Security Information Service Europe. Updated October 2004. http://isis-europe.eu/wp-content/uploads/2014/06/CSDP-Overview-October-2014.pdf.

Dale, Catherine, and Pat Towell. *In Brief: Assessing the January 2012 Defense Strategic Guidance (DSG)*. Washington, DC: Congressional Research Service, August 13, 2013. Accessed February 22, 2015. http://fas.org/sgp/crs/natsec/R42146.pdf.

Daase, Christopher, and Julian Junk. "Strategische Kultur und Sicherheitsstrategien in Deutschland [Strategic culture and security strategies in Germany]." *Sicherheit und Frieden* [Security and peace] 30, no. 3 (2012): 152–57.

Davis, William. "The Public Opinion–Foreign Policy Paradox in Germany: Integrating Domestic and International Levels of Analysis Conditionally." *European Security* 21, no. 3 (2012): 347–69. doi: 10.1080/09662839.2012.655271.

Dawisheh, Housam. "Trajectories and Outcomes of the 'Arab Spring': Comparing Tunisia, Egypt, Libya, and Syria." *IDE Discussion Paper*, no. 456. Mihamaku, Japan: Institute for Developing Economies, March 2011.

Dehner, Dagmar, Ulrike Scheffer, and Michael Schmidt. "Was mehr deutsche Soldaten in Afrika ausrichten können [What more German soldiers could achieve in Africa]." *Der Tagesspiegel*, January 28, 2014. http://www.tagesspiegel.de/politik/ auslandseinsaetze-der-bundeswehr-was-mehr-deutsche-soldaten-in-afrika-ausrichten-koennten/9392336.html.

De Maizière, Thomas. *Internationale Verantwortung wahrnehmen: Deutschlands Rolle in der Welt von heute, Rede des Bundesministers der Verteidigung, Dr. Thomas de Maizière, bei der Heinrich-Böll-Stiftung am Montag, 25. Februar 2013, in Berlin* [Exercise international responsibility: Germany's role in today's world, speech by Federal Minister of Defense, Dr. Thomas de Maizière at the Heinrich-Böll Foundation on Monday, February 25, 2013, in Berlin]. Accessed April 1, 2015. http://www.bmvg.de/portal/ a/bmvg/!ut/p/c4/NYvBCsIwEET_aDcRFOrNUgR79KL1Im mzhIUm-Keu2Xvx4k0Nn4MHwGHxhaXIbB6eck5vxicPE5_ELY9wCR E78URJeI3iS975ByFPCR717gikn0kqlpFwYxGkWWLLoXM0q Ugywx8HYrjXW7LG_5njq-2vTHLpbe8clxssfXL-MOg!!/.

De Maizière, Thomas. "Mali durch Ausbildungsmission nachhaltig stabilisieren [Stabilize Mali sustainably through a training mission]." Interview by Dirk-Oliver Heckmann. Deutschlandfunk, January 14, 2013. http://www.deutschlandfunk.de/de-maiziere-mali-durch-ausbildungsmission-nachhaltig.694.de.html?dram:article_id=234115.

———. "Neuausrichtung der Bundeswehr entschieden [Reorientation of the Bundeswehr decided]." Interview by Tom Buhrow, *ARD Tagesthemen*, May 18, 2011. https://tsarchive.wordpress.com/2011/05/19/bundeswehrrefo rm166/.

De Maizière, Thomas. *Rede des Bundesministers der Verteidigung anlässlich der 8. Handelsblatt Konferenz am 25. Oktober 2011 in Berlin* [Speech by Federal Minister of Defense on the cccasion of the 8th Handelsblatt Conference on October 25, 2011 in Berlin]. Accessed March 12, 2015.
http://www.bmvg.de/portal/a/bmvg/!ut/p/c4/NY3BCsIwE ET_KGmQovVmKYKHXrxovYQ0WdKFJimbbQXx422Fzs C7vIGRL7k2mgW9YUzRjPIpO4vn_i36sHgRMGJmIJyD8JDt gHZg0H-
3ADGgQz9Hn_ehzoCsVVWWgocUTNYOdDD4QSCQj-3OgbApAm9kiIwrPRlOJKZEPG5mJlqNQCe7QjV1oYo96ntq u2tZH45Vc6vvcgrh8gO9ubH1/.

———. *Rede des Ministers zu den Mali Mandaten im Bundestag* [Speech by the Minister on the two Mali mandates]. *BMVg.* Updated Febuary 20, 2013.
http://www.bmvg.de/portal/a/bmvg/!ut/p/c4/NYvBCsIwE ET_aDdBFPVmKYI38aLtRdJmCQtNUtZtvfjxJofOwIPhMdhj aXIrB6eck5vwhd3I5-
ELQ1wDRE78URJeIniS97ZByFPCZ717gjEn0kqlpFwYxGkW mLPoVM0iUgywx87YtjHWbLG_0_5w7e92d2xvzQPnGC9_Y O2o_g!!/.

———. "Regierungserklärung des Bundesministers der Verteidigung zur Neuausrichtung der Bundeswehr [Governmental declaration by minister of defense on the reorientation of the Bundeswehr]." In *Plenarprotokoll* 17/112 [Plenary Protocol 17/112] (May 27, 2011): 12815–18. Accessed October 10, 2014.
http://dipbt.bundestag.de/dip21/btp/17/17112.pdf.

———. "We Will Not Get Involved in Syria." Interview by Ralf Beste and Dirk Kurbjuweit. *Spiegel Online*, June 20, 2011.
http://www.spiegel.de/international/germany/spiegel-interview-with-defense-minister-de-maiziere-we-will-not-get-involved-in-syria-a-769339.html.

De Maizière, Thomas. "Wir haben aus Afghanistan gelernt [We have learned from Afghanistan]." Interview by Sueddeutsche Zeitung, *Bundesregierung*. Updated November 5, 2012. http://www.bundesregierung.de/ContentArchiv/DE/Archiv17/Interview/2012/11/2012-11-05-de-maiziere-sz.html.

———. *Unser Auftrag ist Ausgangspunkt und Ziel der Neuausrichtung: Rede des Bundesministers der Verteidigung, Dr. Thomas de Maizière, anlässlich der Bundeswehrtagung am Montag, 22. Oktober 2012, in Strausberg* [Our task is starting point and aim of the reorientation: Speech by Federal Minister of Defense, Dr. Thomas de Maizière, on occasion of the Bundeswehr Convention on Monday, October 22, 2012, in Straußberg]. Berlin: Federal Ministry of Defense, 2012.

"De Maizière erwägt Einsatz in Mali [De Maizière contemplates mission in Mali]." *Spiegel Online*, November 3, 2012. http://www.spiegel.de/politik/deutschland/verteidigungsminister-de-maiziere-erwaegt-bundeswehr-einsatz-in-mali-a-865123.html.

"De Maizière erwägt Einsatz ohne Bundestagsmandat [De Maizière contemplates mission without Bundestag's approval]." *Die Welt*, November 3, 2012. http://www.welt.de/politik/deutschland/article110587708/De-Maiziere-erwaegt-Einsatz-ohne-Bundestagsmandat.html.

"De Maizière gegen Lammert: CDU zofft sich wegen deutschen Mali-Einsatzes [De Maizière against Lammert: CDU has a row about the German Mali mission]." *Spiegel Online*, January 19, 2013. http://www.spiegel.de/politik/ausland/mali-einsatz-de-maiziere-gegen-lammerts-forderung-a-878517.html.

"De Maizière kritisiert militärische Drohungen [De Maizière criticizes the use of military threats]." *Frankfurter Allgemeine Zeitung*, March 11, 2011. http://www.faz.net/aktuell/politik/ausland/naher-osten/libyen-de-maiziere-kritisiert-militaerische-drohungen-1611689.html.

"De Maizière schließt Kampfeinsatz aus [De Maizière excludes combat mission]." *Süddeutsche*, November 19, 2012. http://www.sueddeutsche.de/politik/bundeswehr-in-mali-de-maizire-schliesst-kampfeinsatz-aus-1.1527416.

"De Maizière will Mali-Einsatz ausweiten: Mandat für Luftbetankung gesucht [De Maizière wants to extend Mali mission: Mandate for air refueling wanted]." *TAZ*, January 31, 2013. http://www.taz.de/!110120/.

"Demokratische Republik Kongo [Democratic Republic of Congo]—EUSEC RD Congo." *BMVg*. Updated September 30, 2014. http://www.einsatz.bundeswehr.de/portal/a/einsatzbw/!ut/p/c4/LclBDoMwDAXRs3CBeN9dbwHdWE7yFaJQG8UpSJy-VKpm9TT0ojuVoxYZ1VQ2mmlJ9RHPEM8MRlWXcd2UWOBp3cwd-h8YF0LG21rnjp2babGAjyNxz5x-pL09py-aZ9F0/.

Depasquale, Ron. "France's Hollande Urges Intervention in Mali to Root Out Islamists." *Star*, September 26, 2012. http://www.thestar.com/news/world/2012/09/26/frances_hollande_urges_intervention_in_mali_to_root_out_islamists.html.

Department of Defense. *Sustaining U.S. Global Leadership: Priorities for 21st Century Defense*. Washington, DC: Department of Defense, January 2012. Accessed February 2, 2015. http://www.defense.gov/news/Defense_Strategic_Guidance.pdf.

Dettke, Dieter. "Deutschland als europäische Macht und Bündnispartner [Germany as a European power and alliance partner]." *Aus Politik und Zeitgeschichte* [From politics and contemporary history] 15-16 (April 2009): 41–46.

"Deutsche wollen sich nicht einmischen [Germans don't want to butt in]." *Stern*, March 16, 2011. http://www.stern.de/politik/ausland/umfrage-zu-unruhen-in-libyen-deutsche-wollen-sich-nicht-einmischen-1664001.html.

Deutscher Bundestag. "Beschlussempfehlung und Bericht des Auswärtigen Ausschusses (3. Ausschuss) zu dem Antrag der Abgeordneten Omid Nouripour, Hans-Christian Ströbele, Marieluise Beck, weiterer Abgeordneter und der Fraktion BÜNDNIS 90/DIE GRÜNEN—Drs. 17/5099—Prüfkriterien für Auslandseinsätze der Bundeswehr entwickeln: Unterrichtung und Evaluation verbessern [Recommendation for decision and report of Committee for Foreign Affairs at the the request of the Representatives Omid Nouripour, Hans-Christian Ströbele, Marieluise Beck, and other representatives of the Faction BÜNDNIS 90/DIE GRÜNEN—Drs. 17/5099—Development of criteria for missions abroad of the Bundeswehr: Improve reporting and evaluation]." Drs.17/8697. Berlin: Bundesanzeiger Verlagsgesellschaft, February 17, 2012.

———. "Beschlussempfehlung und Bericht des Auswärtigen Ausschusses (3. Ausschuss) zu dem Antrag der Bundesregierung–Drucksache 17/12367–Entsendung bewaffneter deutscher Streitkräfte zur Beteiligung an der EU-geführten militärischen Ausbildungsmission EUTM Mali auf Grundlage des Ersuchens der Regierung von Mali sowie der Beschlüsse 2013/34/GASP des Rates der Europäischen Union (EU) vom 17. Januar 2013 und vom 18. Februar 2013 in Verbindung mit den Resolutionen 2071 (2012) und 2085 (2012) des Sicherheitsrates der Vereinten Nationen [Recommendation for decision and report of the Committee for Foreign Affairs at the request of the federal government—Drs. 17/12367—Deployment of German armed forces for participation in the EU-led military training mission EUTM Mali on the basis of the request by the Malian government as well as the EU Council Decisions 2013/34/CFSP on January 17, 2013 and February 18, 2013 in connection with UN Resolutions 2071 (2012) and 2985 (2012)]." Drs. 17/12520. Berlin: Bundesanzeiger Verlagsgesellschaft, February 27, 2013. Accessed March 11, 2015.
http://dipbt.bundestag.de/dip21/btd/17/125/1712520.pdf.

Deutscher Bundestag. "Beschlussempfehlung und Bericht des Auswärtigen Ausschusses (3. Ausschuss) zu dem Antrag der Bundesregierung–Drucksache 17/12368–Entsendung bewaffneter deutscher Streitkräfte zur Unterstützung der Internationalen Unterstützungsmission in Mali unter afrikanischer Führung (AFISMA) auf Grundlage der Resolution 2085 (2012) des Sicherheitsrates der Vereinten Nationen [Recommendation for decision and report of Committee for Foreign Affairs at the request of the federal government—Drs. 17/12368—Deployment of German armed forces in support of the international support mission under African lead (AFISMA) on the basis of UNSC Resolution 2085 (2012)]." Drs. 17/12522. Berlin: Bundesanzeiger Verlagsgesellschaft, February 27, 2013. Accessed January 20, 2015.
http://dipbt.bundestag.de/dip21/btd/17/125/1712522.pdf.

———. "Entschließungsantrag der Fraktionen der CDU/CSU und der FDP zu der Abgabe einer Regierungserklärung durch die Bundeskanzlerin zur Aktuellen Lage in Japan [Resolution by the CDU/CSU and the FDP on the Governmental Declaration by the federal chancellor on the current situation in Japan]." Drs.17/5048. Berlin: Bundesanzeiger Verlagsgesellschaft, March 16, 2011. Accessed February 3, 2015.
http://dipbt.bundestag.de/dip21/btd/17/050/1705048.pdf.

Deutscher Bundestag. "Entschließungsantrag der Abgeordneten Wolfgang Gehrcke, Paul Schäfer, Jan van Aken, Christine Buchholz, Sevim Dagdelen, Dr. Diether Dehm, Nicole Gohlke, Annette Groth, Heike Hänsel, Inge Höger, Andrej Hunko, Harald Koch, Stefan Liebich, Niema Movassat, Thomas Nord, Alexander Ulrich, Kathrin Vogler, Katrin Werner, und die Fraktion DIE LINKE zu der Abgabe einer Regierungserklärung durch den Bundesminister des Auswärtigen: Umbruch in der Arabischen Welt [Resolution by the Representatives Wolfgang Gehrke et al. and the Faction DIE LINKE on the governmental declarion of the federal minister of foreign affairs: Turmoil in the Arab world]." Drs. 17/5040. Berlin: Bundesanzeiger Verlagsgesellschaft, March 16, 2011. Accessed February 6, 2015. http://dipbt.bundestag.de/dip21/btd/ 17/050/1705040.pdf.

———. *Schriftliche Fragen: mit den in der Woche vom 4. April 2011 eingegangenen Antworten der Bundesregierung* [Written questions with response of the federal government on April 4, 2011]. Drs.17/5422. Berlin: Bundesanzeiger Verlagsgesellschaft, August 26, 2011. http://dipbt.bundestag.de/dip21/btd/17/054/1705422.pdf.

———. *Stenografischer Bericht: Plenarprotokoll 11/228* [Stenographic Record: Plenary Protocol 11/228]. Bonn: Dr. Hans Heger, October 4, 1990. Accessed January 20, 2015. http://dipbt.bundestag.de/doc/btp/11/ 11228.pdf#P.18018.

———. *Stenografischer Bericht: Plenarprotokoll 12/6* [Stenographic Record: Plenary Protocol 12/6]. Bonn: Dr. Hans Heger, January 31, 1991. Accessed January 20, 2015. http://dipbt.bundestag.de/doc/btp/12/ 12006.pdf.

———. *Stenografischer Bericht: Plenarprotokoll 12/60* [Stenographic Record: Plenary Protocol 12/60]. Bonn: Dr. Hans Heger, November 27, 1991. Accessed January 15, 2015. http://dipbt.bundestag.de/doc/btp/12/ 12060.pdf.

Deutscher Bundestag. *Stenografischer Bericht: Plenarprotokoll 13/248* [Stenographic Record: Plenary Protocol 13/248]. Bonn: Bundesanzeiger Verlagsgesellschaft, October 16, 1998. Accessed January 13, 2015. http://dipbt.bundestag.de/doc/btp/13/13248.pdf#P.23127.

———. *Stenografischer Bericht: Plenarprotokoll 14/187* [Stenographic Record: Plenary Protocol 14/187]. Berlin: Bundesanzeiger Verlagsgesellschaft, September 19, 2001. Accessed January 15, 2015. http://dipbt.bundestag.de/doc/btp/14/14187.pdf#P.18301.

———. *Stenografischer Bericht: Plenarprotokoll 16/60* [Stenographic Record: Plenary Protocol 16/60]. Berlin: Bundesanzeiger Verlagsgesellschaft, October 26, 2006. Accessed September 20, 2014. http://dipbt.bundestag.de/dip21/btp/16/16060.pdf.

———. *Stenografischer Bericht: Plenarprotokoll 17/11* [Stenographic Record: Plenary Protocol 17/11]. Berlin: Deutscher Bundestag, December 16, 2009. Accessed January 16, 2015. http://dipbt.bundestag.de/doc/btp/17/17011.pdf.

———. *Stenografischer Bericht: Plenarprotokoll 17/93* [Stenographic Record: Plenary Protocol 17/93]. Berlin: Bundesanzeiger Verlagsgesellschaft, February 24, 2011. Accessed February 10, 2015. http://dipbt.bundestag.de/dip21/btp/17/17093.pdf#P.10468.

———. *Stenografischer Bericht: Plenarprotokoll 17/95* [Stenographic Record: Plenary Protocol 17/95]. Berlin: Bundesanzeiger Verlagsgesellschaft, March 16, 2011. Accessed February 6, 2015. http://dipbt.bundestag.de/dip21/btp/17/17095.pdf#P.10814.

———. *Stenografischer Bericht: Plenarprotokoll 17/96* [Stenographic Record: Plenary Protocol 17/96]. Berlin: Bundesanzeiger Verlagsgesellschaft, March 17, 2011. Accessed February 3, 2015. http://dipbt.bundestag.de/dip21/btp/17/17096.pdf#P.10882.

———. *Stenografischer Bericht: Plenarprotokoll 17/97* [Stenographic Record: Plenary Protocol 17/97]. Berlin: Bundesanzeiger Verlagsgesellschaft, March 18, 2011. Accessed February 3, 2015. http://dipbt.bundestag.de/dip21/btp/17/17097.pdf#P.11137.

Deutscher Bundestag. *Stenografischer Bericht: Plenarprotokoll 17/99* [Stenographic Record: Plenary Protocol 17/99]. Berlin: Bundesanzeiger Verlagsgesellschaft, March 24, 2011. Accessed February 6, 2015. http://dipbt.bundestag.de/doc/ btp/17/17099.pdf.

———. *Stenografischer Bericht: Plenarprotokoll 17/121* [Stenographic Record: Plenary Protocol 17/121]. Berlin: Bundesanzeiger Verlagsgesellschaft, July 8, 2011. Accessed February 26, 2015. http://dipbt.bundestag.de/dip21/ btp/17/17121.pdf#P.14290.

———. *Stenografischer Bericht: Plenarprotokoll 17/215* [Stenographic Record: Plenary Protocol 17/215]. Berlin: Bundesanzeiger Verlagsgesellschaft, December 12, 2012. Accessed February 26, 2015. http://dipbt.bundestag.de/dip21/btp/17/17215.pdf.

———. *Stenografischer Bericht: Plenarprotokoll 17/225* [Stenographic Record: Plenary Protocol 17/225]. Berlin: Bundesanzeiger Verlagsgesellschaft, February 28, 2013. Accessed February 15, 2015. http://dipbt.bundestag.de/ dip21/btp/17/17215.pdf.

———. *Stenografischer Bericht: Plenarprotokoll 18/30* [Stenographic Record: Plenary Protocol 18/30]. Berlin: Bundesanzeiger Verlagsgesellschaft, April 10, 2014. Accessed March 26, 2015. http://dipbt.bundestag.de/dip21/ btp/18/18030.pdf.

"Deutsche Stiefel für die Mission in Mali [German boots for the mission in Mali]." *Die Welt*, January 27, 2013. http://www.welt.de/politik/ausland/article113158983/Deutsche-Stiefel-fuer-die-Mission-in-Mali.html.

Deutschlands Zukunft gestalten: Koalitionsvertrag zwischen CDU, CSU und SPD, 18. Legislaturperiode [Shaping Germany's future: Coalition treaty between CDU, CSU, and SPD, 18th Legislative Period]. Berlin: 2013. Accessed August 10, 2014. http://www.bundesregierung.de/Content/DE/ Anlagen/2013 /2013-12-17-koalitionsvertrag.pdf?__blob=publicationFile.

Diallo, Tiemoko. "Military Planners Prepare for War in Mali." Reuters, November 6, 2012. http://www.reuters.com/article/2012/ 11/06/us-mali-crisis-idUSBRE8A50UO20121106.

Dicke, Rachel. "The European Union Training Mission in Mali: A Case Study," *CIRR* 20, no. 71 (2014): 91–119. doi: 10.2478/cirr-2014-0010.

"Die EU-geführte zivile Mission am Horn von Afrika [The EU-led civil mission at the Horn of Africa]—EUCAP Nestor." *BMVg*. Updated April 1, 2015. http://www.einsatz.bundeswehr.de/portal/a/einsatzbw/!ut/p/c4/04_SB8K8xLLM9MSSzPy8xBz9CP3I5EyrpHK9pPKU1PjUzLzixJIqIDcxKT21ODkjJ7-4ODUPKpFaUpWql1qanFiQl1pckl-kX5DtqAgA8A74Ag!!/.

Dilanian, Ken. "Obama Administration Weighs Intervention in Mali." *Los Angeles Times Blog* (blog), July 27, 2012. http://latimesblogs.latimes.com/world now/2012/07/obama-administration-weighs-intervention-in-mali.html.

DPA. "Germany Participated in Libya War without Parliamentary Approval: 100 Germans Involved in NATO Libya Mission." *Global Research*. Updated September 11, 2011. http://www.globalresearch.ca/germany-participated-in-libya-war-without-parliamentary-approval/26481.

Duffield, John S. "Why Germany Confounds Neorealism." *International Organizations* 53, no. 4 (Autumn 1999): 765–803.

Ebert, Philipp. *Die Geschichte der Wiederbewaffnungsdiskussion in der Bundesrepublik, 1949-1955: Argumente, Alternativen, öffentliche Meinung* [The history of the rearmament debate in the FRG, 1949–1955: Arguments, alternatives, and public opinion]. Study work, Norderstedt, Germany: Grin-Verlag, 2010.

"ECOWAS Imposes Sanctions on Mali." *Voice of America*, April 1, 2012. http://www.voanews.com/content/west-african-leaders-impose-sanctions-on-mali-145801255/180314.html.

Ehrenstein, Claudia. "Westerwelles bewegender Besuch auf dem Tahrir-Platz [Westerwelle's moving visit at Tahrir Square]." *Die Welt*, February 24, 2011. http://www.welt.de/politik/ausland/article12636464/Westerwelles-bewegender-Besuch-auf-dem-Tahrir-Platz.html.

"Einsatzzahlen: Die Stärke der deutschen Einsatzkontingente [Mission Numbers: The Strenght of German Mission Contingents]." *Bundeswehr*. Updated May 18, 2015. http://www.bundeswehr.de/portal/a/bwde/!ut/p/c4/04_SB8K8xLLM9MSSzPy8xBz9CP3I5EyrpHK9pPKUVL3UzLzixNSSKiirpKoqMSMnNU-_INtREQD2RLYK/.

Endres, Fabian, Harald Schoen, and Hans Rattinger. "Außen- und Sicherheitspolitik aus der Sicht der Bürger: Theoretische Perspektiven und ein Überblick über den Forschungsstand [Foreign and security policy from the view of the citizens: Theoretical perspectives and an overview about the state of reseach]." In *Sicherheitspolitik und Streitkräfte im Urteil der Bürger: Therorien, Methoden, Befunde* [Security policy and armed forces under judgment of the citizens: Theories, methods, results], edited by Heiko Biehl and Harald Schoen, 39–65. Wiesbaden: VS Springer Fachmedien, 2015.

Engel, Ulf. *Die Afrikapolitik der Bundesrepublik Deutschland, 1949-1999: Rollen und Identitäten* [The Africa policy of the Federal Republic of Germany, 1949–1999: Roles and identities]. Hamburg: LIT, 2000.

———. "The G8 and Germany's Africa Policy: A Case of Hegemonic Mainstreaming." *Global Governance* 18, no. 4 (October-December 2012): 471–76.

Engelberg, Katarina. *The EU and Military Operations: A Comparative Analysis*. New York: Routledge, 2014.

"Erneuter Ausbildungsstart in Mali [New start of training in Mali]." *BMVg*. Updated January 27, 2015. http://www.einsatz.bundeswehr.de/portal/a/einsatzbw/!ut/p/c4/LYvBCoMwEET_KGvaQrW3ipdCenF6qWsZpGlMZG4VpB-fBNwBgZmHgMtRDv88oDC3qGFFzQ9X7pVdauhN7GbUbZY8SMLWbtPJBtBnc6GVO8dSUohJxxzCCg-qMkHsYksIUSi2ECT6arU51O2S_-Ke563j0NxrG7lE6ZxvP4BtoW_uQ!!/.

"European Union Drawing Up Plans for Military Intervention in Mali." *London Evening Post*, October 16, 2012. http://www.thelondoneveningpost.com/european-union-drawing-up-plans-for-military-intervention-in-mali/.

Federal Constitutional Court. *BVerfGE 90, 286—out-of-area Einsätze*. Karlsruhe: Federal Constitutional Court, 1994.

"Federal Foreign Minister Westerwelle on the Libya Resolution of the UN Security Council." *Permanent Mission of Germany to the United Nations*. Updated March 17, 2011. http://www.new-york-un.diplo.de/Vertretung/newyorkvn/en/pr/press-releases/2011/110317_20Westerwelle_20on_20Libya.html.

Federal Foreign Office. "Außenminister Westerwelle: Schutz der Menschenrechte ist Grundpfeiler deutscher Außenpolitik [Foreign Minister Westerwelle: Protection of human rights is a cornerstone of German foreign policy]." *Auswaertiges Amt*. Updated December 12, 2010. http://www.auswaertiges-amt.de/DE/Infoservice/Presse/Meldungen/2010/101210-BM-Tag_der_MR.html.

———. "Federal Minister Westerwelle Welcomes Naming of UN Special Envoy to Libya." *Auswaertiges Amt*. Updated March 7, 2011. http://www.auswaertiges-amt.de/EN/Infoservice/Presse/Meldungen/2011/110307_VN_Libyen.html.

Federal Foreign Office. "Rede von Außenminister Westerwelle im Deutschen Bundestag zum Mali-Einsatz der Bundeswehr, 20. Februar 2013 [Speech by Foreign Minister Westerwelle at the German Bundestag on the Mali mission of the Bundeswehr, February 20, 2013]." *Auswaertiges Amt*. Updated February 28, 2013. http://www.auswaertiges-amt.de/sid_6BF78E917193A5DC0ABED7A7814B221A/DE/Infoservice/Presse/Reden/2013/130220-BM-BT-Mali-Rede.html?nn=352220.

Federal Ministry of Defense. *Defense Policy Guidelines: Safeguarding National Interests—Assuming International Responsibility—Shaping Security Together*. Berlin: Federal Ministry of Defense, 2011.

———. "EU berät über Militäreinsatz in Mali [EU consults about military intervention in Mali]." *BMVg*. Updated November 21, 2012. http://www.bmvg.de/portal/a/bmvg/!ut/p/c4/NYtNC8IwEET_UTYRoerNUhBBL1603tI0pKv5YrutF3-8ycEZeId5DDyhNOoVnWZMUXt4QG_wMHzEEFYnXmm hsooZzWRpsshzTh4Z33Cv19EKk6LlSraRsdCR5kQiJ2JfzUJUj MAReqm6Vir5j_ruN83petk12-7c3iCHcPwByVzcGQ!!/.

———. *The Bundeswehr on Operations: Publication to Mark the 15th Anniversary of the First Parliamentary Mandate for Armed Bundeswehr Missions Abroad*. Berlin: Federal Ministry of Defense, 2009.

———. "Pressekonferenz am 5. Dezember 2002 mit Bundesminister Dr. Peter Struck zur Weiterentwicklung der Bundeswehr [Press conference with Federal Minister Dr. Peter Struck on the further development of the Bundeswehr on December 5, 2002]." *BMVg*. Updated December 5, 2013. http://www.bmvg.de/portal/a/bmvg/!ut/p/c4/NY3BCsIwE ET_KGkOFetNUUEPetR6KWmypItNUjabevHjTYXOwBzm DYx8yeKgZ3SaMQY9yqdsDe76j-j97ITHgImBMHvhIJkBzcDQ_dkMxIAWXQ4urcMuAXKnmr oWli-YoTWLK5i0fy5MFYWIAXpIhMJZ0pDmSmCLxuJBMVIhA K9tKHQ-Vqlap72bbXk9NqS63811O3u9_-L2Ycw!!/.

Federal Ministry of Defense. *The White Paper 2006: On German Security Policy and the Future of the Bundeswehr.* Berlin: Federal Ministry of Defense, 2006.

Fiebiger, Rüdiger, and Carsten Pietsch. "Die Deutschen und ihre Streitkräfte [The Germans and their armed forces]." *Aus Politik und Zeitgeschichte* [From politics and contemporary history] 48 (November 2009): 36–41.

Fiorenza, Nicholas. "EU Launches Training Mission for Mali." *Aviation Week*, February 18, 2013, http://aviationweek.com/blog/eu-launches-training-mission-mali.

Fischer, Joschka. "Außenpolitik: Ein einziges Debakel [Foreign policy: A sole debacle]." Interview by Erich Follath and Ralf Neukirch. *Spiegel Online*, August 29, 2011. http://www.spiegel.de/spiegel/a-782871.html

———. "Deutsche Außenpolitik: Eine Farce [German foreign policy: A farce]." *Süddeutsche Zeitung*, March 24, 2011. http://www.sueddeutsche.de/politik/2.220/streitfall-libyen-einsatz-deutsche-aussenpolitik-eine-farce-1.1075362.

Fischer, Sebastian, and Veit Medick. "Bundeswehr in Afghanistan: Köhler entfacht neue Kriegsdebatte [Bundeswehr in Afghanistan: Köhler sparks new war debate]." *Spiegel Online*, May 27, 2010. http://www.spiegel.de/politik/deutschland/ bundeswehr-in-afghanistan-koehler-entfacht-neue-kriegsdebatte-a-696982.html.

"Foreign Minister Westerwelle on Libya." *Permanent Mission of Germany to the United Nations.* Updated March 13, 2011. http://www.new-york-un.diplo.de/Vertretung/newyorkvn/en/ pr/press-re-leases/2011/110313_20Westerwelle_20on_20Libya.html?archive=2990092.

Formuszewicz, Ryszarda. "Waiting for Germany's European Choices." *Polish Quarterly of International Affairs*, no. 2 (2013): 5-10.

Franke, Ulrike Esther. "A Tale of Stumbling Blocks and Road Bumps: Germany's (Non-) Revolution in Military Affairs." *Comparative Strategy* 31, no. 4 (2012): 353–75.

Frankenberger, Klaus-Dieter, and Hanns W. Maull. "'Gimme a Break': Germany Takes Time Out from a Complex World." *Deutsche Aussenpolitik*. Updated March 24, 2011. http://www.deutsche-aussenpolitik.de/digest/op-ed_inhalt_59.php.

Friedrichs, Hauke. "Die Bundeswehr ist längst in Mali [The Bundeswehr is already in Mali]." *Zeit Online*, October 29, 2012. http://www.zeit.de/politik/deutschland/2012-10/bundeswehr-mali-einsatz-ausbildung.

Fröhlich, Stefan. "Herausforderungen der deutschen Außen- und Sicherheitspolitik bis 2030: Grundlegende Problemstellungen [Challenges of German foreign and security policy until 2030: General problems]." *Zeitschrift für Außen- und Sicherheitspolitik* 5, no. 3 (2012): 404-13.

"Gaddafi Tells Benghazi His Army Is Coming Tonight." *Reuters*. March 17, 2011. http://uk.reuters.com/article/2011/03/17/libya-gaddafi-address-idUKLDE72G2E920110317.

Gahler, Michael. "Kein Konflikt der Anderen [No conflict of the Others]." *The European,* February 7, 2013. http://www.theeuropean.de/michael-gahler/5831-deutsches-engagement-in-mali.

Gareis, Sven Bernhard. *Deutschlands Außen- und Sicherheitspolitik* [Germany's foreign and security policy]. 2nd ed. Opladen, Germany: Verlag Barabara Budrich, 2006.

Gareis, Sven Bernhard. "Die Organisation deutscher Sicherheitspolitik: Akteure, Kompetenzen, Verfahren und Perspektiven [The organization of German security policy: Actors, competencies, procedures, and perspectives]." In *Deutsche Sicherheitspolitik: Herausforderungen, Akteure und Prozesse* [German security policy: Challenges, actors, and processes]. 2nd ed. Edited by Stephan Böckenförde and Sven Bernhard Gareis, 89–112. Opladen, Germany: Verlag Barbara Buderich, 2014.

———. "Militärische Auslandseinsätze und die Transformation der Bundeswehr [Military missions abroad and the transformation of the Bundeswehr]." In *Deutsche Außenpolitik: Sicherheit, Wohlfahrt, Institutionen und Normen* [German foreign policy: Security, welfare, institutions, and norms]. 2nd ed. Edited by Thomas Jäger, Alexander Höse, and Kai Oppermann, 148–70. Wiesbaden: Springer Fachmedien, 2011.

———. "Militärische Beiträge zur Sicherheit [Military contributions to security]." In *Deutsche Sicherheitspolitik: Herausforderungen, Akteure und Prozesse* [German security policy: Challenges, actors, and processes]. 2nd ed. Edited by Stephan Böckenförde and Sven Bernhard Gareis, 115–47. Opladen, Germany: Verlag Barbara Buderich, 2014.

———. "The Making of Germany's Security and Defense Policy: Actors, Responsivities, Procedures, and Requirements." In *German Defense Politics*. Edited by Ina Wiesner, 49–77. Baden-Baden: Nomos, 2013.

Gauck, Joachim. *Germany's Role in the World: Reflections on Responsibility, Norms, and Alliances*. Speech by Federal President Joachim Gauck at the opening of the Munich Security Conference, January 31, 2014. Accessed November 6, 2014. http://www.bundespraesident.de/SharedDocs/Downloads/DE/Reden/2014/01/140131-Muenchner-Sicherheitskonferenz-Englisch.pdf?__blob=publicationFile.

"Gaza Rockets Land near Jerusalem as Fears of Ground Offensive Grow." *Guardian*, November 17, 2012. http://www.theguardian.com/world/2012/nov/17/gaza-attacks-israeli-reserve-troops.

Gearan, Anne. "UN Security Council Will Be Asked to Approve Force to Confront Al-Qaeda in Mali." *Washington Post*, October 3, 2012. http://www.washingtonpost.com/world/national-security/un-security-council-will-be-asked-to-approve-force-to-confront-al-qaeda-in-mali/2012/10/03/3836405e-0d6b-11e2-a310-2363842b7057_story.html.

———. "U.S. Pushes Algeria to Support Military Intervention in Mali." *Washington Post*, October 29, 2012. http://www.washingtonpost.com/world/us-pushes-algeria-to-support-military-intervention-in-mali/2012/10/29/fee8df44-21a3-11e2-92f8-7f9c4daf276a_story.html.

Gebauer, Matthias. "Geplante EU-Trainingsmission: Bundeswehr schickt Erkundungsteam nach Mali [Planned EU training mission: Bundeswehr sends reconnaissance team to Mali]." *Spiegel Online*, February 13, 2013. http://www.spiegel.de/politik/ausland/eu-trainingsmission-bundeswehr-schickt-erkundungsteam-nach-mali-a-883236.html.

Gebauer, Matthias, and Philipp Wittrock. "Germany's Mali Predicament: Trapped between France and War." *Spiegel Online*, January 17, 2013. http://www.spiegel.de/international/world/french-mission-in-mali-puts-germany-in-a-tight-spot-a-878187-druck.html.

Geis, Anna. "Die Zivilmacht Deutschland und die Enttabuisierung des Militärischen [The Civil Power Germany and the removal of taboos on the military]." *HSFK Standpunkte* 2. Frankfurt am Main: Hessische Stiftung Friedens- und Konfliktforschung, 2005.

"German Foreign Policy: The Unadventurous Eagle." *Economist*, May 12, 2011. http://www.economist.com/node/18683155.

German Institute for International and Security Affairs, and German Marshall Fund of the United States. *Neue Macht—Neue Verantwortung: Elemente einer deutschen Außen- und Sicherheitspolitik für eine Welt im Umbruch* [New power—New responsibility: Elements of a German foreign and security policy in a world in change]. Berlin: German Institute for International and Security Affairs, 2013.

"Germany Considers Options to Aid Mali Intervention." *Deutsche Welle*, January 14, 2013. http://www.dw.de/germany-considers-options-to-aid-mali-intervention/a-16520168-.

"Germany's Libya Contribution: Merkel Cabinet Approves AWACS for Afghanistan." *Spiegel Online*, March 23, 2011. http://www.spiegel.de/international/world/germany-s-libya-contribution-merkel-cabinet-approves-awacs-for-afghanistan-a-752709.html.

Gießmann, Hans J., and Armin Wagner, ed. *Armee im Einsatz: Grundlagen, Strategien und Ergebnisse einer Beteiligung der Bundeswehr* [Armed forces on a mission: Principles, strategies, and results of Bundeswehr participation]. Baden-Baden: Nomos, 2009.

———. "Auslandseinsätze der Bundeswehr [Missions abroad of the Bundeswehr]." *Aus Politik und Zeitgeschichte* [From politics and contemporary history] 48 (November 2009): 3–9.

Ginsberg, Roy H., and Susan E. Penska. *The European Union in Global Security: The Politics of Impacts.* New York: Palgrave Macmillan, 2014.

Glenn, John. "Realism versus Strategic Culture: Competition and Collaboration?" *International Studies Review* 11 (2009): 523–51.

Goebel, Nicole. "Germany Defends Cautious Approach to Libya, Denies Isolation." *Deutsche Welle*, March 23, 2011. http://www.dw.de/germany-defends-cautious-approach-to-libya-denies-isolation/a-14926360.

Golaszinski, Ulrich. *Subsahara-Afrika: Die Wiederentdeckung eines Kontinentes* [Sub-Saharan Africa: The reexploration of a continent]. Berlin: Friedrich-Ebert-Stiftung, 2007.

Göler, Daniel. "Die strategische Kultur der Bundesrepublik: Eine Bestandsaufnahme normativer Vorstellungen über den Einsatz militärischer Mittel [The strategic culture of the federal republic: A survey of normative notions about the use of military means]." In *Friedensethik und Sicherheitspolitik: Weißbuch 2006 und die EDK-Friedensdenkschrift 2007 in der Diskussion* [Peace ethics and security Policy: White paper 2006 and the EDK-Peace Memorandum 2007 in the debate], edited by Angelika Dörfler-Dierken and Gerd Portugall, 19185-99. Wiesbaden: VS Verlag für Sozialwissenschaften, 2010.

Gortney, Bill. "U.S. Department of Defense News Briefing on Operation Odyssey Dawn." *U.S. Department of Defense*. Update March 19, 2011. http://www.defense.gov/transcripts/transcript.aspx?_transcriptid=4786.

Gräßler, Bernd. "Germany Backs French Intervention in Mali." *Deutsche Welle*, January 14, 2013.
http://www.dw.de/germany-backs-french-intervention-in-mali/a-16520834.

Greiner, Lena. "Auf Libyen folgt Syrien? [Does Syria follow Libya?]." *Blätter für deutsche und internationale Politik* [Pages for German and international politics], no. 7 (2012): 73–78.

Grundgesetz für die Bundesrepublik Deutschland [Basic law of the Federal Republic of Germany]. Berlin: Bundesministerium für Justiz und Verbraucherschutz, 2014. Accessed January 15, 2015. http://www.gesetze-im-internet.de/bundesrecht/gg/_gesamt.pdf.

Guérot, Ulrike. "Merkel's European and Foreign Policy Legacy on the Eve of the German Elections: European Hegemon or Global Player?" *Polish Quarterly of International Affairs*, no. 2 (2013): 11–27.

Guérot, Ulrike, and Mark Leonard. "The New German Question: How Europe Can Get the Germany It Needs," *ECFR Policy Brief*. London: European Council on Foreign Relations, 2011.

Habermas, Jürgen. "Germany's Mindset Has Become Solipsistic." *Guardian*, June 11, 2010. http://www.theguardian.com/commentisfree/2010/jun/11/germany-normality-self-absorption.

Hacke, Christian. "Deutschland und der Libyen Konflikt: Zivilmacht ohne Zivilcourage [Germany and the Libyan conflict: Civil power without civil courage]." *Aus Politik und Zeitgeschichte* [From politics and contemporary history] 61, no. 39 (September 2011): 50–53.

Haftendorn, Helga. *Coming of Age: German Foreign Policy since 1945*. Lanham, NY: Rowman & Littlefield, 2006.

———. *Deutsche Außenpolitik zwischen Selbstbeschränkung und Selbstbehauptung, 1945—2000* [German foreign policy between self-restraint and self-assertion, 1945–2000]. München: Deutsche Verlags-Anstalt, 2001.

———. "Deutschlands Rückkehr in die Weltpolitik [Germany's comeback to global politics]." *Politische Studien* [Political studies] 60, no. 425 (2009): 49–57.

———. "Zur Theorie außenpolitischer Entscheidungsprozesse [On the theory of foreign policy decision-making processes]." In *Theorien der internationalen Beziehungen: Bestandsaufnahme und Forschungsprozesse* [Theory of international relations: Survey and research processes]. Edited by Volker Ritterberger, 401–423. Opladen, Germany: Westdeutscher Verlag, 1990.

Hanrieder, Wolfram. "Compatibility and Consensus: A Proposal for the Conceptual Linkage of External and Internal Dimensions of Foreign Policy." *American Political Science Review* 61, no. 4 (December 1967): 971–82.

Harnisch, Sebastian, and Kerry Longhurst. "Understanding Germany: The Limits of 'Normalization' and the Prevalence of Strategic Culture." In *German Culture, Politics, and Literature into the Twenty-First Century: Beyond Normalization*. Edited by Stuart Taberner and Paul Cooke, 49–60. Rochester, NY: Camden House, 2006.

Harsch, Michael F. "A Reluctant Warrior: The German Engagement in Afghanistan." Oslo: Peace Research Institute Oslo (PRIO), 2011. Accessed February 4, 2015. http://www.operationspaix.net/DATA/DOCUMENT/6352~v~A_Reluctant_Warrior_The_German_Engagement_in_Afghanistan.pdf.

Hasenclever, Andreas. "Liberalismus [Liberalism]." In *Handbuch der Internationalen Politik* [Handbook of international politics]. Edited by Carlo Masala, Frank Sauer, and Andreas Wilhelm, 77–101. Wiesbaden: VS Verlag für Sozialwissenschaften, 2010.

Hastings, Michael. "Inside Obama's War Room." *Rolling Stone*, October 13, 2011. http://www.rollingstone.com/politics/news/inside-obamas-war-room-20111013.

Hawley, Charles. "The World from Berlin: French Mission in Mali 'Is Not Without Risk.'" *Spiegel Online*, January 14, 2013. http://www.spiegel.de/international/world/germany-offers-support-to-france-in-mali-as-commentators-warn-of-risk-a-877401.html.

Haysom, Simone. *Security and Humanitarian Crisis in Mali: The Role of Regional Organizations*. HPG Working Paper. London: Humanitarian Policy Group, March 2014. Accessed March 4, 2015. http://www.odi.org/sites/odi.org.uk/files/odi-assets/publications-opinion-files/8829.pdf.

Hellmann, Gunther. "Berlins Große Politik im Fall Libyen [Berlin's big policy in the case of Libya]." *WeltTrends* 19, no. 80 (2011): 19–22.

———. "Das neue Selbstbewusstsein deutscher Außenpolitik und die veränderten Standards der Angemessenheit [The new self-confidence of German foreign policy and the changed standards of appropriateness]." In *Deutsche Außenpolitik* [German foreign policy], 2nd ed. Edited by Thomas Jäger, Alexander Höse, and Kai Oppermann, 735–58. Wiesbaden: VS Verlag für Sozialwissenschaft 2011.

Hellmann, Gunther. "Wider die machtpolitische Resozialisierung der deutschen Außenpolitik: Ein Plädoyer für offensiven Idealismus [Against the power-political resocialization of German foreign policy: A plea for an offensive idealism]." *WeltTrends* 12, no. 42 (2004): 79–88.

Hellmann, Gunther, Christian Weber, Frank Sauer, and Sonja Schirmbeck. "'Selbstbewusst' und 'stolz': Das außenpolitische Vokabular der Berliner Republik als Fährte einer Neuorientierung ['Self-confident' and 'proud:' The foreign political vocabulary of the Berlin Republic as a trace of a reorientation]." *Politische Vierteljahresschrift* 48, no. 4 (2007): 650–79.

Hellmann, Gunther, Reinhard Wolf, and Siegmar Schmidt. "Deutsche Außenpolitik in historischer und systematischer Perspektive [German foreign policy in a historical and systematical perspective]." In *Handbuch zur deutschen Außenpolitik* [Handbook for German foreign policy]. Edited by Sigmar Schmidt, Gunther Hellmann, and Reinhard Wolf, 15–48. Wiesbaden: Verlag für Sozialwissenschaften, 2007.

Hellmann, Gunter, Wolfgang Wagner, and Rainer Baumann. *Deutsche Außenpolitik: Eine Einführung* [German foreign policy: An introduction]. 2nd ed. Wiesbaden: VS Springer Fachmedien, 2014.

Hermann, Charles F. "Changing Course: When Governments Choose to Redirect Foreign Policy." *International Studies Quarterly* 34, no. 1 (March 1990): 3–21.

Hickmann, Christoph, and Caroline Ischinger. "Deutschland will Hilfe für Mali-Einsatz ausweiten [Germany wants to extend help for Mali mission]." *Süddeutsche*, January 31, 2013. http://www.sueddeutsche.de/politik/krisengebiet-in-westafrika-deutschland-will-hilfe-fuer-mali-einsatz-ausweiten-1.1587730.

Hippler, Jochen. "Bedingungen, Kriterien und Grenzen militärischer Intervention [Conditions, criteria, and limits of military interventions]." *Jochenhippler*. Accessed October 10, 2014. http://www.jochenhippler.de/Kriterien_von_Interventionen_L angfassung.pdf.

Hilz, Wolfram. "Kontinuität und Wandel deutscher Außenpolitik nach 1990 [Continuity and change of German foreign policy after 1990]." *Informationen zur Politischen Bildung* [Information on political education] 304 (September 2009): 33–51.

Hollande, Francois. S*peech by M. Francois Hollande, President of the Republic at the High-Level Meeting on Sahel, September 26, 2012.* New York: Embassy of France in Washington, DC, September 27, 2012. http://www.ambafrance-us.org/spip.php?article3911.

Holsti, K.J. "National Role Conceptions in the Study of Foreign Policy." *International Studies Quarterly* 14, no. 3 (September 1970): 233–309.

"Hopeless Africa." *Economist*, May 11, 2000. http://www.economist.com/node/333429.

Howorth, Jolyon. *Security and Defense Policy in the European Union.* 2nd ed. New York: Palgrave Macmillan, 2014.

Institute for Strategic Studies. "War in Libya: Europe's Confused Response." *Strategic Comments* 17, no. 18 (April 2011): 1–3. Accessed April 2, 2015. http://www.tandfonline.com/doi/pdf/10.1080/13567888.2011.596314.

Institut für Friedensforschung und Sicherheitspolitik an der Universität Hamburg. *Auslandseinsätze der Bundeswehr: Viele Bedingungen müssen erfüllt sein* [Missions abroad of the Bundeswehr: Many conditions have to be fulfilled]. Hamburg: Institut für Friedensforschung und Sicherheitspolitik an der Universität Hamburg, 2007. Accessed January 20, 2015.
http://ifsh.de/pdf/profil/IFSH_Auslandseinsaetze_der_Bundeswehr_2007.pdf.

International Crisis Group. *Mali: The Need for Determined and Coordinated International Action.* Policy Briefing—Africa Briefing, no. 90. Brussels: ICG, September 24, 2012.
http://www.crisisgroup.org/~/media/Files/africa/west-africa/mali/b090-mali-the-need-for-determined-and-coordinated-international-action-english.pdf.

Irish, John, and David Lewis. "Military Intervention in Mali 'Probable': French Foreign Minister." Reuters, July 12, 2012. http://www.reuters.com/article/2012/07/12/us-france-mali-idUSBRE86B0XS20120712.

Ischinger, Wolfgang. "Germany after Libya: Still a Responsible Power?" In *All Alone? What U.S. Entrenchment Means for Europe and NATO*. Edited by Tomas Valasek, 47–51. London: Center for European Reform, 2012.

Jacobs, Jörg. "Germans to the Front?: Attitudes Towards a German Contribution to Worldwide Military Missions." *Journal of Contemporary Central and Eastern Europe* 14, no. 3 (2006): 271–81. doi: 10.1080/09651560601042993.

Janes, Jackson. "Merkel 3.0: German Foreign and Security Policy in the Aftermath of the 2013 Bundestag Election," *German Politics and Society* 112, no. 3 (Autumn 2014): 86–97.

Jepperson, Ronald L., Alexander Wendt, and Peter J. Katzenstein. "Norms, Identity, and Culture in National Security." In *The Culture of National Security*. Edited by Peter J. Katzenstein, 33–75. New York: Columbia University Press, 1996.

Jervis, Robert. "Cooperation under the Security Dilemma," *World Politics* 30, no. 2 (January 1978): 167–214.

———. "Do Leaders Matter and How Would We Know?" *Security Studies* 22, no. 2 (2013): 153–79. http://dx.doi.org/10.1080/09636412.2013.786909.

Joffe, Josef. "Friedensarbeit 2.0: Gauck rüttelt an deutschen Selbstgewissheiten – und niemand tobt [Peace work 2.0: Gauck rocks German self-assurances—And nobody storms]." *Die Zeit*, February 6, 2014. http://pdf.zeit.de/2014/07/gauck-rede-aussenpolitik.pdf.

Johnson, Dominic. "Bundesregierung beschließt Mali-Einsatz: Deutsche in den Sand gesetzt [Federal government decides Mali mission: Germans put into the sand]." *TAZ*, February 19, 2013. http://www.taz.de/!111377/.

Johnston, Alastair Lain. "Thinking about Strategic Culture." *International Security* 19, no. 4 (Spring 1995): 32–64.

Jung, Franz Josef. *Deutsche Sicherheitsinteressen und die Rolle der Bundeswehr. Punktation des Bundesministers der Verteidigung bei der Konrad Adenauer Stiftung* [German security interests and the Bundeswehr: Commentary by the defense minister at the Konrad Adenauer Foundation]. Berlin: Bundesministerium der Verteidigung, June 18, 2007. Accessed September 20, 2014. http://www.kas.de/upload/dokumente/2007/070618_jung.pdf.

Jungholt, Thorsten. "'Der ganzen Region droht die Eskalation [Escalation threatens the entire region].'" *Die Welt*, November 19, 2012. http://www.welt.de/politik/ausland/article111289917/Der-ganzen-Region-droht-die-Eskalation.html.

———. "Deutscher Mali-Beitrag sorgt für Ärger bei Franzosen [Germany's contribution to Mali causes French resentment]." *Die Welt*, February 3, 2013. http://www.welt.de/politik/ausland/article113350416/Deutscher-Mali-Beitrag-sorgt-fuer-Aerger-bei-Franzosen.html.

———. "Paris ruft—doch Berlin schickt nur zwei Flieger [Paris calls—But Berlin sends only two airplanes]." *Die Welt*, January 16, 2013. http://www.welt.de/politik/deutschland/article112818164/Paris-ruft-doch-Berlin-schickt-nur-zwei-Flieger.html.

———. "Westerwelle rechtfertigt deutschen Libyen-Sonderweg [Westerwelle justifies German special path in Libya]." *Die Welt*, March 20, 2011. http://www.welt.de/politik/deutschland/article12898795/Westerwelle-rechtfertigt-deutschen-Libyen-Sonderweg.html.

Jungholt, Thorsten, and Karsten Kammholz. "Bundesregierung sucht noch eine Strategie für Mali [Federal government still seeks for a strategy on Mali]." *Die Welt*, January 15, 2013. http://www.welt.de/politik/deutschland/article112764631/Bundesregierung-sucht-noch-eine-Strategie-fuer-Mali.html.

Junk, Julian. "Vom Gestaltungsunwillen einer 'Gestaltungsmacht:' Ein Kommentar zur deutschen Malipolitik [Of an indignation of shaping of a 'shaping power': A commentary on Germany's Mali policy]." *Sicherheit und Frieden* [Security and Peace] 32, no. 2 (2014): 91–97.

Junk, Julian, and Christopher Daase. "Germany." In *Strategic Cultures in Europe: Security and Defense Policies Across the Continent*. Edited by Heiko Biehl, Bastian Giegerich, and Alexandra Jonas, 139–52. Wiesbaden: Springer VS, 2013.

"Kabinett beschließt Mali-Einsatz der Bundeswehr [Cabinet decides Mali mission of the Bundeswehr]." *Zeit Online*, February 19, 2013. http://www.zeit.de/politik/ausland/2013-02/mali-einsatz-bundeswehr-soldaten-mandat.

Kaim, Markus. "Deutsche Auslandseinsätze in der Multilateralismusfalle? [German missions abroad in a multilateralism trap?]" In *Auslandseinsätze der Bundeswehr: Leitfragen, Entscheidungsspielräumen und Lehren* [Missions abroad of the Bundeswehr: Guiding questions, freedom to decide, and lessons]. Edited by Stefan Mair, 43–49. Berlin: German Institute for International and Security Affairs, 2009.

———. "Deutsches Interesse versus Bündnisverpflichtung: Zur Frage nationaler Handlungsspielräume bei Auslandseinsätzen der Bundeswehr [German interests versus alliance solidarity: A question of national policy discretion by the Bundeswehr's missions abroad]." In *Armee im Einsatz: Grundlagen, Strategien und Ergebnisse einer Beteiligung der Bundeswehr* [Armed forces in mission: Principles, strategies, and results of Bundeswehr participation]. Edited by Hans J. Gießmann and Armin Wagner, 176–85. Baden-Baden: Nomos: 2009.

———. *Deutschlands Einsatz in Afghanistan: Die sicherheitspolitische Dimension* [Germany's mission in Afghanistan: The security policy dimension]. Note du Cerfa 76. Paris: Institut Français du Relations International, 2012.

Kaiser, Karl, and Manuel Munitz. "Global Europe: Europe, too, Needs an Asian 'Pivot.'" *Europe's World.* Updated June 1, 2013. http://europesworld.org/2013/06/01/europe-too-needs-an-asian-pivot/#.VSVGqvmG8XQ.

"Kampf gegen Islamisten: Sicherheitsrat genehmigt Militäreinsatz in Mali [Fight against Islamists: Security Council approves military intervention in Mali]." *Spiegel Online,* December 20, 2012. http://www.spiegel.de/politik/ausland/uno-sicherheitsrat-genehmigt-militaereinsatz-in-mali-gegen-islamisten-a-874218.html.

Kappel, Robert. "Deutsche Afrikapolitik: Uneinig und Inkohärent [German Africa policy: Discordant and incoherent]." *Internationale Politik und Gesellschaft* [International policy and society], March 17, 2014. http://www.ipg-journal.de/kolumne/artikel/deutsche-afrikapolitik-uneinig-und-inkohaerent-317/.

———. "Global Power Shifts and Germany's New Foreign Policy Agenda." *Strategic Analysis* 38, no. 3 (2014): 341–52. doi: 10.1080/09700161.2014.8952.

Karp, Regina. "The New German Foreign Policy Consensus." *Washington Quarterly* 29, no. 1 (Winter 2005-2006): 61–82.

Katsioulis, Christos. "Deutsche Sicherheitspolitik im Parteiendiskurs: Alter Wein in neuen Schläuchen [German security policy in party debate: Old wine in new skins]." In *Deutsche Sicherheitspolitik: Eine Bilanz der Regierung Schröder* [German security policy: A record of the Schröder government]. Edited by Sebastian Harnisch, Christos Katsioulis, and Marco Overhaus, 227–52. Baden-Baden: Nomos, 2004.

Klose, Hans-Ulrich, and Ruprecht Polenz. "Wahre Werte, falsche Freunde: Deutschlands Partner sitzen im Westen: eine Erinnerung aus gegebenem Anlass [True values, false friends: Germany's partners are sitting in the West—A reminder in view of the occasion]." *Internationale Politik* [International politics] 5 (September/October 2011): 18–27.

Knapp, Manfred. "Vereinte Nationen [United Nations]." In *Handbuch zur deutschen Außenpolitik* [Handbook for German foreign policy]. Edited by Sigmar Schmidt, Gunther Hellmann, and Reinhard Wolf, 727–46. Wiesbaden: Verlag für Sozialwissenschaften, 2007.

Knuf, Thorsten. "Konsequent in die Isolation [Consequent into isolation]." *Frankfurter Rundschau*, March 23, 2011. http://www.fr-online.de/aegypten-syrien-revolution/libyen-konsequent-in-die-isolation,7151782,8260742.html.

"Koblenzer Forum zur Verteidigungspolitik: Lehren aus dem Afghanistan-Einsatz [Koblenz forum for defense policy: Lessons from the Afghanistan mission]." *BMVg*. Updated January 21, 2013. http://www.bmvg.de/portal/a/bmvg/!ut/p/c4/NYu7DsIwE AT_yGdHCGQ6ojR0KA2EznEs5yB-6HIJDR-PXbArTbGjhSeUR-rOjN4wpmgUeMFg8jx8xht2LV9qorGJFOzuaHfKa04KMb7jX 6-SETdFxJbvIWOjJcCKRE_FSzUZUjMA JBqm6Vir5j_rqw1HfTo1uumvbQw7h8gO5hIXC/.

Köcher, Renate. ed. *Allensbacher Jahrbuch der Demoskopie, 2003–2009* [Allensbach yearbook of public opinion polls, 2003–2009]. Berlin: deGruyter, 2009.

Koenig, Nicole. "The EU and the Libyan Crisis: In Quest of Coherence?" *IAI Working Paper* 11, no. 19 (July 2011): 1–21.

Kohl, Helmut. "'Wir müssen wieder Zuversicht geben:' Helmut Kohl über eine Außenpolitik, der es an Verlässlichkeit mangelt ["We must give again confidence": Helmut Kohl about a foreign policy that lacks reliability]." *Internationale Politik* [International politics] 5 (September/October 2011): 10–17.

Köhler, Horst. *Einsatz für Freiheit und Sicherheit: Rede von Bundespräsident Horst Köhler bei der Kommandeurtagung der Bundeswehr am 10. Oktober 2005in Bonn* [Commitment for peace and security: Speech by Federal President Horst Köhler at the convention of the Bundeswehr Commanders on October 10 in Bonn]. Accessed October 3, 2014. http://www.bundespraesident.de/SharedDocs/Reden/DE/Horst-Koehler/Reden/2005/10/20051010_Rede_Anlage.pdf;jsessionid=A4F37B0175C96252B7B4FBBAA1872E91.2_cid388?_blob=publicationFile&v=2.

———. Interview by Christopher Ricke. *Deutschlandradio*, May 22, 2010. http://www.deutschlandradio.de/sie-leisten-wirklich-grossartiges-unter-schwierigsten.331.de.html?dram:article_id=203276.

Körber-Stiftung, ed. *Einmischen oder zurückhalten?: Die Sicht der Deutschen auf die Außenpolitik* [Intervene or retain: The view of German citizens on foreign policy]. Hamburg: Körber-Stiftung, 2014.

Korte, Karl-Rudolf. "Bundeskanzleramt [Federal chancellery]." In *Handbuch zur deutschen Außenpolitik* [Handbook for German foreign policy]. Edited by Sigmar Schmidt, Gunther Hellmann, and Reinhard Wolf, 203–209. Wiesbaden: Verlag für Sozialwissenschaften, 2007.

Kraak, Jan. "Opération Serval." *Air International* 84, no. 3 (2013): 74–79.

Kratochwill, Friedrich. "On the Notion of 'Interests' in International Relations." *International Organization* 36, no. 1 (1982): 1–30. doi: http://dx.doi.org/10.1017/S0020818300004768.

"Krieg gegen Libyen: Über 60 Prozent der Deutschen befürworten den Angriff, Aber: Große Mehrheit lehnt Beteiligung der Bundeswehr ab [War against Libya: Over 60 percent of the Germans support an attack, but big majority refuses participation of the Bundeswehr]." *Bild*, March 20, 2011. http://www.bild.de/politik/2011/libyen-krise/aber-mehrheit-lehnt-beteiligung-ab-16933388.bild.html.

"Krise in Nahost: Merkel macht Hamas für Gewalt verantwortlich [Crisis in the Near East: Merkel blames Hamas for violence]." *Spiegel Online*, November 16, 2012. http://www.spiegel.de/politik/ausland/nahost-merkel-macht-hamas-fuer-gewalt-verantwortlich-a-867638.html.

Kümmel, Gerhard. "The Winds of Change: The Transition from Armed Forces for Peace to New Missions for the Bundeswehr and Its Impact on Civil-Military Relations." *Journal of Strategic Studies* 26, no. 2 (2003): 7–28.

Kundnani, Hans. "Germany as a Geo-Economic Power." *Washington Quarterly* 34, no. 3 (Summer 2011): 31–45.

Lacher, Wolfram, and Denis M. Tull. "Mali: Jenseits von Terrorismusbekämpfung [Mali: Beyond the fight against terrorism]." *SWP-Aktuell* 9. Berlin: German Institute for International and Security Affairs, February 2013.

"Lammert findet deutsches Mali-Engagement zu gering [Lammert finds German Mali engagement as too meager]." *Die Welt*, January 19, 2013. http://www.welt.de/politik/deutschland/article112901467/Lammert-findet-deutsches-Mali-Engagement-zu-gering.html.

Lantis, Jeffrey S. *Strategic Dilemmas and the Evolution of German Foreign Policy since Unification.* Westport, CT: Praeger Publishers, 2002.

Lau, Jörg. "Macht mal—ohne uns! [Do it—Without Us!]" *Die Zeit*, March 24, 2011. http://www.zeit.de/2011/13/Deutschland-Aussenpolitik.

Laub, Zachary, and Jonathan Masters. "Al Qaeda in the Islamic Maghreb (AQIM)." Council on Foreign Relations. Updated March 27, 2015. http://www.cfr.org/terrorist-organizations-and-networks/al-qaeda-islamic-maghreb-aqim/p12717.

Le Monde, AFP, and Reuters. "Mali: Réunion de la Cédéao pour envisager une intervention [Mali: CEDAO union for an intervention]." *Le Monde Afrique*, April 5, 2012. http://www.lemonde.fr/afrique/article/2012/04/05/mali-reunion-de-la-cedeao-pour-envisager-une-intervention_1681185_3212.html#9QevkTdt4hUh5Wau.99.

Leininger, Julia. "Mehr Einsatz in Afrika [More missions in Africa]." *Die Aktuelle Kolumne.* Bonn: German Development Institute, February 11, 2014.

Leithäuser, Johannes. "Mehr Verantwortung für Afrika [More responsibility for Africa]." *Frankfurter Allgemeine Zeitung*, January 26, 2014. http://www.faz.net/aktuell/politik/von-der-leyen-plaene-mehr-verantwortung-fuer-afrika-12770671.html.

"Libya: Governments Should Demand End to Unlawful Killings." *Human Rights Watch*, February 20, 2011. http://www.hrw.org/de/news/2011/02/20/libya-governments-should-demand-end-unlawful-killings.

"Libya Protests: Defiant Gaddafi Refuses to Quit." *BBC News*, February 22, 2011. http://www.bbc.co.uk/news/world-middle-east-12544624.

Lindström, Madelene, and Kristina Zetterlund. *Setting the Stage for the Military Intervention in Libya: Decisions Made and Their Implications for the EU and NATO.* Stockholm: Swedish Defense Research Agency, 2012.

Link, Werner. "Vom Elend des 'offensiven Idealismus': Eine Antwort auf Hellmanns 'Traditionslinie' und 'Sozialisationsperspektive' [From the misery of an 'offensive idealism': A response to Hellmann's 'line of tradition' and 'perspective of socialization']." *WeltTrends* 12, no. 3 (2004): 47–51.

Lohre, Matthias. "Die Grünen zu Libyen: Krieg ja, aber ohne uns [The greens on Libya: War yes, but without us]." *TAZ*, March 21, 2011. http://www.taz.de/!67775/.

Longhurst, Kerry. *Germany and the Use of Force: The Evolution of German Security Policy, 1990–2003.* New York: Manchester University Press, 2004.

Lynch, Colum. "Amb. Rice: Leading From Behind? That's 'Whacked.'" *Foreign Policy.* October 31, 2011. http://foreignpolicy.com/2011/10/31/amb-rice-leading-from-behind-thats-whacked/.

Mair, Stefan. ed. *Auslandseinsätze der Bundeswehr: Leitfragen, Entscheidungsspielräumen und Lehren* [Missions abroad of the Bundeswehr: Guiding questions, freedom to decide, and lessons]. Berlin: German Institute for International and Security Affairs, 2009.

———. "Kriterien für die Beteiligung an Militäreinsätzen [Criteria for the participation in military missions]." In *Auslandseinsätze der Bundeswehr: Leitfragen, Entscheidungsspielräumen und Lehren* [Missions abroad of the Bundeswehr: Guiding questions, freedom to decide, and lessons]. Edited by Stefan Mair, 11–19. Berlin: German Institute for International and Security Affairs, September 2007.

Major, Claudia, and Christian Mölling. "Die europäische Armee kommt [The European Army will come]." *Neue Züricher Zeitung*, April 29, 2015. http://www.nzz.ch/meinung/debatte/die-europaeische-armee-kommt-1.18531717.

———. *German Defense Policy in 2014 and Beyond: Options for Change*. Note du Cerfa 113. Paris: Institut Français du Relations International, 2014.

Major, Claudia, and Elisabeth Schöndorf. "Umfassende Ansätze, vernetzte Sicherheit [Comprehensive approach, networked security]." *SWP-Aktuell* 22. Berlin: German Institute for International and Security Affairs, April 2011.

Mair, Stefan, and Denis M. Tull. *Deutsche Afrikapolitik: Eckpunkte einer Strategischen Neuausrichtung* [Germany's Africa policy: Key parameters of a strategic reorientation]. Berlin: German Institute for International and Security Affairs, 2009.

"Mali bittet UN um Militäreinsatz gegen Islamisten [Mali pleads to the UN for a military intervention against the Islamists]." *Die Welt*, September 25, 2012. http://www.welt.de/politik/ausland/article109438915/Mali-bittet-UN-um-Militaereinsatz-gegen-Islamisten.html.

"Mali Crisis: African Union Backs Plan to Deploy Troops." *BBC News*, November 13, 2012. http://www.bbc.com/news/world-africa-20315423.

"Mali: Mehrheit für logistische und medizinische Unterstützung durch Deutschland [Mali: Majority for logistical and medical support by Germany]." *Infratest Dimap*. Accessed April 12, 2015. http://www.infratest-dimap.de/umfragen-analysen/bundesweit/umfragen/aktuell/mali-mehrheit-fuer-logistische-und-medizinische-unterstuetzung-durch-deutschland-fdp-mehrheit-f/.

"Mali-Mission: Westerwelle schließt Entsendung von Kampftruppen aus [Mali mission: Westerwelle excludes deployment of combat forces to Mali]." *Spiegel Online*, October 23, 2012. http://www.spiegel.de/politik/ausland/westerwelle-schliesst-entsendung-deutscher-kampftruppen-nach-mali-aus-a-862978.html.

Matthay, Sabine. "Raus aus Afghanistan, rein nach Afrika? [Getting out of Afghanistan, Getting into Africa?]" *Deutschlandradio*, February 19, 2014. http://www.deutschlandradiokultur.de/ sicherheitspolitik-raus-aus-afghanistan-rein-nach-afrika.1005.de.html?dram:article_id=277830.

Maull, Hanns W. "Außenpolitische Entscheidungsprozesse in Krisenzeiten [Foreign policy decision-making processes in times of crisis]." *Aus Politik und Zeitgeschichte* [From politics and contemporary history] 62, no. 10 (March 2012): 34–40.

———. "Außenpolitische Kultur [Foreign political culture]." In *Deutschland-Trendbuch: Fakten und Orientierungen* [Germany's trendbook: Facts and orientations]. Edited by Karl-Rudolf Korte and Werner Weidenfeld, 645–72. Bonn: Bundeszentrale für Politische Bildung, 2001.

———. "Deutsche Außenpolitik: Orientierungslos [German foreign policy: disorientated]." *Zeitschrift für Politikwissenschaft* [German journal for political science] 21, no. 1 (2011): 95–119.

———. "Deutschland als Zivilmacht [Germany as a civil power]." In *Handbuch zur deutschen Außenpolitik* [Handbook for German foreign policy]. Edited by Siegmar Schmidt, Gunther Hellmann, and Reinhard Wolf, 73–84. Wiesbaden: Verlag für Sozialwissenschaften, 2007.

Maull, Hanns W. "Germany and Japan: The New Civilian Powers." *Foreign Affairs* 69, no. 5 (1990): 91–106.

———. "Germany and the Use of Force: Still a Civilian Power?" *Trierer Arbeitspapiere zur Internationalen Politik* 2. Trier: Lehrstuhl für Außenpolitik und Internationale Beziehungen, 1999.

———. "Intervenieren? [Intervene?]" *Internationale Politik und Gesellschaft* [International policy and society]. September 1, 2014. http://www.ipg-journal.de/schwerpunkt-des-monats/interventionen/artikel/detail/intervenieren-557/.

———. "Nationale Interessen! Aber was sind sie?: Auf der Suche nach Orientierungsgrundlagen für die deutsche Außenpolitik [National interests! But what are they?: On a search for orientation principles for German foreign policy]." *Internationale Politik* [International politics] (October 2006): 62–76.

———. "'Normalisierung' oder Auszehrung?: Deutsche Außenpolitik im Wandel ['Normalization' or depletion?: German foreign policy in a state of flux]." *Aus Politik und Zeitgeschichte* [From politics and contemporary history] B11 (2004): 19–23.

McClanahan, Paige. "Mali's Humanitarian Crisis May Worsen if Intervention Calls Heeded, UN Warned." *Guardian*, September 27, 2012. http://www.theguardian.com/global-development/2012/sep/27/mali-humanitarian-crisis-worsen-intervention-un.

McNamara, Sally. "The Crisis in Libya Exposes a Litany of Failed EU Policies." WebMemo, no. 3178 (Heritage Foundation, March 4, 2011): 1–2. Accessed February 6, 2015. http://thf_media.s3.amazonaws.com/2011/pdf/wm3178.pdf.

Medick, Veit, and Severin Weiland. "Frankreichs Syrien-Vorstoß: Hollande irritiert Berlin [France's Syria thrust: Hollande confuses Berlin]." *Spiegel Online*, May 30, 2012. http://www.spiegel.de/politik/deutschland/deutschland-lehnt-militaerische-intervention-in-syrien-ab-a-835956.html.

"Mehrheit der Deutschen lehnt Auslandseinsätze ab [Majority of Germans refuse missions abroad]." *Zeit Online*, December 28, 2014. http://www.zeit.de/politik/deutschland/2014-12/umfrage-deutsche-ablehnung-internationale-bundeswehr-einsaetze.

Meiers, Franz-Josef. "The German Predicament: The Red Lines of the Security and Defense Policy of the Berlin Republic." *International Politics* 44 (2007): 623–44.

Meiers, Franz-Josef. "Von der Scheckbuchdiplomatie zur Verteidigung am Hindukusch: Die Rolle der Bundeswehr bei multinationalen Auslandseinsätzen, 1990–2009 [From checkbook diplomacy toward the defense at the Hindu Kush: The role of the Bundeswehr in missions abroad, 1990–2009]." *Zeitschrift für Außen- und Sicherheitspolitik* [Journal for foreign and security policy] 3, no. 2 (2010): 201–222.

Meno, Rajan. "The French Mess in Mali and Libya." *Atlantic Council*, January 24, 2013. http://www.atlanticcouncil.org/blogs/new-atlanticist/the-french-mess-in-mali-and-libya.

Merkel, Angela. *Deutschland weiß um seine Verantwortung in der Welt: Rede der Bundeskanzlerin anlässlich der Festveranstaltung zu '50 Jahre Bergedorfer Gesprächskreis' der Körber-Stiftung in Berlin am 9. September 2011* [Germany knows about its responsibility in the world: Speech by the federal chancellor on the occasion of the gala for '50 Years Bergedorfer Circle' of the Körber Foundation in Berlin, September 9, 2011]. Accessed March 12, 2015. http://www.bundeskanzlerin.de/ContentArchiv/DE/Archiv17/Reden/2011/09/2011-09-09-rede-merkel-au%C3%9Fen-u-sicherheitspolitik.html.

———. "Kanzlerin Angela Merkel kündigt Überprüfung aller Atomkraftwerke an [Chancellor Angela Merkel announced audit of all nuclear plants]." Interview by Werner Kolhoff und Hagen Strauß. *Saarbrücker Zeitung*, March 17, 2011. http://www.saarbruecker-zeitung.de/nachrichten/berliner_buero/art182516,3679553,5#.

Merkel, Angela. *Rede der Bundeskanzlerin auf der 47. Münchner Sicherheitskonferenz* [Speech by the federal chancellor on the occasion of the 47th Munich Security Conference]. Munich, February 5, 2011. Accessed, August 4, 2014. http://www.bundesregierung.de/ContentArchiv/DE/Archiv17/Reden/2011/02/2011-02-05-bkin-m%C3%BC-si-ko.htm.

———. *Rede von Bundeskanzlerin Angela Merkel anlässlich der Eröffnung der Internationalen Afghanistan-Konferenz* [Speech by Federal Chancellor Angela Merkel on the occasion of the opening of the International Afghanistan Conference]. December 5, 2011. http://www.auswaertiges-amt.de/cae/servlet/contentblob/604006/publicationFile/162769/Germany_Merkel.pdf.

———. *Rede von Bundeskanzlerin Angela Merkel anlässlich der Tagung des zivilen und militärischen Spitzenpersonals der Bundeswehr in der Akademie der Bundeswehr für Information und Kommunikation, am 22. Oktober 2012, in Straussberg* [Speech by Federal Chancellor Merkel on the occasion of the convention of civilian and military top staff members of the Bundeswehr at the Bundeswehr Academy for Information and Communication, on October 22, 2012, in Straussberg]. Accessed November 7, 2014. http://www.bundesregierung.de/ContentArchiv/DE/Archiv17/Reden/2012/10/2012-10-22rede-merkel-bundeswehr.html.

"Merkel rechtfertigt deutsche Militärhilfe in Mali [Merkel justifies German military support in Mali]." *Süddeutsche*, January 16, 2013. http://www.sueddeutsche.de/politik/krieg-gegen-rebellen-merkel-rechtfertigt-deutsche-militaerhilfe-in-mali-1.1574329.

Meyer, Berthold. "Von der Entgrenzung nationaler deutscher Interessen: Die politische Legitimation weltweiter Militäreinsätze [On the dissolution of boundaries of national German interests: The political legitmation of global military missions]." *HSFK-Report 10*. Frankfurt am Main: Hessische Stiftung Friedens- und Konfliktforschung, 2007.

Meyer, Christoph, O. *The Quest of a European Strategic Culture: Changing Norms on Security and Defense in the European Union*. New York: Palgrave Macmillan, 2006.

Meyer, Simone. "'Das, was wir tun, liegt im deutschen Interesse' ['That what we do lies in German interests']." *Die Welt*, March 18, 2013. http://www.welt.de/politik/ausland/ article114527292/Das-was-wir-tun-liegt-im-deutschen-Interesse.html.

Milosevic, Nik. *Deutsche Kriegsbeteiligung und—verweigerung: Analyse der Einflussfaktoren im politischen Entscheidungsprozess der Fälle Kosovo, Afghanistan, Irak, und Libyen* [German participation and nonparticipation in wars: Analysis of influencing factors within the political decisison-making process of the cases of Kosovo, Afghanistan, Iraq, and Libya]. Hamburg, Diplomica Verlag, 2012.

Mirow, Wilhelm. *Strategic Culture Matters: A Comparison of German and British Military Interventions since 1990*. Forschungsberichte International Politik 38. Berlin: LIT Verlag, 2009.

Miskimmon, Alister. "German Foreign Policy and the Libya Crisis." *German Politics* 21, no. 4 (December 2012): 392–410.

Mix, Derek E. *The European Union: Foreign and Security Policy*. Washington, DC: Congressional Research Service, April 2013.

Monath, Hans. "Westerwelle und de Maizière: Zwei für Krieg und Frieden [Westerwelle and de Maizière: Two for war and peace]." *Der Tagesspiegel*, May 21, 2011.

Müller, Andreas. "Todesfälle im Einsatz [Fatalities in missions]." *Presse- und Informationsstab BMVg*. Updated July 22, 2014. http://www.bundeswehr.de/portal/a/bwde/!ut/p/c4/DcjBD YAgDAXQWVyA3r25hXohRT7YgMUE1ITpJe_2aKdB-ZXITYpyppW2Q2b3Gfd5mAgPTVDT-cxQ-6i3gVMb04pHDYycYeWyEK3cOt1pmX5GIQYT/.

Müller, Harald. "Ein Desaster: Deutschland und der Fall Libyen [A disaster: Germany and the Libyan case]." *HSFK Standpunkte*, no. 2 (2011): 1–12.

Munich Security Conference. *Munich Security Report 2015: Collapsing Order, Reluctant Guardians?* Munich: Munich Security Conference, 2015. Accessed April 4, 2015. http://www.eventanizer.com/MSC2015/MunichSecurityReport2015.pdf.

Murphy, Joe, and Tom Harper. "David Cameron Proposes Libya No-Fly-Zone and Tells Gaddafi: 'Go Now.'" *London Evening Standard.* February 28, 2011. http://www.standard.co.uk/news/david-cameron-proposes-libya-nofly-zone-and-tells-gaddafi-go-now-6571718.html.

Mützenich, Rolf. "Der ungewollte Krieg [The unwanted war]." *The European,* February 2, 2013. http://www.theeuropean.de/rolf-muetzenich/5820-deutsche-beteiligung-bei-mali-intervention.

———. "Gemeinsame Erklärungen reichen nicht aus!: Weshalb wir in der Außenpolitik statt einer deutschen Kultur der Zurückhaltung eine europäische Kultur der Verantwortung brauchen [Joint declarations are not enough!: Why do we need in foreign policy instead of a German culture of reticence and European culture of responsibility]." *Internationale Politik und Gesellschaft* [International policy and society], February 10, 2014. http://www.ipg-journal.de/kolumne/artikel/gemeinsame-erklaerungen-reichen-nicht-aus-255/.

"Namentliche Abstimmungen: Bundeswehreinsatz in Mali [Roll-call vote: Bundeswehr mission in Mali]." *Deutscher Bundestag.* Updated February 28, 2013. http://www.bundestag.de/bundestag/plenum/abstimmung/grafik/?id=210.

NATO. *Chicago Summit Declaration Issued by the Heads of State and Government Participating in the Meeting of the North Atlantic Council in Chicago on 20 May 2012.* Brussels: NATO, 2012. Updated August 1, 2012. http://www.nato.int/cps/en/natolive/official_texts_87593.htm.

———. "NATO Secretary General's Statement on Libya No-Fly Zone." Updated March 25, 2011. http://www.nato.int/cps/en/natolive/news_71763.htm.

NATO. "Operation Unified Protector: NATO No-Fly Zone over Libya Fact Sheet." Accessed February 24, 2015. http://www.nato.int/nato_static/assets/pdf/pdf_2011_03/unified-protector-no-fly-zone.pdf.

"NATO Forces Needed in Mali, Says AU's Thomas Boni Yayi." *BBC News*, January 9, 2013, http://www.bbc.com/news/world-africa-20957063.

Naumann, Klaus. *Einsatz ohne Ziel?: Die Politikbedürftigkeit des Militärischen* [Missions with objectives?: The political indigence of the military]. Bonn: Hamburger Edition, 2010.

———. "Wie strategiefähig ist Deutschland? [How strategy-capable is Germany?]" *Aus Politik und Zeitgeschichte* [From politics and contemporary history] 48 (November 2009): 10–17.

Neukirch, Ralf, and Gordon Repinski. "Germany abroad: 'Mealymouthed' foreign policy angers allies." *Spiegel Online*, January 22, 2013. http://www.spiegel.de/international/germany/german-approach-to-crisis-regions-frustrates-allies-a-878717.html.

Nonnenmacher, Günther. "Deutschland und die Militäreinsätze: Gaucks Leitfaden [Germany and military interventions: Gauck's guidelines]." *Frankfurter Allgemeine Zeitung*, February 1, 2014. http://www.faz.net/aktuell/politik/deutschland-und-die-militaereinsaetze-gaucks-leitfaden-12778867.html.

Nouripour, Omid. "Vorbeugen ist besser als Heilen [Preventing is better than curing]." *The European*, February 16, 2013. http://www.theeuropean.de/omid-nouripour/5861-klare-ziele-fuer-mali.

Nouripour, Omid, Hans-Christian Ströbele, Marieluise Beck, Volker Beck, Viola von Cramon-Taubadel, Ulrike Höfken, Ingrid Hönlinger, Thilo Hoppe, Uwe Kekeritz, Katja Keul, Ute Koczy, Tom Koenigs, Agnes Malczak, Kerstin Müller, Konstantin von Notz, Claudia Roth, Manuel Sarrazin, Frithjof Schmidt, Wolfgang Wieland, and the Faction of BÜNDNIS 90/DIE GRÜNEN. *Antrag: Prüfkriterien für Auslandseinsätze der Bundeswehr entwickeln—Unterrichtung und Evaluation verbessern* [Request: Development of criteria for missions abroad of the Bundeswehr; Improve reporting and evaluation]. Berlin: Bundesanzeiger Verlagsgesellschaft, March 16, 2011. Accessed January 20, 2015. http://dip21.bundestag.de/dip21/btd/17/050/1705099.pdf.

Nünlist, Christian. "Mehr Verantwortung?: Deutsche Außenpolitik 2014 [More responsibility?: German foreign policy 2014]." *CSS Analysen zur Sicherheitspolitik* 149. Zürich: Center for Security Studies, 2014.

Nyiri, Zsolt, and Ben Veater-Fuchs. "Transatlantic Trends 2011: Key Findings." The German Marshall Fund of the United States. Accessed March 12, 2015,
http://www.gmfus.org/publications/transatlantic-trends-2011.

"Die Operation Pegasus [Operation Pegasus]." *Bundeswehr*. March 3, 2011. Accessed February 2, 2015. http://www.bundeswehr.de/portal/a/bwde/!ut/p/c4/NUzBCoMwFPujP-guDjt0Ud9jYycvmLqXapzzQVt6eE2Qfv3awBBJCQuAJicG9aXRCMbgJHtD2dOo21W0eFVJ4OZQdFc32F2S3w4psPQY7MGFyuOeX-tO5jQMkqGISSjuwksloiy5SblTk1ijy0ha4rbYo_9Od4vl3r0phDfakaWOa5_AIEa6xO/.

"Operation Serval: SPD fordert deutsche Beteiligung an Mali-Einsatz [Operation Serval: SPD demands German participation in Mali mission]." *Die Welt*, January 14, 2013.
http://www.welt.de/politik/ausland/article112743916/SPD-fordert-deutsche-Beteiligung-an-Mali-Einsatz.html.

Oppelland, Torsten. "Parteien [Parties]." In *Handbuch zur deutschen Außenpolitik* [Handbook for German foreign policy]. Edited by Siegmar Schmidt, Gunther Hellmann, and Reinhard Wolf, 269–79. Wiesbaden: Verlag für Sozialwissenschaften, 2007.

Oppermann, Kai. "National Role Conceptions, Domestic Constraints and the New 'Normalcy' in German Foreign Policy: The Eurozone Crisis, Libya and Beyond." *German Politics* 21, no. 4 (December 2012): 502–519. http://dx.doi.org/10.1080/09644008.2012.748268.

Oppermann, Kai, and Alexander Höse. "Die innenpolitischen Restriktionen deutscher Außenpolitik [The domestic political constraints of German foreign policy]." In *Deutsche Außenpolitik: Sicherheit, Wohlfahrt, Institutionen und Normen* [German foreign policy: Security, welfare, institutions, and norms]. 2nd ed. Edited by Thomas Jäger, Alexander Höse, and Kai Oppermann, 44–76. Wiesbaden: Springer Fachmedien, 2011.

Oppermann, Kai, and Henrike Viehrig. "The Public Salience of Foreign and Security Policy in Britain, Germany, and France." *West European Politics* 32, no. 5 (2009): 925–42.

Overhaus, Marco, Sebastian Harnisch, and Christos Katsioulis, "Schlussbetrachtung: Gelockerte Bindungen und eigene Wege der deutschen Sicherheitspolitik? [Conclusions: Loosened relations and the own way of German security policy?]" In *Deutsche Sicherheitspolitik: Eine Bilanz der Regierung Schröder* [German security policy: A record of the Schröder government]. Edited by Sebastian Harnisch, Christos Katsioulis, and Marco Overhaus. 253–62. Baden-Baden: Nomos, 2004.

Pabst, Martin. "Staatliche Schwäche begünstigt Dschihadisten: Neuer Risikoraum Sahelzone [State weakness facilitated jihadists: New risk area Sahel]." *Sicherheit und Frieden* [Security and peace] 31, no. 1 (2013): 1–12.

Pannier, Alice, and Schmitt, Oliver. "Institutionalized Cooperation and Policy Convergence in European Defense: Lessons from the Relations between France, Germany, and the UK." *European Security* 23, no. 3 (2014): 1–20.

"Peace Operations 2013/2014." zif-berlin. Accessed October 17, 2014. http://www.zif-berlin.org/fileadmin/uploads/analyse/dokumente/veroeffentlichungen/ZIF_World_Map_Peace_Operations_2013.pdf.

Peel, Quentin. "Merkel Explains Berlin's Abstention." *Financial Times*, March 18, 2011. http://www.ft.com/intl/cms/s/0/2363c306-51b8-11e0-888e-00144feab49a.html#axzz3SKrTyG7E.

"Per la Bild la satira non esiste: 'Alla Merkel attacco maligno' [For the Bild journal, satire does not exist: 'A malicious attack on Merkel']." *Libero*, August 8, 2011. http://www.liberoquotidiano.it/news/esteri/799538/Per-la-Bild-la-satira-non.html.

Permanent Mission of Germany to the United Nations. "Responsibility, Reliability and Commitment: Germany in the UN Security Council." *Auswaertiges Amt*. Updated January 3, 2011. http://www.auswaertiges-amt.de/EN/Infoservice/Presse/Meldungen/2011/110102_DEU_Sitz_VN_Sicherheitsrat.html.

Perthes, Volker. "Wie? Wann? Wo? Wie oft?: Vier zentrale Fragen müssen vor Auslandseinsätzen beantwortet werden [How? When? Where? How Often?: Four questions that have to be answered before missions abroad]." *Internationale Politik* [International politics] (May 2007): 16–21.

Peters, Dirk. "Ansätze und Methoden der Außenpolitikanalyse [Approaches and methods for the analysis of foreign policy]." In *Handbuch zur deutschen Außenpolitik* [Handbook for German foreign policy]. Edited by Sigmar Schmidt, Gunther Hellmann, and Reinhard Wolf, 815–35. Wiesbaden: Verlag für Sozialwissenschaften, 2007.

Pew Research Center. *Germany and the United States: Reliable Allies-But Disagreements on Russia, Global Leadership, and Trade*. Washington, DC: Pew Research Center, May 7, 2015. Accessed March 25, 2015.

http://www.pewglobal.org/files/2015/05/Pew-Research-Center-U.S.-Germany-Report-FINAL-FOR-WEB.pdf.

Pillath, Sandra. *Motive und Rollenkonzepte deutscher Außenpolitik; Die Auslandseinsätze der Bundeswehr im Kongo und Libanon* [Motives and role concepts of German foreign policy: Missions abroad of the Bundeswehr in the Congo and Lebanon]. Studien zur Internationalen Politik, edited by August Pradetto, Anette Jünemann, and Michael Staack. Hamburg: Institut für Internationale Politik an der Helmut-Schmidt-Universität, 2008.

Pond, Elizabeth, and Hans Kundnani. "Germany's Real Role in the Ukraine Crisis: Caught Between East and West." *Foreign Affairs* (March/April 2015). Accessed April 8, 2015. http://www.foreignaffairs.com/articles/143033/elizabeth-pond-and-hans-kundnai/germanys-real-role-in-the-ukraine-crisis.

Poulton, Robin-Edward, and Ibrahim ag Youssouf. *La paix de Tombouctou: Gestion démocratique, développement et construction africaine de la paix* [The Peace of Timbuktu: Democratic governance, African development and implementation of peace]. New York: United Nations Institute for Disarmament Research, 1999.

Pradetto, August. "Ganz und gar nicht ohne Interessen: Deutschland formuliert nicht nur Ziele—Es setzt sie auch durch [Not at all without interests: Germany does not only formulate objectives—It enforces them]." *Internationale Politik* [International politics] 1 (January 2006): 114–21.

———. "The Polity of German Foreign Policy: Changes since Unification." In *Germany's Uncertain Power: Foreign Policy of the Berlin Republic*. Edited by Hanns W. Maull, 15–28. New York: Palgrave Macmillan, 2006.

Putnam, Robert D. "Diplomacy and Domestic Politics: The Logic of Two-Level Games." *International Organizations* 42, no. 3 (Summer 1988): 427–60. http://www.janes.com/article/35743/reformulation-of-germany-s-foreign-policy-towards-active-military-engagements-is-likely-over-the-next-three-years.

"Putschisten übernehmen Macht in Mali [Putschist take over power in Mali]." *Zeit Online*, March 22, 2012. http://pdf.zeit.de/politik/ausland/2012-03/mali-putsch.pdf.

"Reformulation of Germany's Foreign Policy towards Active Military Engagements Is Likely over the Next Three Years." *IHS Jane's Intelligence Weekly,* March 20, 2014.

"Regierung will 330 Soldaten nach Mali schicken [Government wants to send 300 troops to Mali]." *Die Welt*, February 18, 2013. http://www.welt.de/politik/deutschland/article113733174/Regierung-will-330-Soldaten-nach-Mali-schicken.html.

"Regierung wirbt um Zustimmung für Mali-Einsatz [Government solicits for support to Mali mission]." *Deutscher Bundestag*. Accessed March 11, 2015. http://www.bundestag.de/dokumente/textarchiv/2013/43100677_kw09_sp_mali/211048.

Reuters. "Militäreinsatz für deutsche Wirtschaftsinteressen? [Mission abroad for German economic interests?]" *Zeit Online,* May 27, 2010. http://pdf.zeit.de/politik/deutschland/2010-05/koehler-bundeswehr-wirtschaft-2.pdf.

Riemer, Dietmar. "Merkels Realpolitik setzt Putin unter Druck [Merkel's realpolitik puts Putin under pressure]." *Tagesschau*, February 11, 2015. http://www.tagesschau.de/kommentar/merkel-ukraine-105.html.

Rinke, Andreas. "Eingreifen oder nicht?: Warum sich die Bundesregierung in der Libyen-Frage enthielt [Intervene or not?: Why the federal government abstained in the Libyan Case]." *Internationale Politik* [International politics] (July/August 2011).

Rinke, Bernhard. "Auslandseinsätze der Bundeswehr zwischen Bündnisverpflichtungen und einer außenpolitischen Kultur der Zurückhaltung [Missions abroad of the Bundeswehr between alliance commitments and a foreign policy culture of restraint]." *Politik Unterrichten* 1 (2014): 27–35.

Rinke, Bernhard. "Die Auslandseinsätze der Bundeswehr im Parteienstreit [Missions abroad of the Bundeswehr in party controversy]." In *Armee im Einsatz: Grundlagen, Strategien und Ergebnisse einer Beteiligung der Bundeswehr* [Armed forces on a mission: Principles, strategies, and results of Bundeswehr participation]. Edited by Hans J. Gießmann and Armin Wagner, 163–75. Baden-Baden: Nomos, 2009.

Risse-Kappen, Thomas. "Kontinuität durch Wandel: Eine 'neue' deutsche Außenpolitik? [Continuity through change: A 'new' German foreign policy?]" *Aus Politik und Zeitgeschichte* [From politics and contemporary history] B11 (2004): 24–31.

———. "Public Opinion, Domestic Structure, and Foreign Policy in Liberal Democracies." *World Politics* 43, no. 4 (July 1991), 479–512.

Rogge, Ronald. "Hand in Hand für Mali [Hand in hand for Mali]." *Y: Magazin für die Bundeswehr* [Y: Magazine for the Bundeswehr] 13, no. 6/7 (2013): 44–51.

Roos, Ulrich. *Deutsches Außenpolitik: Eine Rekonstruktion der grundlegenden Handlungsregeln* [*German Foreign Policy: A Reconstruction of fundamental rules of action*]. Wiesbaden: VS Verlag für Sozialwissenschaften, 2010.

———. "Deutsche Außenpolitik nach der Vereinigung: Zwischen ernüchterndem Idealismus und realpolitischem Weltordnungsstreben [German foreign policy after reunification: Between illusioning idealism and real-political striving for global governance]." *Zeitschrift für Internationale* Beziehungen 19, no. 2 (2012): 7–40.

Rosenau, James N. "Pre-Theories and Theories of Foreign Policy." In *Approaches to Comparative and International Politics*. Edited by R. Barry Farrell, 27–92. Evanston, IL: Northwestern University Press, 1966.

Rühl, Lothar. "Deutschland und der Libyenkrieg [Germany and the Libyan War]." *Zeitschrift für Außen- und Sicherheitspolitik* 4 (2011): 561–71.

Rühl, Lothar. "Militärisch erfolgreich, politisch konfus: Die Alliierten über Libyen [Militarily successful, politically confused: The allies over Libya]." *Frankfurter Allgemeine Zeitung,* March 22, 2011. http://www.faz.net/aktuell/politik/militaerisch-erfolgreich-politisch-konfus-1606092.html?printPagedArticle=true%20-%20pageIndex_2.

Rühe, Volker. "Vorwort: Sicherheitspolitik und Auslandseinsätze [Preface: Security policy and missions abroad]." In *Bewährungsproben einer Nation: Die Entsendung der Bundeswehr ins Ausland* [Litmus test of a nation: The deployment of the Bundeswehr into foreign countries]. Edited by Christoph Schwegmann, V–XV, Berlin: Duncker & Humblot, 2011.

Rühle, Michael. "In was für einer Welt leben wir?: Sicherheitspolitische Folgerungen aus einer globalisierten Welt [In what a world do we live?: Security policy conclusions from a globalized world]." In *Bewährungsproben einer Nation: Die Entsendung der Bundeswehr ins Ausland* [Litmus test of a nation: The deployment of the Bundeswehr into foreign countries]. Edited by Christoph Schwegmann, 13–24. Berlin: Duncker & Humblot, 2011.

"Saarbrücker Zeitung: Merkel lehnt deutsche Beteiligung an Militäreinsatz in Libyen ab [Saarbruecker Journal: Merkel refuses German participation in military intervention in Libya]." *Presseportal*, March 16, 2011. http://www.presseportal.de/pm/57706/2009198/saarbr-cker-zeitung-merkel-lehnt-deutsche-beteiligung-an-milit-reinsatz-in-libyen-ab.

Schmid, Bernhard. *Die Mali-Intervention: Befreiungskrieg, Aufstandsbekämpfung oder neokolonialer Feldzug?* [The Mali intervention: War of liberation, counterinsurgency, or neocolonial campaign?] Münster, Germany: Unrast, 2014.

Saleh, Hebah, and Andrew England. "Defiant Gaddafi Vows Fight to Death." *Financial Times*, February 23, 2011.

http://www.ft.com/intl/cms/s/0/5b307dd4-3e9d-11e0-9e8f-00144feabdc0.html#axzz3SUtUlhHA.

Sandschneider, Eberhard. "Deutsche Außenpolitik: Eine Gestaltungsmacht in der Kontinuitätsfalle [German foreign policy: A shaping power in a continuity trap]." *Aus Politik und Zeitgeschichte* [From politics and contemporary history] 62, no. 10 (March 2012): 3–9.

Sangar, Eric. "The Weight of the Past(s): The Impact of the Bundeswehr's Use of Historical Experience on Strategy-Making in Afghanistan." *Journal of Strategic Studies* 38, no. 3 (2013): 411-444.

Sanger, David E., and Thom Shanker. "Gates Warns of Risks of a No-Flight Zone." *New York Times*, March 2, 2011. http://www.nytimes.com/2011/03/03/world/africa/03militar y.html?pagewanted=all&_r=0.

Scheffer, Ulrike, and Albrecht Meier. "Verteidigungsministerin setzt auf mehr Auslandseinsätze [Defense minister emphasizes more missions abroad]." *Tagesspiegel*, January 27, 2014. http://www.tagesspiegel.de/politik/bundeswehr-verteidigungsministerin-setzt-auf-mehr-auslandseinsaetze/9386838.html.

Schiltz, Christoph B. "Bundeswehr wird EU-Ausbildungsmission leiten [Bundeswehr will lead the EU training mission]." *Die Welt*, May 7, 2015. http://www.welt.de/politik/ausland/article140591706/Bundes wehr-wird-EU-Ausbildungsmission-leiten.html.

Schmitt, Oliver. "Strategic Users of Culture: German Decisions for Military Actions." *Contemporary Security Policy* 32, no. 1 (2012): 59–81.

Schockenhoff, Andreas. *Kriterien für Auslandseinsätze der Bundeswehr: Orientierungsmaßstab für den jeweiligen Einsatz* [Criteria for missions abroad of the Bundeswehr: Orientation standard for the respective mission]. Berlin: CDU/CSU Fraktion im Deutschen Bundestag, September 11, 2006. Accessed January 20, 2015.

https://www.cducsu.de/presse/ texte-und-interviews/kriterien-fuer-auslandseinsaetze-der-bundeswehr.

Schuhkraft, Corina. "Die Afrikapolitik Deutschlands—Von der 'freundlichen Vernachlässigung' hin zu einem stärkeren Engagement [Germany's Africa policy: From a 'friendly negligence' toward a stronger engagement]." In *Die Afrikapolitik der Europäischen Union: Neue Ansätze und Perspektiven* [The Africa policy of the EU: New approaches and perspectives]. Ed. Gisela Müller-Brandeck-Bocquet, Sigmar Schmidt, Corina Schuhkraft, Ulrike Keßler, and Philipp Gieg, 195–220. Würzburg: Barbara Budrich, 2007.

Schwarz, Hans-Peter. *Die Zentralmacht Europas: Die Rückkehr Deutschlands auf der Weltbühne* [Europe's central power: Germany's comeback on the world stage]. Berlin: Siedler Verlag, 1994.

"Security Council Press Statement on Libya." UN Security Council press release, on the United Nations website. Updated February 22, 2011.
http://www.un.org/press/en/2011/sc10180.doc.htm.

"Security Council Press Statement on Mali." UN Security Council press release SC/10590-AFR/2359, on the United Nations website. Updated March 22, 2012.
http://www.un.org/press/en/2012/ sc10590.doc.htm.

"Security Council Press Statement on Mali." UN Security Council press release, SC/10603-AFR/2370, on the United Nations website. Updated April 10, 2012.
http://www.un.org/press/en/2012/ sc10603.doc.htm.

"Security Council Press Statement on Mali." UN Security Council press release SC/10676-AFR/2407, on the United Nations website. Updated June 18, 2012.
http://www.un.org/press/en/2012/ sc10676.doc.htm.

Seibel, Wolfgang. "Libyen, das Prinzip der Schutzverantwortung und Deutschlands Stimmenthaltung im UN-Sicherheitsrat bei der Abstimmung über Resolution 1973 am 17. März 2011 [Libya, the responsibility to protect, and Germany's abstention from the vote on UNSC Resolution 1973 on March 17, 2011]." *Die Friedens-Warte* 88, no. 1-2 (2013): 87–115.

Shurkin, Michael. *France's War in Mali: Lessons for an Expeditionary Army*. Santa Monica, CA: RAND Corporation, 2014.

Sikorski, Radek. *Poland and the Future of the European Union: Speech by the Foreign Minister of Poland Radek Sikorski at a Debate at the German Association for Foreign Policy*. Berlin: Deutsche Gesellschaft für Auswärtige Politik e.V., November 28, 2011. Accessed March 6, 2015. https://dgap.org/sites/default/files/event_downloads/radoslaw_sikorski_poland_and_the_future_of_the_eu_0.pdf.

Silberhorn, Thomas. *Deutschlands Interessen und Deutschlands Verantwortung in der Welt: Leitlinien für Auslandseinsätze der Bundeswehr* [Germany's interests and Germany's responsibility in the world: Guidelines for missions abroad of the Bundeswehr]. Berlin: CSU-Landesgruppe im Deutschen Bundestag, January 10, 2007. Accessed December 10, 2014. http://www.thomas-silberhorn.de/fileadmin/pdf/positionspapiere/070201_Auslandseinsaetze_Bundeswehr.pdf.

Sinjen, Svenja. "Der Preis der Freiheit—Fall Libyen: Was wir neu denken müssen [The price of freedom—Casa Libya: What we have to rethink]." *Internationale Politik* [International politics] (May/June 2011): 78–83.

Snyder, Richard C., H.W. Bruck, and Burton Sapin. *Foreign Policy Decision Making: An Approach to the Study of International Politics*. New York: Free Press of Glencoe, 1962.

Sold, Katrin. "Frankreichs Werk und Europas Beitrag [France's work and Europe's contribution]." *The European*, February 2, 2013. http://www.theeuropean.de/katrin-sold/5850-europaeischer-einsatz-in-mali.

Sold, Katrin. "Krise in Mali: Frankreich treibt internationalen Einsatz voran [Crisis in Mali: France impels international mission]." *Deutsche Gesellschaft für Außen- und Sicherheitspolitik* (DGAP). Updated November 15, 2012. https://dgap.org/de/article/22762/print.

"SPD-Politiker fordert deutsche Hilfe für Mali [SPD politician demands German help for Mali]." *Zeit Online*, January 13, 2013. http://www.zeit.de/politik/ausland/2013-01/mali-frankreich-deutschland.

Spyer, Jonathan. "Syrian Regime Strategy and the Syrian Civil War." *Rubincenter.* Updated November 14, 2012. http://www.rubincenter.org/2012/11/syrian-regime-strategy-and-the-syrian-civil-war/.

Staack, Michael. "Deutschland als Wirtschaftsmacht [Germany as economic power]." In *Handbuch zur deutschen Außenpolitik* [Handbook for German foreign policy]. Edited by Sigmar Schmidt, Gunther Hellmann, and Reinhard Wolf, 85–97. Wiesbaden: Verlag für Sozialwissenschaften, 2007.

Staack, Michael. "Normative Grundlagen, Werte und Interessen deutscher Sicherheitspolitik [Normative foundations, values, and interests of German security policy]." In *Deutsche Sicherheitspolitik: Herausforderungen, Akteure und Prozesse* [German security policy: Challenges, actors, and processes]. 2nd ed. Edited by Stephan Böckenförde and Sven Bernhard Gareis, 53–87. Opladen, Germany: Verlag Barbara Buderich, 2014.

"Statement by EU High Representative Catherine Ashton on the Situation in Mali." *EEAS*, January 11, 2013. Accessed March 7, 2015. http://www.consilium.europa.eu/uedocs/cms_Data/docs/pressdata/EN/foraff/134646.pdf.

"Statt in Libyen fliegt Deutschland in Afghanistan [Instead in Libya, Germany flies in Afghanistan]." *Handelsblatt.* March 18, 2011. http://www.handelsblatt.com/politik/deutschland/awacs-aufklaerer-statt-in-libyen-fliegt-deutschland-in-afghanistan/3966958.html.

Steinberg, Guido. "Schlussfolgerungen: Deutsche Politik gegenüber dem Nahen und Mittleren Osten und Nord-Afrika [Conclusions: German policy toward the Near and Middle East and North Africa]." In *Deutsche Nah-, Mittelost- und Nordafrikapolitik—SWP Studie* [German Near-, Middle East, and North Africa Policy—SWP Study] S15. Edited by Guido Steinberg, 74–80. Berlin: German Institute for International and Security Affairs, May 2009.

Steiniger, Michael. "Military Intervention in Syria? Germany Pushes Back Hard on French Warning." *Christian Science Monitor*, May 31, 2012. http://www.csmonitor.com/World/Europe/2012/0531/Military-intervention-in-Syria-Germany-pushes-back-hard-on-French-warning.

Steinmeier, Frank Walter. *Schlussrede von Außenminister Frank-Walter Steinmeier anlässlich der Konferenz 'Review 2014 - Außenpolitik Weiter Denken'* [Closing Remarks by Foreign Minister Frank-Walter Steinmeier on occasion of the conference 'Review 2014 – Thinking Foreign Policy Broader'].' May 20, 2014. Accessed August 8, 2015. http://www.auswaertiges-amt.de/DE/Infoservice/Presse/Reden/2014/140520-BM_Review2014_Abschlussrede.html.

———. *Rede des Außenministers anlässlich der 50. Münchner Sicherheitskonferenz, 01. Februar 2014* [Speech by federal foreign minister on the occasion of the 50th Munich Security Conference, February 1, 2014]. Accessed November 6, 2014. http://www.riga.diplo.de/contentblob/4118688/Daten/3880778/Download2014RedeBMSteinmeier.pdf.

„Steinmeier gegen Einsatz deutscher Kampftruppen [Steinmeier against the engagement of German combat troops]." *Die Welt*, January 20, 2014. http://www.welt.de/politik/deutschland/article124022914/Steinmeier-gegen-Einsatz-deutscher-Kampftruppen.html.

Stelzenmüller, Constanze. "Germany's Unhappy Abstention from Leadership." *Financial Times,* March 28, 2011. http://www.ft.com/intl/cms/s/0/2490ab8c-5982-11e0-baa8-00144feab49a.html#axzz3F6o3ea00.

———. "Mit Gewehr, aber ohne Kompass: Eine Bilanz von vier Jahren rot-grüner Außenpolitik [With rifle, but without compass: A four-year record of red-green foreign policy]." *Die Zeit,* September 12, 2002. http://pdf.zeit.de/2002/38/Mit_Gewehr_aber_ohne_Kompass.pdf.

Strachwitz, Helga, Gräfin. "Außenpolitisches Regionalkonzept für Afrika [Foreign policy regional concept for Africa]." In *Afrika zu Beginn des 21. Jahrhunderts: Herausforderungen und Entwicklungspotenziale – Handlungsoptionen für eine strategische Entwicklungspolitik, Dokumentation des Afrika-Tages des BMZ und DIE am 3. Mai 2001* [Africa at the beginning of the 21st century: Challenges and potentials for development—Options to act for a strategic development policy, documentation of the Africa Day of the Federal Ministry of Development and DIE on May 3, 2001]. Edited by Deutsches Institut für Entwicklungspolitik, 11–20. Bonn: Deutsches Institut für Entwicklungspolitik, 2001.

Taylor, Claire. "Military Operations in Libya." *Commons Library Standard Note,* SN05099. London: Library House of Commons, October 21, 2011.

Theiler, Olaf. "Bundeswehr und NATO: Multilateralismus und Integration als Grundlagen deutscher Sicherheitspolitik [Bundeswehr and NATO: Multilateralism and integration as principles of German security policy]." In *Armee im Einsatz: Grundlagen, Strategien und Ergebnisse einer Beteiligung der Bundeswehr* [Armed forces on a mission: Principles, strategies, and results of Bundeswehr participation]. Edited by Hans J. Gießmann and Armin Wagner, 186–99. Baden-Baden: Nomos, 2009.

Theiler, Olaf. "Deutschland und die NATO [Germany and NATO]." In *Deutsche Sicherheitspolitik: Herausforderungen, Akteure und Prozesse* [*German security policy: Challenges, actors, and processes*]. 2nd ed. Edited by Stephan Böckenförde and Sven Bernhard Gareis, 321–70. Opladen, Germany: Verlag Barbara Buderich, 2014.

Thiels, Christian. "Bundeswehrmission im Nordirak: Dienstreise in den nächsten Krieg? [Bundeswehr mission in North Iraq: Duty trip into the next war?]" *Tagesschau*, December 10, 2014. http://www.tagesschau.de/ausland/bundeswehr-irak-107.html.

Thies, Cameron G. *Role Theory and Foreign Policy*. Iowa City: University of Iowa, Department of Political Science, 2009.

Thießen, Jörn, and Ulrich Plate. "Bundeswehr und Parlament [Bundeswehr and the parliament]." In *Armee im Einsatz: Grundlagen, Strategien und Ergebnisse einer Beteiligung der Bundeswehr* [Armed forces on a mission: Principles, strategies, and results of Bundeswehr participation]. Edited by Hans J. Gießmann and Armin Wagner, 148–59. Baden-Baden: Nomos: 2009.

Tisdall, Simon. "France's Lonely Intervention in Mali." *Guardian*, January 14, 2013. http://www.theguardian.com/commentisfree/2013/jan/14/france-lonely-intervention-mali.

Touchard, Laurant. "Aguelhok: Qui es responsable du massacre? [Aguelhok: Who is responsible for the massacre?]" *MaliActu*, October 23, 2013. http://maliactu.info/nord-mali/aguelhok-qui-est-responsable-du-massacre.

Tramond, Olivier, and Philippe Seigneu. "Operation Serval: Another Beau Geste of France in Sub-Saharan Africa?" *Military Review* 94, no. 6 (November/December 2014): 76–86.

Tull, Denis M. *Deutsche Afrikapolitik: Ein Beitrag zu einer überfälligen Debatte* [German Africa policy: A contribution to an overdue debate]. Berlin: Friedrich-Ebert-Stiftung, February 2014.

Tull, Denis M., and Wolfram Lacher. "Die Folgen des Libyen-Konfliktes für Afrika: Gräben zwischen der AU und dem Westen, Destabilisierung der Sahelzone [The consequences of the Libyan conflict on Africa: Gaps between the AU and the West, destablization of the Sahel region]." *SWP Studie S8.* Berlin: German Institute for International and Security Affairs, March 2012.

"Umfrage: Unterstützung für deutschen Beitrag bei Militäreinsatz in Mali." *Zeit Online*, January 25, 2013. http://www.zeit.de/news/2013-01/25/deutschland-umfrage-unterstuetzung-fuer-deutschen-beitrag-bei-militaereinsatz-in-mali-25131218.

"Umfrage zu Unruhen in Libyen [Survey on turmoils in Libya]." *Stern*, March 16, 2011. http://www.stern.de/politik/ausland/umfrage-zu-unruhen-in-libyen-deutsche-wollen-sich-nicht-einmischen-1664001.html.

United Nations Security Council. *UNSC Resolution 1970.* New York: UNSC, February 26, 2011. Accessed January 27, 2015. http://www.icc-cpi.int/NR/rdonlyres/081A9013-B03D-4859-9D61-5D0B0F2F5EFA/0/1970Eng.pdf.

———. *UNSC Resolution 1973.* New York: UNSC, March 17, 2011. Accessed February 2, 2015. http://www.nato.int/nato_static/assets/pdf/pdf_2011_03/20110927_110311-UNSCR-1973.pdf.

———. *UNSC Resolution 2085.* New York: UNSC, December 20, 2012. Accessed February 12, 2015. http://www.globalr2p.org/media/files/sres2085-on-mali.pdf.

———. *UNSC Resolution 2056.* New York: UNSC, July 5, 2012. Accessed March 2, 2015. http://www.un.org/en/ga/search/view_doc.asp?symbol=S/RES/2056(2012).

———. *UNSC Resolution 2071.* New York: UNSC, October 12, 2012. Accessed March 2, 2015. http://www.un.org/ga/search/view_doc.asp?symbol=S/RES/2071(2012).

"US-Sicherheitsstrategie und ihre Auswirkungen auf Europa, Rede von Kerstin Müller, Staatsministerin im Auswärtigen Amt, auf der 4. Außenpolitischen Jahrestagung der Heinrich-Böll-Stiftung, Berlin, 13.11.2003 ["U.S. security strategy and its implications for Europe," Speech of Kerstin Müller, Minister of State in the Federal Ministry of Defence, on the 4th Foreign Policy Convention of the Heinrich-Böll Foundation, Berlin, November 13, 2002]." *Auswaertiges Amt.* Updated November 19, 2003. http://presseservice.pressrelations.de/standard/result_main.cfm?aktion=jour_pm&r=140036&quelle=0&pfach=1&n_firmanr_=109207&sektor=pm&detail=1.

Van Dam, Nikolaos. "How to Solve or Not to Solve the Syrian Crisis?" *Orient—Deutsche Zeitschrift für Politik und Wirtschaft des Orients* [*Orient—German Journal for Politics and Economy of the* Orient] 53, no. 3 (2012): 31–37.

Van der Lijn, Jair, and Jane Dundon. *Peacekeepers at Risk: The Lethality of Peace Operations.* Stockholm: SIPRI, February 2014. Accessed January 22, 2015.
http://books.sipri.org/files/misc/SIPRIPB1402.pdf.

Varwick, Johannes. "Bundeswehr." in *Handbuch zur deutschen Außenpolitik* [Handbook for German foreign policy]. Edited Siegmar Schmidt, Gunther Hellmann, and Reinhard Wolf, 246–58.Wiesbaden: Verlag für Sozialwissenschaften, 2007.

———. "Deutsche Sicherheitspolitik im Rahmen der Vereinten Nationen [German security policy in the framework of the United Nations]." In *Deutsche Sicherheitspolitik: Herausforderungen, Akteure und Prozesse* [German security policy: Challenges, actors, and processes]. 2nd ed. Edited by Stephan Böckenförde and Sven Bernhard Gareis, 371–403. Opladen, Germany: Verlag Barbara Buderich, 2014.

Varwick, Johannes. "Deutsche Sicherheits- und Verteidigunspolitik in der Nordatlantischen Allianz: Die Politik der rot-grünen Bundesregierung, 1998–2003 [German security and defense policy in NATO: The politics of the Social Democrat–Green Federal Government, 1998–2003]." In *Deutsche Sicherheitspolitik: Eine Bilanz der Regierung Schröder* [German security policy: A record of the Schröder government]. Edited by Sebastian Harnisch, Christos Katsioulis, and Marco Overhaus, 15–36. Baden-Baden: Nomos, 2004.

———. "Neue deutsche Außenpolitik: Kultur der Zurückhaltung versus Kultur des Engagements [New German foreign policy: Culture of reticence versus culture of engagement]." *Europäische Sicherheit und Technik* 63, no. 6 (2014) 15–19.

———. "Nordatlantische Allianz [North Atlantic Alliance]." In *Handbuch zur deutschen Außenpolitik* [Handbook for German foreign policy]. Edited by Sigmar Schmidt, Gunther Hellmann, and Reinhard Wolf, 763–78. Wiesbaden: Verlag für Sozialwissenschaften, 2007.

Vogel, Hannes. "Antwort auf Libyen-Resolution: Deutschland verrät die Freiheit-und seine Verbündeten [Response on Libyan resolution: Germany betrayed freedom and its allies]." *Handelsblatt*, March 18, 2011. http://www.handelsblatt.com/politik/international/antwort-auf-libyen-resolution-deutschland-verraet-die-freiheit-und-seine-verbuendeten/3964624-all.html.

Von Bredow, Wilfried. "Mühevolle Weltpolitik: Deutschland im System internationaler Beziehungen [Troublesome global politics: Germany in the system of international relations]." In *Deutsche Außenpolitik: Sicherheit, Wohlfahrt, Institutionen und Normen* [German foreign policy: Security, welfare, institutions, and norms]. 2nd ed. Edited by Thomas Jäger, Alexander Höse, and Kai Oppermann, 719–24. Wiesbaden: Springer Fachmedien, 2011.

Von der Leyen, Ursula. *Rede der Bundesministerin der Verteidigung anlässlich der 50. Münchner Sicherheitskonferenz, 31. Januar 2014* [Speech by federal minister of defense on the occasion of the 50th Munich Security Conference, January 31, 2014]. Accessed November 6, 2014. http://www.nato.diplo.de/contentblob/4123416/Daten/3885836/redevdleyensiko2014.pdf.

———. *Speech by the Federal Minister of Defense, Dr. Ursula von der Leyen, on the Occasion of the 51st Munich Security Conference.* Munich: NATO, February 6, 2015. Accessed April 2, 2015. https://www.securityconference.de/fileadmin/MSC_/2015/Freitag/150206-2015_Rede_vdL_MSC_Englisch-1_Kopie_.pdf.

Von Hammerstein, Konstantin, Ralf Neukirch, Gordon Repinski, Holger Stark, Gerald Traufetter, and Klaus Wiegrefe. "German Weapons for the World: How the Merkel Doctrine Is Changing Berlin Policy." *Spiegel Online*, December 3, 2012. http://www.spiegel.de/international/germany/german-weapons-exports-on-the-rise-as-merkel-doctrine-takes-hold-a-870596.html.

Von Mallinckrod, Marie. "Zweifel an Verfassungsmäßigkeit: Irak-Einsatz auf wackeligen Füßen [Doubts about constitutionality: Iraq mission on shaky ground]." *Tagesschau*, January 15, 2015. http://www.tagesschau.de/ausland/bundeswehr-irak-117.html.

Von Krause, Ulf. *Die Afghanistaneinsätze der Bundeswehr: Politischer Entscheidungsprozess mit Eskalationsdynamik* [The Afghanistan missions of the Bundeswehr: Political decision-making process with escalation dynamic]. Wiesbaden: VS Verlag für Sozialwissenschaften, 2011.

———. *Die Bundeswehr als Instrument deutscher Außenpolitik* [The Bundeswehr as an instrument of German foreign policy]. Wiesbaden: Springer, 2013.

Von Rimscha, Robert. "Ein Land tut sich schwer: Bundeswehr-Einsätze seit 1991 [A country struggles: Missions abroad of the Bundeswehr since 1991]." In *Bewährungsproben einer Nation: Die Entsendung der Bundeswehr ins Ausland* [Litmus test of a nation: The deployment of the Bundeswehr into foreign countries]. Edited by Christoph Schwegman, 65–76. Berlin: Duncker & Humblot, 2011.

"Wachstum—Bildung—Zusammenhalt: Koalitionsvertrag zwischen CDU, CSU und FDP, 17. Legislaturperiode [Growth—Education—Cohesion: Coalition Treaty Between CDU, CSU, and FDP, 17th Legislative Period]." *Federal Ministry of the Interior.* Accessed January 28, 2015. https://www.bmi.bund.de/SharedDocs/Downloads/DE/Ministerium/koalitionsvertrag.pdf?_blob=publicationFile.

Wagner, Martin. *Auf dem Weg zu einer 'normalen' Macht?: Die Entsendung deutscher Streitkräfte in der Ära Schröder* [On the way to a 'normal' power?: The deployment of the German Armed Forces in the Schröder era]. Trierer Arbeitspapiere zur Internationalen Politik 8. Trier: Lehrstuhl für Außenpolitik und Internationale Beziehungen, 2004.

———. "Normalization in Security Policy?: Deployments of Bundeswehr Forces Abroad in the Era Schröder, 1998–2004." In *Germany's Uncertain Power: Foreign Policy of the Berlin Republic.* Edited by Hanns W. Maull, 79–92. New York: Palgrave Macmillan, 2006.

Walt, Stephen M. "Alliance Formation and the Balance of World Power." *International Security* (Spring 1985): 3–43.

———. "International Relations: One World, Many Theories." *Foreign Policy*, no. 110 (Spring 1998): 29–46.

Waltz, Kenneth. *Theory of International Politics.* New York: McGraw Hill, 1979.

Walz, Christian. "Merkel verurteilt Gaddafis 'Kriegserklärung' [Merkel condemns Gaddafi's 'declaration of war']." *Deutsche Welle*, February 23, 2011. http://www.dw.de/merkel-verurteilt-gaddafis-kriegserkl%C3%A4rung/a-14861369.

"Was macht eigentlich der Auswärtige Ausschuss? [What does the Foreign Affairs Committee actually do?]" *Deutscher Bundestag*. Accessed February 27, 2015.
http://www.bundestag.de/dokumente/textarchiv/2011/34434192_kw21_pa_polenz/205362.

Watt, Nicholas. "U.S. Defense Secretary Robert Gates Slams 'Loose Talk' About No-Fly Zones." *Guardian*, March 3, 2011. http://www.theguardian.com/politics/2011/mar/03/robert-gates-dismisses-no-fly-zone.

Wehrenfels, Isabelle. "Maghreb." In *Deutsche Nah-, Mittelost- und Nordafrikapolitik—SWP Studie* [German Near-, Middle East, and North Africa Policy—SWP Study] S15. Edited by Guido Steinberg, 7–15. Berlin: German Institute for International and Security Affairs, May 2009.

Weiland, Severin. "FDP-Chef Westerwelle: Der Außenseiterminister [FDP Leader Westerwelle: The outsider minister]." *Spiegel Online*, March 23, 2011.
http://www.spiegel.de/politik/deutschland/fdp-chef-westerwelle-der-aussenseiterminister-a-752269.html.

Weiland, Severin, and Philipp Wittrock. "Libyen-Enthaltung in der Uno: Wie es zu dem deutschen Jein kam [Libyan abstention in the UN: How it came to the German Yes and No]." *Spiegel Online*, March 23, 2011.
http://www.spiegel.de/politik/deutschland/libyen-enthaltung-in-der-uno-wie-es-zu-dem-deutschen-jein-kam-a-752676.html.

Weller, Christoph. "Bundesministerien [Federal ministries]." In *Handbuch zur deutschen Außenpolitik* [Handbook for German foreign policy]. Edited by Sigmar Schmidt, Gunther Hellmann, and Reinhard Wolf, 210–224. Wiesbaden: Verlag für Sozialwissenschaften, 2007.

Wergin, Clemens. "Der Zorn der Südländer auf Deutschland [The South European's anger toward Germany]." *Die Welt*, August 20, 2012. http://www.welt.de/debatte/article108701761/Der-Zorn-der-Suedlaender-auf-Deutschland.html.

"West Africa Bloc ECOWAS Agrees to Deploy Troops to Mali." *BBC News*, November 11, 2012. http://www.bbc.com/news/world-africa-20292797.

"West African ECOWAS Leaders Impose Mali Sanctions." *BBC News*, April 3, 2012. http://www.bbc.com/news/world-africa-17591322.

Westerwelle, Guido. "Gaddafi muss weg-ohne Frage [Gaddafi has to go away—Without a question]." Interview by Ralf Neukirch, Erich Follath, and Georg Mascolo. *Spiegel Online*, March 21, 2011. http://magazin.spiegel.de/EpubDelivery/spiegel/pdf/77531597.

Westerwelle, Guido. "Entwicklungen in und um Libyen [Developments in and around Libya]." Interview by Rudolf Geissler. *SWR2*, February 28, 2011. http://www.swr.de/swr2/programm/sendungen/tages-gespraech/-/id=7530064/property=download/nid=660264/7visfy/swr2-tag-esgespraech-20110228.pdf.

———. *Rede des Bundesministers des Auswärtigen, Dr. Guido Westerwelle, MdB, Afghanistan-Konferenz Eröffnung, am 05. Dezember 2011, in Bonn* [Speech by Federal Minister for Foreign Affairs, Dr. Guido Westerwelle, MP, opening of Afghanistan Conference, on December 2011, in Bonn]. Accessed February 26, 2015. http://www.auswaertiges-amt.de/cae/servlet/contentblob/602938/publicationFile/162593/Germany.pdf.

Westerwelle, Guido. "Regierungserklärung durch Bundesminister Westerwelle vor dem Deutschen Bundestag zur aktuellen Entwicklung in Libyen (UN-Resolution) [Governmental declaration of Federal Minister Westerwelle in front of the German Bundestag to the latest developments in Libya (UN Resolution)]." Updated March 18, 2011. http://www.auswaertiges-amt.de/DE/Infoservice/Presse/Reden/2011/110318_BM_Regierungserkl%C3%A4rung_Libyen.html.

———. "Regierungserklärung durch Bundesaußenminister Westerwelle vor dem Deutschen Bundestag zum Umbruch in der arabischen Welt [Governmental declaration of Federal Minister for Foreign Affairs Westerwelle before the German Bundestag on the turmoil in the Arab world]." Updated March 16, 2011. http://www.auswaertiges-amt.de/DE/Infoservice/Presse/Reden/2011/110316_BM_BT_arab_Welt.html.

———. "Wir sind nicht isoliert [We are not isolated]." Interview by Damir Fras. *Frankfurter Rundschau*, April 14, 2011. http://www.fr-online.de/politik/interview-mit-westerwelle--wir-sind-nicht-isoliert-,1472596,8341026.html.

———. "Zur aktuellen Lage in Libyen [On the current situation in Libya]." Interview by Christoph Heinemann. *Deutschlandfunk*, March 17, 2011. http://www.auswaertiges-amt.de/DE/Infoservice/Presse/Interviews/2011/110317_BM_DLF.html.

"Westerwelle Pledges German Solidarity with Mali." *Deutsche Welle*, November 1, 2012. http://www.dw.de/westerwelle-pledges-german-solidarity-with-mali/a-16348029.

"What is EUCAP Nestor?" *European Union External Action Service*. Accessed May 6, 2015. http://www.eucap-nestor.eu/en/mission/general_overview/what_iseucap_nestor_online.

Wiefelspütz, Dieter. *Das Parlamentsheer: Der Einsatz bewaffneter deutscher Streitkräfte im Ausland, der konstituive Parlamentsvorbehalt und das Parlamentsbeteiligungsgesetz* [The parliamentary army: The use of German armed military forces abroad, the mandatory requirement of parliamentary approval, and the Parliamentary Participation Act]. Berlin: Berliner Wissenschafts-Verlag, 2005.

Wiegold, Thomas. "Bundeswehr weltweit: 17 Einsätze, von einem bis 1.600 [The global Bundeswehr: 17 missions, from one to 1,600 Soldiers]." *Augengeradeaus* (blog). October 20, 2014. http://augengeradeaus.net/2014/10/bundeswehr-weltweit-17-einsaetze-von-einem-bis-1-600-soldaten/.

———. "Gegen Einsatz in Mali?: Die de-Maizière-Exegeten [Against the mission in Mali?: The de Maizière exegetes]." *Augengeradeaus* (blog). January 20, 2013. http://augengeradeaus.net/2013/01/gegen-einsatz-in-mali-die-de-maiziere-exegeten/.

Wilhelm, Andreas. *Außenpolitik: Grundlagen, Strukturen und Prozesse* [Foreign policy: Principles, structures, and processes]. München: Oldenbourg, 2006.

Wilke, Tobias M. *German Strategic Culture Revisited: Link the Past to Contemporary German Strategic Choices*. Forschungsberichte International Politik 36. Berlin: LIT Verlag, 2007.

Wingert, Nico. "Die Operationen der Bundeswehr im Nirgendwo [The operations of the Bundeswehr in the middle of nowhere]." *Die Welt*, October 13, 2014. http://www.welt.de/politik/deutschland/article133229488/Die-Operationen-der-Bundeswehr-im-Nirgendwo.html.

Winkler, Heinrich August. "Gehört Deutschland noch zum Westen? [Does Germany still belong to the West?]" Interview by Richard Herzinger and Claus Christian Malzahn. *Die Welt*, June 6, 2011. http://www.welt.de/politik/ausland/article13426251/Gehoert-Deutschland-noch-zum-Westen.html.

Winkler, Heinrich August. "Politik ohne Projekt: Gedanken über Deutschland, Libyen und Europa [Politics without a project: Thoughts about Germany, Libya, and Europe]." *Internationale Politik* [International politics] 5 (September/Oktober 2011): 28–37.

Wlezien, Christopher. "On the Salience of Political Issues: The Problem with 'Most Important Problem.'" *Electoral Studies* 24, no. 4 (2005): 555–79.

Wolfrum, Rüdiger. "Grundgesetz und Außenpolitik [Basic law and foreign policy]." In *Handbuch zur deutschen Außenpolitik* [Handbook for German foreign policy]. Edited by Sigmar Schmidt, Gunther Hellmann, and Reinhard Wolf, 157–68. Wiesbaden: Verlag für Sozialwissenschaften, 2007.

"Zentralafrikanische Republik [Central African Republic]—EUFOR RCA (European Union Force République Centrafricaine)." *BMVg*. Updated April 1, 2015. http://www.einsatz.bundeswehr.de/portal/a/einsatzbw/!ut/p/c4/04_SB8K8xLLM9MSSzPy8xBz9CP3I5EyrpHK9pPKU1Pj UzLzixJIqIDcxKT21ODkjJ7-4ODUPKpFaUpWql1qall9UlJyoX5DtqAgAvelJGg!!/.

Carola Hartmann Miles-Verlag

Politik, Gesellschaft, Militär

Uwe Hartmann, *Innere Führung. Erfolge und Defizite der Führungsphilosophie für die Bundeswehr*, Berlin 2007.

Hans Joachim Reeb, *Sicherheitskultur als kommunikative und pädagogische Herausforderung – Der Umgang in Politik, Medien und Gesellschaft*, Berlin 2011.

Hans-Christian Beck, Christian Singer (Hrsg.), *Entscheiden – Führen – Verantworten. Soldatsein im 21. Jahrhundert*, Berlin 2011.

Eberhard Birk, Winfried Heinemann, Sven Lange (Hrsg.), *Tradition für die Bundeswehr. Neue Aspekte einer alten Debatte*, Berlin 2012.

Angelika Dörfler-Dierken, *Führung in der Bundeswehr*, Berlin 2013.

Cornelia Fedtke, Kai-Uwe Hellmann, Jan Hörmann, *Migration und Militär. Zur Integration deutscher Soldaten mit Migrationshintergrund in der Bundeswehr*, Berlin 2013.

Wolf Graf von Baudissin, *Grundwert Frieden in Politik – Strategie – Führung von Streitkräften*, hrsg. von Claus von Rosen, Berlin 2014.

Wolf Graf von Baudissin, *Der Widerstand. „… um nie wieder in die auswegslose Lage zu geraten…"*, hrsg. von Claus von Rosen, Berlin 2014.

Marcel Bohnert, Lukas J. Reitstetter (Hrsg.), *Armee im Aufbruch. Zur Gedankenwelt junger Offiziere in den Kampftruppen der Bundeswehr*, Berlin 2014.

Arjan Kozica, Kai Prüter, Hannes Wendroth (Hrsg.), *Unternehmen Bundeswehr? Theorie und Praxis (militärischer) Führung*, Berlin 2014.

Angelika Dörfler-Dierken, Robert Kramer, *Innere Führung in Zahlen. Streitkräftebefragung 2013*, Berlin 2014.

Eberhard Birk, Heiner Möllers (Hrsg.), *Luftwaffe und Luftkrieg*, Berlin 2015.

Phil C. Langer, Gerhard Kümmel (Hrsg.), *„Wir sind Bundeswehr." Wie viel Vielfalt benötigen/vertragen die Streitkräfte?*, Berlin 2015.

Jahrbuch Innere Führung

Uwe Hartmann, Claus von Rosen, Christian Walther (Hrsg.), *Jahrbuch Innere Führung 2009. Die Rückkehr des Soldatischen,* Eschede 2009.

Helmut R. Hammerich, Uwe Hartmann, Claus von Rosen (Hrsg.), *Jahrbuch Innere Führung 2010. Die Grenzen des Militärischen,* Berlin 2010.

Uwe Hartmann, Claus von Rosen, Christian Walther (Hrsg.), *Jahrbuch Innere Führung 2011. Ethik als geistige Rüstung für Soldaten,* Berlin 2011.

Uwe Hartmann, Claus von Rosen, Christian Walther (Hrsg.), *Jahrbuch Innere Führung 2012. Der Soldatenberuf zwischen gesellschaftlicher Integration und suis generis-Ansprüchen,* Berlin 2012.

Uwe Hartmann, Claus von Rosen (Hrsg.), *Jahrbuch Innere Führung 2013. Wissenschaften und ihre Relevanz für die Bundeswehr als Armee im Einsatz,* Berlin 2013.

Uwe Hartmann, Claus von Rosen (Hrsg.), *Jahrbuch Innere Führung 2014. Drohnen, Roboter und Cyborgs – Der Soldat im Angesicht neuer Militärtechnologien,* Berlin 2014.

Einsatzerfahrungen

Kay Kuhlen, *Um des lieben Friedens willen. Als Peacekeeper im Kosovo,* Eschede 2009.

Sascha Brinkmann, Joachim Hoppe (Hrsg.), *Generation Einsatz, Fallschirmjäger berichten ihre Erfahrungen aus Afghanistan,* Berlin 2010.

Artur Schwitalla, *Afghanistan, jetzt weiß ich erst… Gedanken aus meiner Zeit als Kommandeur des Provincial Reconstruction Team FEYZABAD,* Berlin 2010.

Uwe Hartmann, *War without Fighting? The Reintegration of Former Combatants in Afghanistan seen through the Lens of Strategic Thought,* Berlin 2014.

Rainer Buske, *KUNDUZ. Ein Erlebnisbericht über einen militärischen Einsatz der Bundeswehr in AFGHANISTAN im Jahre 2008,* Berlin 2015.

Standpunkte und Orientierungen

Daniel Giese, *Militärische Führung im Internetzeitalter – Die Bedeutung von Strategischer Kommunikation und Social Media für Entscheidungsprozesse, Organisationsstrukturen und Führerausbildung in der Bundeswehr,* Berlin 2014.

Dirk Freudenberg, *Auftragstaktik und Innere Führung. Feststellungen und Anmerkungen zur Frage nach Bedeutung und Verhältnis des inneren Gefüges und der Auftragstaktik unter den Bedingungen des Einsatzes der Deutschen Bundeswehr,* Berlin 2014.

Uwe Hartmann (Hrsg.), *Lernen von Afghanistan. Innovative Mittel und Wege für Auslandseinsätze,* Berlin 2015.

Fouzieh Melanie Alamir, *Vernetzte Sicherheit – Quo Vadis?,* Berlin 2015.

Hartmut von Schubert, *Integrative Militärethik. Ethische Urteilsbildung in der militärischen Führung,* Berlin 2015.

Uwe Hartmann, *Hybrider Krieg als neue Bedrohung von Freiheit und Frieden. Zur Relevanz der Inneren Führung in Politik, Gesellschaft und Streitkräften,* Berlin 2015.

Erinnerungen

Blue Braun, *Erinnerungen an die Marine 1956–1996,* Berlin 2012.

Harald Volkmar Schlieder, *Kommando zurück!,* Berlin 2012.

Reinhart Lunderstädt, *Aus dem Leben eines Hochschullehrers. Persönlicher Bericht,* Berlin 2012.

Wulf Beeck, *Mit Überschall durch den Kalten Krieg. Mein Leben für die Marine,* Berlin 2013.

Jan Becker, *Aufgewühltes Wasser,* 3 Bde., Berlin 2014.

Klaus Grot, *So war's, damals. Dienstchronik eines Pionieroffiziers im Kalten Krieg 1954–1991,* Berlin 2014.

Gustav Lünenborg, *Bürger und Soldat. Innere Führung hautnah 1956–1993, 1993–2015,* Berlin 2015.

Monterey Studies

Uwe Hartmann, *Carl von Clausewitz and the Making of Modern Strategy*, Potsdam 2002.

Zeljko Cepanec, *Croatia and NATO. The Stony Road to Membership*, Potsdam 2002.

Ekkehard Stemmer, *Demography and European Armed Forces*, Berlin 2006.

Sven Lange, *Revolt against the West. A Comparison of the Current War on Terror with the Boxer Rebellion in 1900–01*, Berlin 2007.

Klaus M. Brust, *Culture and the Transformation of the Bundeswehr*, Berlin 2007.

Donald Abenheim, *Soldier and Politics Transformed*, Berlin 2007.

Michael Stolzke, *The Conflict Aftermath. A Chance for Democracy: Norm Diffusion in Post-Conflict Peace Building*, Berlin 2007.

Frank Reimers, *Security Culture in Times of War. How did the Balkan War affect the Security Cultures in Germany and the United States?*, Berlin 2007.

Michael G. Lux, *Innere Führung – A Superior Concept of Leadership?*, Berlin 2009.

Marc A. Walther, *HAMAS between Violence and Pragmatism*, Berlin 2010.

Frank Hagemann, *Strategy Making in the European Union*, Berlin 2010.

Ralf Hammerstein, *Deliberalization in Jordan: the Roles of Islamists and U.S.-EU Assistance in stalled Democratization*, Berlin 2011.

Ingo Wittmann, *Auftragstaktik*, Berlin 2012.

www.miles-verlag.jimdo.com